The Vote,
the Pill
and the Demon Drink

The Vote,
the Pill
and the Demon Drink

A History of Feminist Writing in New Zealand
1869–1993

Selected and introduced by Charlotte Macdonald

First published in 1993 by Bridget Williams Books Limited,
P.O. Box 11-294, Wellington, New Zealand

Introductions and selection © Charlotte Macdonald 1993

ISBN 0 908912 40 4

Design by Mission Hall Design Group
Typeset by Archetype, Wellington
Printed by GP Print, Wellington

Contents

Sources

With the exception of items 3.1 and 3.3, all the documents included have been drawn from the collections of the Alexander Turnbull Library and the National Library, Wellington. The Library's permission to reproduce the documents is gratefully acknowledged. Every effort has been made to gain permission from authors and appropriate publishers to reproduce the items here. Some authors and organisations could not be contacted, however, and for these acknowledgement is made now.

Documents have been reproduced in their entirety in all but a few cases, which are indicated. They are reproduced without alteration other than the occasional insertion of punctuation to assist a modern reading, and the silent correction of typographical errors.

Abbreviations

ATL   Alexander Turnbull Library

BNZW   *The Book of New Zealand Women/Ko Kui Ma te Kaupapa*, edited by Charlotte Macdonald, Merimeri Penfold and Bridget Williams, Wellington, 1991

NCW   National Council of Women

NZJH   *New Zealand Journal of History*

NZLP   New Zealand Labour Party

WCTU Women's Christian Temperance Union

Acknowledgements

The possibility of reflecting on a feminist tradition in Aotearoa/New Zealand would not have arisen had there not been courageous women who put their views forward in the hope they would bring about change. To them goes my greatest tribute.

The possibility of recovering that feminist tradition would have been extremely difficult without the Alexander Turnbull Library. Special thanks go to its staff – both those who directly assisted with this project, and those former staff who assiduously deposited a miscellany of items in the Ephemera collection (from which many documents in the later chapters are drawn). Staff at the Victoria University Library have also been most helpful.

Moira Long has worked on the project through most of its life. Her inestimable skills and experience as a researcher and librarian, her judicious use of the editorial pencil, and formidable rigour at all stages have been of enormous value. To her go my special thanks for the very considerable work she has done in shaping the book and in sustaining its author.

Students in my women's history class at Victoria University over the last three years have helped me formulate ideas about the pre-1945 period of New Zealand feminism. I also appreciate the suggestions made by a large number of people; and especially discussions with Barbara Brookes, Claire-Louise McCurdy, Jackie Matthews, Dorothy Page, Margot Roth, Gay Simpkin and Margaret Tennant.

The Internal Grants Committee and the History Department of Victoria University gave practical support. Thanks also to Craig Cherrie, Jan Robinson, Alisa Hogan and Victoria Upton for their assistance.

To the patient, and painstaking, publishers – Bridget Williams, Andrew Mason and Adrienne Howard – go final but by no means least thanks.

Charlotte Macdonald

Introduction

The centenary of women's suffrage has sharpened interest in New Zealand's feminist heritage. The women who campaigned to win the right to vote are now gaining some general recognition. But was the franchise agitation of the 1890s an isolated outbreak of feminism in New Zealand's history? Has New Zealand a feminist tradition beyond the 'first wave' of the 1890s and the 'second wave' movement which emerged around 1970 as 'women's liberation'? The answer to these questions is an emphatic 'yes'. 'The woman question' was the subject of articles and lively public discussion several decades before Kate Sheppard stirred the Franchise Department of the Women's Christian Temperance Union into action, while equal pay and abortion were only two of a range of social, political and personal issues to be addressed during the so-called 'trough' between the two 'waves'.

From the 1860s and early 1870s, when the 'three Marys' (Mary Ann Müller, Mary Taylor and Mary Colclough) first put their ideas into the public arena, to the 1980s and 1990s, there has been debate in New Zealand about how women might improve their situation. The discussion has not proceeded at an even pace. At times it amounted to little more than a few isolated advocates speaking to an indifferent, bemused or apparently complacent public. At other times it emerged as the voice of a small, determined group. Occasionally (in the 1890s and in the 1970s and 1980s) it was the expression of a large scale social and political movement.

This collection has been put together to provide a broader base for reflection on New Zealand's feminist history, and to provide an historical account of the development of feminism both as a set of ideas and as a political movement. In doing so it supplements Margaret Lovell-Smith's *The Woman Question: Writings by the women who won the vote*[1] and Pat Rosier's *Been Around for Quite a While: Twenty years of Broadsheet magazine*[2], which have focused on the two notable periods of feminist activism: the 1890s and the contemporary movement of the 1970s on. The centenary of women's suffrage provides a timely occasion to survey and reflect upon the character and achievements of not only the suffrage feminists of the 1890s, but also their predecessors and their more numerous successors. It is also hoped that this book will provide an enduring base to enable that reflection to continue beyond 1993.

In presenting an historical survey of New Zealand's feminist voices it has not been my intention to set out a triumphal path showing 'how far we have come'. No underlying progressivist agenda is intended. As a woman born in the

1

mid-1950s, who came to adulthood as women's liberation reached full force, I have lived through the most recent feminist movement, both as an actor in it and as a member of the society on which that movement has had and continues to have a profound effect. I now teach university courses in the history of Aotearoa/New Zealand to classes comprised predominantly (the more so since recent fee increases) of women and men who have little, if any, memory of the 1970s. 'Liberation' feminism, the United Women's Conventions (and the society from which those events so riotously arose) and indeed events such as the 1981 Springbok Tour (which occurred when the nineteen-year-old students of 1992 were just eight years old) are, for increasing numbers of New Zealanders, past history. I believe, therefore, that there is a need to present the contemporary movement in its historical context. Inevitably, the more recent past is more difficult to see in perspective. Readers will have their own view of the significant points in the last two or three decades. What is presented here attempts to survey the breadth of material and issues in the 1970s and 1980s. It is by no means definitive.

For those who wish to find out about earlier feminist activity in New Zealand, there is a problem of access. Many feminist writings are now out of print. Others, probably the majority, were originally published in a relatively ephemeral form – as pamphlets, newspaper articles or letters. This is true not only of documents we might think of as 'historical' – dating from the nineteenth and early twentieth centuries – but also of writing from the 'second wave' feminist movement. Many of the documents produced in the 1970s and 1980s are no longer easily available to us.

The recent past can often be almost as hard to lay hands on as the more distant past. This is especially the case with the contemporary feminist movement, which eschewed the centralised and formally organised structures that tend to leave records of their activity in the form of minutes of meetings, agendas, correspondence, accounts, etc. For primary material from this period two collections are particularly important: the 'Women' section of the Alexander Turnbull Library's Ephemera collection, and the Rosemary Seymour collection at the University of Waikato. For this work the former has been the major source for the contemporary period. Wellington groups and activities may consequently appear rather over-represented. Hopefully, this does not skew the picture of the kinds of ideas and events that were occurring throughout the country.

Many of the writings of earlier feminists are no longer easily available outside research libraries. The 1930s feminist magazine, *Woman Today*, for example, is held in only a few libraries in its original form, and although the Alexander Turnbull Library has recently made additional copies available on microfiche, these are not easily accessible to general readers, or indeed to those at a distance from a well-resourced public or university library. A further aim of this book then is to bring much of this less well-known and less accessible material to a wider readership.

In the selection of material for this collection some consideration has been given to including items that have not recently been reproduced elsewhere. *The*

SOUTHERN CROSS SOCIETY.

ITS OBJECTS.

ADDRESS BY LADY STOUT

DELIVERED AT THE

INAUGURAL MEETING

OF THE

SOUTHERN CROSS SOCIETY

WELLINGTON, AUGUST 22, 1895.

Wellington.
J. H. CLAYTON, PRINTER, 43 LAMBTON QUAY
1895.

Cover of Anna Stout's inaugural address to the Southern Cross Society, Wellington, 1895 – see Document 2.9. *Alexander Turnbull Library*

Woman Question and *Twenty Years of Broadsheet Magazine* provide detailed surveys of the writings of the 1890s, and of the 1970s and 1980s respectively. Therefore this selection has concentrated on complementing rather than replicating the contents of these books and of specialist collections of individual authors, such as Gillian Boddy and Jackie Matthews' edition of Robin Hyde's journalism: *Disputed Ground*.[3] The overall objective has been to provide as representative as possible a survey of the development of feminist thought throughout the period covered. Many more documents were collected in the process of preparing this book than the number finally included. As well as the practical constraint of producing a book acceptable to publisher and readers, the aim was not to be exhaustive but to depict a broad profile of feminist writing across New Zealand history.

'Feminism' has been given a wide definition. Here it has been applied to those writings that were penned consciously to advance the cause of women, or to draw attention to a disparity between women and men. With such a broad scope there is clearly no uniformity of approach or of analysis, and no underlying consensus. There is tremendous variety. Another of the purposes of this collection is, indeed, to demonstrate the extent of that variety. The ways in which women have written and thought about their position have changed through our history; yet at any one time there have been various perspectives from which women's situation has been viewed. These differences can be recognised and usefully studied.

As for the nature of material included, the boundary has been drawn somewhat tighter. The focus has been placed on feminism as a movement for social and political change. Thus the emphasis is on the public face of feminism. Most of the documents included in this collection originally appeared in some public form: as published pamphlets or handbills, letters to newspapers, magazine articles, or reported speeches. They were, in the main, composed for a general readership rather than for a specific audience. There are a few exceptions, but generally the focus has been on writings that put the feminist case in order to persuade and shape public opinion, rather than on more esoteric pieces written for consumption *within* limited circles. Overall, this first survey has been concerned with what appeared in the public domain, how feminists sought to shape public opinion and challenge public attitudes and, latterly, how feminist issues have come to be addressed in public policy. It has not entered the realm of private writings – letters, diaries, journals and unpublished manuscripts.

The style of these documents varies a good deal. They have been selected not on the basis of literary merit but for their content and their capacity to illustrate the ways in which feminist causes have been advanced. Leaflets hastily prepared to distribute at demonstrations, broadsheets circulated at conventions and conference brochures have been included alongside more reflective pieces. In some there is evidence of considerable capacity to present a persuasive case; in others the urgency of the issue or campaign has overridden literary considerations. For those writers whose only weapon was the pen (e.g., Mary Ann Müller), the power to persuade, to enchant and to cajole with rhetoric was considerable. The style varies with the occasion, and also with the period. Twentieth-century newspaper readers and editors are far less patient with time and less generous with space. A feature as long as Müller's article rarely finds a place in a later twentieth-century newspaper.

The following chapters proceed chronologically. They vary in length and in the number and nature of items. The volume of feminist writing was not consistent over time; nor did the issues remain the same. As the principal aim of this collection is to provide an historical context for the development of feminism in New Zealand, the pieces are arranged in strictly chronological order within each chapter, according to the date on which they first appeared. This contrasts with the thematic arrangement often used in collections of this kind, where items are grouped by subject.

The language used by women to reflect on their own position and to present their concerns to the world has clearly changed over the 120 or so years since 1869. To take one example: when applied to women in the late nineteenth century, the term 'disabilities' commonly referred to the constitutional and legal inequalities between women and men. Removing these disabilities was the aim of their agitation. To women in the late twentieth century the term is more likely to suggest women differently abled. In the nineteenth century the term 'feminist' was not often used, and the word 'suffragettes' had not come into existence (it was coined as a pejorative and diminutive to refer to members of the Women's Social and Political Union, the militant section of the British suffrage movement in the early 1900s). Women described themselves as working for the franchise, or as speaking on 'women's rights', or referred to themselves as 'white ribboners'. Similarly, the word 'housewife' was seldom used in the nineteenth century and first came into use in the early twentieth century. From the 1930s to the 1960s, women who were in paid employment, or who pursued a vocational training were frequently termed 'career girls'. In the 1970s women advocating feminist goals called themselves women's liberationists, socialist feminists, women seeking equality, or advocates of human rights for women. The changing language itself tells us a good deal about changes in thinking about women and the political context of feminism.

The term 'feminist' has more often been used by opponents as a tag to deride or scorn a person or a position than as a description of a set of political or social views. Not all of the women whose writings are represented here called themselves feminists, but they all sought to advance the interests of women. They all wrote in the hope of achieving some kind of social change.

Most of these documents have been selected because of the influence they had in shaping opinion at the time they first appeared, or because they present a key issue of the time. It is not always easy to assess just what impact a pamphlet, article or letter had on those who might have read it. The way in which public opinion is shaped changes over time. In the nineteenth century, when more people received a weekly message from the pulpit and local news from fellow church-goers, and when many people read newspapers from cover to cover (or had them read aloud to them), ideas were digested more slowly and probably more thoroughly. The church played a greater part as a social gathering place and was more influential in shaping ideas. In the twentieth century, we are presented

Housewives or Human Beings?

MARGOT ROTH'S "Point of View" broadside against the domestic role imposed on—and accepted by—so many New Zealand women may have sparked a thousand arguments in suburban living rooms. But the results have not been announced. Being, in any case, dedicated to the proposition that it is not who is right that is important but what is the truth, "The Listener" canvassed for intelligent comment on Mrs Roth's argument. We print here the text of the talk, slightly abridged, together with what some fellow New Zealanders had to say about it.

A FRIEND of mine has a large and highly intelligent family. When she went along to enrol her eldest daughter at secondary school, the headmistress said yes, the child's record definitely showed she should join the top third form. Very gratifying. But Mother's pride soon changed to fury. The headmistress added that there must be a lot of chores falling to the eldest girl in such a big family, so she'd place the child in the second stream in case she couldn't keep up. Fortunately for this pupil, her mother's indignation at the idea of school work having to take second place won the day. But this is the point. Can you imagine a head-master of a boys' secondary school putting a child into the second stream because of all the lawns he had to mow? No, of course you can't. And neither can I. What's the reason for this shatter-ing distinction between what's expected for boys and what for girls? Why have so many of our Kiwi males got the same attitude towards women as my son at the age of three? He remarked: "We like Mummy because she makes our food and looks after us." Well, fair enough at three, but it jars twenty or thirty years later. Could it be that many Kiwi females don't deserve more than this? I think for the answer we've got to delve into our past. The idea of men's role in society being of primary import-ance, with women as contributing sub-ordinates rather than partners, isn't it simply a hangover from out-of-date British working-class customs? . . .

But today in our mainly middle-class lives, these old distinctions are out-of-date and meaningless. We no longer need to build Father up to withstand the strains of being overworked and under-paid. These adjectives though, do des-cribe many mothers with small children. They're the ones who most emphatically need half an hour or so of oblivion be-hind the evening paper at six o'clock. In spite of this, we—and I do mean women as well as men—go on thinking and behaving in the same old way, pre-serving the same stale old distinctions and taboos. Listen to this. It's the testi-mony of an English visitor, Amabel William Ellis. She says: "I can still hear in my mind the gentle, rather weary voice of a young suburban mother in New Zealand above four-year-old son was playing near by. 'You don't want to play with dolls,' said the tired voice. 'Dolls are for girls! You play with your nice engine . . . No Ronnie, not that . . . You don't want to play with dolls.'"

You know, I don't think it's odd that New Zealand's two international con-tributions to woman's welfare are the Plunket system and marching girls. The Truby King system of mothercraft—

what was it but an authority encour-aging women to be manly? It's sissy to play with dolls is it? All right, we'll show you. Our babies are going to be little engines that keep to the rails. The railway timetable rules of the early Plunket days were really a negation of motherhood. In the same way, I feel, marching girls are a negation of femininity. Women are a different shape from men, if you've noticed, and all that masculine vigour simply develops the wrong muscles. Anyway, what's the point of marching like men? I know that marching teams give girls a chance of fun with others of their own age; they get gay uniforms and rhythmical exer-cise in the open air. These are all normal needs. But our society's way of filling them is an abnormal travesty of men being drilled for war.

Quite obviously, our society's out of plumb somewhere. And I'm suggesting that one way of helping to correct it is to get nearly half of it—the women—out of the mould of inferiority in which they're settling themselves more and more firmly. And again I'd like to stress that it's something which is largely their own fault. You see, over the years I believe we have been busily cultivating a myth—the myth of the overworked housewife. Like most myths, it has a definite basis of fact.

Looking backwards again, our pioneer women coped with conditions we just can't picture. Although the majority of the earliest assisted immigrants were classified as servants, such a label didn't necessarily mean that they had any clues about dealing with what they found here. As for the women who weren't herded into the steerage with the lower orders on the way out, some of them were even more helpless . . . So house-work came hard to a great number. It was a sort of moral challenge, met, we can proudly say, with courage and ingenuity . . .

But once again, times have changed, and once again our attitudes haven't changed with them. Today the hard-worked housewife stuff is propped up by the Homemakers' cult. We make a virtue of necessity and cling to our housework like a miser to his gold. Ours being a competitive society, we're encouraged to buy lots of labour-saving devices. Not to save our labour, but as ends in them-selves—to keep up with the Joneses and

to put money in advertisers' pockets. If we're honest, though, we must admit that housework, or homemaking as some advertisers prefer to call it, produces nothing that is directly useful to society. It opens no door to the future. Domestic chores should take their proper place as a background necessity, like brushing the teeth. This happens only if the per-son doing them is a creative worker of some kind, or making some contribution to society.

But all the forces in our lives bring pressure to bear to cast a false glamour over what's called "the creative role of wife and mother." Of course I know it is creative up to a point, and certainly it may be emotionally satisfying. But the permanent company of children and the kitchen sink is hardly stimulating ment-ally. True creative work implies a steady development. And you can't tell me anybody's developing if all she ever thinks about is food for the family and her resentment at their lack of apprecia-tion for her often self-imposed drudgery. It seems to me utterly fantastic that our children should grow up with the belief that women fall into two classes. The married, despised for their intensely personal, housebound preoccupations, and the unmarried, despised because they lack that magic gold band that immediately transforms women into superior beings with no effort on their part. Oh yes, there are plenty of women who do realise that just being that other mother's daughter, or a Married Woman —in capital letters—doesn't provide them with instinctive knowledge. So they go in hordes to learn about arrang-ing flowers or cooking or sewing or child development. But—and this is a very big but—such studies too quickly be-come an end in themselves instead of forming just one part in an all-round development of the personality. We don't take ourselves seriously because we're so conditioned to the idea that domesticity comes first, last and all the time—the one really important thing in our lives. And this in turn leads straight to the old, old story that women, as such, aren't capable of really extend-ing themselves individually.

Actually we do have another, better tradition, which stems from the old liberal middle-class in New Zealand. We used to have leisured women from this class who took their community responsibilities seriously. As well as

other social reformers, they worked like beavers all over the country to get the vote for women in 1893. This in spite of opposition from their husbands, other brewers. Most of these women came from families who could afford education . . . Until the last war, anyway, New Zealand has always had such a leisured minority.

And today? Well, the point I want to make is that today it's no longer a small minority. Growing numbers of women have, or could have, the leisure to devote to activities which benefit the whole community. This isn't because we can employ help, but because of our generally smaller families, our better health, longer lives and high standard of living. Yet our false commercialised pic-ture of the Little Homemaker means that, with few exceptions, all this spare time hasn't led to wide social or cultural reforms. What it has led to is a women's organisation at every lamp-post. And if the majority of them were laid end to end round our coastline they wouldn't be much loss. Why? Because most women's organisations, if you come to grips with them, devote their time to organising their organisations. They elect officers, frame constitutions, argue among themselves and battle with their rival associations for prestige. But when you get down to it, you find that few of their members are anxious to do away with injustices and abuses, which would make their association unnecessary.

For instance, there are several hard-working organisations catering for mothers and children. I've benefited from them myself. But generally speak-ing they're slaving so hard to organise a ball that's to be a highlight of the social season, or arranging lectures to tell us where we're going wrong in bringing up our children, that they've overlooked the basic need of many mothers with babies. I mean relief from social isola-tion and the physical and mental exhaus-tion caused by a 24-hour day. Surely more mothers would be helped and more babies saved from the effects of Mum's fatigue, if some of this time were spent in hanging out washing for tired young mothers, or baby-sitting while they went out with their husbands leaving the dishes in the sink. And with all our chatter about children's welfare, it takes

N.Z. LISTENER, NOVEMBER 20, 1959.

Margot Roth, 'Housewives or Human Beings', copy of original article as it appeared in the *New Zealand Listener*, 20 November 1959 – see Document 5.6. *New Zealand Listener* with a very much greater volume of information, which we absorb more rapidly, but possibly less thoroughly.

In assessing the influence of these writers on their contemporaries, we need to consider their personalities as well as the ideas they presented. In the earliest phase we have one of the greatest contrasts. Mary Ann Müller was known to the world only as 'Femina' from the time she wrote, in 1869, until the late 1890s. It was only several years after the death of her husband that she felt able to let go the protection of her pseudonym. Mary Colclough, by contrast, was known first to readers of Auckland newspapers simply as 'Polly Plum', but soon became a well-known public figure when she gave a series of lectures to eager audiences. That her speech, demeanour and public appearance were as effective an advertisement for the ideas she espoused as the ideas themselves was demonstrated in the way she was received by the Auckland public. Yet unlike many of their successors, neither Müller nor Colclough became the centre of an organised group of women.

A survey of women's writing about their position in New Zealand over the last 150 years or so reveals strong elements of both continuity and contrast. Throughout, women have sought greater economic independence, the elimination of the double standard of sexual morality (and protection from harmful male sexuality), greater equality within marriage and a larger place in political life. The contrasts between different generations of feminists can be seen in changing perceptions of sexuality (especially female sexuality), attitudes towards 'home and family', in parallel issues such as temperance or the Treaty, and in the way in which feminist women have orchestrated social change.

In New Zealand, as in other parts of the world, feminist debate began with the economic issues: married women's property rights, access to a wider range of employment, and the right to education (the last not solely, but partly, an economic issue). Employment, pay equity and financial security are central issues to New Zealand women in the late 1980s and 1990s. In between were the mid-twentieth-century campaigns for a motherhood allowance, entitlement to unemployment benefits and equal pay.

Economic self-determination preceded political emancipation as a goal. Only later in the nineteenth century did an organised campaign arise, focused on attaining political and constitutional rights, in particular the right to vote. The franchise movement of the 1880s and 1890s fomented a much wider debate on the nature of men's and women's intellectual and physical capacities, social position, need for employment, etc. While women won the right to vote in 1893, they were not eligible to stand as parliamentary candidates until 1919. Only a very small number of women have occupied seats since then. The continued imbalance between women and men in political participation has been a frequent subject for comment. In the 1980s attempts were made to form a women's political party.

The National Council of Women, set up in 1896 to pursue the broader feminist agenda after the vote had been won, had as one of its main goals the removal of the obstacles to women's parliamentary candidature. The NCW, however, went into recess in 1905 and active feminism disappeared for some years.

Women's energies were directed into other organisations of a more philanthropic or charitable nature. Apart from the courageous campaigns launched by a small group of women against militarism, it was patriotic societies that largely soaked up women's time in the First World War.

The years that followed – the 1920s and 1930s – present, in many ways, the greatest enigma of New Zealand's feminist history. Ostensibly, the 1920s were a quiet, unremarkable, somewhat conservative decade, dominated by a conservative farmers' government led by William (Bill) Massey. Some attention was given to improving conditions in which women gave birth, but this was in the context of a strong pro-natalism. The greatest concern was for increasing the birth rate and promoting Plunket methods of infant and maternal care rather than the welfare of women in a wider sense. Yet, during that time, women were campaigning for the endowment of motherhood (with a little success), standing for parliament (with no success), joining political parties, lobbying for women police and establishing their own organisations as never before.

The early twentieth century has, indeed, often been thought of as 'the black hole' of New Zealand's feminist history, appearing as a trough of inactivity between the two great 'waves' of nineteenth-century and contemporary feminism. This interpretation deserves revision. The 1920s and 1930s were in fact years of considerable activity. During the depression, the working women's movement was formed, and, in the later 1930s, *Woman Today* appeared as a serious forum for the debate of women's position. Issues of peace, international politics and birth control predominated in the later 1930s.

In the 1940s, as the Second World War had an impact on the home economy, economic issues again came to the fore. The effects were felt not only in women's work but also in such things as rationing and wage controls. However, it was the issue of women's paid work that aroused feminist agitation, and an organised campaign for equal pay in the Public Service was mounted, supported by the National Council of Women and its constituents. Sustained throughout the 1950s, the campaign came to a successful conclusion with the passing of the Government Service Equal Pay Act in 1960, which introduced equal pay for government employees.

With changing family size, life expectancy, general prosperity and full employment, the focus in the 1960s shifted from economic issues to questions of self-fulfilment and social values. The phrase of those years was 'the changing role of women' and the mood one not so much of indignation as of social questioning. People began to recognise that convenient houses, piped hot water, indoor bathrooms, electric appliances, healthy children and regular pay packets – however welcome – were not in themselves life-fulfilling. It was more a crisis of the spirit than of sustenance. Sexual concerns, once submerged, were now increasingly coming to the surface. The great diversity of individual expectations of marriage was explored. Attention turned to the consequences of pre- and extra-marital sex: high illegitimacy rates, venereal disease, stranger adoption and the social attitudes that went along with them. All of these issues lay just below the surface of post-war New Zealand life.

In the 1970s, the women's liberation movement flared up and spread like a bush fire. Never before had women been so well educated. Yet many, married as young as twenty, found that, as suburban housewives, they were leading mundane lives on the margins of society and were condemned to inequality. Combining the roles of attractive wife/sexual partner with those of efficient housekeeper and attentive mother presented too many contradictions to this generation of women. A vast social and political movement grew up. It was not, however, an organised movement in the sense that the nineteenth-century movement had been. There *was* organisation, but it was largely confined to co-ordinating activities: newsletters, mailing lists, workshops, consciousness-raising and reading groups. It was not a highly structured system. What united these groups and gatherings were common experiences and ideas found in books, articles and magazines. Copies of Germaine Greer's *The Female Eunuch*, Kate Millet's *Sexual Politics*, Juliet Mitchell's *Women's Estate, Spare Rib, Off Our Backs* and, from 1972, *Broadsheet* formed the currency of the new movement.

In the 1980s and early 1990s the spontaneity of those early years of discovery was replaced by a greater sophistication and a more dispersed movement. Groups worked for particular goals. The social movement that had existed largely outside mainstream institutions moved inside them, as equal oppportunity programmes, women's officers and women's caucuses appeared. Recognition at a national and parliamentary level was achieved in 1984 with the establishment of a Ministry of Women's Affairs. The era of street politics had largely ended. Feminists were now making submissions to select committees, to vice chancellors and to chief executives. Subtle but fundamental changes occured as sexist language disappeared, first from job advertisements, and later from the Anglican prayerbook.

One of the continuing concerns, which was identified in the nineteenth century and has become more conspicuous in the later 1980s and 1990s, is feminist awareness of sexual danger to women. In the nineteenth century this was perceived largely in terms of young women's vulnerability to sexual predations. Feminists in the 1890s succeeded in having the age of consent raised from fourteen to sixteen. They also sought the repeal of the Contagious Diseases Act, and the reform of the divorce law in order to eliminate the moral double standard. In the twentieth century, feminists have campaigned for female police and for women in the judicial system, partly to provide greater protection for women. In the 1970s, rape crisis centres and women's refuges have provided women with places of sanctuary from male violence, including sexual violence.

Most of the writers in this collection have been, explicit or implicitly, concerned with conceptualising the differences between men and women in earnings, political rights or other areas. Some have highlighted socially observable inequalities, while others have analysed the origins of these differences. In the nineteenth and twentieth centuries certain feminist thinkers (or theorists, as they have increasingly been described) have ascribed separate natures to men and women. They have not necessarily claimed that different natures entail 'separate spheres' (a notion which Kate Sheppard had little patience with). The idea of separate natures was often used to suggest complementarity and equivalence, and led its supporters to draw up demarcations between masculinity and femininity,

NOW

NATIONAL ORGANISATION FOR WOMEN

Box 2946 Auckland

For EQUALITY
Against DISCRIMINATION

"Feminism is believing women are people and that they therefore have at least as much to offer as men; it is against discrimination and oppression, and for equality of opportunity and free choice of life styles."
UN Status of Women definition.

National Organisation for Women pamphlet, 1975 – see Document 7.16.
Ephemera Collection, Alexander Turnbull Library (Ephemera A Women ca 1975)

though these terms were not always meant to refer to men and women. In the late nineteenth century, they came to have a moral content and force – hence the links between temperance, social reform and feminism.

In the early 1970s, New Zealand feminists regarded their nineteenth-century predecessors with some ambivalence. The women of the 1890s had won something, and something important. Their early success pre-empted any heroics of the sort that emerged in the British suffrage movement, with its Emily Davison martyrdom, or imprisonment and force feeding. However, Patricia Grimshaw's *Women's Suffrage in New Zealand*[4] challenged the prevailing picture of the nineteenth-century movement. Until then most New Zealanders believed that New Zealand women had been handed the vote on a plate, as William Pember Reeves had stated categorically in his early and influential history. Grimshaw's account documented the campaign, showing just how energetically New Zealand women had had to press their case, how vehemently they had been opposed, and how narrowly they had won in 1893.

Yet to 1970s feminists it seemed that, despite the effort made and the goal achieved, all had been to little effect. How had New Zealand women benefited from the vote? Why had such an early and apparently important victory made so little difference to the position of women in the twentieth century? Nowhere was this more succinctly encapsulated than in the banner that hung above the heads of three women who chained themselves to railings in Christchurch's Cathedral Square in 1972: 'Yesterday's suffragettes; today's marionettes'.[5]

In 1993 we are marking the centenary of that suffrage victory, largely in a mood of celebration. The Suffrage Centenary Trust has taken as its slogan 'Celebrating the past, challenging the future'. We are less critical and less ambivalent than we (or at least some of us) were twenty or so years ago. Why is this?

Several things have, I believe, contributed to this change in attitude. There has been, first of all, a growth in confidence, which has fostered a desire to celebrate the women who fought for a goal that is still seen to have some value. Thanks to this new assurance, women are eager to celebrate women, and the fact of being a woman, if not to celebrate feminism or being a feminist. The vote itself is still valued by the vast majority of New Zealand women and men as legitimate and beneficial, even if belief in the elected representatives and the parliamentary system has never sunk so low. Indeed, we are now in the midst of a major constitutional review of *how* that vote is to be exercised. Current levels of non-voting, cynicism and the poor reputation of politicians (especially of political leaders) indicate that the public are disillusioned with *politicians*, not with the right to vote or with the democratic process. Indeed, the current constitutional debate about proportional representation is about maximising the effect of that vote.

More New Zealand women can probably be mobilised now to take part in, or feel themselves part of, a celebration of their sex. Women who might never have called themselves feminist or been in any explicit way part of the feminist movement can be persuaded that things have changed – and that some of this change has been beneficial. There has been some recognition of the legitimacy of campaigns with which feminists have been associated – against domestic violence, for example. Unequal earnings, sexist language and advertising, sexual harassment, domestic violence and other concerns are recognised, and measures exist to combat them. Issues like these are no longer the butt of derision and jokes in all but a feminist enclave, as they were in the early 1970s. And while there is still considerable opposition to women and antagonism to feminist ideas and arguments, the hostility is not as open, explicit or unreserved as it once was. In most public gatherings obviously sexist remarks are likely to meet a disapproving reception.

In the early 1990s there is also a greater appreciation of the forces working against social change, and of the tremendous effort needed to move things even a little. This has resulted in greater sympathy for the nineteenth-century women who campaigned for so much and, apparently, gained so little. It also stands in contrast with the tremendous indignation, impatience, fervour, expectation and hope of the early 1970s. Such a mood of impatience for change was not confined to women and the feminist movement, but was shared also by other social activists. The naivety and political exuberance of the early 1970s were more pronounced in the conflict of the later 1970s. But this mood has mellowed or become transmuted in the succeeding decades: economic recession has hit; political parties and other organisations (especially in late 1970s and early 1980s) have absorbed some of the political impetus, and have changed, along with the causes and style of their advocacy.

The 1993 celebration of 1893 is also occurring at a time when interest in New Zealand history is very much greater than it was even twenty years ago. More New Zealanders have a genuine interest in knowing about their own past. There is, too, I think, a desire among women to celebrate, to act positively, to draw attention to their achievements and to claim the recognition they deserve. So much of feminist politics (though not feminism as a whole) is concerned with documenting and redressing the injustices, and inequalities suffered by women. Therefore a time of celebration, where the emotional tide can be reversed, is welcome.

1. *Margaret Lovell-Smith (ed.),* The Woman Question: Writings by the women who won the vote, *Auckland, 1992*
2. *Pat Rosier (ed.),* Been Around for Quite a While: Twenty years of Broadsheet magazine, *Auckland, 1992*
3. *Robin Hyde,* Disputed Ground: the journalism of Robin Hyde. *Introduced and selected by Gillian Boddy and Jacqueline Matthews, Wellington, 1991*
4. *Patricia Grimshaw,* Women's Suffrage in New Zealand, *Auckland, 1972*
5. *Christine Dann,* Up from Under: Women and liberation in New Zealand, 1970–1985, *Wellington, 1985, p. 1*

Sources and Further Reading

Dann, Christine. *Up from Under: Women and liberation in New Zealand, 1970–1985*, Wellington, 1985

Grimshaw, Patricia. *Women's Suffrage in New Zealand*, Auckland, 1972

Lovell-Smith, Margaret (ed.). *The Woman Question: Writings by the women who won the vote*, Auckland, 1992

Rosier, Pat (ed.). *Been Around for Quite a While: Twenty years of Broadsheet magazine*, Auckland, 1992

Chapter 1

Early Awakenings
1850s–1870s

Three women raised the question of women's rights in New Zealand in the 1860s and early 1870s. They were Mary Ann Müller, whose pamphlet *An Appeal to the Men of New Zealand*, written under the pseudonym 'Femina', appeared in the *Nelson Examiner* in 1869; Mary Taylor, a Yorkshirewoman, who spent fourteen years in Wellington (1845-59) running her own business, and who subsequently wrote a series of articles published in 1870 as *The First Duty of Women*; and Mary Colclough, who instigated a lively debate in the Auckland newspapers in the early 1870s as the correspondent 'Polly Plum'.

Their writings introduced the novel idea of women's rights to colonial readers. As Mary Ann Müller noted, the subject 'is one which has been but little alluded to in New Zealand, but it is seething, yeasting in many minds' (1.1). All three were primarily concerned to point out the injustice of the inequalities between women and men before the law and within the constitution. Their fundamental argument – that men and women should possess equal legal and political rights – was radical in the mid-nineteenth century.

Women at this time could exercise only limited power within the economic, political and legal structures of colonial society. They were not entitled to vote in national elections (though a small number of women ratepayers gained the right to vote in municipal elections in Otago and Nelson in 1867, and in the rest of the country from 1875). They were not members of the professions (apart from teaching), and, upon marriage, they relinquished most rights to own property. Very few women indeed had the means to obtain for themselves any degree of economic security.

The case that each of these three women advanced in support of women gaining the right to vote (and to own property as married women, to be educated and to enter employment) was based strongly on arguments of natural justice. They took the reasons used to advance universal male suffrage and applied them to women. If all men could vote as a matter of right, what disqualified women from the entitlement of citizenship? What capacity did women lack to be excluded from political participation? On what grounds were women as a whole now denied the vote?

The basic democratic tenet of 'no taxation without representation' was also raised, though few women commanded resources which made them liable for tax. More important, these writers put forward the proposition that women's interests could be represented in the political process only through the direct exercise of a vote, not through the vote of husbands, fathers and brothers. It is important to recognise the radical nature of this claim, given Müller's apparently light dismissal of the idea that women would ever want to sit in parliament. Within a few years many would also claim this as a fundamental right.

The extension of universal suffrage to men made the disenfranchisement of women patently anomalous. When the majority of men as well as women were excluded from the political process, the distinction was not so obvious. When women were excluded simply because they were women, while all men – of whatever status, calling, education or wealth – were enfranchised, the differentiation by gender became conspicuous, and was seen as unjust by increasing numbers of women and by some men. At times such arguments led these early feminist advocates to assert the entitlement of educated, middle- and upper-class women over the illiterate labouring men. 'Is she as capable', asked Mary Ann Müller, 'as our bullock-drivers, labourers, and mechanics?'(1.1).

These were the grounds on which Müller and Colclough, especially, challenged their readers to defend the status quo. John Stuart Mill's attempts to gain British women the vote at the time of the Second Reform Bill and his *Subjection of Women*, published in England in 1869, were an important influence on their ideas. Mill's treatise was read in New Zealand and helped popularise the ideas that flowed from the pens of 'Femina' and 'Polly Plum' (1.5).

The 'three Marys' were well-educated women. Their personal experience as well as their intellectual and political convictions contributed to the views they advanced. Mary Ann Müller wrote under the closely guarded cover of her pseudonym 'Femina' (her identity was not disclosed until the 1890s). Her *Appeal*, written as a plea to the men in whose hands power and political rights lay, was 'penned in jealous secrecy from every human eye' (1.1). Her second husband, Dr Müller, did not share her views on women's emancipation; she had to write clandestinely and could not reveal her identity in public. This was clearly not ideal, but Müller's second marriage was a distinct improvement on her first. Müller's first husband had, it seems, been either negligent or abusive, or both. She seems to be speaking from personal experience when she emphasises the disabilities suffered by women when disenfranchised, and their helplessness as married women dependent economically and in other ways on husbands who might exercise their authority in a cruel manner. Mary Ann left her husband, emigrating to New Zealand at the age of thirty with her two sons, and marrying a second time when news of his death reached her in Nelson. The *Appeal* was published with the co-operation of the sympathetic editor of the *Nelson Examiner*, Charles Elliott. It was reprinted a number of times after its initial appearance in 1869.

Müller and Taylor wrote their pieces as manifestos – statements of belief designed to challenge, provoke and persuade. Colclough was more impulsive and dialogic, engaging directly with her audience both in her columns and, following their success, in a series of public lectures. Mary Colclough, or as she was better known 'Polly Plum', presented the abstract principles of justice in an immediate and practical way. Championing the case of a widow with six children who was in gaol for debt (1.3), she asked what a woman in this situation was to do when 'indifferently educated' and 'trained in the erroneous system that fits women solely for dependence.' A woman in this plight was subject to the law but forbidden a vote. How could she ever climb out of poverty and deprivation if denied access to education and, through that, a path to better-paid work?

In 'What Women Want' (1.4) she describes 'the women's cause' as 'a holy cause', using the golden rule to support her argument for reform of laws that distinguish between men and women in property and political rights. She does not see differences between women and men as a justifiable basis for a disparity in earnings or in power. Colclough herself was a widow in her early thirties when she wrote to the papers. She describes some of her own experience in 'Answers to "Jellaby Pater" ' (1.7).

All three writers believed that women's unequal position in law had a detrimental effect on their social and economic situation. They were at pains to point out that, whatever the ideals of a society based on Christian principles, the reality was one of failed and imperfect human and social relationships, in which women were frequently the casualties. Of particular concern was the economic vulnerability of women, especially married women, who relied on their husbands for support, and were unable to control property or earnings – their own or their husbands'.

Mary Taylor's book was devoted almost entirely to this subject. The remedy she offers is the most emphatic of those proposed by the three writers. *The First Duty of Women*, from which the piece included here is an excerpt (1.2), is an uncompromising statement in which she asserts not only that it is desirable for women to have the opportunity and capacity to be economically independent, but that they have a duty to be so. She decries the situation in which middle class women, to whom the piece is addressed, must look upon the decision to marry as a mercenary one, with the only alternative a life of miserable poverty. The first duty, she declares, is 'for every woman to protect herself from the danger of being forced to marry' (1.2). For men too, she says, the view of marriage as fundamentally an economic relationship is corrupting, and contorts human relationships. The man who marries for money, or in the expectation of securing a wife's services in exchange for material support, is, she writes, 'like the naturalist trying to secure possession of that fish that has the power of dropping off its limbs when touched. He seizes one after another and destroys them all' (1.2).

Mary Taylor knew from experience the cost of economic insecurity. Her family suffered a serious loss of fortune, and in New Zealand she had to earn her own living. She succeeded and found in the experience a rewarding sense of satisfaction as well as a high degree of personal freedom. This was not enough, however, to make her stay in colonial Wellington – a place she found totally devoid of stimulating company. Mary Taylor did not return to New Zealand after her departure in 1859 and lived the rest of her life in England. She did not marry.

The 'three Marys' made important statements of their beliefs which were read and taken up by their contemporaries. Published in England and writing principally for the metropolitan audience, Mary Taylor was probably the one whose ideas received least circulation in New Zealand. Today the only copy of *The First Duty of Women* held in any New Zealand library is a microfilm copy in the Alexander Turnbull Library. Some copies of Mary Taylor's book probably did find their way to New Zealand in private hands, and it is extremely likely that there were New Zealand subscribers to the *Victoria Magazine*, where the chapters of

The First Duty of Women were originally published.

Mary Colclough's correspondence in the Auckland newspapers stimulated an extremely lively debate on the subject of women's rights during 1871 and 1872. The pieces selected here represent only a small portion. Soon after, in 1874, 'Polly Plum' left Auckland for Melbourne, where she continued her activities as a public advocate for women's causes. She was reported to have become 'an advanced thinker' on marriage. With her departure the issue faded from public attention. There was no one else at that time prepared to take up the cause. Mary Colclough later returned to New Zealand, where she died in Picton in 1885 at the age of forty-nine.

By contrast, the appearance of Mary Ann Müller's *Appeal* brought no outward change to her life. She continued to live in Nelson, her views unknown to all but a few friends. Years later she told Kate Sheppard how satisfying she found it 'to watch the efforts of those younger and abler women striving bravely to succeed in obtaining rights, so long unjustly withheld'.[1] She died, aged 81, in 1901.

There were other women in New Zealand at this time who shared some, if not all, of the views of Müller, Taylor and Colclough on the advancement of women. In Dunedin, Learmonth Whyte Dalrymple worked hard for a secondary school for girls to be established at the same time as a school for boys was opened. Otago Girls' High School took its first pupils in 1871, offering an intellectually stimulating education rather than the conventional smattering of accomplishments that passed as standard schooling for girls. Similarly, Jane Maria Atkinson was one of a group of Nelson women who sought 'a boy's education' (i.e., an academic one) for the girls in the town.[2] The Edger family in Auckland encouraged their daughter Kate to continue her education beyond school to Auckland University College. Their determination, and that of others in Canterbury, Otago, and later, Wellington, meant that degree courses became available to women students as well as to men. The number of women students who followed Kate Edger (BA, Auckland, 1877), Helen Connon (MA, Canterbury, 1881) and Caroline Freeman (BA, Otago, 1885) was never large but it was significant.

As far as employment was concerned, the options available to women in nineteenth-century New Zealand were limited. The vast majority of young single women worked as domestic servants and were better paid but harder worked in the colony than in the United Kingdom. A small number of women found work as teachers, while others – often widows or women coping on their own – ran businesses: shops, post offices, hotels and the like. Colonial life threw up many circumstances in which the ideal of the home-nurturing, dutiful, financially dependent wife was thrown into conflict with day-to-day reality, for example, husbands who shot off to the goldfields or to Australia and were never seen again. For women, this meant earning a living, supporting children and running a household single-handed, or with only the erratic assistance of an unlucky, improvident or mobile spouse. In the circumstances of their daily lives many women were forced to develop independence, self-reliance and practicality – qualities which they may not in any way have recognised or expressed as feminist, but which were a long way from the simpering passivity or meek gentility often associated with 'Victorian womanhood'. The problem of married women's right to control property and earnings was a real one in colonial New Zealand and had a direct bearing on the situation of many women, not simply those in the upper echelons of society. Reforms to the law occurred in 1860, 1870 and 1884 – not as a matter of abstract justice, but in response to the economic plight of a considerable number of settler women who were otherwise likely to become a charge on the meagre public purse.

Women in New Zealand in the mid-nineteenth century may have lived at some distance from the capitals of sophisticated urban culture but they were not unaware of the ideas and movements that were occurring in other parts of the world. Mary Ann Müller noted: 'women in the colony read, watch, and reflect' on events in other parts of the world. She was referring particularly to the progress of the first women's suffrage group, formed in England in 1865. Her *Appeal* makes reference to Lydia Becker's well-known 1867 article on women's suffrage, which was published in the *Contemporary Review*. News was eagerly absorbed from newspapers, books and visitors. One of the most important of these was Maria Susan Rye, a talented if rather rumbustious person, who had been part of the group working for reform of married women's property law in England in the mid-1850s. She travelled through New Zealand in 1863-64, staying with Mary Ann Müller in January 1864. She had an important influence in shaping Müller's ideas. Mary Taylor was in constant correspondence with friends and family in England throughout her time in New Zealand.

Mary Ann Müller, Mary Taylor and Mary Colclough may have been isolated voices in New Zealand but they had echoes in other parts of the world. Their writings did not prompt widespread agitation, sudden changes in the law or even a sustained debate on the position of women. But their ideas were read and discussed. They had raised the question of women's rights.

1. *Quoted in Aorewa McLeod, 'Mary Ann Müller', BNZW, p.464*
2. *Frances Porter, 'Jane Maria Atkinson', BNZW, pp.25–29*

Sources and Further Reading

Dalziel, Raewyn. 'The Colonial Helpmeet: Women's role and the vote in nineteenth-century New Zealand', in Barbara Brookes, Charlotte Macdonald and Margaret Tennant (eds), *Women in History*, Wellington, 1986, pp.55–68
Elphick Malone, Judith. 'What's Wrong with Emma? The feminist debate in colonial Auckland', in Barbara Brookes, Charlotte Macdonald and Margaret Tennant (eds), *Women in History*, Wellington, 1986, pp.69–85
Elphick Malone, Judith. 'Mary Colclough', *BNZW*, pp.142–145
Grimshaw, Patricia. *Women's Suffrage in New Zealand*, Auckland, 1972
Macdonald, Charlotte. *A Woman of Good Character*, Wellington, 1990
McLeod, Aorewa. 'Mary Ann Müller', *BNZW*, pp.461–464
Rendall, Jane. *The Origins of Modern Feminism: Women in Britain, France and the United States, 1780–1860*, London, 1985
Sargison, Patricia. 'Mary Taylor', *BNZW*, pp.657–660
Stevens, Joan. *Mary Taylor, Friend of Charlotte Bronte: Letters from New Zealand and elsewhere*, Auckland, 1972

1.1.   An Appeal to the Men of New Zealand
by Femina (Mary Ann Müller) (1869)

A wise ancient declared that the most perfect popular government was that 'where an injury done to the meanest subject is an insult upon the whole constitution'. What, therefore, can be said for a Government that deliberately inflicts injury upon a great mass of its intelligent and respectable subjects; that virtually ignores their existence in all that can contribute to their happiness as subjects; that takes a special care to strike at the root of their love of country by teaching them that they have no part in forming or maintaining its glory, while it rigidly exerts from them all penalties, even unto death? What can be said, what urged, in extenuation of this crying evil, this monstrous injustice? 'Custom; use; it has always been so'. This may be enough to say of the past – 'let the dead past bury its dead'; but is it to be remedied for the future? How long are women to remain a wholly unrepresented body of the people? This is a question that has of late been agitated in England, and women in this colony read, watch, and reflect. Though their household cares chiefly occupy them, yet many find leisure in the quiet evening hours to read not only their fashions, and colonial papers, but the English papers also. They cannot remain ignorant of the agitation of this, to them, great matter, and it has struck the writer of these few pages that I might not be wholly vain to make an appeal to the men of this our adopted land.

America has in many things stepped in advance of the mother country. How often has she shown us the advantages of things the English mind feared to attempt, though it does not disdain often to adopt these innovations, and, as Mr Gladstone says, 'Americanise our institutions'? Why should not New Zealand also lead? Why ever pursue the hard-beaten track of ages? Have we not enough cobwebs and mists to cloud our mental gaze, enough fetters to impede our onward progress here, that we must voluntarily shackle ourselves with old world principles in the way of Government. But to come to the point. Why has a woman no power to vote, no right to vote, when she happens to possess all the requisites which legally qualify a man for that right?

She may be a householder, have large possessions, and pay her share of taxes towards the public revenue; but sex disqualifies her. Were it a question of general knowledge and intelligence as compared with men, women might submit unmurmuringly; but this is not the case. The point is, is she as capable as our bullock-drivers, labourers, and mechanics?

It may surely be confidently asserted that when a woman is possessed of sufficient skill and management to retain unassisted the guidance of her family, and remain a householder, she develops more than a moderate degree of capability. The weak and incapable generally elect to live in the homes of others, they naturally shrink from the responsibility of such a position and are thus placed out of the question.

The true position is, that educated thinking members of the State are degraded below the level of the ploughman, who perhaps can neither read nor write. And this is 'law' – called 'justice'! How is the word 'just' weakened and falsified! It is enough to 'make the angels weep'. But we must not despair. We have in our General Legislature statesmen, justly so called, whose powers of intellect, aye, of oratory, would make them shine in the English Parliament. Champions from among these men will step forth and fight the good fight for those fettered weak ones who can only think and suffer. Women's eyes turn in hope – nay trust – on some leading spirits who will not fail them. They but need rousing – the knowledge that we claim our right – that we wake and watch.

It is not difficult to learn in whom dwells the fine old chivalrous spirit towards which the world will ever warm. The women read the *Hansard* as well as our *Punch* and *Cornhill*, though perhaps – *magna est veritas* – we do skip the figures sometimes.

But let us go a little deeper into the case, and inquire what are the just claims of women to vote, and the objection to their so doing. We live under the dominion of a Queen – England rejects the Salique law. A woman may be an heiress of a county, may nominate a minister who takes charge of the souls of thousands, may vote in joint-stock companies, in vestries for guardians, may, I believe, even be an overseer; while in America women are doctors, lawyers, managers of factories, schools, &c, are Government clerks, and in one place Judges. Indeed, if we ponder on the power of wealth, we are struck with a wholesome feminine awe of Miss Burdett Coutts, who even entered into the matter at issue some time since between the Bishops Gray and Colenso, she having power to withdraw some large endowment bestowed by her upon the Church of Natal. When we consider what great wheels are turned by women, can we fail to wonder at their being so rigidly, so jealously excluded from the touch of this one of voting? And after all, its possession would amount to but a fractional power in our government. What real influence upon society is exercised by a woman like Florence Nightingale? Yet to such women men arbitrarily deny a power granted to a sweep.

It is excellent
To have a giant's strength; but it is
tyrannous
To use it like a giant.

I cannot pretend to follow all the proceedings as they have taken place in England during the close of the last year; but I note that the name of a lady householder had been placed upon the electoral roll in some county, and struck off by the revising barrister. The lady appealed to the Court of Common Pleas, and the Judges dismissed the appeal, simply because she was a woman, and therefore had no *locus standi*, and possessed no right of appeal; though it seems that some time, days even, had been fully occupied in hearing, going into the subject, and finally deciding upon this same appeal, which looks rather paradoxical. It is not worth the trouble to repeat, or even refer to all the reasons given by these astute Judges for their decision in this case; – the majority can but provoke a smile. We are compelled to bend to their law, but decline to receive their logic. One, Justice Probyn, sapiently considers that the right of voting demands 'an improved understanding, which women are not supposed to have.' Ample room for improvement in this Judge's understanding, I fancy. Another, named Bayles, considers that granting this power to them would be 'a premium on women to remain unmarried', or 'to desire that their husbands might die, in order to possess votes as widows'. From these, and such specimens of improved understanding, may we be preserved! This same learned Judge holds to our 'legal incapacity as women'. He says, 'Otherwise aliens might vote'. Aliens we truly are – alienated from natural rights. But it were worse than vain to dwell upon this phase of the proceedings, the law as it now stands is against us. 'Long and undisturbed usage', to quote the words of the Chief Justice, settles it.

About 1300 women in one place (Salford) placed their names upon the list of voters, and more than 5000 in Manchester; but of course the whole question of legal claim is now disposed of.

There was much reference during the proceedings to old and new statutes, inquiries instituted as to whether women were included when the word 'man' was used, which was allowed at once in the words 'manslaughter' and 'mankind', though it appears we are not even 'persons' sometimes. However, the gist of it all is that an express enactment is requisite to enable women to vote. Hence this appeal to the common sense of New Zealand men – of New Zealand law-givers. I cannot appeal to a higher quality in a statesman than common sense, for is it not the sense of the common interest. Let them dispassionately ask themselves whether that interest will not be advanced by the admission of a few female votes. There are but few, comparatively speaking, who could claim to vote on the strength of possessing the minimum amount of property and those few would probably bring pretty keen intelligence on the duty. The infusion of a fresher, purer spirit, and higher tone, would result from the concession of this right to women. As to the *bete noir* of women sitting in Parliament with men, rely upon it there is scarcely a woman in New Zealand who would desire or consent to do so. It is a bugbear, an absurdly exaggerated view of a notion taken by men whose intellect must be as weak as it is intolerant. Besides, who makes the laws? Men. Theirs is the power to grant or to deny; let them so frame our admission to the privilege we desire, as to exclude us from that duty which we consider clearly incompatible with our necessitous ones.

We ask you, our rulers, to disembarrass yourselves of those tenets of Government, built up during ages upon a system of senseless and credulous trust in those principles which guided our ancestors. Shake them aside, or subject them to a rigid scrutiny, and see how they fit the requirements of the present day. Women are now educated, thinking beings, very different from the females of the darker ages. They might have been contented with their lot in those days, and '*ceux-la sont veritable heureux, qui croient l'etre*'; but this is not so now. The stride of advancement is rapid, 'the roaring loom of time flies on', and while our law-givers 'work and weave in endless motion', we yearn to feel ourselves borne on by the stream of progress, to be improving as all should be, to feel that our claims have

June 1, 1878.

NEW ZEALAND MAIL.

Social Topics.

WOMAN'S RIGHTS.

In view of the talked-of changes in the electoral franchise, we reprint, as appropriate to the time, "An Appeal to the Men of New Zealand by a Woman," the work of an eminent hand, which was published in pamphlet form at Nelson in the year 1869. Sir George Grey or Mr. Ballance—we will not venture to use the conjunction copulative and—may be able to answer the question put by the author :— "How long are women to remain a wholly unrepresented body of the people?"

AN APPEAL TO THE MEN OF NEW ZEALAND.

BY FEMINA.

A wise ancient declared that the most perfect popular government was that "where an injury done to the meanest subject is an insult upon the whole constitution." What, therefore, can be said for a Government that deliberately inflicts injury upon a great mass of its intelligent and respectable subjects ; that virtually ignores their existence in all that can contribute to their happiness as subjects ; that takes a special care to strike at the root of their love of country by teaching them that they have no part in forming or maintaining its glory, while it rigidly exerts from them all penalties, even unto death? What can be said, what urged, in extenuation of this crying evil, this monstrous injustice ? "Custom ; use ; it has always been so." This may be enough to say of the past—"let the dead past bury its dead ;" but is it to be remedied for the future? How long are women to remain a wholly unrepresented body of the people ? This is a question that has of late been agitated in England, and women in this colony read, watch, and reflect. Though their household cares chiefly occupy them, yet many find leisure in the quiet evening hours to read not only their fashions, and colonial papers, but the English papers also. They cannot remain ignorant of the agitation of this, to them, great matter, and it has struck the writer of these few pages that it might not be wholly vain to make an appeal to the men of this our adopted land.

America has in many things stepped in advance of the mother country. How often has she shown us the advantages of things the English mind feared to attempt, though it does not disdain often to adopt these innovations, and, as Mr. Gladstone says, "Americanise our institutions !" Why should not New Zealand also lead ? Why ever pursue the hard-beaten track of ages ? Have we not enough cobwebs and mists to cloud our mental gaze, enough fetters to impede our onward progress here, that we must voluntarily shackle ourselves with old world principles in the way of Government. But to come to the point, Why has a woman no power to vote, no right to vote, when she happens to possess all the requisites which legally qualify a man for that right ?

She may be a householder, have large possessions, and pay her share of taxes towards the public revenue ; but sex disqualifies her. Were it a question of general knowledge and intelligence as compared with men, women might submit unmurmuringly ; but this is not the case. The point is, Is she as capable as our bullock-drivers, laborers, and me-

society is exercised by a woman like Florence Nightingale? Yet to such women men arbitrarily deny a power granted to a sweep.

It is excellent
To have a giant's strength ; but it is tyrannous
To use it like a giant.

I cannot pretend to follow all the proceedings as they have taken place in England during the close of the last year ; but I note that the name of a lady householder had been placed upon the electoral roll in some county, and struck off by the revising barrister. The lady appealed to the Court of Common Pleas, and the Judges dismissed the appeal, simply because she was a woman, and therefore had no *locus standi*, and possessed no right of appeal ; though it seems that some time, days even, had been fully occupied in hearing, going into the subject, and finally deciding upon this same appeal, which looks rather paradoxical. It is not worth the trouble to repeat, or even refer to all the reasons given by these astute Judges for their decision in this case :—the majority can but provoke a smile. We are compelled to bend to their law, but decline to receive their logic. One, Justice Probyn, sapiently considers that the right of voting demands "an improved understanding, which women are not supposed to have." Ample room for improvement in this Judge's understanding, I fancy. Another, named Bayles, considers that granting this power to them would be "a premium on women to remain unmarried," or "to desire that their husbands might die, in order to possess votes as widows." From these, and such specimens of improved understanding, may we be preserved ! This same learned Judge holds to our "legal incapacity as women." He says, "Otherwise aliens might vote." Aliens we truly are—alienated from natural rights. But it were worse than vain to dwell upon this phase of the proceedings, the law as it now stands is against us. "Long and undisturbed usage," to quote the words of the Chief Justice, settles it.

About 1300 women in one place (Salford) placed their names upon the list of voters, and more than 5000 in Manchester ; but of course the whole question of legal claim is now disposed of.

There was much reference during the proceedings to old and new statutes, inquiries instituted as to whether women were included when the word "man" was used, which was allowed at once in the words "manslaughter" and "mankind," though it cppears we are not even "persons" sometimes. However, the gist of it all is that an express enactment is requisite to enable women to vote. Hence this appeal to the common sense of New Zealand men—of New Zealand law-givers. I cannot appeal to a higher quality in a statesman than common sense, for it is not the sense of the common interest. Let them dispassionately ask themselves whether that interest will not be advanced by the admission of a few female votes. There are but few, comparatively speaking, who could claim to vote on the strength of possessing the minimum amount of property, and those few would probably bring pretty keen intelligence on the duty. The infusion of a fresher, purer spirit, and higher tone, would result from the concession of this right to women. As to the *bete noir* of women sitting in Parliament with men, rely upon it there is scarcely a woman in New Zealand who would desire or consent to do so. It is a bugbear, an absurdly exaggerated view of a notion taken by men whose intellect must be as weak as it is intolerant. Besides, who

when, and why not be r men believe in the hidd devotion and sympathy unsealing touch—the qui support their best efforts women enter into the top husbands and brothers, preciate all their plans society when their pri *esprit de corps* of whic ceptible.

Go to our Governmen so far behind boys in inte verse in society with girls and compare them with age ;—are they less sensi even venture to assert eighteen are better infor jects of general informati are. After this I grant generally goes in an in young man advances in intellect, the woman's larly if married—narrow her own immediate circle duties she casts herself might preach a sermon t upon the sin of so contra thies. Do but observe th sex with the interest an you. Note the delicatel her wondrous power au unflagging cheerfulness banishment to some bac land, where she toils around her ; where she r her fruit 'and flowers quently digs her potato while she yet cheers he her children with anxi from the social sphere clings. Mark the persi she toils on, till, in sor turns to grace the settl of her days.

Many, alas ! have fa the toilsome march of doing their duty. Pe grim mothers of the la forgotten, but rather l fate deepen your symp

Our women are bra amount of self-reliance ventionalities eminentl great nation. Give th their grasp and powe cabined, and confined" It is weakened and only a close observer force, the unspent e many seemingly ordin

Mark the sudden qu girl, or the quiet re matron, upon a politi paper before her, and prise, or hear the rebu to step beyond their paterfamilias stops th you marvel that the g the new fashions, or in discussions upon chines, and other n Women of the middl this open, systematic deference to the se real civilisation, and will never wantonly g over a woman, even t wife or daughter, and mercy. When wom

Femina (Mary Ann Müller), 'An Appeal to the Men of New Zealand', reproduced in the *New Zealand Mail*, 1 June 1878. *Alexander Turnbull Library* become higher, nobler, and our sympathies wider. Let the laws be fitted to the people and times. Do you still persecute for religious opinions? Do you still burn for witchcraft? Why, when the broad road of progress is cleared for so many human beings, is the Juggernaut car of prejudice still to be driven on, crushing the crowds of helpless women beneath its wheels?

Permit them to take, as their right, an interest, and some small part in the Government of their adopted land. That interest will grow apace, enlarging the scope of their ideas, and in time changing entirely the habit of their thoughts. I cannot more highly compliment the intelligence and equity of those who rule, than quietly to submit to their consideration our bitter grievance.

It is one which has been but little alluded to in New Zealand, but it is seething, yeasting in many minds, I believe, and it must bear fruit.

I do not think we are likely to call together a great female convention, like that over which the Lady Mayoress presided in Manchester; nor is it probable that a society for the promotion of female suffrage will be formed here; yet not the less earnestly do we, in all feminine gentleness, ask redress. Few New Zealand women, I dare say, have read even a review of Miss Becker's thesis on women's rights, which was read before the British Association and excited such deep interest; but we know of such a thesis having commanded public notice, and a feather shows the direction of the wind. A change is imminent – all must feel it to be so. It is but a question of when, and why not be now? Why will not men believe in the hidden wealth of mental devotion and sympathy that waits for their unsealing touch – the quiet strength, ready to support their best efforts? How willingly will women enter into the topics discussed by their husbands and brothers, how much better appreciate all their plans for the well-being of society when their privileges develop the *esprit de corps* of which they are so susceptible.

Go to our Government schools. Are girls so far behind boys in intelligence there? Converse in society with girls of sixteen or twenty, and compare them with youths of their own age – are they less sensible? I think I might even venture to assert that most girls of eighteen are better informed upon many subjects of general information than their brothers are. After this I grant that the improvement generally goes in an inverse ratio, and as the young man advances in the cultivation of his intellect, the woman's

intelligence – particularly if married – narrows more and more to her own immediate circle of duties. Into these duties she casts herself with an energy that might preach a sermon to the men around her upon the sin of so contracting her vast sympathies. Do but observe the idiosyncrasies of the sex with the interest and care they claim from you. Note the delicately-nurtured woman, see her wondrous power and energy, her patient, unflagging cheerfulness during the years of banishment to some back station in New Zealand, where she toils until the waste smiles around her; where she rears her poultry, grows her fruit and flowers – aye, and not unfrequently digs her potatoes and chops her wood, while she yet cheers her husband and teaches her children with anxious care lest they drop from the social sphere to which her heart clings. Mark the persistent faith with which she toils on, till, in some happy cases, she returns to grace the settled town in the evening of her days.

Many, alas! have fallen exhausted, spent in the toilsome march of life, fallen like soldiers, doing their duty. Peace to the martyr pilgrim mothers of the land? Let them not be forgotten, but rather let the memory of their fate deepen your sympathy with the sex.

Our women are brave and strong, with an amount of self-reliance and freedom from conventionalities eminently calculated to form a great nation. Give them scope. At present their grasp and power of mind is 'cribbed, cabined, and confined' to one narrow groove. It is weakened and famished by disuse, and only a close observer can detect the latent force, the unspent energy lying dormant in many seemingly ordinary characters.

Mark the sudden questions of a bright eager girl, or the quiet remark of some sensible matron, upon a political matter in the newspaper before her, and see the cold stare of surprise, or hear the rebuke about women seeking to step beyond their province, with which the paterfamilias stops the innovation, and can you marvel that the girl turns to gossip about the new fashions, or the mother takes refuge in discussions upon servants, sewing machines, and other minor domestic details? Women of the middle class suffer most from this open, systematic 'putting down'; for deference to the sex is the best test of real civilisation, and a truly well-bred man will never wantonly give pain to, or tyrannise over a woman, even though that woman be his wife or daughter, and therefore utterly at his mercy. When women shall be interested in the entire contents of newspapers, there will be found fewer inferior novels and serials upon the table. When her enthusiasm can find vent upon topics of world-wide interest, she will furnish criticisms with fewer startling eccentricities. She will become more truly feminine, and our journals will less abound in smartly satirical articles upon 'the girl of the period', &c. How often now are we pained to read the attacks made upon our dress and manners; many of them, too, having in them the grain of truth that gives a false colouring of sincerity to the whole libel; but the critics of the day delight in nibbling at results instead of dipping deep into causes – they revel in detail, rarely rising to great principles. Thus much venom is spent upon feminine follies, while the cure lies in their own hands – that is, premising them to be male critics, as I take it for granted they be. Men alone can give us the power to rise above our present degradation: they must cease to consider inactivity to be delicacy, and frittering away time upon elegant fancies to be refinement. Women's minds require hardening by the principle of reasoning. Watts says, 'What is it but custom that has for past centuries confined the brightest geniuses, even of the highest rank, in the female world, to the employment of the needle only, and secluded them unmercifully from the pleasures of knowledge, and the divine improvements of reason. But we begin to break these chains, and reason begins to dictate the proper education of youth.' We do but begin now; still having begun, let us make good strides in the noble race for knowledge – knowledge of all kinds tending to the welfare of the community, and some knowledge of and share in the government of our country is imperative. And where, in what land upon the face of the earth, was there ever a finer field for educating the people in the art of government? We have it to satiety. It is a colonial vice, and

The gods are just, and of our pleasant vices
Make instruments to scourge us.

Mushroom provinces crop up, shedding forth showers of embryo senators, whose amusing blunders supply fun for the excluded sex; for on the acknowledged rule that lookers on see the most, women, outside the strife and confusion of party bickerings, often detect the coming storm that will overwhelm the self-satisfied, obtuse senator, and know the mine that will infallibly be sprung

beneath his clumsy incautious tread. Truly, if, as has been said, 'we learn by our failures', we shall become a wise nation in the heart of government. And we are improving, we begin to see our faults, and to use the language of Sir James Macintosh, 'who will be hardy enough to assert that a better constitution is not attainable than any which has hitherto appeared? Is the limit of human wisdom to be estimated in the science of politics alone, by the extent of its present attainments? Is the most sublime and difficult of all arts, the improvement of the social order, the alleviation of the miseries of the civil condition of man [Query, woman also?] to be alone stationary, amid the rapid progress of every other art, liberal and vulgar, to perfection! Where would be the atrocious guilt of a grand experiment to ascertain the portion of freedom and happiness that can be created by political institutions?'

In the face of these thoughts, how small a matter seems the simple concession here pleaded. And for that cause how frail a hope seems these few pages, penned in jealous secrecy from every human eye, for such is the ban we live under that a woman naturally learns to shrink from drawing down upon her devoted head the avalanche of man's condemnation, and travels on with 'bated breath', hiding her noblest, highest aspirations! Yet it is a hope. Though like a rope flung to a drowning creature, when we close our eyes in dread of seeing it fall short, it is sent forth. It is the cry of aliens for naturalisation, the wail of the fettered for freedom, and I feel constrained to put forth the prayer – to strive to utter 'the thoughts that lie too deep for tears'. Fully is the difficulty of the task realised, weakness and inability press painfully, yet the counsel of the gentle Italian prevails:

Tanto ti prego piu gentile spirto
Non lassar la magnanima tua impresa

I do but ask for my sex a calm unprejudiced consideration of their condition. I feel that our claim will be granted, that the time is coming, but the hours are passing, *'Periunt et imputantur'*, and my whole soul yearns to see it 'before I go hence'.

The change is coming, but why is New Zealand only to follow? Why not take the initiative? She has but to inaugurate this new position, all will applaud. 'One touch of nature makes the whole world kin'. It will be the spark to the train now laid in most civilised countries.

Take the instant way:
For honour travels in a strait so narrow.
Where one but goes abreast; keep then the
*   path;*
For emulation hath a thousand sons,
That one by one pursue; if you give way,

Or hedge aside from the direct forthright,
Like to an entered tide, they all rush by
And leave you hindmost.

This version published in the New Zealand
Mail, *1 June 1878, p.7*

1.2. Marriage
by Mary Taylor (1870)

'Why would you upset all the world with your new arrangements? Whoever heard of women working for a living? Of course, they ought to be honest, and to behave properly, and try to learn, and improve, and all that, but they need not plague themselves to do such strange things as you want. Their fathers give them the money they stand in need of, and when they grow older they fall in love, and their husbands do all that about caring for the future, and doing justice, and not coming to poverty.'   .

If this language is not very clear, and not definite enough to explain the conservative side of the question, it is sufficiently so to call to mind the arguments that everybody knows. Why urge on women the duties of forethought, or self-teaching, or even honesty – or point out to them that without watchfulness on their part they may easily drift into a position of such temptation as makes the commonest virtues impossible? 'Their husbands do all that', and so we get rid of all the difficulties we have been conjuring up, and in their place rises the fairest vision, the dearest hopes of happiness that God has granted human kind. This sets all to rights, and the world – for women, at least – is not a world of trial or exertion any more. From him she loves she receives gifts without shame; he shields her from all temptation; she flies to him in all difficulty; accepts his teaching as the perfection of morals; leaves the future soul and body in his care, and sums up all duties in the pleasant one of pleasing him.

Perhaps it is not new information, even to the young ladies who are so willing to fulfil their natural destiny, and who look on the idea of modifying it by their own exertions as so absurd, that this destiny is not always altogether happy; that they may not succeed in finding this director at all who is to take the burdens of life off their shoulders, and that when they do, he may prove such a curse as to make them envy the fate of those who are without. They may even seem with a little attention that the best provided for have a large enough share of

temptation and suffering to make it worth while to ask, could it be lessened? And if it could, how can a rational being cease to strive because some one is striving for them? For the world is so made that we have only what we strive for. There are no blessings given us absolutely. There are circumstances in everybody's life that may yield a blessing if made a proper use of, but the same may become curses by our own misconduct. And there is no more certain way to make marriage a curse than for one party to throw the burden of their duties and responsibilities on the other.

And the first duty in the matter is for every woman to protect herself from the danger of being forced to marry. She must secure an alternative, and one not too repulsive to be accepted. Instead of looking to marriage to provide her with means she needs to get it clearly into her mind that it needs the means to make the marriage probable. Few men are in a position to marry before middle life, and the cause of their inability is just the weight of that burden which women think it so natural they should bear. If a woman leaves out of her list of eligible husbands those who would too rashly undertake the burden without the means, and those who have means but no other desirable quality, can she shut her eyes to the fact that she may live till her habits and character are formed without meeting with her choice, or may never meet with them at all? So the vision fades into common light, and the only means of recalling it is to take her share of the burden – to show by her life that economy and self denial enter into her scheme of existence, and earning too, if needful. She will, at least, save herself the mortification of finding, when youth is past, that she must begin, perforce, ignorant, helpless, and shamed, the work that she ought to have begun long before – begin under the constant necessity of apologising for conduct so different from that she has hitherto followed, and doomed to find, most probably, that her delay has taken away all hope of success, though it has not spared her the necessity of labour.

Since women on the whole possess much less than men, it follows that each woman, of those above the working-class, may be called poor. She is poor compared to the men of the class she lives in. Her means, if any, is small compared to what is required, if she is not to sink in worldly position on her marriage. Such a woman comes, in effect, with this proposition to the men wanting wives –

'I am educated with no other object than to be a wife. My qualifications are – that I know nothing of the fight against poverty, and the struggle with the world. I shall leave the work entirely to you, unhelping, unknowing; only, I expect it to be successful, and only marry when certain that it has been so hitherto, and is likely to be so for the future. I have been carefully kept from learning or practising any means of increasing my income, and all that I could do with that intent would earn or save so very little, that it would be meanness in you to insist on my doing it. The most I can promise is, to be content with the comforts I have been used to; at least so long as you cannot afford more. As soon as you can I think I have a right to them. My main employment I consider ought to be to maintain before the world as great an appearance of wealth as possible, and for this purpose I will lay out what you give me as economically as I can, and for the same reason it shall be my constant endeavour to get as much to spend as I can. I shall probably know nothing of any subject, literary, scientific, or political, wherewith you will fill up your leisure time, for though I promise not to follow any intellectual pursuit farther than you wish it, I by no means undertake to follow it so far.'

Considering the magnitude of these demands, and the limited power and the shortness of life of those who have to meet them, it is not wonderful that the happy solution that was to come of itself to all our difficulties, should come so seldom, and should take the shape, when it comes, of a very doubtful benefit. Women do not unite themselves in youth to a young man, whose fortunes they assist and share; they hold themselves at the disposal of those separated from them by age, pursuits and interests. They do not join fortunes with their husbands as their greatest pleasure, they adopt a set of duties towards them and are paid for doing them.

Thus, not only the earthly happiness they most prize fades away before their sight. The necessity of marriage brings upon them evils, as great as, or greater, than poverty itself.

For of all human feelings that colour their earthly courts the longest, the strongest, the most domineering, is probably the desire to be believed and trusted, and to have some one in whom to believe and trust. No woman with the heart to utter a kindly speech, will willingly face the suspicion that her words are insincere. And few are aware of the blighting effects on their own heart of the total silence to which their position compels them. The hope of appreciation, the eternal good aspirations, the consciousness of half-developed power that belongs to youth, depend almost for their existence on the belief that there is sympathy somewhere. Those feelings that are never shared almost die out of life – how much more those that we refuse to communicate. But a woman will find a dead wall rise round her that will prevent her ever showing to the satisfaction of others the feelings she most earnestly wishes them to have faith in. Now of all misery and baseness in the eyes of a young girl, the greatest lies in the perpetration of a loveless marriage; and of all pleasures the greatest is that her love should be valued where it is given. And, what is odd, though of all qualities this is the one that a man likes best, yet such are the civilised arrangements for re-making the woman's nature that God has already made, that in the middle ranks of life a woman has seldom any power to exercise any choice in the matter of marriage, and consequently her professions on the subject are never believed in. She will find it impossible to acquire a character. All the friends whose good opinion she may think she has, will draw quietly back, and appear not to know what her decision may be, if the opportunity is offered her of making a rich and profligate marriage. She can never be believed. Never. Protestations will do nothing. Proof positive is only good for the moment. She will find all the world silently betray the opinion that her 'girlish fancies' will be given up if the equivalent be satisfactory; that she may be so foolish as to fix her price too high, but a price she has. Only to her the nature of the bargain is not mentioned in plain terms. Not the less does a woman in that position and liable to those temptations lose the respect and confidence of those, whom above all things, she wishes to please. Never can she escape the suspicion of a meanness altogether inconsistent with her age and feelings. Proud protestations are but a trick the more. Under the thinnest veil of courtesy she will continually discern the settled belief that she cannot afford to have either heart or conscience. The knowledge of this will silence her spontaneous kindness, and make her ever on the watch for insult that she can easily trace, though kept in the background and she can neither forget nor be patient under the certainty that all who know her, and all the successive strangers whose acquaintance she may make, are not to be shaken in their conviction that if they chose to pay the money price they would secure all the respect, love and service that she has to give.

And they are right. No matter how much she protests or how well she thinks she knows. It is she who is mistaken; she who is ignorant of the pressure that will force her down. She need not think she can bear what other people cannot. She merely deceives herself; the world's experience is wiser than she. Let her look for a moment at the evidence there is to justify the opinion that so angers her. If it is not true that English girls are often ready to sell themselves in marriage, there is no proof by which a thing can be known to be a fact. They are mocked, denounced, caricatured, scorned, for this baseness by all parties, on all occasions, in all companies, except in their own immediate presence. Even their absent sisters are not spared. They themselves fling the accusation at each other on the slightest grounds, and seem themselves aware of its universal applicability. All the world knows that to so much money they must yield. Seldom, indeed, can a man fail to suspect that half a woman's tastes and habits are hid from him, and half assumed. He becomes accustomed to exaggerated language, and accustomed to find that words and deeds are seldom in concatenation accordingly. The only result is that words and deeds get to be of less and less value. If he hears the strongest in the language he only thinks – 'It may be so', but does not care enough to settle how much they actually mean. And with all possible sincerity on their part, it is a difficult thing to settle. A woman may not be consciously insincere when professing the extremest devotion while leading a life of selfish idleness, for human beings are so constituted that when engaged on work in which they feel but little interest, their labour is scarce worth having. A man grasping at the possession of a woman's services on these terms is like the naturalist trying to secure possession of that fish that has the power of dropping off its limbs when touched. He seizes one after another and destroys them all. So men

when they buy a fellow-creature do but destroy the faculties that were hers when she belonged to herself. An inferior is of less use than an equal; a dependent of less still; a slave is but a burden.

It is a frequent remark that women become possessed of all manner of heroic qualities in extremity; the explanation probably being that only in unusual circumstances have they liberty or motive sufficient to call forth their ability. It has dropped from them in the firm grasp of some one who intended to control and direct its activity.

Suppose, now, that a woman had the strongest possible motive for wishing to give her love to one person rather than to sell it to another; that all the notions of decency and duty in which she had been educated should forbid her to accept the only escape from poverty that custom has provided; that she were ready for great sacrifices and constant exertion, and that she brought to her help in the struggle the health and strength of the prime of life, and the advantages of what is thought a first-rate education; she would look round and see that she could do – nothing. Her dearest pleasure, her evident duty, her only hope become impossible to attain to. Such is the result of protecting women from the struggle with the world, and doing their work for them. The blessing that seems to them above all others, the destiny that their protectors generally believe is the only one they are fitted for they must perforce resign. Their largest part, their power of loving, drops away under the rude grasp of violent seizure, for their choice lies, in very many cases, between frightful poverty and mercenary marriage.

There is a certain advantage in meeting one's destiny with one's eyes open, and a woman who finds few good qualities in her husband is not disappointed if she never expected anything better. But few people live to grow old without observing how a woman may come to a worse fate than even this.

Anyone who may be acquainted with a man whose vicious self-indulgence has brought him to the verge of ruin, is sure to hear the opinion given of him that 'He ought to marry.' 'Can't you get him married?' And they may chance to see too how people recommending this remedy set about providing it for their friends. How they keep total silence as to the main part of his character, and exaggerate, if they do not invent, the little that is fit to tell. How they choose for him a woman whom poverty makes miserable in her present position, and whose friends will connive at the suppression of truth, that will have the effect of falsehood. How little scruple is shown in choosing a woman of such different life and antecedents to his own that they cannot be told her, and in common courtesy she is supposed to be ignorant of them. How the horrible disgust with which a woman of decent training looks on a man in a state of animal excess, the lifelong misery that must be hers, from being at the mercy of a man who looks on women as contemptible, and who has not chosen her because she inspired a different opinion, but because he heard on all hands that he must choose some one – all this is to receive pecuniary compensation. The maintenance secured for her is made the reason and justification of the part played by those who draw the net round her, and put on the pressure from which she cannot escape. No plea of ignorance or deception can avail her when once the die is thrown. 'She should not have married him' is thought answer enough to all complaint.

Perhaps it ought to be. Perhaps – probably – it is not possible to frame laws which shall acknowledge the obligations of marriage and also provide an escape for those who have made a mistake in the matter. So much the more important then becomes the duty of removing causes that tend to make it a necessity; the poverty that makes any change welcome; the custom that makes marriage the only means by which a woman's relations can free themselves of the burden of her maintenance. Let her take upon herself the duty from which they wish to protect her of providing her own, and if her friends have any real goodwill towards her, she

will not forfeit their advice and assistance by so doing.

One can easily see how, to the man 'who ought to marry', and to the friends who are helping him, it will be convenient that there should be women who have no alternative. How they will repeat that it is a woman's natural destiny, how they will prefer that it should be her inevitable one. In proportion as the natural and all-powerful means of winning a woman's love are neglected, this means of forcing her obedience comes into favour. These people look on the inclination to choose, and especially to reject, as a piece of unaccountable perversity, to be met with inflexible severity and condemnation. They hold that women are made up of affection and the capacity to feel affection, and that the indulgence of it consti-tutes their life. Therefore the refusal to feel it just when wanted is a diseased part of them that wants rooting out.

So true is this, that you will constantly hear it recommended as a feminine duty to make use of one class of means only. Whether the object be the winning a man's heart or gaining the control over his purse, 'women's weapons' never yet included hard work or honesty, skill, talent, or knowledge. The persuasion that is thought their best means is distinctly under-stood not to include reasoning. If it involves any reference to just or noble or kindly feeling, it must be, not because the speaker is inspired with such, but because the mind of the hearer can appreciate it. If any baser passion is more active, she must appeal to that.

Excerpt from a chapter in The First Duty of Women, *London, 1870, pp. 207–219*

1.3. A Widow in Gaol for Debt by Polly Plum (Mary Ann Colclough) (1871)

MR EDITOR, – To my surprise, in the latter part of last week I saw in the list of prisoners for debt in Mount Eden Gaol two females. At the time I thought of writing about it, for it seems to me the greatest social anomaly to forbid women to vote, tie their hands with reference to a choice of employments, prate of their domestic sphere as the only proper one for women, curtail their sphere of usefulness so that it is almost im-possible for a self-helpful woman to earn a decent living, and yet, whilst loading her with all these disqualifications, to make her as liable as any man to the pains and penalties of the

law. These thoughts made me contemplate writing when I saw that two female debtors were in gaol; but I forbore. I thought doubtless they were cases of flagrant dishonesty and want of principle – some women who had wantonly and wilfully misappropriated money, and never made an effort to pay – possibly women with means independent of the labour of their hands or their brains, who had made such means an excuse for incurring debts they never meant to pay. Had the cases been such as this, there would have been every reason to believe that the defaulters were rightly served; but the report of the Provincial Council gives it, on Mr Cadman's authority, that one of those debtors is the widowed mother of six children! Tell me, 'Grandmother' from Mauku, who insist on extreme privacy and modesty in the education of girls, how those tender qualities would fit her for the law courts and Mount Eden Gaol? Her lot – that poor mother now there incarcerated – is the lot of many, and may be the future lot of any girl – to strive, to work, to struggle, for fatherless children. Think of the thousands of widows left by the devastating war in Europe. Amongst us the evil may not be so apparent – the widows are not so many, but depend upon it there are cases of severe struggle and heavy responsibility in our very midst – women heartsick and weary with the effort to carry the load on their shoulders, too heavy for them because they are neither fitted by education nor by habit to bear it. What man is to be found so callously cruel as to advocate the weakening of women's mental and physical powers, by an education calculated to unfit them for the heat and struggle of the battle for bread, whilst women are to be found in every place who have to work for their living, and pay their debts? Let me say, in conclusion, that I remark that, in strong, pointed cases like this, the men who

clamour for simple domestic education for women, who usually oppose my theories, conveniently ignore what they cannot refute. They choose to stick to their poetical imaginings in spite of this stern prose of the other side of the question. Some time ago I wrote a short essay, *'What can she do?'* I should have been glad to hear what 'Old Practical', 'Jemmy Jenkins' or 'A Grandmother' had to suggest in reference to such a case, but I did not expect to hear. The argument against the theory of educating women entirely with a view to their being dependent was too strong. Now again, in this case, here is not a supposititious case; here is a real case of hardship. A poor unfortunate woman, certainly not able to pay her debt, or she never would stay in prison away from her little fatherless children; possibly indifferently educated, very likely trained in the erroneous system that fits women solely for dependence. On her behalf, and on behalf of others who are only so much better off than she is that they may have more gentle-hearted creditors to deal with, I again ask the question: What can she do?

POLLY PLUM

Daily Southern Cross, *18 January 1871, p.3*

1.4. What Women Want by Polly Plum (1871)

SIR, – From your frequent kindness and personal courtesy to me, I am sure you will give me space for this letter, thought it is likely to be a very long one.

I am well known and everywhere known as a firm and earnest woman's advocate, and I am content and grateful to be so considered. No amount of contumely, insult, contempt, or ridicule, would make me swerve for one instant from a cause that I consider a high and holy cause. You will believe that I am true when I declare on my honor as a Christian woman that dearly as I love my life, and many and close as are the ties that bind me to it, I would this day gladly and gratefully lay it down, if by so doing I would serve the great work which, next to my God, claims my highest service. No Missionary ever yet went amongst the heathen, who was ever more firmly convinced that he was doing God service, and working to His honour and glory, than I am convinced that I am doing God's best work, in the path I have chosen to follow. I fully believe, and am convinced, that

neither I or my little ones will suffer in this enlightened nineteenth century, by my carrying out my earnest convictions of right; but even were it otherwise, and I should be counted 'worthy to suffer', I hope and believe the strength will be given to say 'Even so Father, for so it seemeth good in Thy sight, not my will but Thine be done.' From this preface you will see that I consider the cause of woman's rights a *holy cause;* I do, apart from all social considerations. I count it a holy cause, and I believe any advocate who does not so consider it, has undertaken the work in a wrong spirit and can hardly hope for a blessing.

I will tell you why it is a holy cause. Christ has said that 'we should do unto others as we would they should do unto us.' Now men dread to give us power, avowedly from the fear lest we should oppress them, as they have hitherto oppressed us, and place them where they have not hesitated to place us. The very dread lest by our emancipation they should be brought to endure some of the ills which hitherto we alone have borne, is the clearest proof that they know they have not acted to us in the spirit of the Golden Rule.

I will ask any young man just entering on life, if he would like to contemplate this fate. That all he has, or can have, or can earn, shall be absolutely at the disposal of his wife, that it shall be in her power to take away from him those dear children – whom I can tell him, good parents love as their very lives, and whom it is hard *hard* to part with, even to the God who gave them – that she shall be able to do all this, to force him to obedience, keep him poor if she please, while she has plenty, and leave him penniless if she dies first and it pleased her to do it. Further, that on this creature he had no further hold than her moral sense of right, supposing her to have any moral sense of right, and even of that there is no guarantee required, he must trust to his insight into character to settle that question, and if he is deceived! – there is no hope: the cruel grave or the scarcely less cruel and more shameful Police Court can alone end the misery of such a life. I will ask the young man entering on life – Would it not take all the aim and energy out of his bright dreams for the future if he had only to contemplate such an uncertain, such an unsettled fate as this? If all his future life's happiness or misery depended on his getting a good tyrant, what would his life be worth to him? No! men could not endure this fate. They would soon become vitiated in principle if it were theirs. Woman has borne it so long that she does not often see it in all its dread uncertainty. Men who have not to bear it are content to leave her to it. She is supposed to be used to it, as 'the eels are to skinning'. Aye and each fresh eel has to bear its own particular skinning, and where bad men bring the burden of the law to bend down women, it comes no easier because other sisters have borne the load. Do not tell me 'God meant it to be so.' That is a vile and wicked perversion of a few texts of Scripture. God meant, and St Paul enjoins, that every Christian wife should practice all the Christian duties towards her husband, but He never meant this Christian obligation to be tortured into a legal bond to bind a woman down as the legal bond slave of her husband, giving him entire power over her children, and the unlimited control of her money. If God gave man mental and physical superiority over woman, as I truly believe He did give it, He gave it to be used for woman's good, to draw out all the noble and chivalrous in man's nature to assist and defend her; and

man has done it of a verity to some purpose. He can stand before the judgement-seat of his Maker, and render account of his stewardship: woman, as man's companion, legally enslaved; without him, little above a pauper. Forced to work, does woman find in her sex a claim to chivalrous kindness and assistance? Oh no; she finds it a bar, a clog, a disqualification. That very womanhood which, if men think what they profess to think, should plead for her, is her bitterest foe. For many spheres it quite incapacitates her, and in others – the telegraph for example – it is made the excuse for imposing harder conditions and poorer pay. And men say they are doing as God would have them by women, and even many of the professed apostles of the meek and lowly Jesus, that dear Saviour who promised to help the weak and heavy laden; even Thy ministers, O Christ! shut their eyes and ears, and will not see the harm and the sin. How will men answer the question, 'Whom have ye oppressed?' How reconcile the legal position of woman with the Golden Rule? The Church tells us we are included in all the promises, that we are 'heirs of God, and joint heirs with Christ'; then if this is so we cannot be inferior beings; nor can it be justifiable to subject us. Teach us to use our freedom aright, inculcate in our hearts every grace and virtue that makes womanhood lovely and Christianity beautiful, but, oh! take away off our necks the iron yoke that weighs on us the weaker vessel with unjust and unequal pressure. The cries of wronged women and helpless children rise to God bearing witness to the deep blot on our country's fair scroll, and believe me, Christian men, so long as you defend the law; so long as you even tacitly oppose reform, no matter how excellent and admirable you may be in your own family relations; no matter how pure and good and holy your moral and religious view may be, as long as you defend the existing marriage laws; so long as you are opposed to the doctrine of perfect legal equality between man and woman, so long do you share the blame of all the sin and shame born of these evils; so long are you in part answerable not only to man, but to your God, for every robbery and every brutality committed under their shelter. It *is* your affair, if you countenance the system that legalizes the sins, and if you do no worse you help to perpetuate abuses and check progress – to my mind two of the greatest political sins a man can commit. I have been asked, 'Who is going to free woman?' and it has been asked of me, with a sarcastic smile by men who, thinking they have *all* the power, fancy that clinches the argument. I answer – 'God is going to do it; God by means of the humble instruments he is using, who are content to work faithfully and wait patiently.' Flippant satire is powerless even to offend women working in such a spirit as this, but are we to be deterred by the argument that the truth we urge is new, or more properly is newly discovered truth. There must be a day of discovery for everything, nor is the long period during which woman has been subject an argument. The same might be urged to defend the subjection of the lower orders and the slavery of the colored races; those are evils that long held sway, but have now happily disappeared before the light of the glorious gospel of Christ. Professed servants of God for a long time held with these abuses, as do many now with this great abuse, the subjection of women, yet slowly and surely is the light approaching, and though it may not be given to me to live to see this black, ugly abuse a thing of the past, others will see it and rejoice. I think I have written enough to show that my advocacy of the cause of woman is firm and unflinching; that my devotion to it is entire and on the highest grounds, and this I want to make clearly understood.

That all may know this and not hope to move me by silly letters and coarse squibs, is my desire; and I hope you will allow me space for this letter in your paper, and believe me, Yours, &c,

POLLY PLUM

New Zealand Herald, *31 July 1871, p.3*

1.5. Polly Plum's Opponents by Polly Plum (1871)

SIR, – In answer to 'F.A.H.', and to everybody else who differs from me, I must make this one answer, that I hold it to be iniquitous that in a Christian country, anyone, male or female should have it in their power to wrong and oppress others, under the shelter of the law. That bad people will wrong and oppress in spite of the law, is, alas! too true, but, in such cases, the law is not to blame. If we do our best to prevent abuses, that is all we can do; and this is what we have not done with regard to the marriage law, or with regard to the law of parents and children.

If any man wants to know what abuses and wrongs women complain of, let him read the *Subjection of Women,* by Mr Mill, and if, after reading it, he is still of opinion that women are fairly treated, and that men can uphold the existing state of the law – knowing what they uphold – and yet call themselves Christians, – if men can do this, I pity them for the black darkness in which prejudice has steeped them. In reply to 'F.A.H.', I beg to say that I think, neither parent should be able to withdraw the children from the guardianship of the other, without clear proof that the parent deprived of the children was incapable, from vice, drink, &c, of being trusted with the charge of children. The balance of power should remain with the one who pays for all, generally the father, but not always. Even now, ill-educated, and untrained as women are, many of them guide the helm with a hand so firm and steadfast that many men might blush for their own incapacity. At present, the most intelligent men are learning to see this, and are led to acknowledge that the doctrine that women are only suited for dependence is not borne out by facts. For my part, I can speak favourably of the intelligence and kindness of men generally. I have made many friends among the opposite sex by my advocacy of 'Women's Rights'. It is generally acknowledged that such people as the Brights, Miss Nightingale, Mr Mill, Miss Faithfull, Miss Tod, and Lady Amberley, are worthy of respect and confidence, and accordingly they have the respect and confidence of large numbers of the British Parliament. For 'Nemo' and others only half instructed in this matter, to set about saying our path is not clean, clear, and Scriptural, call confining the advocates in a lunatic asylum 'a joke', and speak of courteous argument as 'scratching his face', shows such an amount of ignorance of the great question of the day, that all discussion is useless until the other party has more information. I would back Lady Amberley, Mrs Jacob Bright, Miss Nightingale, or Miss Emily Faithfull against 'Janie' or 'Maggie Plum', any day. Of their superior education and opportunities of acquiring information, I think there can be no doubt. We Auckland ladies, however well inclined to be learned, have, comparatively, little opportunity. Therefore, I do not depreciate the amount of culture in my fair sisters. I only urge that, living in a retired way, in an out-of-the-way corner of the world, their opportunities of becoming enlightened are limited. The fact is, the great giants, ignorance and prejudice, are hardly half subdued. In this respect we in Auckland are something before some of the Wellington people. The *Evening Post* of that city, in speaking of my advocacy of Women's Rights, is quite insulting: declares that the meanest personal motives actuate me; that I am 'an intensely disagreeable old maid, who never having had a chance to marry have vowed deadly vengeance against all men'; and further, 'that my story is public property, and is one of disappointed hopes'. Of course I can deal with *that*. People can say what they please of my opinions, but I will not permit them to try to injure me by private slanders, and the editor of that paper will have to apologise, or he will hear more about it. Had I been an old maid I never would have ventured to be a public advocate. The fact of my never having married would, in a prejudiced community, have quite destroyed my influence, no matter how sincere and earnest and talented I might have been. The fact that I fulfilled a wife's duties to the best of my ability, and now try to be a good mother to my children, and am a woman's advocate from conviction only, has its effect with many. This very influence, the story of my private life, the Wellington *Evening Post* has entirely falsified, to injure me. Now, do you not think, Mr Editor, I have many grounds of complaint? Some men ascribe to me mean personal motives, others sneer at me for working for pay, as if clergymen and all others dependent on themselves and their families did not do the same. Some insist on my confining myself to tuition,

without knowing anything of the poverty and difficulties attached to that overcrowded profession; others, again, tell falsehoods of me. I am sure you will admit that it requires a good amount of courage and determination, as well as of sincere conviction, to enable me to bear up against all this opposition. Surely some of the charges are shameful. I give my opponents credit for meaning to be right and conscientious, by thinking they are so. Might they not give me credit for equal sincerity? Every week or so someone writes to say 'Polly Plum' would find this, that, and the other field of work much more creditable than the one she has chosen, and these paths they set out for me are always occupations that require a person to have means and leisure. I have neither; and shall my own children starve whilst I run after the City Arabs? Shall my own little ones grow up to be lost and neglected, whilst I seek after the unfortunates of my sex? No; I am ready to do what I can for anyone, and that is little enough I am sorry to say; but I am no Mrs Jellaby, and my own home and its belongings must first be considered before I run after 'Boria Boolah Ghaa'. Please excuse this long letter. I am sorry to inflict it on you, but there is such a want, not only of kindness, moderation, and logic in those who argue with me, but also of practical common sense, that I feel it right to say a few plain things. I am a woman's advocate, because I am convinced that women are placed in an unjust position by law, and because I have experienced, and do still experience, many of the evils that position entails on women. – Yours, &c,

POLLY PLUM

New Zealand Herald, *14 August 1871, p.3*

1.6.   Questions for Polly Plum
by Jellaby Pater (1871)

SIR, – I would like, through the medium of your columns, to ask 'Polly Plum' to state in a few short petty sentences, without any of that circumlocution which characterises her letters, what she demands as 'Women's Rights'? I have read the whole of the controversy (?) between her and her various correspondents, but as yet fail to see what she aims at. Her letters to me are 'full of sound and fury', but after reading them through they 'signify nothing'. After patiently reading everything emanating from her during the past six months, I am still in a state of bliss-

ful ignorance as to the nature of the so-called 'rights' she claims for women. Her ideas are so wrapt up in a cloud of words that it is impossible to sift the grain of wheat (if there is one) from the bagful of chaff in which her letters are smothered. – Please answer the following questions *seriatim:* – 1st. What rights are they which 'P. P.' desires for women? 2nd. Has not woman a perfectly legal right under the present law to protect her own property and secure it to herself by means of a marriage settlement? 3rd. On what does she ground her idea that women generally are dissatisfied with their present position? 4th. Setting aside the present agitators – Mill, Miss Nightingale, and others – that 'P. P.' is so fond of quoting, can she state on her veracity that she knows six married ladies in Auckland who are dissatisfied with their present legal position? 5th. Can 'P. P.' bring to bear any text of Scripture which is violated by the present legal position of women? In conclusion, I would again ask 'Polly Plum' to reply in terse sentences to these questions, to avoid circumlocution, far-fetched similes, and recondite allusions. – I am, &c,

JELLABY PATER

New Zealand Herald, *16 August 1871, p.3*

1.7. Answers to 'Jellaby Pater' by Polly Plum (1871)

SIR, – The enclosed are answers for 'Jellaby Pater', with 'Polly Plum's' compliments, hoping to see the day when he shall be added to the list of those who, while upholding Christianity, *hate* oppression. – I am, &c,

POLLY PLUM

Wednesday, August 16, 1871.

1st.   The right, as thinking, reasoning beings, to decide for themselves what is best for their own happiness. If they were satisfied with man's decision, this agitation for change would not be.

2nd.   A woman can only protect property she has before marriage. Men, unless proved bad and incapable, can claim all property and earnings *after* marriage. This the writer has experienced, her husband – not a bad, but a thoroughly unbusinesslike, unenergetic man – spent pounds and pounds of his wife's earnings in profitless, and even in ruinous speculations, and on one occasion all the little home comforts she had gathered around her, by unremitting toil, were seized through some of his mistakes, and she and two little children, the eldest not two years old, were left on the bare floor.

3rd.   The immense movement in favour of a change answers *that* question.

4th.   *On my veracity,* 75 per cent of my married lady friends are *opposed* to the present law, many of them happy enough themselves, but knowing of wrongs, evils, and injustice that make them in favour of 'woman's rights'. My experience in Auckland – for I have had no experience in these matters elsewhere – goes to prove that young single ladies are those who are most opposed to the new view, their ideas of marriage being simply ideal, and that married ladies are not always sincere with their husbands in this matter. It is not to their interests to be so. They offend their husband, make domestic broils, and can *at present* gain nothing, and lose much comfort. Thackeray, in *Denis Duval*, says, 'But you don't expect sincerity and subservience.'

5th.   Christ's rule of life, 'Do unto others as ye would they should do unto you', and the whole *spirit* of Gospel doctrine, is *opposed* to arbitrarily deciding for anybody what is best for them.

[We think it but fair to publish our fair correspondent's reply. The correspondence is now closed. – Ed. N.Z.H.]

New Zealand Herald, *18 August 1871, p.3*

Chapter 2

Temperance and Other Feminisms
1885–1905

The writings of the 'three Marys' did not fall on deaf ears in the 1860s and 1870s, but it was not until the end of the century that women's rights were championed in an organised fashion. Ideas were transformed into concerted action following Mary Clement Leavitt's visit to New Zealand in 1885. Leavitt was a travelling representative of the American-based Women's Christian Temperance Union. She inspired New Zealand women to form WCTU branches throughout the country, thereby creating the first autonomous women's organisation that could provide a national framework for a sustained campaign.

Leavitt toured extensively through New Zealand speaking at public meetings, women's circles, and gatherings organised chiefly among Presbyterian, Congregational and Methodist Churches. She was, first and foremost, an advocate of temperance. But in urging women to work for the introduction of temperance in their communities she stressed the interests that they, as women, shared, and the strengths that they could realise in combining together for the cause. In speeches such as the one she gave at Christchurch's St Paul's Church on 'Woman, Her Duties and Responsibilities' (2.1) Mary Leavitt elaborated on women's responsibility in issues of social reform, basing it on the notion of women's 'special mission' and separate nature. Here and elsewhere she referred to the importance of the work of reform being performed 'by pure womanhood'.[1]

Leavitt argued that women's special mission carried with it an obligation to take social and political action. In this she was going much further than other mid-nineteenth century thinkers: on one hand, the advocates of separate spheres for men and women, and on the other, traditional Christians who exhorted women to express their faith through charitable or philanthropic work. The evangelical roots of temperance stressed the link between the spiritual transformation of the individual and the moral transformation of society.

In New Zealand Leavitt met extremely receptive audiences. Branches of the WCTU were formed readily and the first national convention of the New Zealand WCTU was held in 1886. From that time the WCTU grew to become the focus of women's reforming and organising energy. The WCTU led the campaign for women's franchise to its successful conclusion in 1893. But, for women who embraced the whole of the WCTU philosophy, the vote was only one part of a larger programme of social reform. It was the instrument through which other reforms could be achieved.

Beyond the WCTU, the campaign for the vote stimulated a much wider debate in New Zealand society about women's rights and the position of women and men. After the franchise victory, women activists formed the National Council of

Women (NCW) in 1896 to press forward the emancipation cause. Two periodicals were produced, providing a forum for feminist ideas: the *White Ribbon* (1894-) and the Wellington-based *Daybreak* (1895-96).

The pieces in this chapter have been selected to give a representative picture of the late nineteenth-century feminist movement across time and subject, and to complement the more detailed coverage available in *The Woman Question*. The formation of the WCTU in 1885 marks the movement's beginning, while 1905, the year in which the NCW went into recess, marks its conclusion. After the initial two or three years, the campaign for the vote dominated the period until 1893, but the concerns of women were extremely wide, encompassing such things as dress and prison reform as well as political enfranchisement.

This chapter includes documents drawn directly from the suffrage campaign, such as Kate Sheppard's 'Sixteen Reasons . . .' (2.4), which is an expanded version of her 1888 pamphlet *Ten Reasons Why the Women of New Zealand Should Vote*[2]. These documents were tools in the campaign, designed to be used by women collecting signatures for the franchise petition, and at public meetings. Alongside these pieces are more reflective items and detailed programmes of reform. These include Margaret Sievwright's 1894 presidential address to the Gisborne Woman's Political Association (2.7) and Anna Stout's manifesto for the Southern Cross Society (2.9).

In her stirring call to action (2.2), Helen Nicol, the franchise superintendent in the Dunedin WCTU, makes the standard case linking prohibition with women's suffrage. Women want the vote in order to press their view on a political issue of particular interest to them: 'when Prohibition is in motion many other evils will cease to exist which at present fall with an unmerciful hand upon innocent women.' Drink was the source of many social ills of which women bore the brunt. Maori women were also brought into the WCTU's fold (2.10). Auckland's Annie Schnackenberg was particularly involved in forwarding this part of the work.[3]

By 1891 the campaign for women's franchise was well underway and a new Liberal Government was in power. Members of the House of Representatives had had a chance to declare themselves supporters or opponents of the cause. There were some who tried to hold back from either position, and others who swayed with the interest of the moment. 'The Sitter' in Jessie Mackay's satirical poem 'smiles derisively' at the advancing tide of emancipation-minded women with the dismissive response: 'No woman's wits can grapple/ With Church and State and Politics. Who first did eat the apple?'. Her conclusion challenges the political masters directly: 'You've clogged the world's wheels enough, yourself and such as you;/ We know that you can *talk*; it's another thing to *do*.'

Meri Mangakahia's speech to the Paremata Maori, the Maori Parliament (2.5) in the Kotahitanga movement in the 1890s, shows a very different set of arguments advanced for equal enfranchisement. These are arguments of principle, prag-matism and sisterhood. Women should be participants in the Parliament because they are among those whose interests are represented (points 1 and 2). Women should be represented because they have land, are experienced in its management and because the men have tried and so far failed in their aims (points 3, 4 and 5).

33

Finally, the ultimate object of the Parliament is to petition the Queen for redress of grievances arising from the undertakings given in the Treaty of Waitangi. As a woman, surely the Queen is more likely to heed the words of her Maori sisters.

At the same time as women's political rights were being advanced, wider questions of women's social emancipation were also under consideration. To Kate Walker, Alice Burns, James Wilkinson and a small number of others, an equally important part of improving women's position lay in altering dress. They were New Zealand's leading advocates of dress reform and founders of the Rational Dress Association. Freeing the body from the encumbrances of heavy and largely decorative garb would, they argued, lead to an enlarged degree of freedom in all aspects of life. Excerpts from their manifesto, *Notes on Dress Reform*, are included in 2.6.

Margaret Sievwright led the franchise campaign in Gisborne; she was also a national figure, succeeding Kate Sheppard as national president of the National Council of Women. Her determination to achieve much more for women than simply the vote is evident in her activity after 1893. On the anniversary of the franchise victory Margaret Sievwright gave a presidential address to the newly constituted Gisborne Woman's Political Association (formerly the Gisborne Franchise League) (2.7). She refers to the franchise victory as a milestone: 'we pause, but only again to press forward.' In a comprehensive address she discussed current legislation and sought change to enable women to stand as parliamentary representatives. She also argued fervently for the reform of divorce and marriage laws, to reduce what she termed 'the degradation of unblessed wedlock'. Throughout, she counters the idea of the 'widespread notion of women's inferiority' and the belief that men and women belong in 'separate spheres'. At the end she applauds emancipation as something that enhances womanhood, and she encourages women to be proud of their new status. There are still obstacles to overcome, but the five barriers that stand in the way of women's emancipation – the first being 'masculine selfishness', the last, 'Philistine Stupidity' – can, she urges, be surmounted.

Similarly, Anna Stout worked for women's rights well beyond 1893. Wellington's Southern Cross Society was formed largely at her initiative. Educating women, especially in political matters, advancing reforms of benefit to women, and promoting women's independence and equality were its principal objects. While Anna Stout frequently defers to the greater experience, knowledge and wisdom of men in her address, and takes the trouble to reassure her audience that women's interest in public affairs will not 'interfere with the discharge of their home duties', the objects of the Society represent a bold statement of change (2.9).

Economic issues continued to be of central importance in the 1890s. The Southern Cross Society had as one of its objects (clause 4) 'To Secure for Women equal Remuneration with men for equal work'. Within the franchise movement the interests of working women had been represented, especially in Dunedin, where Harriet Morison was active in organising women workers. In 1902 Edith Hodgkinson presented a paper to the NCW on the subject of 'Equal Pay for Equal Work' (2.13). As the number of female wage and salary earners increased, and as the variety of their occupations expanded beyond domestic service, this issue gained importance.

The continuing question of the economic independence of married women was the subject of a paper given by Margaret Sievwright and Ada Wells to the NCW in 1898 (2.12). Also of key importance at this time was the improvement of conditions for women who had to provide for themselves – because they were unmarried, widowed or had no breadwinners.

Another central issue for women in the late nineteenth century was the double standard of morality. Most suffragists felt this keenly as a matter of deep injustice – especially when it was enshrined in law. The main reforms they sought were: the repeal of the Contagious Diseases Act (introduced in 1869, it provided for the compulsory inspection and detention of women on suspicion of carrying venereal disease); the reform of the divorce law to make the grounds of divorce the same for men and women; and the raising of the age of consent for girls from fourteen to sixteen years. In seeking these reforms activists encountered tremendous resistance. Ada Wells presented the case for repealing the Contagious Diseases Act to the 1898 meeting of the NCW (2.11). The reasons she gave on this occasion were reiterated by women throughout these years. The Contagious Diseases Act was not repealed until 1910, though it had been one of the objectives when the WCTU was founded in 1885. *Daybreak*'s 1895 article, 'Unfortunate Women' (2.8), presents a different angle on the subject, consistent with the magazine's iconoclastic stance. The writer urges sympathy with women forced to earn a living on the streets rather than a zealous campaign to eliminate brothels and prostitution.

Throughout the writings from this period ran two distinct, and to some extent conflicting, lines of argument, which were sometimes evident within a single piece. The first based the claims for women's enfranchisement and other rights on the belief that women were the equal of men, and that legally and constitutionally they should have equal rights and duties. This was the argument advanced by John Stuart Mill and was based on the claims of natural rights. The first of Kate Sheppard's 'Sixteen Reasons' (2.4) sets out this argument.

The other line of argument, which was probably more in evidence in the franchise campaign in New Zealand, sought political and constitutional rights for women on the basis of difference. Because women were endowed with a special moral responsibility and sensibility, they should have the vote in order to exercise that moral nature in the political and public sphere. This argument based women's entitlement to political and constitutional rights on their inherent differences from men. Some of these beliefs underlie reasons 6-8, and 11-13 in Kate Sheppard's 'Sixteen Reasons' (2.4). Her strategic acumen, in drawing in as wide an alliance of pro-suffrage opinion as possible, is apparent.

Behind these arguments lay two contradictory concepts of sexual difference. The complementarity of the sexes – the idea that men and women, masculinity and femininity were different but of equal value – had now become imbued with a moral dimension. As Mary Leavitt put it: 'Men needed women for the completion of their intellectual and moral natures as much as for other matters.' (2.1) Women were seen as having higher, truer and superior moral natures. Men were deemed either devoid of or distinctly less endowed with moral judgement and sensibility. Women were therefore encouraged to exercise a purifying and improving influence on the world of politics and public life.

On the basis of this moral difference or superiority, women made a number of claims in this period for greater representation in public office. The NCW, for example, passed resolutions urging that women be appointed to positions within the criminal justice system – as police, jurors, justices of the peace, judges and prison warders. Similar calls were made for women to become charitable aid officers, prison visitors, etc., thereby bringing into the public world the nobler and purer virtues exercised by women in their homes and families. These objectives were largely unfulfilled by the time the active membership of the NCW ceased to be sufficiently large to sustain annual meetings, but they were to be taken up again within a few years.

1. New Zealand Mail, *27 March 1885, p.25*
2. *Margaret Lovell-Smith (ed.),* The Woman Question, *Auckland, 1992, p.66*
3. *Sandra Coney, 'Annie Schnackenberg',* BNZW, *pp.584–589*

Sources and Further Reading

Bunkle, Phillida. 'The Origins of the Women's Movement in New Zealand: the Women's Christian Temperance Union, 1885-1895', in Phillida Bunkle and Beryl Hughes (eds), *Women in New Zealand Society*, Auckland, 1980, pp.52–76

Dalziel, Raewyn. 'The Colonial Helpmeet: Women's role and the vote in nineteenth-century New Zealand', in Barbara Brookes, Charlotte Macdonald and Margaret Tennant (eds), *Women in History*, Wellington, 1986, pp.55–68

Devaliant, Judith. *Kate Sheppard*, Auckland, 1992

Grimshaw, Patricia. *Women's Suffrage in New Zealand*, Auckland, 1972

Labrum, Bronwyn. 'For the Better Discharge of Our Duties: Women's rights in Wanganui, 1893–1903', *Women's Studies Journal*, vol.6 (1990), pp.136–152

Lovell-Smith, Margaret (ed.). *The Woman Question: Writings by the women who won the vote*, Auckland, 1992

Macdonald, Charlotte. 'The Social Evil: Prostitution and the passage of the Contagious Diseases Act (1869)', in Barbara Brookes, Charlotte Macdonald and Margaret Tennant (eds), *Women in History*, Wellington, 1986, pp.13–33

The Suffragists: Essays from the Dictionary of New Zealand Biography, Wellington, 1993

Tyrrell, Ian. *Woman's World, Woman's Empire: the Women's Christian Temperance Union in international perspective*, Chapel Hill & London, 1991

Upton, Victoria. 'Women's Suffrage in Hawkes Bay', Honours research essay, Victoria University of Wellington, 1992

2.1. Mrs Leavitt's Mission
Lyttelton Times (1885)

Last evening Mrs Mary Clement Leavitt lectured at St Paul's Church, Cashel Street, taking for her subject 'Woman, her Duties and Responsibilities.' The attendance was not so numerous as when she previously delivered an address in the same church, but she was listened to with the same amount of attention, and carried her audience with her as usual. The chair was taken by the Rev J. Elmslie, and on the platform were the Rev J. Berry and Mr M. W. Green, with other well-known advocates of temperance.

Before beginning her lecture, Mrs Leavitt desired to disabuse the public of the impression which she feared had got abroad to the effect that the Women's Temperance Union were to visit public-houses and establish a crusade against them similar to that adopted in some parts of America. She then devoted herself to her subject, beginning with the proposition that since God had created women with certain faculties women had a right to have those faculties fully developed. It was now generally admitted that no one human being should have the power to say that another should have only a limited freedom. Tyrannies and old prejudices had, one by one, been beaten down, till all men, or nearly all, were now practically free. She considered that woman, as an integral part of humanity, was entitled to freedom under the law of God, and to take the positions her faculties suited her for. It was said that women could not fulfil certain duties; that they could not, for instance, be Judges, but she contended that though all women were not fit to be Judges, neither were all men. The latter fact did not prevent men from being allowed to study the law, and so fit themselves to become Judges; neither should the former fact prevent women. The same objection had formerly been made to women studying medicine, but experience of late years had proved that women were wonderfully adapted to be physicians, through the fineness of their perception, and the delicacy of their judgment. There was no fear that the greater number of women would still become wives and mothers, even if every profession should be thrown open to them; though she must admit that in some places there were difficulties in the way, as in Massachusetts, where there were 7000 more women than men. It had been objected that women could not study what were called the humanities, and that their physical weakness would cause them to break down under the necessary mental strain; but the fact was that girl graduates enjoyed much better health than fashionable ladies, who danced all night and slept all day. It was very much a question of education and training, for men, with all their boasted superior mental powers, would be unable to make angel cake, or a decent bonnet, unless previously taught, just as much as women were unable to do men's work, for which they had received no preparatory training. Certainly men were larger and stronger physically, but, mentally, were not superior when a fair trial was given to the weaker sex. Men needed women for the completion of their intellectual and moral natures as much as for other matters. It had been objected that woman ought not to have the franchise because she might vote for war, knowing that her incapacity for shouldering a musket would exonerate her from fighting, but the fact was that women would often rather go to war themselves than see their fathers, brothers, or other male relatives go. If the freedom from liability to serve in the army was a reason for the refusal of the franchise, then the clergy, the medical faculty, cripples, and men above 45 years of age, should not be allowed to vote. Let men and women be treated alike; that was all she asked. Some said that women would bring confusion into Government, but she thought there was considerable confusion there already. But why should woman's franchise produce mischief when the proportion of criminals in America was twelve men to one woman, and church membership numbered two women to one man; in England only one woman was a criminal to five men. To her it seemed very strange that Englishmen, at least, should object to women taking part in the Government, when England had been so wisely governed by the present Queen and by other queens. The household franchise in England had given a share in municipal government to widows and single women, and so well had this worked that the same system was being extended to Scotland. In Wyoming ever since the formation of the territory, sixteen years ago, women had been allowed to vote – and this was surely long enough to put the system on its trial – and there every Governor but one, who was hand and glove with the liquor traffickers and holders of gambling saloons, had testified that woman suffrage had been an unmitigated blessing. In Washington territory women had voted once, and so damaged the liquor traffic that one man said he would pay the whole expense of packing Congress so that the women might be deprived of the franchise. Chief Justice Green had testified that women, when on juries, performed their duties better than men, and what else could be expected when, as happened in one protracted trial for murder, the jurywomen had each night a prayer meeting while the men were playing poker. At Boston, since women had voted on the school question, the polling-places had been freed from the abominations attendant on smoking, whereas previously one could scarcely breathe for the smoke which poisoned the atmosphere. Another abuse, that of men bringing drink to the polling-places and treating voters there had been abolished, thanks also to the women voting. These things showed that Legislatures would certainly not be the less orderly were women admitted into them; indeed, the mere presence of women in the Strangers' Gallery caused the members to improve their behaviour. That the woman's vote would have an important influence in suppressing the liquor traffic was fully recognised by the Women's Christian Temperance Union, which had advocated it strenuously from the commencement of its organisation. Illinois and Arkansas were examples of how the women exercised their right in this direction. The lecturer devoted the remainder of her lecture to combating objections which were founded, erroneously as she contended, on the teaching of the Bible. She concluded by deprecating the present system which classed women with children, idiots and criminals, who were the only other classes incapable of voting.

During the evening the choir sang hymns, and after the address a hearty vote of thanks and sympathy was given to Mrs Leavitt, on the motion of Mr Green, seconded by the Rev J. Berry.

Lyttelton Times, *23 May 1885, p.3*

2.2. Female Suffrage and Prohibition
by H.L.N. (Helen Nicol) (1890)

Sir, – It is now about time that we women of Dunedin were rousing ourselves to act in some way or other to gain our right to vote on political questions, especially those affecting ourselves. We have the all-important prohibition question. We want our foot upon that in particular, and I do not hesitate to say when Prohibition is in motion many other evils will cease to exist which at present fall with an unmerciful hand upon innocent women. Have we not ladies in our City with sufficient backbone to call a public meeting of women to test this question? I think we have some fearless women in our Women's Christian Temperance Union who do not hesitate in working with a will for the right. Then we have the Good Templar Order, who was among the first to strike at the prejudice existing against the right of woman to take her place in the lodge room, on the platform, or where else she could maintain her position, based alone upon a mental equality with the sterner sex. Then I would appeal to every lodge to take up this question for the sake of the sisters. All over the world our cause is being taken up by very able and influential ladies and gentlemen, with very marked results, which will soon terminate in our ultimate success. But are we going to sit with our hands folded in the meantime, while our sisters in the neighboring colonies are doing their best to gain this franchise for women? I will here quote from a paragraph from the 'Leader' by F. G. Ewington: 'The women of the Christian Temperance Union did only what might have been expected of them in asking the assistance from Christian and temperance organisations to get them political rights. They are too sensible, influential, and united to be put down. Women of their class who feel that they can do something else than household duties without letting household duties suffer are developing a world-wide federation, which has proved its right to be entrusted with the vote they ask for. In the State of Iowa they gave a majority of 30,000 votes in favor of the constitutional abolition of the liquor traffic in 1882, and through them a similar law was passed in Rhode Island in 1886. They have shown they can organise and carry through a political campaign. We could state numberless cases where women are unjustly treated through bad and cruel laws.'

I would crave your permission on some future occasion to be allowed space in your valuable columns to further prosecute this question of woman's suffrage. I have principally dealt with the question of prohibition of the liquor traffic in this letter. – I am, etc., H.L.N. Dunedin, May 12.

Evening Star, *13 May 1890, p.2*

2.3. The Sitter on the Rail
by Jessie Mackay (1891)

He is sitting in the country, he is sitting in the town,
He's now my Lord Tomnoddy, and now he's Hob the clown;

But if the Rail be easy, or if the Rail be hard,
He's sitting there for ever, like the Raven keeping guard.

His heels serenely tilted, his head serenely
  bowed,
The curling of his meerschaum is round him
  as a cloud.
The world may cry for succour, the world in
  dolour wail,
But like a rock he's planted on his own
  beloved Rail.

When the banner Prohibitional is waving in
  the air,
And the ruby nose of Boniface is ashen in
  the scare,
The Sitter waxes eloquent: 'What cranks
  and rigours cruel!
The British Lion is a beast that loves not
  water-gruel.

We've whipped the world on beef and beer,
  we're game to whip it still:
A man, I take it, with his own can just do
  what he will;
And if, sometimes, he doesn't sup on lacteal
  fluid blue,
And homeward sees a double moon –
  what's that to me or you?

Besides the friendly publican you threaten
  with starvation;
It really wrings my tender heart; and, as to
  compensation,
'Twould not be adequate, you know' – that
  moment I'd gone bail
I saw the shadow of a wink flit somewhere
  o'er the Rail!

Is't an army treading nearer? is it
  swarming bees that hum?
'Tis the women at the polling-booth:
  Emancipation's come.
And manly optics anxiously adown the
  vista strain;
And manly fingers tremble, grasping tighter
  at the rein.

The Sitter smiles derisively: 'No woman's
  wits can grapple
With Church and State and Politics. Who
  first did eat the apple?
Ho, treason there! hold fast the door! they
  haven't passed the Bill;
There's a bitter potion brewing for many an
  ancient ill.

Ho, bring the keys, and lock the gates; for
  man must do or die,
In the oven I smell cooking a prodigious
  humble pie!'
A cruel whisper floats to him while holding
  doors the tighter;

'Perhaps the bills at Bellamy's may be a
  trifle lighter!'

There's a cry from Macedonia, the islands
  of the sea
Lie there in outer darkness. The Sitter, what
  says he?
'Excuse me, I'm not on to fill a missionary
  kit;
This cramming of the heathen with my
  conscience doesn't fit.

The dark New Hebridean needs no
  embroidered vest;
And pockethandkerchiefs are frauds where
  pockets are non est;
And, speaking as a cultured man, by newest
  lamps enlightened,
What right have you to let them be by
  ancient bogies frightened?

They're very happy as they are; they've got,
  as you may see,
Their simple old theology, which suits them
  to a T;
And to cram with Shorter Catechism or the
  Thirty-Nine,
Those unoffending blackamoors should not
  be our design.

What's that you say? You do not think their
  state so beatific,
Making mincemeat of each other in the Isles
  of the Pacific.
You question they've a right to make of
  baby-flesh their diet,
Or to burn a premature Suttee, by no means
  on the quiet?

Well, I have no intentions of chopping logic
  longer;
But take my ultimatum; I think you'll find
  it stronger:
There's a big white heathen army starving
  at our backs;
When they're dressed up, fed, converted,
  you may think about the blacks.'

Alas for that rare jewel – Consistency, its
  name!
When home-abiding poverty his charity
  would claim,
Put not, I pray, the cream-jug his sombre
  visage under;
'Twill sour, as did the banquet of
  Ravenswood in thunder.

With barricades of blue books he fortifies
  the Rail;
And begins, 'Why really, Madam, you'll
  excuse me if I fail

39

The Sitter on the Rail.

—

 E is sitting in the country, he is sitting in the
town,
He's now my Lord Tomnoddy, and now he's
Hob the clown ;
But if the Rail be easy, or if the Rail be
hard,
He's sitting there for ever, like the Raven
keeping guard.

His heels serenely tilted, his head serenely bowed,
The curling of his meerschaum is round him as a cloud.
The world may cry for succour, the world in dolour wail,
But like a rock he's planted on his own beloved Rail.

When the banner Prohibitional is waving in the air,
And the ruby nose of Boniface is ashen in the scare,
The Sitter waxes eloquent :—" What cranks and rigours
cruel !
The British Lion is a beast that loves not water-gruel.

We've whipped the world on beef and beer, we're game to
whip it still :
A man, I take it, with his own can just do what he will ;
And if, sometimes, he doesn't sup on lacteal fluid blue,
And homeward sees a double moon,—what's that to me
or you ?

First page of Jessie Mackay's satirical poem *The Sitter on the Rail*, 1891. *Alexander Turnbull Library*

In sentimentalizing the sin of pauperhood,
And maintaining that a beggar has a right
to dress and food.

I ever to Humanity have been a faithful
friend;
To pauperize Humanity's a crime I can't
defend;
And the truest way to raise it, as everybody
knows,
Is to let it hunt around to find its provender
and clothes!

Now you and I undoubtedly, by Nature's
wise decree,
Have reached, to put it finely, the apex of
the tree;
And Tag and Rag and Bobtail are groaning
down below
Because they didn't want to rise – you
needn't tell me No.

For Nature has ordained it the fittest shall
survive;
And the drones have ne'er a portion in the
honey of the hive;
So to run against the edicts that Nature
framed for us,
And pension off her criminals, is flatly
blasphemous.

'Deliver us,' the Sitter prays, 'from
Socialistic turns;
From Mann, the Man of Gotham wise; from
fiery Johnny Burns,
By name and nature igneous, the torch of
fell sedition;
And Champion, the champion of Capital's
perdition!'

Then the Friend of poor Humanity his
testimony graces
By buttoning up his pocket – and hieing to
the races,
Where, deprecating still the sins of
charitable filchers,
He gives Humanity a hoist – in person of
the Welshers!

When the trembling Arts and Sciences are
weighted in the scale
O a Daniel come to judgment is the Sitter on the
Rail!
Long's marble steps are stearine; and Leighton
he eschews;
And Birket Foster's meadow-greens have given
him the blues.

The Laureate doesn't meet his views, despite his
name's new handle;
There's not a living novelist that's fit to hold the
candle
To their dead predecessors lapped in dim
Elysian clover;
Though Scott's played out, and Dickens' day
is well and justly over.

So he swells and so he puffs, like Froggie in the
fable,
And thinks to reach the bovine bulk he shortly
will be able.
And here's his literary tip, if to gain it you'd
contrive,
It's 'Praise not very many dead and never one
alive!'

'If I took so and so in hand' – the world his
dictum waits;
But like those kine Egyptian that swallowed up
their mates
Without at all improving their attenuated
figure,
A big If swallows all he does and never gets the
bigger.

You've clogged the world's wheels enough,
yourself and such as you;
We know that you can talk; it's another thing
to do.
Come down in the arena; for if e'en therein you
fail,
You'll criticise your neighbours less, good
Sitter on the Rail!

From The Sitter on the Rail and Other Poems,
1891, pp.1–5

2.4. Sixteen Reasons for Supporting Women's Suffrage
Prohibitionist (1891)

1. Because it is the foundation of all political liberty that those who obey the law should be able to have a voice in choosing those who make the law.
2. Because Parliament should be the reflection of the wishes of the people.

3. Because Parliament cannot fully reflect the wishes of the people, when the wishes of women are without any direct represent-ation.
4. Because a Government of the people, by the people, and for the people, should

mean all the people, and not one half.

5. Because most laws affect women as much as men, and some laws affect women especially.

6. Because most laws which affect women especially, are now passed without consulting those persons whom they are intended to benefit.

7. Because some of those laws press grievously on women as mothers. As, for instance, those relating to the guardianship of children.

8. Because some set up different standards of morality for men and women.

9. Because such laws are thereby rendered inefficient for protecting women from wrong.

10. Because the enfranchisement of women is a question of public well-being, and not a help to any political party or sect.

11. Because the vote of women would add weight and power to the more settled and responsible communities.

12. Because the possession of the vote would increase the sense of responsibility amongst women towards questions of public importance.

13. Because public-spirited mothers make public-spirited sons.

14. Because large numbers of intelligent, thoughtful, hard-working women deserve the Franchise.

15. Because the objections raised against their having the Franchise are based on sentiment, not on reason.

16. Because – to sum up all the reasons in one – *it is just*.

Prohibitionist, *7 November 1891, p.3*

2.5. So that Women May Receive the Vote by Meri Mangakahia (1893)

Meri Mangakahia: E whakamoemiti atu ana ahau kinga honore mema e noho nei, kia ora koutou katoa, ko te take i motini atu ai ahan, ki te Tumuaki Honore, me nga mema honore, ka mahia he ture e tenei whare kia whakamana nga wahine ki te pooti mema mo ratou ki te Paremata Maori.

Ka whakamarama ahau i te take i tino tino ai ahau kia whakamana nga wahine maori ki te pooti, a kia tu hoki he mema wahine ki roto i te Paremata Maori.

1. He nui nga wahine o Nui Tireni kua mate a ratou taane, a he whenua karati, papatupu o ratou.

2. He nui nga wahine o Nui Tireni kua mate o ratou matua, kaore o ratou tungane, he karati, he papatupu o ratou.

3. He nui nga wahine mohio o Nui Tireni kei te moe tane, kaore nga tane e mohio ki te whakahaere i o raua whenua.

4. He nui nga wahine kua koroheketia o ratou matua, he wahine mohio, he karati, he papatupu o ratou.

5. He nui nga tane Rangatira o te motu nei kua inoi ki te kuini, mo nga mate e pa ara kia tatou, a kaore tonu tatou i pa ki te ora i runga i ta ratou inoitanga. Na reira ka inoi ahau ki tenei whare kia tu he mema wahine.

Ma tenei pea e tika ai, a tera ka tika ki te tuku inoi nga mema wahine ki te kuini, mo nga mate kua pa nei kia tatou me o tatou whenua, a tera pea e whakaae mai a te kuini ki te inoi a ona hoa

Wahine Maori i te mea he wahine ano hoki a te kuini.

I exult the honourable members of this gathering. Greetings. The reason I move this motion before the principal member and all honourable members so that a law may emerge from this parliament allowing women to vote and women to be accepted as members of the parliament.

Following are my reasons that present this motion so that women may receive the vote and that there be women members:

1. There are many women who have been widowed and own much land.

2. There are many women whose fathers have died and do not have brothers.

3. There are many women who are knowledgeable of the management of land where their husbands are not.

4. There are many women whose fathers are elderly, who are also knowledgeable of the management of land and own land.

5. There have been many male leaders who have petitioned the Queen concerning the many issues that affect us all, however, we have not yet been adequately compensated according to those petitions. Therefore I pray to this gathering that women members be appointed.

Perhaps by this course of action we may be satisfied concerning the many issues affecting us and our land. Perhaps the Queen may listen to the petitions if they are presented by her Maori sisters, since she is a woman as well.

Paremata Maori O Nui Tireni, *Proceedings of the Maori Parliament, 1893 (q499M, ATL)*

Reweti : Me unu tenei korero mo te 2 p.m.

Toroaiwhiti : E tautoko ana ahau.

Pika : Konga mea e pai ana me ki mai Ae. Paahitia ana.

Ka panuitia atu te motini a Meri Mangakahia, he tono kia whai mana nga wahine ki te pooti.

R. Aperahama : Me haere mai a Meri Mangakahia ki te whaka-marama i tenei motini.

H. K. Taiaroa : E tautoko ana ahau i tenei motini, i te mea kanui nga wahine whiwhi whenua a ka mahi noa atu ko tatou ki te mahi ture atu mo o ratou whenua I oti hoki i tera tau kia kohi nga wahine i te £1 0s 0d, na reira me whai mana nga wahine ki te pooti.

Pika : Ka tonoa atu a Meri Mangakahia.

Mo te 2 p.m. ka noho te whare.

---

2 P.M.

Pika : Ko te kai motini i naianei.

Meri Mangakahia : E whaka-moemiti atu ana ahau kinga honore mema e noho nei, kia ora koutou katoa, ko te take i motini atu ai ahan, ki te Tumuaki Honore, me nga mema honore, k a mahia he ture e tenei whare kia whakamana nga wahine ki te pooti mema mo ratou ki te Paremata Maori.

Ka whakamarama ahau i te take i tino tino ai ahau kia whaka-mana nga wahine maori ki te pooti, a kia tu hoki he mema wahine ki roto i te Paremata Maori.

1. He nui nga wahine o Nui Tireni kua mate a ratou taane, a he whenua karati, papatupu o ratou.
2. He nui nga wahine o Nui Tireni kua mate o ratou matua, kaore o ratou tungane, he karati, he papatupu o ratou.
3. He nui nga wahine mohio o Nui Tireni kei te moe tane, kaore nga tane e mohio ki te whakahaere i o raua whenua.
4. He nui nga wahine kua koroheketia o ratou matua, he wahine mohio, he karati, he papatupu o ratou.
5. He nui nga tane Rangatira o te motu nei kua inoi ki te kuini, mo nga mate e pa ara kia tatou, a kaore tonu tatou i pa ki te ora i runga i ta ratou inoitanga. Na reira ka inoi ahau ki tenei whare kia tu he mema wahine.

Ma tenei pea e tika ai, a tera ka tika ki te tuku inoi nga mema wahine ki te kuini, mo nga mate kua pa nei kia tatou me o tatou whenua, a tera pea e whakaae mai a te kuini ki te inoi a ona hoa Wahine Maori i te mea he wahine ano hoki a te kuini.

Akenehi Tomoana : Kia ora nga mema Honore e kimi nei i te ora mo tatou. E tu ake ana ahau ki te tautoko i tenei motini, engari e mea ake ana ahau kia riro rawa mai te Honore i nga tane katahi ano ka pai te korero i tenei motini.

Marara : Ko ahau tetahi e tautoko ana i tenei korero.

Meri Mangakahia's speech to the Paremata Maori, as recorded in the proceedings of the Kotahitanga Parliament, 1893. *Paremata Maori o Nui Tireni, Alexander Turnbull Library.*

2.6. Notes on Dress Reform and What It Implies by Kate Walker and James Wilkinson (1893)

1. It should be recognised and accepted, that women are enlarging their sphere of action, and are taking up professions usually held by men only, thus furnishing a better basis for Rational Dress than has hitherto been obtainable.

2. Accepting the new principle that women as well as men have a right to hold any position for which they can be readily qualified, or indeed to which they can attain, we are led to concede to women the right of using all opportunities enjoyed by men for training in capability and character.

3. While on the one hand we believe that difference of sex in the human race cannot justly be made a ground for refusing to women free choice of livelihood, and while on the same side we believe that difference of sex should create but trifling difference in habit of life of refined people:

4. Yet, on the other hand, we must note that the natural distinction between the male tendency to activity and the female tendency to passivity, and the artificial inequalities that have grown almost into our natures during past ages, will for an indefinite time prevent the realization of our ideals for the sexes.

5. Some of the inequalities are:
   (i) Neglect of girls' physical training.
   (ii) The repressed and in-door life put upon girls.
   (iii) Absence of women from sharing in the national out-door sports.
   (iv) The retaining of girls and women in domestic duties solely, and the discouragement of free choice of a livelihood.
   (v) The wholly different standard of ideal set up for young men and young women.
   (vi) The absence of equal freedom in matter of dress, and the social compulsion placed upon women to cultivate the ornamental at the sacrifice of the rational.
   (vii) The inequality in dress, that of women being fitly associated with repressed life and narrower sphere.

6. Dress has two purposes, utility or adaptation to the wearer's need at the time, and ornament.

7. We believe that adaptation or rational and seasonable fitness should have most weight in deciding dress for times of active move-

ment, and that ornament may decide choice for times of leisure, bodily quietness, and social display.

8. The history of costume shows evolution in utility and continual variety in display. The course of utility is from the simple mat or hide up to the elaborated clothing of the gentleman of the present day, which, without being skin-fitting, follows uniformly the trunk and each limb.

9. Personal display in dress was employed by men until about the end of the seventeenth century, and then practically left to women. It is now popularly considered part of 'women's sphere,' though women are already developing beyond this stage.

10. Again, dress may be considered from the point of view of the age of the wearer. We believe that the school day dress for girls should be mainly decided by suitableness for physical development, and that from this point of view girls' dress is decidedly inferior to boys'.

11. That in the age of youth and personal beauty attention may be given to a definite distinction between dress for times of activity and dress for times of leisure, a legged style being used for the former, and optional style for the latter.

12. The ability of a legged costume to admit of ornamentation has not been yet elaborated, and will be found, we believe, not greatly inferior, if at all, to that of the skirt costume.

13. In the time of youth the sense of right and wrong should be sufficiently established to enable a person of either sex to examine any custom, and to some extent take original action with regard to it.

14. For adult life, when muscular activity gradually lessens, and the full-grown sense of self-importance goes against cut-and-dried rules, we merely recommend the Minor dress reform described in Note 26, deeming it well fitted to maintain as long as possible the physical health and strength acquired in youth.

15. We do not recommend dress reform as an end in life, but as a way out of the greatest obstacle, as we think, that still hinders development in women.

16. Unsuitable dress, we believe, is the chief cause preventing school girls, or such of

them as are naturally active, from acquiring that physical vigour which, in the case of boys, enables them after leaving school to take a strong active part in what goes on around them.

17. Girls, on leaving school, fall still more from physical activity by adopting long dresses, and by giving themselves more or less completely to domestic life; or if on leaving school they take some other means of livelihood, they still closely adhere in dress and personal habits to the style of domestic women.

18. The habit of restricting the sphere of women to domestic duties, especially after marriage, is exemplified in an extreme manner in the customs of the half-civilised peoples of the East.

19. This habit held sway generally even among more civilised nations until late years, when the spread among advanced writers of the new doctrines of the emancipation of women and the equal freedom of the sexes, has been such as to have entirely superseded the old teaching.

20. Opposition to the advancement of women is now found in the opponents of woman suffrage, in the opponents of married women remaining in their maiden professions, in the opponents of the doctrine that a woman should be trained to earn her own living, and in the indifference shown to the question of the athletic development of girls.

21. We, for our part, are in strong sympathy with the matters variously styled women's rights, the emancipation of women, and the giving to the sexes equal freedom of using opportunities of development, and qualifying for any chosen means of livelihood. We emphasise the justice of equal pay for equal work.

22. Many writers now strongly urge parents to see that their daughters take up some profession or calling that will secure them an independent livelihood, and as an argument they show from statistics, women's decreasing chance of marriage, more especially in the older countries and in very respectable classes of society. (In New Zealand it is seen from the 1891 census returns, that of women between 21 and 25 years of age, two-thirds are unmarried, between 25 and 30 one-third are unmarried, and between 30 and 35 one-sixth are unmarried).

23. We strongly approve of an independent livelihood for women, and heartily seek to improve public opinion in the direction of encouraging women to remain after marriage in their maiden profession or calling. In the New Zealand 1891 census twenty-two per cent of the total number of women over 20 years of age are classed as 'breadwinners.'

24. In opening to women – married or single – as wide, practically, a choice of livelihood as men have, we believe that dress reform, such as that explained in these Notes, is essential to success.

25. With regard to books bearing on the question, we can recommend for study Mrs. Godwin's Vindication (1792), Mill's Essay on the Subjection of Women, Colonel Higginson's Common Sense about Women, Mrs. Ashton-Dilke's Women Suffrage, Bebel's Works, Professor Huxley's Essay, Havelock Ellis's Contemporary Science Series, Scientific Meliorism by Miss Clapperton, frequent articles in the chief magazines, notably 'The Arena,' Mr. Stead's notices and comments in the 'Review of Reviews,' and the resolutions and papers of the London Rational Dress Society. As these works do not, in our opinion, sufficiently elaborate the practical treatment of dress reform, we venture to supply their deficiency in this respect.

26. We divide dress reform into two classes, Minor and Higher. Minor is more specially suitable for adult women, for street use, and generally for times of moderate activity.

27. It is practically a reform in the under-things, and advocates the use of divided and combined under-garments, accurately fitted to the body and not baggy about the legs, together with skirt lightened and shortened to a convenient degree. It may also be viewed as an ordinary knickerbocker costume, with light skirt thrown round.

28. This arrangement dispenses with the corset, as the petticoat is replaced by lighter and warmer knickers shaped about the hips and not requiring suspension, while the skirt, if not attached to the bodice, can be suspended by braces or by a body. With this arrangement of under-things there is no bulging of the skirt in front in the sitting position.

28A. With regard to corsets, Dr. Alice B. Stockham, author of 'Tokology,' writes: 'If women had common sense instead of fashion sense the corset would not exist. There are not words in the English language to express my convictions on the subject. The corset, more than any one thing, is responsible for woman being the victim of disease and doctors.' With respect to putting off stays, see Note 84.

28B. Dr. Treves in his recent work on 'Physical Education' (J. & A. Churchill), strongly writes: 'The corset is an abomination;' and indeed, also referring to the ordinary clothes of our girls he says they 'are probably a collection of hygienic errors.'

. . . .

54. Arrived at maturity, young women are the physical opposites of young men, the latter being now qualified to undertake more or less hard muscular work, to maintain the national sports, and to undertake the more arduous callings.

55. Hence, as a rule, a young woman is not the companion of a young man in those things he has had most training in and can do best; and such things form the sphere of his excellence or best conduct.

56. Similarly, instances may be cited in which a young man is not the companion of a young woman in certain lines in which she has attained excellence and shown her highest conduct; but as man's life is usually both wider and intenser than woman's, we believe the greater need for reform lies with the latter.

57. We believe this lack of the higher companionship between the sexes deteriorates the quality of love in youth, tends to confirm male roughness and selfishness and foster larrikinism, produces marriage between unequals, and after marriage ties a woman to her house.

58. We advocate companionship of men and women in work, and in this connection must make an exception to Note 55 in the case of the University Colleges, where the same intellectual training is offered to men and women.

59. When these Colleges create and uphold a sentiment that shall cause equal provision to be made for men and women in other departments of living than the purely studious, we believe we shall then have in these institutions the finest training places the world will yet have seen.

60. We hold that the frequent and regular use of the knicker costume is the first necessary step towards the fundamental development of girls, and that it will enable women, while retaining their loveableness, to become the real companions of men in the higher walks of skill and knowledge.

61. By varying the length, material, and cut of the tunic and knickers, plenty of difference in style can be got. We do not ourselves recommend the baggy Oriental trousers, now being discarded by the higher Turkish ladies.

62. As before stated, the power of the knicker system for the expression of beauty has not been elaborated. Society journals, however, already apply the term 'dainty' to successful examples of this system, as, for instance, to the costume of Madame Bernhardt in Joan of Arc, and to those made by Tantz and Co., London.

62A. We have ourselves seen charming knickerbocker suits, of which Mrs. D. W. M. Burn has designed some of the prettiest; and patterns and photos may be obtained from her and also from the writers of this pamphlet. These suits cannot be considered in any way masculine-looking, and are rapidly winning their way.

Notes on Dress Reform and What It Implies, 1893, pp. 7–13, 19–20

2.7. President's Address, Gisborne Woman's Political Association
by Margaret Sievwright (1894)

Ladies and Gentlemen: 'The world,' it has been well said, 'has never yet seen a fully grown up woman,' and the great woman movement at the close of this wonderful 19th century is, in a word, the revolt of womanhood against a despotism, often apparently unconscious, which authorizes and perpetuates this enforced condition of childhood.

The Legislature of New Zealand has enfranchised woman. This has accentuated N.Z. womanhood, and was the first necessary step towards her complete emancipation. Till, however, she is able to work out her own independence, and to place herself side by side with man, his comrade and his peer, there can be no talk of emancipation.

I read the other day in a Home paper that 'women are organising, in such a way, that they will become a great power in the state. The ball has been set rolling, and those of us who feel impelled to take interest and action in political matters must see to it that that Political ball shall so roll as will be to the advance and solidarity of the great whole.' The Association under whose auspices we are gathered together tonight, is aiming at such issue. Its promoters would fain work so that, in sympathy with Associations of a like nature throughout the Colony, enfranchised women may be found doing what in them lies to unravel the tangled skein of life, to evolve from every local and from every national chaos-cosmos. If they fail to help, they must hinder, and so make confusion worse confounded. Should there be any here this evening who argue that women should leave politics alone, should devote themselves to the social and economic questions of the day, I can only reply; first, that I should like to find the man or woman who could trade for me the boundary lines of these several 'spheres'; second, that, of course, if any woman be of this opinion she will not be likely to engage in purely political work; that that work will be better done by those who do believe in politics, as in everything relating to our common humanity, as being within the province and capacity of woman. Our Association, however, is by no means purely political. Social questions, in fact anything almost, if tending towards mutual improvement, encouragement, and instruction may be discussed or debated at our meetings.

It is a year to-day since Woman's Franchise was granted, and we resolved to celebrate it by assuming a distinctive name, motto, and constitution. It fell to my share to give the opening address, and though woman is a subject of which many among us are growing very weary, it does not seem as if I could speak of anything else to-night. We are admonished not to be weary in well-doing, and we know that all achievement is the result of a struggle. We have reached one milestone, it is true, the milestone of the suffrage, we pause, but only again to press forward.

Retrospect

A few months ago we reviewed the chief events of the political year, the General Elections, the Licensing Elections, and so on down to the beginning of this Session of Parliament, and it was, on the whole, a cheerful and encouraging retrospect. I cannot say, however, that what has subsequently, from time to time, reached our ears from Wellington, is either very cheerful or very encouraging. The attitude of the present House regarding the so-called woman's questions, is not what one would desire. In acting as they do, however, our Representatives are only acting as their predecessors have done before them. When we asked for the Suffrage, we did not expect miracles, we asked it as an instrument, not as an end. We did not, moreover, get exactly what we asked. We gained the right to be represented without the right to represent. It is in vain for men to plead in this Democratic country 'you are not yet politically old enough, or educated enough to represent.' Such a limitation never before accompanied any extension of the Franchise – not even that which gave a vote to every man out of prison in New Zealand. But that is not to say that every man out of prison in New Zealand might be returned as a Member of the House of Representatives. It is for the people, as I have often said before, and not for Parliament to say who shall, or who shall not, represent them, and that quite irrespective of sex. That this disabling clause crept into the Electoral Bill of 1893, is simply another outcome of the widespread notion of women's inferiority as a sex – a notion fostered by unjust laws, and, if possible, still more unjust and irrational, Mrs Grundyism. Where does this notion, consciously or unconsciously, not exist? Have we not had ample opportunity, even within the last few weeks, for noting it in the speeches of Members in both Houses of the Legislature? Judges on the Bench, Barristers at the Bar, Clergymen from pulpit and altar-rail, aye and Doctors in the very sanctuary of sickness – more or less – according to the meanness or nobility of their individual natures – give expression to the same. And if education and culture are so influenced, what shall we say of the uncultured, the rough, the uninstructed ones of our land, and of the victims who are more immediately in their power. I will not enter on the question whether women, as a sex, are inferior in moral and intellectual qualities to men. I believe they are not – I do not know. Few, however, will deny that the average woman is equal in these respects to the average man, and the terms superior and inferior seem to me, unless applied with limitations such as this, altogether stupid. Ruskin says: 'We are foolish, and without excuse foolish, in speaking of the "su-periority" of one sex to the other, as if they could be compared in similar things. Each has what the other has not; each completes the other, and is completed by the other; they are in nothing alike, and the happiness and per-fection of both depends on each asking and receiving from the other, what the other only can give.' These words were written many years ago, but they are true for all time. Failure in the past; Political – Social – Economical failure, may, in a great measure be attributed to the non-recognition of these truths. But surely, friends, the remedy cannot be to emphasize the separation – the separate spheres of the sexes. I have long ago ceased to believe that it is for man, or for other women, to limit woman's sphere – woman's sphere, because she is the complement of man, as he of her, is every-where. A good man will not be found in any place, or amid surroundings, where he would be ashamed to bring his own mother, or the brightest and most beautiful of his girl friends. In fact the question seems to be almost past argument. I believe New Zealand women have only to say the word, and, for instance, Mr G. W. Russell's 'Political Rights Bill' will become the law of the land. The one Operative Clause in the Bill runs thus: 'From and after the passing of this Act, a woman may be appointed, or elected to any public office or position to which a man may be appointed or elected, any Law or Statute to the contrary notwithstanding.' The Bill, as Mr Russell remarked, affirms one principle, i.e. that they shall not bar from public office persons who are otherwise fitted for it. I find that Messrs Seddon, Cadman, and our representative Carroll were among the 41 noes on the division on this question. Stout ap-parently did not vote. With regard to Dr Newman's Bill, which was read a second time in the House, and then shelved, I need only say that it provided for women being called to the Upper House, and clause three repealed that clause of last year's Electoral Act, which debars women from entering the House of Repre-sentatives. Seddon and Stout were here found among the ayes; Cadman, J. Mackenzie, &c., among the noes – Carroll, nowhere. Ladies and Gentlemen, I think these two Bills should become the law of the land. Just let us go over the objections of the various Members; the grounds on which they voted against the Bill. One Hon. gentleman, Mr O'Regan, considered women physically unable to bear the strain of an Electioneering Campaign. Surely that is out

side the Hon. Member's commission. If she be not strong enough, then of course, she can but fail, as man would in like circumstances. Women, however, and men too, are beginning to ask if canvassing itself is an unmixed blessing. Possibly there may be much less of that to do in the years to come. Mr Saunders remarked that 'It would be a pity for women to come to this House so long as they were liable to hear such a succession of slanging matches, as we have heard this afternoon.' Does Mr Saunders forget that had women been present, the slanging matches would probably not have taken place? Mr Allan is perhaps right. He does not think 'Women are so far advanced in the Political sphere that they desire for themselves entry to this House at the present time.' 'Then', one naturally asks, 'where comes in the necessity of debarring them by unnecessary and illogical Legislation?' Mr Mills thinks it very safe to infer that even if the Bill should pass, 'we shall not have a lady in this Chamber for many years to come,' and further that 'we should have an expression of opinion from those interested in it.' Mr Massey too complained 'we have had no petitions,' and voted against the Bill. Capt. Russell, also opposing the measure, said 'If we affirm the principle that women, on the ground that in all respects they are the equal of men, are to be allowed to take their seats in this chamber, there is no reason why they should be exempted from serving as volunteers.' Such reasoning is proof, if more were wanted, of the weakness of their position. In this as in other respects, women are not the equal, but the complement of men, as men of them. Each supplies what the other wants, and in this case woman's share is to do away, as soon as possible, with the necessity of volunteers, and the whole *raison d'etre* of volunteers. Besides there is a law debarring physically weak men from entering the army; it would be against the interests of the whole. There is no law, however, that I ever heard of, in any country, debarring physical delicacy or slightness of form from becoming successful Statesmen, or Scientists. Again, if women could not fight, they equalize matters by bearing the heavier burden of a dual parentage. I believe I have now gone over all objections offered by Members during the late debate, and the message for enfranchised women is simply this, organize and express your wishes. See that these measures do, as soon as possible, become the law of the land. Government should be asked to make them Government measures, as Mr Reeves suggests.

The only other debate I shall notice is that on the Divorce Bill, in the Upper House, now thrown out. I am inclined, as I was at first, to be opposed to the Bill, but I am ashamed of the arguments of those who spoke against it. They are too puerile; too unworthy – I cannot go into them. Read the debate, as reported in Hansard, if you will. We might perhaps have better opportunity for, and more easily obtainable, judicial separation than we have, especially when there are no children, and the present law should certainly be amended to put divorce on an equal footing for men and women. The law of Scotland knows no such inequality, and there is no more unfaithfulness among the married there than elsewhere – perhaps less. With facility of divorce, women would assuredly be again the greater sufferers. Whether any suffering could equal the present degradation of unblessed wedlock is indeed a question but would facility of divorce mend matters? It is a subject calling for the earnest study of both enfranchised men and women. Divorce is in the air, and might, at any moment, become a pressing question of the day. There is one thing, it seems to me, which ought to have preceded or accompanied the Amendment of the Divorce Law, and that is the Consolidation and Amendment of our Marriage Laws. I think I am right in stating that with six lawyers in the Lower House, not one has moved a point in this direction. It is time there was some equality of parental rights and duties, time that our Marriage Laws were based on something like justice. Why should not this Grand Old Century anticipate still more of what is to be:

'*When this old earth is righted;?*
When woman's life no more shall be
The playground of hypocrisy,
But earnest, natural, and free;
And Love shall stay unfrighted,
And reign in sacred, sweet content
And offer service reverent;
For Marriage shall be Sacrament
When this old earth is righted.'

Delay is dangerous. Marriage, in the slang of the period, is becoming a failure, and honest, loving-hearted, clear-headed girls are turning their attention to other vocations. Such girls do not care to have their liberty of thought and action confiscated, even for the sake of wifehood, or woman's crowning blessing motherhood. It is true the young and inexperienced, in the plentitude of their trusting love, will, for the sake of a being whom they, and they alone,

perhaps, have invested with all sorts of virtues, may, and often do, take the terrible leap, and wake up too late to the vain illusion. If girls marry from other motives than love and respect, they deserve to take the consequences; but even then one fails to see why Marriage should reduce them to enrolment in the legal category of 'infants, idiots, lunatics, and married woman.' With enlarging interests, and broader thought, matters are becoming more unbearable. Hence the increasing number of miserable marriages – hence the responsibility of society in permitting a state of matters into the midst of which thousands of children are born, the miserable progeny of unblessed love, to be reared in homes of more miserable discord and dissention. Hence the cry for easy divorce. Frame marriage laws on a basis of equal justice and we shall have less need for easy divorce. 'Only spirits little generous can entertain the idea that liberty is good for everybody except the married woman.'

To-day

We are now beginning to have a glimmer of intelligence as to whither humanity may be tending. Woman is not what she once was, she certainly is yet very far from what she would wish to be; let us be thankful she is what she is. Formerly religious people used to argue of woman's disabilities on the ground of Eve eating a forbidden apple and giving it to her husband. Now Eve is considered to have been the first missionary in that her own eyes being opened to the knowledge of good or evil she immediately proceeded to insist on the same gift being conferred on her husband. Formerly Bishops used to argue whether woman had a soul or not. Now the plaint is that woman is all soul. Formerly scientific men thought that somehow – even in defiance of all evidence – women transmitted to their children only bodily characteristics while men bequeathed all superior or mental. Now, what of such evidence? Find me any great and good man on the face of this wide world and I will venture to believe and so will you, that that man had a good mother. Forty years ago Florence Nightingale went with a few women to the Crimean War. What has been the direct outcome of that proceeding? Thousands, tens of thousands of England's picked women are now earning an honourable living and serving their day and generation in one of the noblest walks of life. Twenty years ago the battle of lady medicals was fought out in Edinburgh by seven brave women. The battled raged loud and long. It was discussed in public and private; in railway carriage and tram car. One recognised the two sides by the names adopted. Professor Christison, a stern opponent, used to call them 'the females.' This became 'Christison's Females,' while among their friends, they were known as the 'women students,' or 'lady medicals.' For the time they were unsuccessful, and had to go to Dublin in some cases, to London in others, for their degree. Seventy women are now practising medicine in Britain, and within the last year or two, not one, but two Medical Schools, for women, have sprung up in the whilom recalcitrant Edinburgh. Glasgow, however, has been the first in the field to grant the degree. On the 26th of July last, when the names of Marion Gilchrist, with high commendation, and Alice Louisa Cumming, with an ordinary degree, were announced, the men students cheered vociferously, and, after the ceremony of capping had been completed, the organ pealed forth the popular ditty 'For She's a Jolly Good Fello,' in which the students joined with great heartiness. Prof. Charteris, who stuck to the early Edinburgh contingent, through good report and through bad, was chosen to deliver the valedictory address. His opening remarks were as follows: 'In our little University World it is an *annus mirabilis.* You have to-day, Sir, I think I may call it the honour of admitting, for the first time in Scotland, two women to a Medical Degree of Bachelor of Medicine, and Master of Surgery. After a long conflict their admirable perseverance has been crowned with success, and we heartily congratulate them,' &c.

Again we cannot but admire and wonder, when we consider the devotion and zeal for good which has been aroused by the women in that great modern movement of the Salvation Army; 'Slum Angels' as Cardinal Manning has well called them. An officer of the Salvation Army, interviewing Sir George Grey in London the other day, asked: 'And what do you think generally of the Army's policy with respect to women?' 'You mean the woman's question. Their place in public affairs?' The man assented. 'She is the hope of the world, and the Army, in recognising her equal right with men, is enforcing a noble truth.' Now if all these things are being done by unenfranchised women, should we, more favored, not be asking ourselves what we can accomplish?

No party

With the granting of the Franchise to women there arose a loud cry, heard before but in an undertone, of there being no Party in Politics. Personally, I fear, I am too Conservative (extremes are said to meet) to believe in this wide-spread notion. If it be so, however, it is a mark of progress, and I am for progress. But instead of No Party what does one see? Turning to England, is she not parcelling herself off into many Parties? We have Home Rule Party, Liberal-Unionist Party, Labour Party, and General Booth was heard the other day appealing for a Starvation Party. Think of it 3,000,000 well-nigh naked, homeless, foodless, voteless ones! Do you not think the great General was right, and that there is room for a Starvation Party there? Thank God we have not yet reached that stage in New Zealand civilization, but to aid in warding it off we think that a Woman's Party might not be altogether an undesirable proposal. Do not suppose for a moment that I mean a Woman's Party v. Man. I mean a strong manly Man's Party, which will make up its mind, once and for all, to put woman on such a footing of perfect legal equality with the other sex, as will redeem her from her present position of childhood; and then appeal to her every higher and holier instinct to be true to the trust that they have imposed in her, appeal to her to die unto silliness, vanity, weakness of every kind, and to live unto all that makes for righteousness, sweet reasonableness, and the womanly side of humanity. Nor here again have we any right to expect miracles. Centuries of past injustice and injury have laid a heavy incubus on woman. She can scarcely be expected to spring to the novel combat like a trained young gladiator. Ask men – men who are in power to do what is right and just. I do not think women on the whole will be found wanting. But to return to the question of No Party. It would be easy to multiply definitions of Liberal and Conservative, and to submit that both are represented in New Zealand. I am satisfied to quote an article which I came across in a late number of the London Speaker: 'The ultimate distinction in politics (says the writer) is between those who believe in the ideal, and those who believe in the actual. The Liberal is essentially the party of ideas, the Tory is essentially the party of comfort and class. The one thing the Liberal Party can never be, and yet remain Liberal, is false to the ideas of justice and freedom, progress and equality. The classes Liberalism can do nothing with are those impervious to ideas; the prejudice that will not hear reason, the privilege that will not be challenged, the interest that conceives its being guaranteed by a right divine, the culture that refuses to feel the touch of humanity, and the class that holds its position as the manifest law of God. The aim of the Liberal is to secure the reign of freedom and justice in society, and of progress and equality in industry; and his hope of reaching his end is by the increased power of those ideas that beget the ideals which he wishes to translate into realities.' ['The Speaker,' April, 1891.] If this writer be correct, and if the Man in The Street, here in New Zealand, be correct, when he tells me 'We all are Liberals here,' then friends we are nearer Heaven than most of us are aware.

Home

Again, we enfranchised women hear much of woman's domain being the home. Whoever denies, or would wish to deny such a self-evident fact? All women, however, have not a home in which to reign. And if they have, perhaps they are only the better-fitted to carry that home influence into the outside world to humanize it a little. At any rate a busy woman, the other day, wrote this: 'It has become a truism that busy people have most time. We think experience will also show that it is the busy mothers who see most of their children. Devotion to regular work never need involve the withdrawal of time and attention from the claims of family life. These claims and duties will always tend to rank higher than ever as the standard of womanhood is raised. It is the endless visiting, for visiting's sake, of indifferent acquaintances, it is the struggle for recognition by those a little richer, or a little more important, it is the truly miraculous absorption in the mysteries of the toilette, for which there will be 'no time' in the life of the busy woman. She, whose day is arranged on the lines of work which must be done, will, in 99 cases out of 100, find her truest recreation in the ordering of her household, and her highest joys in those family ties which she is accused of despising.' ['The Hospital,' May 5, 1893.] A German authoress tells us, by the way that out of 34 lady Doctors in New York, there are only two who have not themselves nursed their own babies [ibid]. And just let me ask, are the men and the women who keep ever repeating, repeating the very same thing, are they the husbands and the wives whose homes can always answer to such

a description of house as has any right at all to the title? Do four brick or wooden walls, with some tables and chairs, crockery, and a sufficiency of screaming children constitute home? John Ruskin knew better. He says: 'This is the true nature of home – it is the place of Peace; the shelter, not only from all injury, but from all terror, doubt and division. In so far as it is not this, it is not home; so far as the anxieties of the outer life penetrate into it, and the inconsistently-minded, unknown, unloved, or hostile society of the outer world is allowed, by either husband or wife, to cross the threshold, it ceases to be home; it is then only a part of that outer world which you have roofed over, and lighted fire in. But so far as it is a sacred place, a vestal temple, a temple of the hearth, watched over by Household Gods, before whose faces none may come, but those whom they can receive with love. So far as it is this, and roof, and fire, are types only of a nobler shade and light – shade as of the rock in a weary land, and light as of the Pharos in the stormy sea. So far it vindicates the name, and fulfils the praise of Home.' These words are written of happy love-encircled homes, and, my friends, it is from happy love-encircled homes that the cry for 'nobler manners, purer laws' must come forth – for justice, equal justice to those who, in the bondage of despair, have no power left even to resist. Let us 'descend by the steps of mercy,' and seek to redeem for our sex that justice which love accords to the loved, and is usually most anxious to bestow upon all. Hear Olive Schreiner, from her African Farm: 'They say that when men and women are equals, they will love no more. Your highly cultured woman will not be loveable, will not love. A great soul draws, and is drawn with a more fierce intensity than any small one. By every inch we grow in intellectual height, our love strikes down its roots deeper, and spreads out its arms wider. It is for love's sake yet more than for any other that we look for, that new time. Then when that time comes, when love is no more bought and sold, when it is not a means of making bread, when each woman's life is filled with earnest independent labor, then love will come to her, a strange sudden sweetness, breaking in upon her earnest work; not sought for but found; then, but not now.' This idea of earnest work suggests another thought. Many are eager for work who cannot get it. People keep asking: 'If there be not work for men now, how will it be when women too crowd the labor market?' The effect may be that something, which some people do not want to come to pass, will come to pass. It may bring matters to a crisis. In any case there is at present much work being very badly done, and if woman's appearance will in any measure improve that work, it will be for the good of the community, as well as simple justice to herself, that she should appear. But with a re-distribution of wealth, there would come a re-distribution of labor, and neither men nor women would be under the necessity of working either so hard, or for so many hours per day, for the means of securing their daily bread. All would be able to spend their leisure on one or other of the 1001 subjects which now engross the minds of the favoured few. You may call this Utopian, you may call it visionary, and possibly such time may be some way off, but we should have an idea of what we are aiming at, especially our young people should, and our ideal cannot be too high. The practical question, however, is how to attain to this standard, how to reach the goal? And this is the very question which is now exercising and puzzling the greatest men of the age. You and I, perhaps, can do but little towards the solution of the problem, but we can all read, mark, learn, and inwardly digest every possible hint on the subject. We can cast our little grains of influence on the right side, and we can help others to do the same. Those who do not wish it, may flatter themselves that that day is a long way off. My own belief is that the time for patching and cobbling the old bottles is drawing to a close. People may close their eyes, but their not seeing the danger will not avert it. Anarchy and Nihilism are the inevitable, and the natural products, not of the cogitations of a few raving fanatics, but of swindling syndicates, trusts, Joint Stock Companies, millionaireism, and all the devilish devices man invents to 'best', as you New Zealanders say, his brother man. They may guillotine 100 Santos. What are they? Poor; often low-typed, well nigh barbarian madmen, who, in the extremity of their misery, see no other way of entering their protest against the inhumanity of man. Pessimists tell us the Santos will multiply into regiments, and the regiments into armies. I know not; but it does not take superhuman prescience to foretell that within a measureable time, something further and deeper down than the execution of our Santos, will have to be done in the direction of equalizing the necessaries and opportunities of life. Do you ask what all this has to do with enfranchised women? Much every way.

Women are asking from all what one-half of men are still asking from the other half of their brother men, and the man of poor estate, who clamors for his own rights as against the dishonorable rich, the man whose cry too is for equality of opportunity for all, must of necessity lend a sympathetic ear to the perhaps weaker, but not less weary wail of either enfranchised or unenfranchised womanhood. The relief of the distressed is preached by Christian philanthropists, and by Christian Ministers. We have Societies for the Prevention of Cruelty to Children, Societies for the Prevention of Cruelty to Animals, but the law of our land admits cruelty and injustice of the deepest dye, towards her married women. Who is there to lift up a word of remonstrance? Is not this a subject for the consideration of enfranchised women? As isolated women we can do something – not much. Let us stand together, and by petitions, and other means, make our wants known. Men, I do believe, are not half aware of what an ordinarily sensitive married woman feels, or would feel, if she only knew the extent of her legal disability.

In conclusion

In conclusion, is the talk of women unsexing themselves by taking more part in public life? Nay, verily, enfranchisement will but emphasize their womanhood. Emancipation will help to perfect it. The woman of the future will not be the hideous caricature some people are fond of portraying her. She will be wise, loveable and wholly womanly. Do not be afraid, my younger friends, of being called names. It is a very easy thing to fling all sorts of ugly epithets about. Any fool can do that. The 'emancipated woman,' or even 'the emancipated female' is a grand idea which I hope many among you may live to see realized. Meanwhile find out, each of you, what your work in life is, and having found, do it. Remember too that you live in stirring times, times of storm and stress, times painful to the thoughtful, and dangerous to the thoughtless woman; nevertheless remember that now is woman's opportunity, that you, even the most insignificant among you, must do something to make or mar the present great movement. Ah! but some wellwisher groans forth 'there are barriers.' We know the barriers, and I will tell you some of them. There is the barrier of masculine selfishness conscious and unconscious. There is the barrier of feminine apathy; women are all right themselves, or imagine they are, and that is enough for them.

There is the barrier of the boycott applied to all who wander in unbeaten tracks; there is the barrier of vested interests, and lastly there is a terrible barrier, for we are told that 'a barrier more unsuperable than Styx is Philistine Stupidity.' Is it? As far, at least, as the woman's question is concerned, I hope the barriers will be bravely assailed, and I believe there are those here to-night who will live to see even the barrier of 'Philistine Stupidity' laid low.

Gisborne Woman's Political Association, President's Address, 19 September 1894 *[Gisborne, 1894]*

2.8. Unfortunate Women
Daybreak (1895)

If we women who are strong, happy and fortunate, and are filled with a desire to raise our sex to an equality with men, really intend to do any practical good we shall have to treat some very unpleasant subjects in a straight-forward, commonsense manner, and deal with them in plain language – not immodestly or unwomanly, however novel. In broaching this subject we feel thoroughly satisfied that no apology is necessary to those readers who are women – in the highest and best sense of the word – and for the opinion of those who are too timid or mock-modest to boldly face an evil which casts a stigma on our sex we do not care. The time has passed when Mrs Grundy ruled that every woman who wished to be thought 'correct and proper' should feign or assume ignorance of the existence of a section of our sex called 'unfortunates' or 'social evils.'

'Ignorance is the worst form of innocence', and the ravages of this growing evil have been so deadly and cruel in its effect on the health, happiness, and welfare of thousands of both sexes; in its destruction of home and family life, and in its power to decrease the marriage rate and doom vast numbers of women to an enforced celibacy, that, however nauseous and difficult the task of combatting it may be, it has to be undertaken.

The prospects of totally eradicating an evil of such long growth and of such dimensions is, of course, almost hopeless. Ancient and Scriptural history record its existence from the earliest period. Hardly any nation or community have been free from it. But that should not discourage us, for when we thoroughly understand how the evil is caused, sustained, aggravated, and fed, we need not despair of reducing or minimising it. In the consideration of this subject it is necessary that we should know something about our unfortunate sisters, whose weakness, folly, or misfortunes have reduced them to this deplorable occupation. The conventional idea of 'orthodox respectability' is that they are naturally 'bad women.' This is not by any means generally true. There are, no doubt, women whose strong passions and indolent dispositions unhappily doom them to such a career; but it is pleasant to know that these are few indeed. In the majority of cases it is force of circumstances, poverty, neglect, bad training and associations, and in numberless instances the perfidy and cruelty of men which swell the ranks of the unfortunates. It must not be forgotten that the merciless law of society – which ostracises and obliterates the woman or girl who has made 'one slip,' and which practically prevents her from regaining her position, and often debars her from obtaining honest employment – has made more prostitutes than ten thousand libertines or *roues*. And it must not also be overlooked that we women have, in the past, applauded and enforced the execution of this Draconian measure with greater zeal and strictness than men have. Those who, in works of philanthropy and relief, have made a sorrowful acquaintance with this class of women, will tell you that the majority of them hate their trade and despise themselves. Like Stern's starling, their continual complaint is – 'I can't get back' (or 'out' if you prefer the correct rendering). Given but a fair opportunity, where they would not have the finger of scorn continually pointed at them, the great majority would be glad to accept honest employment and return to a decent life. Sisters, we entreat you, as you hope to remedy this evil, do not forget the facts we have detailed. No good can be done by police persecution, or by hunting these unfortunate women from house to house and finally into the streets. The women's Political organisations which have favoured or proposed a crusade against brothels are acting in a short-sighted and cruel manner. They are only dealing with effects and neglecting the cause. They are merely cutting branches, which will grow stronger, and leaving the roots of the evil tree untouched.

The only possible way to reduce the evil is by fighting for new social conditions, in which every woman and man (because uncertainty of employment for men restricts marriage and fosters prostitution) will be able to get employment, if they are willing and able to work. Mr G. Bernard Shaw said, very truly, 'that it is not dissolute men who make women 'cheap' and draw them down to ruin and degradation, so much as it is the commercial, industrial, and social system under which we are living.' The impossibility of having decent attractive homes, and healthful intelligent recreation, on the one hand, and the demoralising 'cheapening' of women's labour in factory, shop, and household, by our competitive system, on the other, steadily feeds this evil to an awful extent. Raising the age of consent, and other restrictive legislation, may be necessary, but human beings cannot be made virtuous by Acts of Parliament, which can never reclaim, rescue, and can only to a moderate extent prevent. The only effective remedy for the reduction of this 'hideous social cancer' is change. Change 'with-

out and within.' Improved social conditions, and the growth of a new spirit having a lofty yet true conception of the dignity and sanctity of womanhood as its ideal. A spirit which in dealing with others tries to elevate, purify, and ennoble, not by suppression, law, or force, but by helping the weak, lifting up the fallen, and by inculcating the young with ideas and habits of decency, cleanliness, modesty, and self-respect. Agitate for persecutions if you will, carry on your crusade against the brothels if you will, martyrise and crucify your weaker sisters, but in common justice shut your doors against and refuse friendship and hospitality to their male partners in iniquity – the men who support and frequent houses of ill-fame. And, above all, hesitate to maintain in its cast-iron rigidity the conventional law which denies the seducer's victim one more chance, and which condemns to the 'gutter of prostitution' those whose sole fault has been misplaced confidence and loving 'not wisely but too well.'

Daybreak, 8 June 1895, pp. 4–5

2.9. Southern Cross Society. Its Objects by Anna Stout (1895)

I have been asked to state the objects and aims of this Society. These I will first state generally. The Society has been organised for the purpose of educating women, not women of any one class or opinion, but women from all classes and of all shades of opinions, to take a wide view of the questions of the day and to do all in their power to advocate reforms that will tend to benefit women, to promote their independence and equality and make life and the conditions of living easier and better for those women who have to depend upon their own exertions for their livelihood. Such in general are our aims, but to prevent confusion I shall just say a few words in explanation of each of the objects involved in our programme:

1. THE EDUCATION OF WOMEN IN POLITICAL AND ECONOMIC PRINCIPLES

I am sure we all feel that we require education in politics. It is only lately that women have obtained a voice in politics, and one can scarcely expect that we can be qualified to understand the science of politics and political economy without study and thought any more than one can expect to learn a foreign language by hearing the language spoken, or learn music by listening to the organ grinder. But I have

been asked: What does economics mean? Does it mean economy in house-keeping? Well, yes it does, but applied as it is in our programme it means 'political economy; the science of the production, distribution and exchange of wealth,' and this includes a consideration of the application of the money or wealth of a country so as to procure such a distribution as will promote the well-being and industrial efficiency of the members of the community. I think we should get a good book on political economy, read chapters on the various subjects of general interest, and then we might be able to understand the political and economical questions of the day. It is absolutely necessary that we have a firm grasp of the elements of political economy before we venture to criticise the policy of any Government, take up any line of action, or adopt any particular views. We should not condemn what we only know by hearsay to be a wrong, and it is absurd for us to declare we are for or against any policy when we are in a mist as to wherein the faults or fallacies of such a policy consist.

As to Section 2. THE PROMOTION OF PURITY OF ADMINISTRATION BOTH OF THE GENERAL GOVERNMENT AND OF LOCAL BODIES.

To be able to give an opinion on this subject we must understand the working of institutions and we must not be too ready to jump to conclusions and find fault with any administration without good and sound reasons. Again, we should make ourselves conversant with the methods of Government, and if we find the laws have been broken by such abuses as appointment by favoritism or the dismissal of good officers in any department of general or local Government, so as to make place for friends of the powers that be, we may then be called upon as a society to make our voice heard in protest.

Clause 3. TO INSIST UPON HIGH CHARACTER AS AN ESSENTIAL QUALIFICATION FOR ELECTION TO ANY PUBLIC POSITION.

In this clause I consider our strength and power as women will have the very best and fullest scope for action. But here again caution will be necessary. If we do not wish to brand ourselves as uncharitable or narrow-minded, we must have good and sufficient reasons for objecting before we take action. We women have, I think, in our hands the power to raise the standard of uprightness and purity of character in men. If we could devise any method by which we could make our influence felt in this direction we should be able to strike out the second clause of our programme as accomplished. Once we succeed in securing men of high character and purity of life to all our public positions, we need have no fear that the administration of Government will be disgraced by any abuses. We of course can make a move in attaining the end which we desire, when the occasion arises, by urging the rejection of anyone whom we know to be unworthy, and when we have the power, by choosing the best candidate. In that way and that way alone, I think we will improve the tone of public life, and men who are not able to bear the light upon their characters or actions will soon find it wiser to retire. We must make it known that no matter how clever a man may be we shall not accept him as the Women's candidate, unless his private and public reputation is such as to command respect and reflect credit upon his supporters.

Clause 4. TO SECURE FOR WOMEN EQUAL REMUNERATION WITH MEN FOR EQUAL WORK.

This clause I fear will be the source of a good deal of trouble to us. Many friends disagree with this, insisting that it is better for women that men should command higher pay, that it would be to the disadvantage of women if employers had to pay as high for their work as for the work of men, and that many employments now open to men and women would at once be closed to the latter if they demanded equal wages. I think we must make ourselves conversant with the opinions of leading men of the day upon this point. For my own part I consider this clause would be beneficial to women as it would tend to show how far and in what directions women are competent to compete with men. Where women succeed in doing the work equally well, and only if they do so, they are by right entitled to equal pay, and where women are found unequal to cope with men it is better that they should fall out of competition, and take up another line of work in which they would be more successful.

Clause 5. TO ADVOCATE THE IMPROVEMENT OF LAWS PARTICULARLY RELATING TO WOMEN.

This clause relates to such laws as the divorce law, laws pertaining to the rights of mothers over their children, to the rights of property and social conditions. I think we will all agree that in making men stand upon an equality with women in the divorce law we are only insisting upon justice and right in this matter; and in all social matters it is necessary for the protection of the weaker to put more rigid restrictions upon the stronger. We should study the laws that are brought before Parliament and make our influence felt in promoting justice and the cause of purity and right in our land. I think there is no need to take up the line that all women are angels and all men brutes, when we advocate our right to insist that men shall be judged by the same standard of purity as women, and that what is sin in a woman is equally sinful and reprehensible in a man, and must involve the same punishment. We have too long excused the stronger sex, and blamed and punished the weaker, when we all know that, if the stronger were subject to equal punishment, it would act as a lever to keep them in the right path.

No 6 Clause. TO OBTAIN THE EXTENSION TO WOMEN OF THE RIGHT TO UNDERTAKE SUCH PUBLIC DUTIES AS THE SOCIETY MAY CONSIDER SUITABLE AND BECOMING TO WOMEN.

This clause I find has been the cause of much misapprehension, and many friends have thought we intended to support women as candidates for Parliamentary honors. I may as well emphasize the fact that not one of the originators of this movement is in favor of the candidature of women for seats in Parliament. We all agree that women require some years of education in politics before it would be becoming for them to come forward as politicians. Certainly I think if women were equally well qualified with men they have a perfect right to stand if they wish to do so and I consider it absurd to say women should not stand for Parliament because they should look after their homes and families, and it is not suitable for women to sit in the House and go home at all hours. I think any woman who was qualified to sit in the House, would be very well able to take care of herself and go home without any fear at any time. Do not professional nurses go through the streets at all hours to attend their patients? I never heard of one being molested in any way. Do not brave, noble women belonging to sisterhoods go everywhere quite safely, and are they not treated with respect, and honored by all men with whom they come in contact? We all know that strength is not and has never been our weapon. True virtue needs no bolts and bars. No one would expect girls of eighteen to stand for Parliament. Men never aspire to a seat till they have come to years of discretion. Neither will women. It is very well for women with homes and children to object to women in the House. There are hundreds of women who can never have husbands and children to look after, whose energies might be devoted to helping on the cause of right, justice and good government instead of spending their lives in utter uselessness and becoming a prey to nervous diseases for the want of some object in life. Women need never fear that unsuitable women will come forward, and I don't think we need trouble about objecting to women standing for Parliament till they wish to do so; and when the time comes for a woman to undertake the responsibilities and she has the necessary ability, I hope we will not be narrow-minded enough to reject a woman who is qualified for a man who is not suitable. Our object is to have women on Hospital Boards, Education Boards, School Committees, Charitable Aid Boards and any other position for which women are equally suitable with men. I think we need to go slowly and find really suitable women as candidates, women without domestic responsibilities, who have time and ability to attend to the duties required. It is difficult to get women to come forward, but there must be many who would willingly have some real object in life; and we must try and instil into the minds of such the hope of doing good, and enthusiasm for the good work.

No 7. TO IMPROVE THE ADMINISTRATION OF CHARITABLE AID.

This is or has been our stumbling block. We do not intend or wish to organise any form of charitable aid. We consider there are too many societies dispensing charity. All seems to be in confusion. People who are unworthy in many cases receive assistance, and those who are in want are not even known. Our idea is that there should be something done to prevent the constant overlapping of charitable aid societies, and ensure the deserving poor receiving necessary help without the publicity that is humiliating to them. If a central board with district boards and visiting committees was organised all cases would be properly investigated and no one in need would be overlooked. Of course we would wish women to be district visitors, and members of the different boards. Waste would be done away with to a great extent and unauthorised collectors and distributors would not be required. It would be much easier to raise voluntary subscriptions if the donors were certain that their gifts would be expended for the benefit of the worthy and deserving. Our idea is to endeavor to have a scheme of this sort tried in Wellington but not to collect or distribute as a society. We shall wish to have a voice in the election of visitors and members of the Board.

No 8. TO PROMOTE TEMPERANCE.

To insist upon the licensing laws being rigidly carried out, and the members of the licensing committees being of a reliable character. I don't know whether the members agree with me, but I certainly think that one of the most vital causes of intemperance, amongst our growing youths, is the employment of barmaids. I think it should be against the law for women to dispense drink. Many young men just go to the bar for the sake of a chat with a pretty girl and don't like to come away without taking something. They would never dream of going into a bar if a man was serving. We, as women, can discourage the habit of drinking intoxicants by girls and men, by quiet example and perhaps do much that will tend to help our cause in the end. Individually, I should like to see the sale of drink prohibited, but whatever our views on this subject may be we can have no difficulty in agreeing to support any proper means for the advancement of temperance reform. Unfortunately, temperance is through hereditary, mental and physical weakness, utterly impossible to many. Those we can do our utmost to persuade to adopt total abstinence and make the laws such that it is a crime to give drink to men and women who are thus made unaccountable for their actions and a menace to their fellows.

Clause 9. TO AFFORD FACILITIES FOR MEETINGS FOR THE STUDY AND DISCUSSION, OF SOCIAL, POLITICAL, ECONOMICAL, EDUCATIONAL AND LITERARY SUBJECTS, AND GENERALLY TO CARRY ON SUCH USEFUL WORK AS THE SOCIETY MAY CONSIDER SUITABLE.

I think this clause explains itself, and I shall just say a few words in conclusion. We do not wish to be considered a society for the suppression of mankind. We only desire that the women of the colony should have equal rights with men, and not be debarred by law or prejudice from living the fullest and free life that they may be qualified by education to live. Women need not be compelled to exist on the charity of brothers and relations, if they can earn their own living and make such wages as are necessary to comfortable existence. Women wish to take part in the life and work of the Colony. I don't think there is any need to fear that women will allow public functions to interfere with the discharge of their home duties.

We shall be most happy to elect gentlemen as honorary members and accept 5s as a fee from those who wish to join us. Money will be required for our room etc., and women-like we will permit men to assist us in providing the necessary funds. We shall also be most happy if any of our gentlemen friends will address us from time to time, and let us benefit by their greater experience and wisdom. We are only beginning to use our wings and must sometimes rest upon branches of the tree of knowledge and experience that has taken centuries to come to maturity, or we may get some bruises that will take some time to heal. We shall insist upon our right of equality, not forgetting that in unity of thought, hope and aim our strength lies. We hope that by obtaining equal rights, we shall instead of making life harder for men, make it much better, and that they will see that the recognition of our mental equality, will tend to make those who are destined to become wives and mothers more pleasant and agreeable companions. Homes will be more happy when the wife is able and willing to take part and advise her husband in every department of his work and share his aspirations as well as his daily cares and sorrows.

And so these twain, upon the skirts of Time,
Sit side by side, full summ'd in all their powers,
Dispensing harvest, sowing the To-be,
Self-reverent each and reverencing each
Distinct in individualities
But like each other ev'n as those who love.

Southern Cross Society. Its Objects. Address by Lady Stout delivered at the inaugural meeting of the Southern Cross Society, Wellington, 22 August 1895, *Wellington, 1895, pp.[1–4]*

2.10. The *White Ribbon*, Official Correspondence (Maori section WCTU) by Mihi Schnackenberg (1896)

AKARANA, Tihema.
Hei kupu aroha atu tenei ki nga wahine Maori, ki te hunga e rua rau (200) kua hui huia nei i tenei hui huinga nui, ara te Woman's Christian Temperance Union – W.C.T.U.

Tena Koutou. Whakawhetai tonu au ki toku Atua i nga maharatanga katoatanga ki a koutou. E hari ana hoki toku ngakau no te mea kua rongo ahau i ta koutou pono i tenei whawhai, te patu waipiro. E hoa ma, kia kaha, kia pono, me te inoi tonu ki te Atua. Kei a ia te naha-ma te Atua nui tatou e whakakahangia mo enei mahi nui e rua ko te patu waipiro, me te patu puremu; na te rewera, na Hatana, nga kino katoa, ahakoa, nga te tangata te hara. Me korero hoki koutou ki nga wahina tai tama riki, kei hinga ratou i te hara puremu.

Tenei ahau te mihi atu nei ki aku hoa aroha ki a koutou nga wahine Maori, kua tahuri nei ki te taha Temperance. Kia maharatia nga kupu a Paora Apotoro i tuhi tuhia ki te hunga whakapoua i Epiha, c.6., v.10, 'Heoi, e aku teina, kia whai kaha koutou i roto i te Ariki, i te mana ano hoki o toua kaha; v. 11, Kakahuria iho nga mea whawhai katoa a te Atua, kia taea ai e koutou nga mahi tinihanga a te rewera, ti tu ki te riri; v. 13, Mo konei, kia mau ki nga mea whawhai katoa a te Atua, kia taea ai e koutou te tu atu ki te riri, i tera kino, a ka poto i a koutou nga mea katoa te mahi, kia tu.'

Heoi tenei, tera ano pea tetahi atu kupu kia koutou me he mea e marama ana.

Na te hoa pouo, NA MIHI NAKIPEKA. Tuhi tuhi, c/o Mrs Hewitt.

Free Translation. Auckland, December.

This is a word of loving greeting to the Maori women – to the noble two hundred (200) who have joined the great gathering named the Woman's Christian Temperance Union. W.C.T.U.

Greetings to you all. I thank my God on every remembrance of you all. My heart is very glad because I have heard of your faithfulness in this fight against strong drink (bad water). My dear friends, do you be ever strong, and ever faithful, and pray always to God. With Him is strength, and may He make us all strong for these two great works – to fight against drink and uncleanness. All evil comes from the devil.

Satan is the author of evil, though man commits the sin. I want you to talk to your young women lest they fall into the sin of uncleanness.

Here am I sending salutations to my loving friends, to you, my Maori sisters, who have turned to the side of temperance. I should like you to remember the words of St. Paul, the Apostle, written in 6th chap. Ephesians, v.10, 11, and 13; ponder them well.

This is all at present. I may write to my Maori friends again, if this is clear to you.

From your kind friend, MIHI SCHNACKEN-BERG, Write to me, care of MRS HEWITT.

White Ribbon, vol. 2, no. 18 (December 1896), p. 9

2.11. The C.D. Acts (1898)

Mrs Wells read the following reasons why the Contagious Diseases Acts should be repealed:

1. Because they are a glaring violation of constitutional law. Herbert Spencer says that they 'treat with contempt the essential principles of constitutional rule.' Lord Halsbury, the late Lord-Chancellor, writing of one of the powers conferred by these Acts, says, 'It is contrary to the whole spirit and principle of our law.' The C.D. Acts allow a woman to be urged to criminate herself. They sanction her being intimidated to write herself down as guilty before she has had any kind of trial whatever. They hold her to be guilty until she can prove herself to be innocent. They condemn and punish on the mere suspicion of the police, and no positive proof is required. They grant no open trial.

2. Because they are an insult to the womanhood of the Colony. Under these Acts a pure and modest woman may be subjected to the most disgusting personal outrage. Before these Acts were repealed in England many cruel indignities were inflicted on innocent girls, respectable married women, and even on ladies of good position. Any woman is completely at the mercy of a policeman, who may be either stupid or vicious. It is all but impossible for persons falsely accused and cruelly outraged to get redress. The policeman may plead in excuse of the greatest outrage that a woman can suffer his *intention* to obey the Act. If the verdict is not decided against the policeman, he shall obtain from the women full costs; but if the verdict is for the outraged woman, she shall not have costs (unless the judge shall certify that he approves it). Professor Newman says 'Did ever any stupid, ignorant, reckless barbarians make such a law?'

3. Because they are useless in checking the spread of disease. M. Lecour, Commissaire Interrogateur and Chef de Bureau a la Prefecture de Police, whose duty it is to superintend the administration of these Acts in Paris, says, 'The evil is a moral and social one, and cannot be controlled by the police, who can neither restrain nor destroy it.' Leon Lefort, of the Paris faculty and physician to the du Midi hospital for men, says 'The means employed against syphilis in Paris amount to nothing.' Dr. Armand Despres, for thirty years surgeon to the Lourcine, the great hospital with upwards of 300 beds, devoted solely to the treatment of venereal diseases in women, says, 'There are some police laws destined to regulate debauchery (the French C.D. Acts); thus the liberty of some women has been destroyed in order to give security to debauched men, *but the result has not answered expectation.*' The Sanitary Commissioner of the Panjab reported to the Government, 'That, notwithstanding the preventive arrangements of recent years, there is nowhere any substantial improvement in the condition of the troops as regards venereal diseases.' (These 'preven-

tive arrangements,' the C.D. Acts, have since been repealed.) The Army Sanitary Commission is the highest hygienic authority in the British Army. That Commission, in 1893, forwarded to the Government a memorandum in which it was stated that the re-introduction of the Lock Hospital, on sanitary grounds, could not be recommended. Mr. Campbell-Bannerman, the Secretary of State for War, in reply to questions put in the House of Commons, in June 1894, said 'That, after looking very carefully into the matter, with the assistance of some of the most eminent and competent medical authorities, the conclusion to which he, and every one else who had looked into the subject, came to – was that these Acts had no practical effect whatever in checking the progress of disease. He also stated that, as a matter of fact, the number of men affected by this disease had diminished since the repeal of these Acts.'

4. Because the C.D. Acts actually help to spread disease by creating a false sense of security. M. Lecour says: 'All these results prove that it (Prostitution) is now more dangerous than ever to the public health.' Dr. Jeannel acknowledges that the number of diseased persons is greater in Paris than in London (which has twice the population). Dr. Drysdale made the same assertion before the most eminent Continental medical authorities at the Venereal Medical Congress held at Paris, and the truth of the assertion was frankly acknowledged. When

the French introduced the C.D. Acts into Algeria, venereal disease amongst the soldiery increased until in a comparatively short time it had doubled. The smallest amount of disease in the French army was among the troops who were quartered in Rome, where the Pope refused to allow the C.D. Acts to be put in operation. Mr. Acton, in his work on Prostitution, says, 'The hope of escaping punishment multiplies vicious habits, and many men are tempted by the health examinations who otherwise would never incur the risk.' He tells of men who have travelled hundreds of miles, lured by a false security, to visit French brothels, where periodical examinations are carried out, and have immediately contracted a foul disorder. Professor Andrews says: 'As a professional man, I have been compelled to laugh at the frequent instances where young Americans have, with infinite gullibility, cohabited with loose women in Paris, because they supposed it safe there, but were utterly astonished afterwards to find that they had contracted syphilis.'

Many other reasons could be given. For example: The C.D. Acts should be repealed because 'it is immoral for the State to legalise vice.' But the 'Four Reasons' alone should be sufficient to show that the example set by England – years ago – in repealing these abominable Acts should be followed by New Zealand without delay.

NCW 3rd Session, April 1898, pp.36–38 (MS Papers 1376, folder 4, ATL)

2.12. The Economic Independence of Married Women by Margaret Sievwright (1898)

At the evening sitting of the Council, on Thursday, April 28, Mrs. Sievwright read a paper on 'The Economic Independence of Married Women.' She also read the following draft Bill, which had been prepared by the Executive of the National Council of Women:

A Bill intituled an Act to abolish coverture, and to equalise the economic relations of husband and wife.

Whereas serious evils to society arise from the inequalities of the law in regard to the economic relations of husband and wife, by which the wife is often placed at a disadvantage and may be greatly injured and unfairly treated; and it is just and expedient, in the interests of

society, that the law of coverture and all the incidents thereof should be abolished, and that complete equality between husband and wife in all their relations as such should be established.

Be it enacted by the General Assembly of New Zealand in Parliament assembled and by the authority of the same as follows:

1. The short title of this Act is * * * and it shall come into operation on the passing thereof.

2. Coverture both as to person and property, and all the incidents thereof, as known and established by law in the Colony of New Zealand shall be and are hereby abolished; and all laws and customs in force, in the said

colony, relating to coverture, are hereby repealed.

3. From and after the passing of this Act, every man and every woman, already married, or who may marry, shall in all their economic relations be, and be deemed to be, separate persons in law and in equity as to all property, means and estate which shall belong to each before or at marriage, or which either may succeed to acquire or earn during marriage; provided always that every man and every woman before marriage may enter into such lawful contracts as they judge suitable to provide for the maintenance of the household and the management of their domestic concerns as freely as if they were entering into a co-partnership in business.

4. From and after the passing of this Act, the wages or earnings during marriage of every husband, and the wages or earnings during marriage of every wife, subject always to existing contracts of marriage relating thereto, shall form a common fund appropriated to the maintenance of their household and family expenses and the education and outfit in life of the children of their marriage in such way and manner as the parents may see proper. And in like manner, when only the husband is in receipt of wages or earnings during marriage, that income shall always form a common fund appropriated as aforesaid. In either case the wife shall be entitled, if she sees proper to do so, to require one-half of such wages or earnings to be paid to herself, or to her credit in a bank, and the same shall be regarded in law as her own separate wages or earnings just as if she were in receipt of the same as wages or earnings, to be applied, however, equally with her husband's share towards the support of the household.

5. The husband and wife together, or either of them separately, may at any time apply in a summary manner to the courts, or any of them, hereinafter mentioned, for such order as may be necessary to give practical effect to such appropriation of wages or earnings received during marriage, and may by such order, attach, secure, and protect the same, to such extent and in such manner as the court may see proper, and may give authority to the wife or to the husband to see to the application thereof for the purposes aforesaid.

6. Every question, dispute and difference, which may arise under this Act, and every matter relating thereto, shall be determined in a summary manner by the judge or magistrate appointed under the 'Magistrates' Courts' Act, 1893,' or by any other judge or court, in the colony, which magistrates, judges and courts shall have and exercise full jurisdiction to determine the same, and to make all proper orders, awards or judgments consequent thereon.

7. No formal procedure of any kind whatever, shall be necessary or required in any such application, but the matter shall be disposed of upon such facts and evidence as the parties concerned may bring before the judge or court, but no order, award or judgment shall be made unless and until due notice of the application shall have been given to any wife or husband concerned therein.

8. An appeal from the decision of a magistrate, in terms of the provisions for appeal contained in the 'Magistrates' Courts' Act, 1893,' may be taken to a judge of the Supreme Court, and the decision of such judge shall be final and conclusive in regard to the particular application.

Mrs. Sievwright also read the following commentary, which had been contributed by 'A Lawyer Husband' to the *Lyttelton Times* of August 21, 1896:

Preamble. The truth of the statements herein can hardly be disputed, and it should not be necessary to prove the preamble before the Committee by any elaborate evidence.

Clause 1. The Bill might be called 'The Abolition of Coverture Act, 1897.'

Clause 2. This clause is intended to have the effect, and will have the effect, of putting an end to all existing economic inequalities between husband and wife. It will create a fundamental change in prevailing ideas, and the legal position of husband and wife. Coverture, in English law, is based upon, but mistakenly based upon, the New Testament doctrine that the husband is the head of the wife. That, however, is surely a misapplication even of the Apostle's teaching, because the Apostle does not teach that the man is the head in material or economic matters, but only in a spiritual sense, resembling Christ's relation to the Church. Common sense must be allowed play in the solution of the question. As a matter of fact, he is very often not the head of the woman in any sense, whatever he may be in the eye of the law, or of the Gospel.

Clause 3. This expresses the practical effect of abolition of coverture as to estate. Women are to be treated as separate persons in the most complete sense after marriage. Is this right? Is it wise? Is it expedient? This clause will have to be in a special manner fought for, because it goes to disturb the relations of persons already married. In those cases (and it is to be hoped they are not a few) in which marriages have been, or shall be, 'made in Heaven' – those cases in which 'whom God hath joined let not man put asunder' (not those in which the Church only has said the words) – there is probably no need whatever for any legal enactment, because such husbands and wives will be of one mind, and will regulate their domestic and economic concerns in the way proposed. They will have separate purses, but in practice they will have but one purse. As to all future marriages, the clause leaves all men and women to arrange for the conduct of their household affairs as they judge best at marriage; and if they make no such arrangement, then each will continue responsible for the support of the family out of the separate estates, so far as concerns the interest of the State or Society. They are so now, under present law, by natural obligation, and can be made by the State to provide for their families out of their separate estates, the husband's first and always, and, failing his, the wife's. Is this clause a right one? If it be right to do justice, then it is so. *Fiat justitia, ruat coelum.* Is it wise? Can it be other than wise to do right? Dislodge a prejudice from our mind, put a true idea in its place, and what is now regarded by many as unwise, will be found to be wisdom. That is the question in a nutshell. Is it expedient? We live in an age of changes, more and more rapidly developing, and the general tendency is undoubtedly towards betterment. The mind and feeling of the people must be educated; but put human feelings and ideas on the right track, and what now to some may seem an unsafe experiment will soon be regarded as the only proper thing to do. Human nature is accommodating, and fashions and custom change.

Clause 4. This will no doubt be found to be the crucial clause when the Bill gets into Parliament, and I believe the vote on the second reading will turn on it. Why shall the man be required to forego his rights? Why shall the wife, because she is the mother of children, be entitled by law to a half share of her husband's income, and to have the same placed to her credit in a bank? It will disorganise family relations; it will lead to confusion and trouble in the supply of the family wants; there will be divided counsels, 'ructions,' and so on, and so on. As a matter of theory or principle it will be admitted, because it cannot be denied, that it is proper, when the husband is the only breadwinner, that his earnings should be appropriated by law, first and foremost, to the support of the family. If that be admitted to be sound and proper the necessary sequence is that the principle should be practically applied by law. It is established law now that wherever there is a wrong there is a remedy; and all that is asked is that that law shall be made available to married women who 'elect' to become mothers, and to supervise and to manage household affairs, by which they necessarily are prevented from earning independent incomes. Law will never be appealed to, it may be assumed, unless under necessity. The married woman's true position and rights are expressed in Will Carleton's 'Betsy and I are out':

'Write on the paper, lawyer, the very first paragraph,
Of all the farm and live stock, that she shall have her half,
For she has helped to earn it through many a weary day,
And it's nothing more than justice that Betsy has her pay.'

Clauses 5, 6, 7, and 8. These are the clauses that probably will be objected to and censured by the common lawyer mind. Summary and informal procedure in such a serious, important matter! Nothing but ruin can come of it ! No! No! There must be a verbose statute, without perspicuity, and accompanied by elaborate rules and regulations to deal with such extensive interests. Wigs and gowns are necessary to clear up intricate questions. That, no doubt, is the general characteristic of New Zealand legislation in matters of judicial procedure. But speedy justice is wanted, otherwise the proposed law will prove to be a dead letter so far as regards the mass of married women. And the machinery created by this proposed Act must be of the simplest kind, and as expeditious in action as possible. The wife of the commonest labourer must be cared for. An easy and cheap appeal from the Magistrate will be all that is needed to insure safety and propriety in administration.

Mrs. Wells upheld the Economic Independence of Married Women, on the following grounds:

1. *Because it is just.* A wife is an individual equally with her husband, and as such she is entitled to the rights of an individual. Under present conditions the person without money is bound, seeing that it commands the commodities of life. It follows that the husband who holds the purse has control of the freedom of action of the wife dependent on him. Marriage is considered to be partnership, but it exists under an anomalous condition in that, though both partners contribute their share of work, the work of one only is considered to have money value. The wife's work may be as arduous as that of her husband, she may toil from morning till night, yet she is entitled to nothing except by the good-will of her husband. While some men are better than the law, there are many who take full advantage of the legal situation. A woman who before marriage may be economically independent, is rendered by marriage economically dependent, though she has by no means withdrawn from active work, but has merely changed the direction of her energies. Surely this is a wrong inflicted on her, especially as wifehood is said to be the noblest profession of a woman.

2. *Because Society has a right to protect the individual.* The noblest and most sensitive women refrain, on principle, from obtaining money by ignoble methods. They feel the indignity of using artifice to secure what should be their natural right. The pain, consequent on this disability, unfits the noblest women in adverse conditions from fulfilling their duties as wives and mothers to the best of their natural ability, and society is the loser thereby.

3. *Because it would improve the status of women.* The average man's actions are influenced strongly by current law. As the law does not consider the married woman's right to a separate estate (except where, as under the present 'Married Women's Property Act,' her property is settled upon her, and to this class we are not referring), the husband too often holds the same view, and acts upon it. To those who trim their opinions to the law of the land, a statute, declaring a married woman to be entitled to a first share of her husband's income, would bring about the recognition of the woman to independence. The mass of people follow suit and conventional opinion and the status of women would go up with a bound.

4. *Because it makes for woman's freedom and for the freedom of the race.* It is axiomatic that every human being has a right to unimpeded development of the higher faculties. A just law would help weak and selfish men to do the right, thereby benefiting themselves and their wives. Economic dependence tends to degrade woman, in that it removes her liberty of action and gives her the position of a minor. Self-reliance is ever being held up as a goal towards which the weak should tend. The spirit of the age is striving to discountenance gifts as being detrimental to both donor and recipient.

'Brother, if Jove to thee a gift would make,
Be sure thou from his hands no present
take.'

There is a subtle feeling of degradation engendered in the recipient of gifts, which is bad morally and spiritually. The idea that husband and wife are one – and that one, the husband – is being exploded. Perfect vision comes from the blending of the vision of the two. Sometimes it is argued women want their husbands' incomes to spend on their own pleasure, but that is not what is asked for. The wife would be equally responsible with her husband for domestic expenditure, and each partner would be responsible to the other. Economic freedom is not the end women have in view, a question of more importance is involved – it is a question concerning the race. Only when the woman is free, can the wife be free, and free motherhood is the end in view. Evolution demands the birth of the fit, and the fit are those who are born of love, who come welcomed into the world. If we were wise and scientific in our humanitarian researches, how often should we find the criminal, the lunatic, the morally irresponsible, the vagrant, the harlot, unwelcome children.

NCW 3rd Session, April 1898, pp.22–25
(MS Papers 1376, folder 4, ATL)

2.13. Equal Pay for Equal Work
by Edith Hodgkinson (1902)

The proposition that equal amounts of labor should be rewarded with equal pay might well seem so obvious as not to need defence. To one unacquainted with the anomalies of our social system – say a visitor from Mars or a wanderer from Bellamy's perfected republic dropping by mischance into our century – the thing to arouse surprise and call for defence would be that workers should be rewarded unequally solely on account of their sex. But we are the creatures of habit and tradition; what is customary is right, unless self interest plead very loudly on the other side; and the inequality of payments to men and to women is so ancient and so general that the proposal to equalise them strikes many as rash and unreasonable.

As a matter of fact abstract justice has had little to do with determining wages at any time or place. The usual rule has been for the employer, whether private individual or public body, to pay as little as need be for work done, and for the employee to hold out for as much as there is a reasonable chance of getting. Thus it is easy to see why women workers have everywhere received far less remuneration than men.

Fewer kinds of employment have been open to them, therefore the need of accepting any available is more pressing; they have been far less able to combine and hold out for better pay than men; and up to recent years they have been less educated and less ambitious, and hence slower in bringing their claims before the public; while the old opinion of the essential inferiority of women, though far less openly stated than in former years, still influences the general estimate of the value and of the adequate remuneration of women's labour and time.

The inferiority of women's pay carries with it no demonstration of the inferiority of their work compared to that of men. In some cases, as of nurses, governesses, and most domestic servants, as well as of those engaged in sewing, millinery, etc., women have had the field to themselves, and could not well be replaced by men. Nor is their work of trifling value. Yet they are paid far less than men engaged in employments demanding similar amounts of labour and intelligence. That they have accepted the lower pay without protest, and have been, as a rule, thankful to get it, is no proof that they felt themselves adequately rewarded.

After saying at the outset that abstract justice has little to do in determining payment of work, it may seem superfluous to bring arguments to show the justice of equalising payment between men and women. But it is one thing to say that custom, prejudice, caprice, the law of supply and demand and the power of workers to combine in their own interest, have hitherto been stronger than considerations of justice and reason; quite another to say that such considerations are of no weight whatever with the public. The former statement denies that the low remuneration of women is justified by the quality of their work; it does not forbid them to hope for a hearing if they can prove the justice of their claim for higher remuneration. In the case of salaries paid by the State and by public bodies, we may expect more attention to what is in itself just and fitting than can reasonably be looked for with the mass of private individuals. 'Buy in the cheapest and sell in the dearest market' is the maxim followed in the case of labor as of other commodities. Yet public opinion has force; and the public has some conscience even in matters economic – it only needs awakening. Every year justice and humanity are surely if slowly widening their sway in our social mechanism. Tradition or conventions of what is right and fitting have also much power. The doctor, lawyer, and others receive their stated fees without attempts to beat them down. Now, we want to overthrow the tradition that women are to be paid less than men.

We need specially to arouse women. If women workers are once convinced that their claim to equal emolument with men is just, the world at large will soon tacitly accept its justice. But women are often disposed to acquiesce in what is customary, unless they have some strong personal motives to rouse them. Many women workers find their pay sufficient. They have a vague idea that a man in the same position may need or should get more, and they do not see why they should make themselves obnoxious by joining in a demand for which they feel no necessity. Here we are met by the difficulty that many women are not solely dependent on their earnings. They are partially dependent on relatives, or at all events work for only a few years to fill up the time before marriage. Thus they feel no need for a 'living wage' that shall maintain them wholly and adequately, and allow them to provide for sickness and old age. The harm done by girls who need work only for dress and pocket money is little regarded by themselves or those who employ them.

In urging better pay for women we must be consistent and thorough. I suspect that some who demand it are thinking solely of the improvement that would take place in their own salaries, without regarding that the principle 'equal pay equal work' would, if carried out, mean their paying much more than they have before done to many female workers. The application of this principle is plainest when the work is absolutely identical, as in the case of teachers, clerks, shop assistants, etc. Yet it is plain also on consideration, that labor of equivalent though not identical kinds, making the same demands on the strength or skill of the workers, should be equally, or, at least, similarly rewarded. A woman who goes out washing gets at most five shillings a day and one or two meals. A man who goes out digging or doing similar manual work certainly receives more. Yet the washerwoman's work demands at least as much intelligence as his, and is probably more physically taxing to her than his is to him; while she usually has a family to support in whole or in part. On stations a woman cook never, I believe, gets more than £1 a week; a man receives £1 10s; and the woman will do a deal of housework in addition to the cooking. We need not, perhaps, go out of our way to offer women servants more than they ask for; but should they raise their demands, we should be prepared to see justice in them.

But it is where men and women work side by side under precisely the same conditions that the inconsistency of their scales of remuneration is most apparent. Where woman's work is demonstrably inferior to that of men, either in quantity or quality, it is reasonable that they should be paid less in proportion. Then I think all women will concede that they cannot fill all positions equally well with men. But when the work is equal the pay should, as a matter of abstract justice, be equal. Practical considerations to the contrary can be urged, but these on examination will be found less convincing than they appear at first sight.

In the profession of teaching, the inequality of men's and women's salaries has hitherto been very striking; and though something has been done to remove this, some injustice may still be found. As I have more acquaintance with the conditions of teachers' lives than with those of other workers, I will review the arguments for higher pay of women with special reference to teaching; but most that I say will apply to any field where men and women are engaged together.

The arguments usually adduced to support the claim of men teachers to higher pay than women are as follows:

1. Women have only themselves to support; men have their families.
2. Women can live more cheaply than men.
3. Women entail more expense on the country, as they frequently quit the service after a few years: and thus the cost of their training is wasted.
4. Women are liable to require more frequent sick leave than men, thus the work is more irregular, and the schools where they are employed suffer in consequence.

As to argument 1, I have always thought it proved too much. If we are to allow for a man always having a wife and children to support, while a woman is supposed to have only her own needs to provide for, an addition of £10 to £40 to the salary of a man seems very inadequate. The addition seems rather a concession to the old idea that men must as men receive more than women – a principle universally upheld by school arithmetics which give us such problems as – 'A man leaves £3000 to each of two sons, and £1000 to each of three daughters, what was his estate?' or 'Divide £100 between two men and two women so that each man may get twice the share of a woman.' As the authoress of 'Elizabeth and her German Garden' says in speaking of Russian field labourers, 'The women are paid less than the men, not because they work less, but because they are women, and must not be encouraged.' As a matter of fact probably few men in the lowest paid positions of the teaching profession have families dependent on them. If they should have, it would seem to display an economic rashness that should not be rewarded. I believe that banks make it a rule that their clerks must not marry under a certain salary. As to the assumption that women have only themselves to provide for, I believe that a far greater proportion of women workers than is usually suspected have relatives wholly or partially dependent on them. Then all should be able to save for a time when they may be past working.

It may be urged that exceptions cannot be considered; that though some women may have to maintain others and some men them-selves only, yet as a general rule the contrary is the case. No doubt this has force. But we do not find that payment is elsewhere apportioned to needs. Different kinds of workers are paid according to their value and scarcity, and among workers of the same class the married are not paid more than the unmarried, those with many dependent on them more than those with few, nor the feeble more than the robust. If the end sought were to proportion reward to need, nothing more than a very rough approximation could be achieved. To make reward proportionate to work is the only principle that can be consistently carried out.

As to argument 2; women no doubt do as a rule live more cheaply than men. This does not prove that it is right and reasonable that they should do so. I will leave out of the question the case of young women who are helped by their relatives, and consider only those who support themselves entirely. It does not seem that there would naturally be much difference between the cost of food, clothing and lodging for a man and a woman. Women, no doubt, often pay less for board and lodging than men, and they get a good deal less. It is well recognised that the table kept in a boarding-house for women only may be expected to be very inferior to that of one where men have to be provided for. Take the cheaper kind of boarding houses, also the case of lodgers in a family. A woman pays from twelve to eighteen shillings a week, a man from eighteen to twenty-five. But the women boarders are often expected to subsist on a diet consisting mainly of weak tea and bread and butter; men must have a good hot dinner, and meat on the table three times a day. Then women boarders in a family will do their own rooms; perhaps also their washing and ironing. Many do most of their sewing; those who have sufficient skill often do their own dressmaking and millinery. I know that many women teachers in the country, whether living in residences or boarding out, spend the greater part of their Saturdays in sweeping and cleaning, washing and mending. Women can do these things, it may be said, men have to pay for them to be done. But women might prefer to pay rather than work, if they could, and men, where there is need, as in the case of up country settlers and surveyors, prove themselves well capable of wielding a broom or plying a needle. Is there any reason in the nature of things why a woman who already does what is considered, a day's work for a man, should in addition be

her own housemaid, laundress and sempstress? The hardship of a female teacher having to spend her supposed leisure in this way is more noticeable if it be remembered that she has also several additional hours work a week over the school sewing – a subject the man teacher is happily ignorant of. Then it is said that women are not expected to subscribe for charitable or social objects as freely as man, and that they escape other social obligations. But the tend-encies of modern life are to assimilate the modes of life of men and women; and many of the latter would be glad to take more part in social schemes, and to live a wider intellectual life did their circumstances permit it. Most women workers could well live a little more expensively with benefit to themselves and those around them; and men could cut their expenses down to a level with those of women.

There is undoubtedly force in the argument as to the short time that many women remain teachers. But it seems rather hard that women who remain a lifetime in the service should all that lifetime be fined because of their fellows who quit the service early. If women must be paid less to start with, surely an increase of salary might be made for a term of years spent in teaching. Then the training of women teachers cannot be considered to be wholly lost, even if they soon quit their occupation for marriage, since it is of a kind that cannot fail to be beneficial to their families, and to the com-munity generally.

Here it may be noted that the fact of such a large proportion of women teachers quitting the service after a few years tells somewhat against the plea that because so many girls seek to become teachers, therefore the salaries and positions attainable by women are very tempt-ing. The girls teach for a few years, but do not reckon on continuing teachers for life. Hence so long as they can pay their way for those few years, young women teachers will come forward.

As to the fourth argument, I wonder to how many it seems that smaller pay and harder work have anything to do with ill-health among women teachers. Women, of course, are much inferior in physical strength to men. But muscular strength and healthiness of consti-tution are very different things. Girl students have as a rule more application than young men, and are more prone to overwork them-selves. Apart from this, if conditions were equally favorable, it does not appear that there should be such a difference in the amount of sick leave required by men and by women teachers as is said to be the case. But is it conducive to health to spend an hour or two in a close schoolroom after dismissal employed in setting sewing, or to take it to one's lodgings and sit over it, perhaps in a fireless room, till ten or eleven o'clock? Or to spend Saturdays in housework and sewing instead of in rest and outdoor exercise? A man can indulge in outdoor sports and other amusements when his teaching is over; a woman's school work is often indefinitely prolonged, and few spend enough time in the open air for good health. Of course irregularity caused by ill-health does detract from the value of a woman's work; on the other hand it greatly increases her own expenses. Thus argument four annuls argument two – that a woman can live on less than a man.

At the sittings of the late Teachers' Salaries Commission, it was generally conceded that as sole teachers of small schools and as assistants, women were fully equal to men. If they were not, they would not be so freely employed as they all along have been. Then, in reason and equity, their pay should in all cases be the same as that of men in like positions. As a matter of fact women work more than men in the same positions. The mistresses and assistants in large schools find the sewing a formidable task, and a female sole teacher of a small school may have to teach sewing to twenty or twenty-five girls in addition to all the work a man would do in her place. On sewing afternoons she must do her best to keep the boys profitably employed while her whole attention is demanded by the sewing; and I have not found that inspectors are more lenient in judging of her work because she loses two hours a week from other subjects and has additional work and worry which a man teacher escapes. The late Salaries Bill has equalised – very properly – the salaries of male and female teachers in this class of schools, but the work is not equalised.

The Canterbury women teachers who have taken up this subject complain that under the new regulations the best positions are still allotted to men. It is enacted that out of the first six assistants in large schools three must be females, while apparently there is nothing to prevent the heads of large schools from being females also. No doubt in practice the preference will be given to men in appointing heads of schools over fifty, and first assistants in large schools. And the first assistants are specially favoured, the discrepancy between first and second assistants' salaries being very marked. In America the preponderance of women over men teachers seems to be greater than here; and I believe they are commonly employed as heads, and in all departments. Personally, I think that men are preferable as heads of large mixed schools, and in most cases as teachers for large classes of fifth and sixth standard boys. Yet I do not think the latter position demands either so much physical strength or so much power of control as a country school with a roll of fifty and over, where a woman is often placed. There is much to be said in favour of separate schools for boys and girls in towns, and this would mean more good positions for women.

I should regard it as a misfortune if men of ability and force of character were no longer to come forward as teachers; and thus I am ready to admit the practical argument that higher salaries must be offered them than are requisite to induce women to enter the calling. Teaching is in itself none too attractive a calling, and probably very few, either men or women, take it up or persevere in it for pure love of it. There are scores of other occupations in which a youth of brains and energy may hope to win more distinction and wealth. For women, even now, comparatively few paths in life are easily accessible. The salaries offered to them as teachers have in the past been sufficient to attract more than places could be found for. But there are indications, at present, that teaching is losing its popularity in the case of girls as of young men. No doubt the best thing women teachers can do to secure better pay and more consideration, is to limit their supply. It is hard for those whose path in life is already chosen to quit it for a fresh one, demanding perhaps time and money to prepare for it. But young women choosing a calling and their relatives might do well to strike out in fresh lines rather than seek the beaten and overcrowded fields of a few long established callings, as nursing and teaching. Meanwhile it is asked with point, are women teachers to receive less than the value of their services, or men more than the value of theirs? Well, we certainly do not want to receive less than the value of ours. So let us keep up our courage, and strive to increase the feelings of esprit de corps and public spirit among women. We may be thankful for what has been gained and still go on urging our claims, for the principle that equal services should bring equal rewards is the only one that satisfies reason and justice, and the only one that can be carried out with consistency.

Miss Henderson moved, Mrs Daldy seconded, 'That this Council is of opinion, that in all cases where men and women are engaged in the same work, either in the employment of Government or of private individuals, equal wage should be paid for equal work.' – Carried unanimously.

NCW 7th Session, 1902, pp.64–70 (MS Papers 1376, folder 3, ATL)

Chapter 3

Patriotism and Dissent
1905–1919

During the years in which the NCW was in recess, from 1905 to the end of the First World War, there was very little feminist debate going on in New Zealand. The position of women was rarely the subject of public discussion; no group took over from the NCW in championing women's rights. This is not to say that women ceased to be interested or active in political and social campaigns, or that they lapsed wholly into complacency and domesticity, though some of the activists of the suffrage era rather feared that they had. Small groups of women were vitally concerned with particular issues – peace, reforming the criminal justice system and 'social hygiene'.

Many women during these years directed their efforts towards organisations such as the Society for the Protection of Women and Children (founded in 1898) and church-based groups, which were primarily concerned with providing welfare for women and children rather than political reform.[1] The WCTU continued to be a major national women's organisation, but increasingly it came to focus its efforts on prohibition at the expense of issues of direct relevance to women.

When war broke out in 1914, women were called to patriotic service, and societies were formed throughout the country. The scale of women's involvement in these activities should not be underestimated. The officers of the Otago Women's Patriotic Society, for example, met every day 'for the duration' to organise fund raising and to collect, sort and pack parcels for despatch to soldiers serving overseas. Eight hundred women attended the inaugural meeting of the Society.[2] With women's organisational resources being heavily diverted, it is hardly surprising that political debate waned during these years. Most of the patriotic societies continued their work beyond 1918 – first, to deal with the influenza epidemic which struck within days of the Armistice celebrations, and then, to aid soldiers returning to civilian life.

Military training, questions of peace and war, and, later, conscription became major issues in this period. Against a largely patriotic and pro-government tide of opinion, a small number of women were among those who spoke out against the preparation of a society for war.[3] This was not a subject on which there was general agreement among women. At the time of the Boer War women's organisations discussed the question of women's attitudes to military conflict, but it became a much more important source of division at the end of the first decade of the twentieth century.

The first major controversy was stirred by the 1909 Defence Act, which established a system of compulsory military training for boys and young men from the age of fourteen. This was the first time New Zealand had had a system of compulsory military training. Two organisations were founded to oppose it – the Anti-Militarist League, and the National Peace Council, both originating in Christchurch. Women were among the members of both. The Canterbury Women's Institute also took a stand against the Defence Act. In October 1913, three representatives of the Canterbury Women's Institute: Ada Wells, Sarah Saunders Page and Mrs Nuttall, travelled from Christchurch to Ashburton to put their case. Reports of the two public meetings they attended featured in the *Lyttelton Times* (3.1) and reveal just how lively an issue this was.

Speaking to an audience of 150 women in the afternoon, Page, Wells and Nuttall gave their reasons for opposing the Act. These ranged from the broad principle of anti-militarism – that it prepared New Zealanders for war rather than peace and incited international hostility among nations – to specific objections against the draconian powers of the police to enforce the Act. Ada Wells told the audience that women in other countries were refusing to bear children because of the harsh treatment young people received during their military training. Mrs Nuttall spoke as the mother of a boy who had resisted the Defence Act. In their objections to the Act the women were essentially upholding principles of peace, but they also spoke as mothers in defence of young and unprotected boys, mothers who feared what these boys might encounter during training. They were presenting the views of a very small minority. In their mission to Ashburton, Sarah Page, Ada Wells and Mrs Nuttall were singularly unsuccessful: the women's meeting rejected their motion en masse, while the mixed evening meeting expressed its virulent hostility by refusing to give the speakers any kind of hearing whatsoever.

Within three years of the Ashburton meeting, not only were the New Zealand people at war, but the Government was faced with the need to fulfil its commitment to the war in Europe by introducing conscription. The best known resistance to World War One conscription was led by Te Puea on behalf of her Waikato people. A small number of Pakeha women from different parts of the country also opposed the measure. Some were socialists who opposed the war, and especially conscription, on the grounds that the war was no more than the sacrifice of working people for capital and enabled a small number to make large profits. Others were pacifists, opposed to the war on principle. A deputation of women was organised while the Military Service Bill was being debated in June 1916. Mrs Donaldson declared the women's common interest in opposing conscription: 'As the mothers of the nation we protest against bringing lives into the world to be used, when reaching manhood, in the interests of a class which does not represent our interests.' The report of the deputation's meeting with Prime Minister Massey in the *Lyttelton Times* (3.3) does not so much discuss the women's political views as belittle their attempt at lobbying by ridiculing their 'feminine qualities'.

But treatment like this did not deter the small group of women working for peace. Later in 1916, a New Zealand branch of the Women's International League for Peace and Freedom was founded, and groups formed in Auckland and Wellington. Their manifesto appeared in the *Maoriland Worker* (3.4), a labour and socialist paper founded in 1910 with Ettie Rout as its first editor. Since its foundation the League has worked for peace and international understanding. While never a large organisation it has consistently made its voice heard.[4]

Apart from peace, the other issue of major concern during this period of relative inactivity by feminists was prostitution and venereal disease, referred to euphemistically as 'the social evil', 'the red plague' or 'the social hygiene' question. Because of concern about a perceived increase in venereal disease, especially during the war years, legislative measures to suppress venereal disease were frequently debated. The Contagious Diseases Act was finally repealed in 1910, bringing satisfaction to the WCTU, to former members of the NCW, and to other women's groups who had fought for its repeal since the 1880s. But fears continued that new measures would be introduced with the same objectionable features, i.e. the detention and compulsory treatment of women, while men were exempt. In the 1910s the rationale for new legislation was couched in terms of health rather than morality, and was intended more to control venereal disease than simply to suppress prostitution, but it still fell heavily upon women.

In 'The Social Evil and the Degradation of Womanhood' (3.6), one of two articles written towards the end of her life, Eveline Cunnington calls for an awakening of the public conscience on this issue. She does not equivocate but urges just and practical action. Rejecting the idea of regulated houses, she advocates stronger measures against prostitution, and, above all, the eradication of poverty, which she regards as the underlying cause of prostitution. Cunnington's piece stands out from the contemporary debate because it locates 'the social evil' firmly in the context of injustice to women and sees prostitution as a transaction between powerless women and powerful men.

Another issue with which Eveline Cunnington was deeply concerned was reform of the criminal justice system, especially as it related to women (3.5). A Christian socialist and one of the first two women appointed as official prison visitors in 1896, Eveline Cunnington argued for greater justice and more compassionate treatment for women in the courts and in prison. A woman apprehended and brought before the court, she asserted, was 'from the hour of her trial until her sentence is finished in prison' subject to men and male authority, 'not one woman has any legal power over her – to try her, to judge her, to control her!' To remedy this she called for the appointment of women police, justices of the peace and jurors – a plea made by the NCW in the 1890s, which would continue to be voiced in the 1920s. Cunnington also called for a reconsideration of the perspective from which criminals were viewed – suggesting that they were 'patients' who needed to be reformed in 'moral hospitals', rather than punished in retributive prisons. With these ideas she was articulating the philosophy of the broader movement for prison reform, which emanated from the United States. New Zealand's first women's prison was established at Addington in 1910. Its management, and that of women criminals generally, was a minor but ongoing issue for women's organisations in the early twentieth century.

Kate Sheppard's two pieces – one written in September 1914 on the twenty-first anniversary of the women's suffrage victory (3.2), and the other in 1919, inaugurating the NCW's second phase (3.7) – are much broader in view than the other items in this section. In both Sheppard reviews the position of women, reflects on their achievements and suggests directions for the future. The 1914 article, written in response to two questions posed by Dunedin's *Evening Star*, is restrained. The effects of women's suffrage have not, she says, led to social revolution. 'Public credit has not been shaken. The average woman has not neglected her home and children, stockings and socks are darned as usual, families have not been rent asunder by political feuds.' Sheppard lists a number of laws passed since 1893 that have a direct bearing on the lives of women. She words this section carefully however, not suggesting that these laws were the direct result of women exercising their vote, but only that they had some impact upon women and children. She concludes her generally positive account with a clear summary of reforms still needed: economic equality between husbands and wives; guardianship rights over children; equal pay and equal access to government employment; women officers within the justice system; and a rise in the age of consent.

All of these issues are mentioned again in her 1919 President's address (3.7). But the tone here is more rousing and more positive. The enfranchisement of British women is lauded as a great sign of progress (though it was restricted to women over the age of thirty). The English campaign had, of course, been the centre of public attention in the years before the First World War, as it reached its militant peak. It did not disappear altogether during the War. In 1916 Adela Pankhurst visited New Zealand, speaking in various parts of the country about the British suffrage movement.[5] Many women living in New Zealand at this time still came from Britain, or had family and friends there who were directly involved.

Kate Sheppard sees the war as contributing directly to the erosion of opposition to the women's movement: 'fossilized prejudices crashed in all directions'. She looks forward to the removal of the anomaly that New Zealand women could not stand for Parliament (British women gained this right along with the franchise in 1919). In discussing the endowment of motherhood and the importance of appointing women to the criminal justice system, Sheppard points to the issues that were to become prominent in the next decade, while reiterating those concerns from the 1890s that were still to be addressed.

Most telling, perhaps, is the justification given at the beginning of her address for women's involvement in public life: the 'Home and the State are one', she says, and 'all the work of the State is for the welfare and protection of the Home'. These arguments, used in the 1880s and 1890s, were not to disappear altogether in succeeding decades. but would find a different formulation. Indeed, women's experience of home and family life had changed and would continue to change markedly over the late nineteenth and early twentieth centuries, as families declined in size from an average of six to two children, and as the pattern of women's paid labour and unpaid work in the home changed hugely.

1. Margaret Tennant, 'Matrons with a Mission: Women's Organisations in New Zealand, 1893–1915', MA thesis, Massey University, 1976
2. Bronwyn Dalley, 'Women's Patriotic Associations', in Anne Else (ed.), Women Together, forthcoming, 1993
3. Elsie Locke, Peace People: a history of peace activities in New Zealand, Christchurch, 1992, chapters 7–13

4. *Betty Holt,* Women for Peace and Freedom: a history of the Women's International League for Peace and Freedom, *Wellington, 1985*
5. Maoriland Worker, *24 May 1916*

Sources and Further Reading

Dalley, Bronwyn. 'Women's Imprisonment in New Zealand, 1880–1920', PhD thesis, Otago University, 1992

Devaliant, Judith. *Kate Sheppard*, Auckland, 1992

Fleming, Philip. 'Fighting the Red Plague: Observations of the response to venereal disease in New Zealand 1910–1945', PhD thesis, Massey University, 1989

Holt, Betty. *Women for Peace and Freedom: a history of the Women's International League for Peace and Freedom*, Wellington, 1985

Locke, Elsie. *Peace People: a history of peace activities in New Zealand*, Christchurch, 1992

McCurdy, Claire-Louise. 'Eveline Cunnington', *BNZW*, pp.162–164

Rice, Geoffrey. *Black November: the 1918 influenza epidemic in New Zealand*, Wellington, 1988

Tennant, Margaret A. 'Matrons with a Mission: Women's organisations in New Zealand, 1893–1915', MA thesis, Massey University, 1976

Tolerton, Jane. *Ettie. A Life of Ettie Rout*, Auckland, 1992

3.1. Peace Propaganda Rejected by Ashburton People

Lyttelton Times (1913)

Ashburton is nothing if not patriotic. It has perpetuated Empire Day while larger towns have let it fall into desuetude. Ashburton has its live branch of the Navy League. It does not own an anti-militarist organisation. Its young men are not passive resisters. Therefore the overtures of anti-militarists have been frowned on in Ashburton. A week or two ago, a party of proselytisers were refused a hearing in the Theatre Royal. Thereupon an advance party of ladies went south yesterday to discuss the question of military training at a women's meeting in the afternoon, while the main assault was reserved for the evening. The afternoon meeting was hostile to the propagandists, and a motion in favour of military training was carried almost unanimously.

Into the hand of each person who attended the meeting was put a leaflet, containing a telegram from the Rev W. J. Elliott to Lady Stout, and her reply. The telegrams were as follows:

'Lady Stout, Wellington – If no objection, kindly give your opinion of military training – W.J. Elliott.'

'Elliott, Ashburton – Beneficial physically, mentally, morally; absolutely necessary for national safety. – Stout.'

Mrs Page, who presided, said that the ladies on the platform represented the Canterbury Women's Institute, whose motto was 'For Humanity.' It might be considered 'cheeky' for a body of women from another town to dictate to the ladies of Ashburton, who had given

Christchurch a lead in the adoption of no-license. However, there were those among the speakers whose sons had suffered fines and imprisonment for remaining loyal to the principles that they had been taught at their mothers' knee. Never before had anybody in New Zealand been called to go to prison for the sake of their principles. The Defence Act had established a principle abhorrent to every Britisher, and a menace to public liberty, and under it a boy of fourteen was compelled to go to prison (for military detention came to the same thing) if he refused to take the oath of allegiance, an oath never before demanded in the Empire. The Act had been rushed through at the end of a session by a Liberal Government, of which better things were to have been expected. That Government would never have dared to appeal to the country on the principle.

Mrs Page read the oath of allegiance, which was received with hearty applause. She replied that the oath was not so bad if it was designed for men of mature age, but it was absurd for a youth of fourteen, who did not understand its import. She went on to say that those who objected to military training could still be found other work to do. It was not necessary for all the men to go to war, and if New Zealand were attacked it would be by sea.

'If you are for peace you should prepare for peace,' said Mrs Page.

'No,' cried members of the audience. 'Prepare for war.'

Mrs Page said that preparations for war were most likely to precipitate a collision, and it was preparations for aerial war that were going to shock the world next. The adoption of a more Christian attitude towards the other nations would avoid the necessity of training fourteen-year-old boys. It was only because the women were for peace that the politicians were for military training. For her own part, she had allowed her own boys to drill because she could not bear to see them go to prison; but they had learned no more in two years than an intelligent woman could grasp in two weeks.

Mrs Wells, the next speaker, described the hardships of women workers in Germany and France as the result of their sons' and husbands' service in the military. French women, she said, had refused to bear children, because their sons came from their period of conscription physically and morally wrecked. Mrs Wells stated that she had been told by a gentleman from England that he believed that Krupps were behind the race for armaments in England. She was ashamed of the National Service League, which was unpatriotic, and had inspired Sir Joseph Ward to offer a Dreadnought as a step towards conscription. 'War is organised murder,' said Mrs Wells, and she advocated the abandonment of armaments and the cultivation of internationalism. She was astounded, she said, that there were boys brave enough to resist the Defence Act. She declared that the press had suppressed thousands of prosecutions that had taken place under the Defence Act. The best boys were being driven from New Zealand because they would not serve. New Zealand was losing its best blood and the girls their sweethearts. (Laughter.) Mrs Wells condemned Mr Herdman for introducing an Act that would permit a constable to arrest her in the hall for talking treason. She was proceeding to stoutly berate the Imperial authorities for spending £100,000 to bring the Dreadnought to New Zealand when the audience broke into continued applause, and Mrs Wells gave place to the next speaker.

Mrs Nuttall, who was introduced as 'the mother of one of the persecuted youths,' said that she had done a grand thing in bringing her sons to New Zealand, but she had never thought that they would have had to become conscripts.

A lady: If it had not been for British arms, there would have been no British colonies.

Mrs Nuttall declared that if the anti-militarists met martyrdom it would be due to the inconsistencies of the ministers of religion.

In reply to an invitation to opponents of anti-militarists to speak, a lady in the audience said that British colonies had been established by British arms, which had done away with barbarities and had allowed Christianity to follow.

Mrs Wells replied that India, Canada, Australia and New Zealand had not been won by the sword. Canada would not have military training. It was building up a great nation, whose public men had ten times more culture than those of New Zealand.

A question from the audience as to whether the sons of those on the platform would become volunteers met with grim shakes of the head, and Mrs Page explained that it was a matter of free will.

Mrs W. G. Roberts moved – 'The women of Ashburton fully recognise that the principle of universal military training is in the best interests of the dominion of New Zealand.'

The motion was seconded by Mrs H. Willis.

Another lady in the audience quoted Bishop Averill as stating that military training was good for the moral fibre of the nation. She stated that she was ashamed of women who would encourage their sons to resist the Defence Act.

Some sharp passages took place between women on the stage and women in the audience regarding what their sons should and would do for their country.

Eventually Mrs Page put the motion, which was carried with four dissentients in an audience of about 150, and a vote of thanks to the chairwoman closed the meeting.

Lyttelton Times, 10 October 1913, p.8

3.2. A Symposium on the Effects of Female Enfranchisement: What the reform has accomplished and is capable of achieving
Evening Star (1914)

To those who assisted in bringing about the passage of the Electoral Act of 1893, which for the first time in Australasia conferred political rights on the womanhood of New Zealand, we addressed a circular inviting replies to these questions:

(1) Have your expectations in regard to the operation of female enfranchisement been realised, and will you kindly state whether in your opinion the exercise of the Vote by the women has in any way helped to raise the moral, social, industrial, or political status of the women of this Dominion?

(2) In what directions should the activities of our women be encouraged, with the object of attaining fully reforms of a pressing but beneficent nature?

We append the replies that have reached us:

SOME THOUGHTS ON THE WORKING OF THE WOMEN'S FRANCHISE MOVEMENT IN NEW ZEALAND: What it has succeeded in accomplishing for the social, moral, industrial, and political betterment of our women, and to what further reforms we ought to direct our future effort.

By MRS KATHERINE W. SHEPPARD.

In endeavouring to comply with your request the first thought that comes is the difficulty of proving all the results that may flow from one simple act of bare justice, such as the granting of the parliamentary franchise to women. The mere doing of such an act of justice was the outcome of a larger vision of rights and duties – a growing enlightenment – a broader conception of humanity as it now is, and as it may become. So that while a large number of women in New Zealand fought a long and hard fight for the right to be governed only with their own consent, that right could not have been gained had it not been that a number of earnest men also preached the gospel of 'the government by all for the good of all.' Briefly, the enfranchisement of women was in itself an expression of the growing sense of justice and humanitarianism in New Zealand. That sense, once aroused, could not stop short at one legislative Act, but found further expression, and the women's vote gave it an added political force.

The next thought that presents itself is the difficulty of separating the 'social,' 'moral,' 'industrial' and 'political.' All are so interwoven. Probably no legislative enactment (in itself political) is without some effect on the social, moral and industrial life. I therefore abandon all attempt to make any strict classification. Following the enfranchisement of women there was great legislative activity, and it would be easy to compile quite a long list of enactments of what may be termed a social, moral, and

industrial character. Some of our most prominent men publicly declared in 1907 that more humanitarian legislation had been passed in New Zealand since women had had the vote than during all the previous years of her existence as a British colony. Most of the more important of these enactments were initialled and agitated for by our women. Others were proposed by legislators, and received such hearty support from the women voters as to hasten their passage through Parliament.

The dire evils prognosticated by opponents of womanhood suffrage have not come to pass. Public credit has not been shaken. The average woman has not neglected her home and children, stockings and socks are darned as usual, families have not been violently rent asunder by political feuds. Indeed, there is probably much greater companionship between husbands and wives, brothers and sisters, than ever before, politics having a common interest for both sexes. One instant effect of women at the polls was to stamp out all the old-time election rowdyism. The closing of hotels on polling day was a direct result of the enfranchisement of women, and has been most beneficial. It was said that if the women had the vote they would not use it. The very first election proved the folly of this remark, and subsequent elections have shown that women have not ceased to value their franchise. It cannot be claimed that every woman appreciates the right to vote. Nor can it be claimed that every man does. As Mr Poyser aptly said:

'I ain't denyin' the women are foolish. The Almighty made 'em to match the men.'

It may be well to call attention to some of the legislation passed since the enfranchisement of women which has a direct bearing on the social, moral, and industrial life of the community in general, and of women and children in particular.

There have been passed The Infants' Life Protection Act (which is to prevent baby farming), an Act to regulate the adoption of children. Amendments have been made to the Industrial Schools Act for better classification and general methods. Amendments to the Illegitimacy Act, whereby a child born out of wedlock may claim a share of the father's property after his death (the claim to be settled by the Court); also providing that, where parents are willing, the child may be registered in the name of the father as well as of the mother.

The Widows' Pension Act grants a small

pension to widows who have a child or children born in New Zealand. There is an Act making it unlawful to sell alcoholic liquor to persons under 21 years, and an Act prohibiting the sale to and smoking of cigarettes by young persons under 15. Scientific temperance instruction is now part of the curriculum of our State schools. Juvenile courts have been set up, so that young people, first offenders, shall not be subjected to the environment of the ordinary open court. The divorce law has been altered to make the standard of morality equal for both sexes. The Summary Separation Act gives protection to working women against worthless husbands at little expense. By the Slander of Women Act women who have been slandered may recover damages without having to prove special (economic) damage. The further employment of women as barmaids has been discontinued, the 'age of consent' has been raised from 14 to 16 years, and the infamous C.D. Acts have been repealed. The Testator's Family Maintenance Act prevents a man from willing away his property without making suitable provision for his wife and family. Pensions for the aged poor have been provided, both sexes being treated equally. Women have been admitted to the practice of law in our courts. Labor laws have been passed which safeguard the health of women and young workers; their hours of work have been limited, their holidays fixed, and the payment of a minimum wage enforced. Servants' registry offices have been brought under regulation, greatly to the advantage of women and girls. A beginning has been made in prison reform, and inebriate asylums have been established.

Technical schools have been established, giving equality of opportunity to both sexes. The municipal franchise has been extended to women who are ratepayers or the wives of ratepayers. Both husband and wife can vote by virtue of the qualification of the other. The Licensing Act Amendment makes 10 o'clock closing universal, does away with bottle licenses and the locker system, and gives electors the right to vote on Dominion Prohibition.

Omitting any further dry reference to legislative enactments, a word might be said as to the change that has come over women in regard to what one may be allowed to call the corporate life of our people. Women are working more side by side with men in many ways. Especially in regard to charitable and educational affairs is this so. Then women have shown a greater power of organisation and better executive ability than they were formerly deemed to possess. The Society for the Health of Women and Children, whose labors have had such marvellous results in saving precious lives, is a notable example. But while there is so much of good to be recorded, there is great need for further reform. The ideal that we aim at is legal freedom regardless of sex. To place legal letters on the ability and usefulness of one sex is a crime not only against that sex but against the community. For the community has ample need for every power for good possessed by any and every member. Women must be free to work for humanity in whatever capacity for which God has fitted her. And so we ask to-day, as we have asked for years past, for the removal of all the civil and political disabilities of women.

To protect and uphold the dignity of wifehood and motherhood we ask for economic equality or partnership between husband and wife; for the co-guardianship of children by wife and husband; for equal pay for equal work and equality of opportunity for men and women to fill all Government posts, capacity for the work and not sex to be the test. We want to see women appointed as visiting justices to the women's prisons, and to be able to take their places on juries – especially where cases of women and children are being tried. We want the age of consent to be raised to an age when a sense of responsibility may be expected to be arrived at. We want a much larger annual grant to the Education Department – a larger supply of teachers and better salaries. We want a majority rule on all questions, and the abolition of the totalisator. We want an Elective Executive, and thus minimise the evils of party government. And, for the furthering of these and other reforms, we want to see women sitting side by side with men in the legislative assemblies, helping to make laws which will be beneficial to the community as a whole.

Evening Star, *19 September 1914, p.10*

3.3. Feminine Deputationists
Lyttelton Times (1916)

A women's anti-conscription deputation to the Prime Minister on Saturday consisted of thirty people, thoroughly in earnest, but the display of essentially feminine qualities made the whole proceedings very entertaining. Mr J. M'Combs, M.P., introduced the deputation as representative of women's organisations and a large body of public opinion which was honestly and strenuously opposed to the Military Service Bill. Three ladies were named as 'speakers,' but the whole thirty got in their verbal shots at various times.

Mrs Donaldson, a well known platform speaker in Wellington, said the workers had given so strenuously of their life that the women felt that the Bill was uncalled for. The result of voluntary effort showed there was no need for compulsion. 'Wherever you have military power you have degradation – history proves that,' said Mrs Donaldson. 'As the mothers of the nation we protest against bringing lives into the world to be used, when reaching manhood, in the interests of a class which does not represent our interests. The working classes have always fought the battles, paid the debts, and lost their liberties when great wars have been fought.'

'We as mothers object to our boys being forced to go to the war if they don't want,' said Mrs Aitken. 'I have never done anything to hinder recruiting, and I'll never do anything to advance it!' As for the 'spying clauses' of the Act, she would 'do time' rather than 'put away' anyone for not going to fight for her if he didn't wish to.

The Prime Minister: 'Supposing the Germans came along, what would you do?'

Mrs Aitken: 'I'd fight them if they interfered with me, but not otherwise. We should fight for liberty and freedom, but not give it away in this manner!'

Mrs Taylor, who had a son at Gallipoli, considered the Bill a direct insult to the boys who had gone. Conscription was not wanted to win the war but to keep down the workers and get a tighter grip of the worker.

The Prime Minister: 'You must not say that!'

Mrs Taylor: 'If I'm out of order I won't say it.'

The Prime Minister: 'No, you're not out of order, but you are mistaken.'

Mrs Taylor declared that it was simply the workers' bodies which the Government wanted. People in high places would be let off.

Mrs Snow stated that all her sons had enlisted except a married one, who could not go unless the Government could do better for married men. 'I really think you only want the Bill so as to get the single men cheaper,' continued the lady. 'Now look at me –'

The Prime Minister: 'I have been looking at you with a great deal of admiration!' (Laughter.)

Mrs Snow: 'I forgot you are an Irishman.' (Loud laughter, in which the Prime Minister joined heartily.)

'Too drastic for words – absolutely taking the last shred of liberty,' declared another lady, who held that it would go against the conscience of any woman to give away the fact that a young eligible man was not enrolled.

Seizing an opportunity

Another lady spoke of the sanitary conditions in the camps, but admitted she had never seen either Featherston or Trentham.

'Then I'll give you a pass to both camps. You can see for yourself,' replied the Prime Minister.

'And a railway pass?' asked the lady.

'I'll pay for it out of my own pocket,' said Mr Massey.

'And can I take a friend, poke about and see underneath – not only on the surface?'

'Yes, we'll give you a guide and a pass to go anywhere.'

No class distinctions

The Prime Minister, having ascertained that there were no more speakers, commenced to reply twenty minutes after the deputation had opened. He found himself still replying forty minutes later to the ladies' afterthoughts. They were loth to let him have the last word. He conceded that the deputation was quite honest in its objection to the Bill, but there was a good deal of misapprehension, and he doubted if many of his hearers had read it. The Bill did not do away with the privilege of volunteering. Unless some great emergency came along which we could not foresee at the moment, each district would send its monthly quota voluntarily, and only resort to the ballot if the voluntary enlistments failed. There was absolutely no class distinction about it.

'Oh, Mr Massey!' said a lady in a shocked tone. 'How could you say that?'

The Prime Minister explained that to the millionaire's son and the worker's son the Bill would impartially apply. 'I suppose you suggest I am not a worker?' he remarked during a little argument on the point he sustained with several ladies. 'I was working in my office till three o'clock this morning, and I don't get paid overtime.'

'But you got more than £2 a week!' exclaimed the lady in the triumphant tone of one who has found an unanswerable argument. The Premier's reply was that if the rich man's son did not volunteer under the voluntary system the bill would enable the State to get the man.

'And his money?' queried a deputationist sharply.

'All we want,' said the Premier.

An expressive chorus of 'Oh's' provoked Mr Massey to ask that surely the deputation did not want the Government to take more than it needed. The Government took £2,000,000 last year and it might take more this year, because we were spending nearly a million a month. 'We want to avoid taxing the worker, and there is no country where his exemption from direct taxation is so high as here.' Coming back to his original point the Prime Minister said it would be impossible for a man to escape because he was rich.

'None of our butter merchants have gone!' declared a lady.

The Prime Minister referred to the importance of the Military Service Boards in seeing fair play. The Government would appoint to those boards the straightest men possible to find.

'What about putting a woman there?' came a suggestion.

The Prime Minister: 'I don't know but that we might. The matter has not been decided.' He recognised that without good boards there would be serious trouble. And in every case they were going to have military doctors.

The ladies: 'Oh! worse still!'

The Prime Minister: 'Well, you are hard to please! It might be possible to influence a local or family doctor, so the men will be examined by strangers to them. The first class to be called will be the single men without dependents.'

Voices: 'Shame!'

Mrs Donaldson: 'The young man may not have dependents, but he may have a moral conscience.'

'Send the fellows over forty,' was one of the suggestions, which now came fast and furious.

'I don't mind having this out but we cannot all speak at once,' said the Prime Minister good humouredly.

The deputation wanted a written guarantee that the principle of compulsion would end with the end of the war. Mr Massey said this was in the Bill.

When a lady asked if a man with a religious objection would have to go, the Prime Minister brought about his head a perfect buzz of protest when he declared with an emphatic gesture: 'The State comes first!'

'You'll drive him at the point of the bayonet!' interjected a lady whose excellent voice enabled her to be heard above the uproar.

'If he won't do his duty he must be driven!' said the Prime Minister, with a stronger gesture of emphasis.

It was impossible to note all the interesting things said, sometimes in chorus, but a lady who made an entirely fresh and amusing suggestion suddenly obtained a good listening audience by suggesting to the Prime Minister: 'What about closing up Parliament and all you old men going?'

There was loud laughter, especially when the lady, who happened to be at the Prime Minister's elbow, assured him that 'if the Premier went, she would go too, and nurse him!'

The Prime Minister: 'It's very good of you! When I go to the war I shall make it the condition that I have the selection of the nurse.' (Loud laughter.)

'Every man will fight for his country when it is really necessary,' said the next lady to 'hold the floor.'

The Prime Minister: 'Why, is it not necessary now, when civilisation is trembling in the balance?'

'The whole thing comes down to this,' declared the Prime Minister towards the end of his lively hour. 'You have to choose between the British rule and German rule. I give you credit for being every bit as patriotic as I am, but that's the choice!'

'Not your patriotism,' suggested a deputationist.

'There may be varieties, and we must agree to differ,' replied the Prime Minister, 'but we want our armies to win the war, and we must win! Now,' he ended, 'I have cleared up the important points.'

'Stirred them up!' corrected a lady, who atoned for her sharp interruptions by assuring the Prime Minister, 'We have a better impression of you, but not of the Bill.'

'The nicest compliment I've had for many a day,' declared Mr Massey, as he bowed out the deputationists, answering more questions all the time.

Lyttelton Times, *12 June 1916, p.9*

3.4. Women's International League
Maoriland Worker (1916)

The Women's International League states its objects:

To Ensure that in future National differences shall be settled by some other means than war.

To demand that women shall have a direct voice in the affairs of the nation.

Our Hope – Universal Peace with Justice.

Our Aim – to elevate and cement sisterhood.

Our Effort – To serve and uplift humanity.

The following is the Manifesto issued by the Conference held September 30th and October 1st, 1915 to form the organisation.

Upon women as non-combatants lies a special responsibility at the present time for giving expression to the revolt of the modern mind of humanity against war. Therefore, we women of the Women's International League, assembled in conference, do band ourselves together to unite with women of all nations to demand that international co-operation between the peoples, secured by goodwill and organisation, shall supersede the outworn system of warfare.

We ask that women may be given equal rights of citizenship in order that their voice may be heard in all national and international councils.

We see that alliances contracted in the hope of maintaining peace by a Balance of Power have often brought forth war because they are an effort to balance the forces of two opposing camps. We propose to work for a different kind of alliance, one which shall be a co-operation of the nations, one that shall bring forth peace. We recognise that, were such an alliance established, the healthy development not only of individuals but of nations, would be so fostered that causes of strife would be removed before they could lead to all the various kinds of warfare, economic, social and international.

We believe that peace is no negative thing: it is not only the condition of all fruitful work, but the result of the most strenuous and adventurous effort of mind and spirit. We dedicate our organisation to the task of encouraging in ourselves and others this ceaseless effort, and of helping to mould institutions in accordance with the vital policy laid down by the International Congress of Women at The Hague, April, 1915.

The Objects include: The establishment of the principle of right rather than might, and of co-operation rather than conflict, in National and International affairs and for this purpose to work for:

1. The development of the ideals underlying modern democracy in the interests of Constructive Peace.

2. The emancipation of women and the protection of their interests.

Maoriland Worker, *2 August 1916, p.3*

3.5. Women in Our Criminal Courts: the need for reform
by Eveline Cunnington (1916)

From the moment a woman commits a crime, or is supposed to have committed one, she passes into the hands of men. Men arrest her, men question her in the lower court, a man defends her, a man directs her committal to the Supreme Court. The grand jury – all men – consider her case. She is cross-examined by men, twelve men pronounce her guilty or not guilty; if guilty a man passes sentence upon her. A man controls her prison life; the inspector who visits her in prison is a man, the authorities of the Justice Department are all men, the Prison Board is composed entirely of men.

In short, from the hour of her trial until her sentence is finished in prison not one woman has any legal power over her – to try her, to judge her, to control her!

It is absurd, it is preposterous, it is unjust. It is a record of sex stupidity – on the part of the man who assumes this great responsibility, on the part of the woman who permits and consents to such a state of gross unfairness in a land where women possess political weapons.

Women do not realise the shame and suffering endured by their unfortunate sisters in the criminal courts.

Something should be done to amend matters and to soften the nerve-racking conditions to which females are now subjected in our public courts.

We must ask for some equality of control between the sexes where all women and children are concerned; women police, if possible women lawyers, women on the grand and petty juries, women detectives.

We must have women serving on our prison board, women inspectors of prisons to work conjointly with men inspectors (for all the prisons in the Dominion); we must have a woman colleague with the under-secretary of the Minister of Justice.

These reforms in the Department of Justice are themselves based on justice and right, and should no longer be delayed or hindered in their passage through the legislature of any liberal and enlightened government.

But women are not only needed on behalf of their sisters charged with crime, but also on behalf of the victims of crime who, too often, present a truly tragic appearance in our criminal courts.

Look at this little one standing in the open court, surrounded by men. A mere slip of a girl – a little child in short petticoats and hair down her shoulders! There is something in her face that any woman of discernment could quickly read and interpret – an expression of pathetic weakness, accentuated by lines of awakening sexuality. Her modesty is outraged, her innocence is destroyed, her girlhood gone – she stands there the victim in laws of a criminal assault.

She is a daughter of the poor. She has never been watched and guarded, because no one had time to watch and guard her. Her danger years, 'wonder years,' found her an easy prey. A child of rich parents is carefully tended until those danger years are safely passed. Think of it reader! For years and years I have noticed this fact. The victims are from the least protected of all classes. They are also little girls of retarded mental development, of arrested moral growth, the weakest and the most helpless of the community.

And the predatory man gets off and goes off. On what plea? Of previous good character, perhaps, or from a laudable reluctance on the part of a judge to send a first offender to 'herd with hardened criminals.'

Now, the grounds upon which these lenient positions are based are unsound and dangerous.

Imagine a doctor saying to a patient attacked with influenza: 'This is your first illness, your previous health has been excellent, therefore I shall not attend you. I shall leave you to get well as best you may. I feel also unwilling to send you to a hospital to 'herd with infectious patients,' therefore I shall let you loose on society.' We should acclaim that medical man as a very shortsighted and foolish doctor. But this is precisely what we do to our first offenders. We fail to recognise the importance and significance of first symptoms in moral diseases. Assuredly if a person commits a demoral action, either from passion or premeditation, he is suffering from moral ill-health – acute or morbid as details of the case may denote: he has, therefore, a claim on our skilled consideration. We have no right to let him go free; it is a wrong to him and to the public at large.

The offender – this first offender – needs treatment. Why do we not give it to him? Isolation is no treatment: it may be a deterrent to crime until its pressure is removed, but it is certainly 'no cure or attempted cure.'

There are two salient reasons why the legal authorities either refuse to commit first offenders to prison or are anxious to liberate them too soon.

The judicial mind has been partially influenced by the modern physio-psychologist's point of view with regard to criminals. It dallies with theories of free will – moral irresponsibility, morbid tendencies and many other cryptic aspects of the anti-social offender, thus confusing and obscuring practical issues. Secondly, our present penal system, being so ineffective and repugnant to the modern judge, he prefers to let the convicted criminal go free rather than send him to our more or less archaic institutions.

As a matter of bold fact, we go to great expense to create cumbersome machinery to deal with crime in our prisons, and then set all our wits together to dodge those prisons or to escape from them as speedily as possible.

The remark made recently by one of our judges that he did not wish a certain convicted person to go to prison to 'herd with hardened criminals,' is a tremendous indictment of our punitive establishments.

All this points to the crying need of moral hospitals where patients suffering from a first or second attack of moral disorder can be treated without loss of time.

Prompt and early treatment are quite as imperative for our so-called criminals as for our consumptives. In short, we have a right to claim for the morally sick the same advanced and progressive treatment as we bestow on the inmates of our general and mental hospitals.

In order to effectively achieve those reforms of our penal system women must enter in all departments dealing with first offenders of each sex. Chronic cases can be safely left to the charge of male warders in completely separated establishments. Chronic criminals are the germ-carriers of moral disorders, and as such must be rigorously isolated.

When public and judicial confidence in our reformative institutions is at last firmly secured, we shall find that the irritating oscillation of opinion between Judge and Prison Board will cease. The Judge's sentence of prolonged cura-

tive detention will not be tampered with by a few amiable gentlemen sitting in judgment of a Judge's wisdom, as they now do under the present confused management of prisons and prisoners.

This Government can be credited with the best intentions; it is the most alive Government in regard to prison reform that this Dominion has ever experienced, but it is of prime importance that our judges should at once cease to liberate first offenders on the grounds that they must not herd with 'hardened prisoners,' and we have every right to ask that our moral offenders be treated in highly equipped hospitals while moral disease is still in its earliest and most hopeful stage.

Assuredly for this work the influence of women is absolutely indispensable.

Women's Column, Maoriland Worker, *18 October 1916, p.7*

3.6. The Social Evil and the Degradation of Womanhood by Eveline Cunnington (1916)

From time to time it becomes imperatively necessary to call public attention to one of the most painful and repellent aspects of social life, viz., the degradation of womanhood. Under the veil of various names, we attempt to conceal the real horrors of the subject: The Red Plague; the Social Evil; the Social Menace are covers we use for the loathsome sore of modern civilisation.

The obligation of discussing the subject in our public papers finds its excuse in the fact that society is a capricious and forgetful creature, its memory and conscience are liable to spasmodic attacks of activity intercepted by more or less lengthy periods of quiescence and indifference. Just now we are agitated by authoritative accounts of the inroads made on public health and morality by that class of women who prey upon the susceptibilities and passions of young manhood. The massing of large numbers of men taken from their usual wholesome modes of life into congested areas and subjected to great nervous excitement, accompanied by a relaxation from home influence, has created a grave menace to the physical and moral condition of society at large.

The question arises in all thoughtful persons: 'Can anything be done to check or eradicate the social evil?'

Let us strike a note of warning at the outset

of this article. There is no one panacea for the evil: its roots lie too deep, its origins are too complex and varied, its sources too intricate and entangled for any specific line of action to stop it or cure it promptly or adequately.

There are three different systems which have been brought to bear upon the public degradation of women. And all three have completely failed.

Suppression, regulation and masterly inactivity.

Suppression usually took the form of grotesque and brutal punishments for women, and women only. In the Middle Ages women of the type under discussion were sometimes put in iron cages and dipped into the river; their noses were cut off; they were publicly whipped; they were forced to wear a distinguishing dress; they were the victims of blackmail or of heavy extortionate fines (divided between their accuser and the city government.)

In more recent times harsh police raids are the mode of suppression most favoured by rash social reformers who never stop to question what becomes of the persecuted women turned out of house and home.

Suppression failed. Now what about regulation?

The so-called continental system of the

regulation of vice is subject to the gravest disapproval by all deep thinking social workers; the system varies in details in different countries of Europe. The Scandinavian is the least objectionable: it comprises a certain amount of police supervision, with compulsory reporting of venereal diseases, and ample free medical service. The German and French systems are most repugnant to all sense of justice and humanity. Terrific powers are vested in the police, supported by a spy system of plain clothes men and anonymous letters. The head of the 'Moralé Police' in Paris, when asked wherein lay the chief strength of the system replied: 'Arrests; always arrests; that is our only hope.'

In the German Reichstag a member once said: 'It is well known that these marked women can never reform.'

This dreadful system of the regulation of vice and the patronage of 'tolerated houses' has been strongly condemned by public commissions in France; it has been discarded in Italy, given up in Switzerland, except in Geneva.

Harriet Martineau, Florence Nightingale, Josephine Butler fought the battle of the notorious C.D. Acts in England. The history of that magnificent war of the women is too well known to be repeated here.

The masterly inactivity system is also a failure. Ignoring and neglecting the subject of woman's public degradation is stupid and dangerous. It is the English system, and has led to most disastrous effects and consequences on the physical and moral condition of the people. Two schemes of reform alone are left to us: Repression and prevention.

To repress an evil is not so drastic as to suppress it. Suppression invites clandestine and secretive activities. 'Virtue through fear is vice in handcuffs,' said Emerson, and vice in handcuffs can be a very power factor for evil.

Repression – The remedies under this system are legislative and social.

1. All procurors, male or female, should be subjected to heavy penalties at the hand of the law.
2. No girl under 21 should be allowed to carry on a life of public immorality. This is no fanciful suggestion of an irresponsible lay person, but is the pondered opinion of many medical men. Dr. Pileur, himself an advocate of regulation, urges the reduction of prostitution to a minimum by cutting off from the 'trade' all girls under 21. He substantiates his plea with very impressive facts gathered from a wide field of practical knowledge. He states that 25 per cent of these unhappy women begin their life of immorality before the age of 21; that of these minors 60 per cent are afflicted with 'social disease' – which they contract much more easily than other women. These are most important physiological and psychological reasons supporting the claim upon the public conscience in demanding this humanitarian reform. It is also the daughters of the poor who are the least protected from the onslaught of the 'White Slave' traffic, for they are compelled to go away from home to earn a living at an earlier age than the children of well-to-do people.

3. All men found living on the immoral earnings of women should be most severely punished and greater supervision of such persons must be insisted upon.
4. Public solicitation must be kept severely in check. The disgrace of appearing in court keeps many young women out of the life and drives them off the pavement into better modes of existence. This is the experience of many social workers.
5. Women police are an absolute necessity in dealing with young girls just entering the life of vice. It is astonishing to me that the women of New Zealand have not already accomplished this reform.
6. Houses of ill-fame should be occasionally raided so as to give the occupants a sense of discomfort and insecurity, thereby disgusting them with their trade. Continuous and harsh raiding is not at all advisable from social or moral points of view.

There is no sound reason why the men found in these disreputable houses should not be arrested as well as the poor unfortunates. Such legislation would go on all fours with the raiding of gambling houses.

Social Measures – In brief, get rid of poverty and you will abolish its worst disease – prostitution. Thousands and thousands of the unfortunates are the victims of our cruel and stupid social order. All medical and social experts on this subject are convinced of this appalling fact. Out of 100,000 cases studied by Dr Minod in France and personally known to him, he had not found one hundred who did not loathe the life! Quite four-fifths of the women loathe their occupation! Sweated industries claim and make victims of the social evil. Neglected children, cruel parents, miserable homes, drink, lack of technical and industrial education of the young woman, all these are tremendous factors in the production of 'fallen women.'

The awakening of the public conscience is absolutely necessary if we are to combat this great social sore as effectually as we are fighting tuberculosis and other diseases.

The fight should call all men and women into the ranks, because it is not the physical ills alone that devastate our fellow creatures: the moral ruin is appalling, tragedy follows closely on the steps of vice, nothing but misery and shame, agony, the ruin of homes, the wreck of human lives accompany the degradation of our womanhood and let us add of our manhood also!

Maoriland Worker, *29 November 1916, p. 7*

3.7. President's Address to the National Council of Women by Kate Sheppard (1919)

It is with a spirit of great hopefulness that our Conference should meet this year. The terrible tragedy of a world war has been ended – a peace between the most powerful of the combatants has been signed, and a League of Nations to preserve peace is being established.

In the four years of conflict, systems of government, class distinctions, national and international laws, have been cast into a fiery crucible and tested, until those which were faulty have crumbled into ashes, and those which were basically right are emerging, purified of much dross.

Truer and clearer perceptions of truth and justice, of rights and of duties have been gained, and already attempts are being made for a fairer and more equitable adjustment of power and responsibility. Amid the crash of high explosives and the din of battle a more vivid sense of the value of the common people – of the rights of the individual – has been evolved. It has been realised that the peer and the peasant, the male and the female, are fashioned out of one common clay; that the accident of birth or the incidence of sex cannot be allowed to bar the right of each human being to self-development.

And, further, it has been borne in upon us that our greatest and truest liberty can only be attained by our voluntary submission to divine law – the law of service – the law of 'each for all.'

Although the range of subjects which might be profitably discussed is most invitingly large, I propose to confine myself to those which bear more directly upon the position and work of women. It is gratifying that the opposition to the admission of women to full citizenship is breaking down. The desire among women for a change in their political status may be said to be world-wide. The organised women's societies in the twenty-six countries where National Councils of Women have been established are all working in this direction. All are working for the removal of the civil and political disabilities which hinder women from developing their capacities for service, whether in the home or in the State. For it must not be forgotten that the Home and the State are one. A very little consideration will show that, in its ultimate issue, all the work of the State is for the welfare and protection of the Home. It therefore follows that any community which deliberately excludes women from its government is lacking in a true perception of the functions of government.

I have said that the opposition to the right of women to full citizenship is breaking down. How could it be otherwise? Continuous appeals to reason and justice for more than half a century had convinced the more thoughtful and unprejudiced that to class women politically with criminals and lunatics was worthy only of tyrants or of fools. But the majority of the people (I am paraphrasing Carlyle) are foolish, and neither thoughtful nor unprejudiced. And, curiously enough, it did not hurt the self-love of most men to have their mothers, sisters, wives and daughters classed with criminals and lunatics. Therefore, progress was slow, and came first in the smaller centres of population. Then came the tremendous upheaval of the war, and fossilized prejudices crashed in all directions. Women were welcomed in professional and industrial capacities that had hitherto been deemed sacred to men. And most splendidly did the women rise to meet the need for their help. Societies for relief were rapidly organised, hospitals were established, and, as doctors and nurses, as orderlies and clerks, as motor drivers and teamsters, in town and on the land, in munition factories, and even on the field of battle, they wrought side by side with their obdurate brother man. And he – well, I suppose he scratched his head and began to think!

It was difficult to continue to dogmatise about 'woman's sphere' while a woman bound up his wounds, and washed him and fed him, and her sisters were doing the work that he and his brothers used to do. And so the idea grew that as women were capable of all this, they might be also trusted to mark a name on a ballot paper! An indication of the growth of this idea is found in the facts that six millions of British women over thirty years of age have been enfranchised and made eligible for Parliament, and that the House of Commons passed a bill giving the franchise to all women over twenty-one years of age. That the House of Lords refused to pass this bill is but an indication that the most privileged class is most opposed to progress. One of the happiest auguries for the woman's outlook in Britain is found in a manifesto issued by Mr Lloyd George and Mr Bonar Law on November 22nd, which outlines the programme of the coalition. In this they say: 'It will be the duty of the Government to remove all existing inequalities in the law as between men and women.' When Radical and Conservative send forth a whole-souled statement of duty such as this, it is, indeed, a happy augury.

'But,' you may say, 'How has the war helped the liberation of women in other countries?' Let me give a brief outline of the position in other countries. But I wish first to call attention to the fact that the Peace Conference at Paris, in defining the Articles of the League of Nations, agreed to Clause 3, Article VII, which reads thus: 'All positions under, or in connection with, the League, including the secretariat, shall be open equally to men and women.' The passage of this Clause gives the final evidence not only of the coming world-wide change in the status of women, but also of the strong desire among the representatives of the world's most powerful nations to deal even-handed justice. Whether the League succeeds or fails it will always remain a glorious attempt.

In the United States of America the defeat of the Federal Suffrage Amendment Bill was disappointing to women workers. There are, however, good prospects of a renewal of that vote in the near future. In any case, more than half of the States in the Union possess womanhood suffrage, and the women in those States will be voting at the next Presidential Election, while one woman, Jeannette Rankin, from the State of Montana, has been elected to Congress. As you are aware, women in Denmark, Norway and Finland have enjoyed the vote and

eligibility for Parliament for years past, and recently Canada, Austria, Germany and Poland have granted these rights to women. In Holland, strangely enough, women were eligible for Parliament but did not possess the franchise. This curious anomaly has now been rectified, and women may now vote and sit in Parliament. The French Senate, like our English House of Lords, does not reflect public opinion as closely as the Lower House, for it rejected a motion to give women the vote and eligibility by eight votes to five. On the contrary, the Chamber of Deputies voted in favour of women's franchise with eligibility for all elected bodies by 344 to 97. Australia granted Womanhood Suffrage in all her States years ago and eligibility for the Commonwealth Parliament, and at least four of her States now possess Parliamentary eligibility. Swedish women have gained suffrage and eligibility, Switzerland and Italy are working hard for voting powers, and we are informed by cable that the Union Parliament of South Africa has passed a motion for womanhood suffrage by 44 votes to 42.

Women in Parliament

While wishful to avoid any encroachment on our Secretary's report, I cannot refrain from mentioning the present position and prospects of women's eligibility for Parliament in this Dominion. You will remember that when, more than a quarter of a century ago, we were enfranchised, special care was taken to prevent the electors from choosing any woman to represent them in Parliament. At the moment this seemed to be of little importance, for the prohibition against women being members of Parliament was so illogical and unfair that it appeared certain that in a short time it must be removed. Yet the years have passed while women electors that were young became elderly, and many that were middle-aged have grown old, and the frequent efforts for justice that have been made by earnest women and chivalrous men have been met by indifference and a scarcely-veiled hostility. It would not be right to blame Parliament altogether for the continuance of this injustice. Under our faulty system of Party Government, Parliament, which should be all powerful, has really little choice of action. Every member is supposed to belong to, and obey the instructions of, one party or another. And while Governments may come and go, no strong party has yet included justice to women in its programme. Yet, as I have said, since the war there has been a stirring of the dry bones. Systems of Government are on their trial, and the idea of justice may yet become a living force. During the last session of our Parliament a proposal to make women electors eligible for election was favourably received. The proposal was lost on the plea of unconstitutional procedure. Mr Massey declared that while he accepted Sir Francis Bell's dictum on the question of procedure, he was not opposed to the reform, and would himself bring the question before the House at its next session, and give members an opportunity of voting upon it. Sir Joseph Ward said that he 'felt that women should be admitted to Parliament,' while Sir Francis Bell, replying to a deputation of women who interviewed him, said that he 'needed no deputation to persuade him that what it asked for was just.' He further said, 'It is an accurate and absolute fact that if the Lower House had passed the amendment, it would have passed the Legislative Council without question or objection.'

It would therefore seem that the accomplishment of this long sought for reform is assured.

I am glad to note that Mr Massey, in ratification of his promise, has already given notice in the House to ask for leave to introduce the Women's Parliamentary Rights Extension Bill.

It may be asked by some of the unthinking, 'Why this desire to make women eligible for Parliament?' This question may be answered by another. 'Why should the electors be denied the right to select as their representative the person they wish to represent them?' Or, 'If a woman be the Sovereign of our mighty Empire, why should a woman elector be prohibited from being the servant of a constituency, if the constituents so desire?' Such a prohibition is not only an interference with the liberty of women citizens, but an interference with the men citizens also, and cannot be defended on reasonable grounds. Further, it is my belief that the one-sided laws which operate against women and the welfare of the family will not be repealed until we have women representatives in Parliament. It may be interesting here to quote from an address given by Miss Mary Macarthur, a candidate for Parliament, to the electors of Stourbridge, England. 'It takes a man and a woman,' she said, 'to make an ideal home, and I believe that neither can build the ideal world without the help of the other. In the new Parliament, where laws affecting every household in the land will be framed, the point of view of the mother as well as that of the father,

should find expression. If I am returned to the House of Commons I shall try to voice in a special sense the aspirations of the women workers of this land . . . I shall also feel entitled to speak for the woman whose work never ends, the woman in the home who faces and solves every day a multitude of problems, the woman who has been too often neglected or forgotten by politicians, the mother of the children upon whom the future pride and strength of the nation depends.'

With the wider opportunities for service that seem to be opening for women, there should be a continuous effort to expand their outlook, and to deepen their knowledge of many of the questions which call for legislative action.

Education

Take, for example, the question of Education, which affects almost every home directly, and which is so important to us as a young nation. Possibly the Education Department has tried to do its best, but Governments have been parsimonious in providing funds, and Parliament seems quite to have forgotten that the power of the purse is one of its most important functions. And so we have schoolrooms in a state of decay, and so overcrowded as to be injurious to health. The grants made to school committees are so scanty that it is practically impossible to cleanse and keep sweet the rooms in which healthy and unhealthy children are huddled together. The means for personal cleanliness and necessaries for sanitation are frequently grossly deficient and neglected. In sparsely settled districts the rooms are small, and, generally speaking, it is difficult to procure decent boarding accommodation.

Yet it is to these schools that our youngest women teachers, often barely out of their teens, are sent. One would think that young men teachers should be more aptly chosen for these back-blocks, where the conditions of life are rude. But, it will be said, the young men won't go. Why? Because they can get better positions in town. And why can they get better positions? Because women are treated unfairly. In what way? In two ways. First, in the matter of salary. Watch the Education Boards' advertisements in your local paper. You will often see such advertisements as this: 'Wanted, assistant teacher for – – school. Salary, male £150; female, £120.' The female has to gain the same certificates as the male, why should there be this unequal pay? She has to teach the same subjects, and an extra one, namely, sewing, and when the male inspector examines her class or her school, he makes no concession because she is a female teacher.

Secondly, women teachers are treated unfairly in the matter of promotion. The best paid positions are always given to men. We know of women of good attainments, of mature years, with a long record of meritorious service, who, when promotion was possible, have been passed over in favour of a youthful male teacher with a most inferior record. And if you ask 'Why?' you will be told 'Oh, the head teacher must be a man.' And if you again ask 'Why?' you will probably be told, 'Because he can maintain discipline better.'

There is only one suitable reply to this kind of argument, and that is 'Fudge!' Discipline is not a matter of physical strength. If it were, many male teachers would have to give place to women teachers. It is simply a question of power of control inherent in the individual, with, possibly, some cultivation. And power of control is not a matter of sex but of temperament. We all know that in families where the children are well-behaved and well-mannered it is usually the mother who has been the disciplinarian.

Sole charge women teachers in back-blocks schools, where they teach unruly boys of twelve and fourteen, have, perforce, cultivated the power of control, while a young male teacher in a town or suburban school has been under no such necessity. The question of discipline should not be allowed to block a woman's promotion until she has been proved to be deficient. And, by the same reasoning, a man should not be assumed to be a disciplinarian until he has been tested.

One other matter should be made prominent. All our school Inspectors are men. This is not right. An Inspector should be a counsellor and guide as well as a critic. And I gladly admit that many of our Inspectors are. But to many of our young women teachers, lonely, far from home and friends, often badly, and sometimes horribly, boarded, a visit from a woman Inspector would be a comfort and a boon. No man Inspector could be so helpful to such a girl, who is often suffering from causes that she could hardly explain save to a sympathetic woman. Our Education Department has no right to send its young women teachers to such places and feel free of all responsibility for their welfare, and it cannot fulfil its duty towards them without

the aid of women Inspectors.

Hygiene should be given a leading part in the curriculum of all our schools, primary and secondary, for what is more important than the preservation of health? I admit that the grubby and unsavoury condition of many of our schoolrooms is an object lesson of the worst kind. But we hope that a few women in Parliament may lead to better provision being made for the health and cleanliness of our school children. Then lessons on health and the necessity for cleanliness will seem less ironical. The lack of co-ordination between teachers, parents and pupils is now being recognised as a serious hindrance to true education. Our New Zealand Council of Education has forwarded resolutions on this question to the various Education Boards, and the matter has been discussed by some of our women's societies. In connection with this problem I may remind you that Mrs Rhodes, a lecturer from the United States of America, recently told us that a 'Parent-Teachers Association' had been formed in her State. The Association organised monthly meetings, at which the parents and teachers exchanged ideas and consulted together as to the welfare of the children. These meetings have proved to be very beneficial and helpful, and I think that our women's societies might be useful in helping to organise and support this movement.

Co-guardianship of children

Among the many legal injustices which the presence of a few women in our Parliament would be useful in removing, few, I think, are more glaring than the question of the Guardianship of Children. That a mother has no legal right to her own child or children is so outrageous an anomaly that one would suppose could not be tolerated in these enlightened days. Yet for years past women's societies have sent requests, resolutions and petitions to Parliament asking for the co-guardianship of mother and father, without avail. Justice to mothers was not in the game of party politics, and our modest requests have fallen upon deaf ears. The late Dr McNab, in reply to a deputation of women, promised that if he were returned to Parliament, he would certainly do his best to introduce a Bill on the question, or, if the Government did so, he would strongly support the measure. He said that he did not believe that there was a man in the House who would not support such a Bill. Unfortunately, Dr McNab was not successful in his candidature, and by his lamented death we lost a warm advocate of justice to women.

The old Roman law, by which the mother and children became the property or dependents of the husband or father, was imposed on the British when the domination of Rome was imposed upon them, and the question of the Guardianship of Children is necessarily bound up with the general status of Woman as Citizen, Wife and Mother.

Endowment of motherhood

A subject that has been much discussed in England of late is the Endowment of Motherhood, or, as some prefer to term it, the Endowment of Families.

With the dreadful loss of life in the great war, attention has again been drawn to what is termed 'Race Suicide.' For many years the population of France has been practically stationary, and at the present time it is estimated to be four millions less than it was at the beginning of the war. In Great Britain the birth-rate has been steadily declining, and in the Dominions overseas the same tendency is noticeable. In the United States of America the birth-rate has been mainly sustained by the foreign population. Among the people of British descent, which we may be pardoned for calling the finest element in that great nation, the diminution in the size of the family has been most marked. There is no reason for supposing that the limitation is other than voluntary, for certainly in the severe test of virility which the war imposed on the peoples who took part therein, no races have displayed greater vigour and capability than have the Anglo-Saxons and our gallant Allies, the French. Yet the German and Russian birth-rate far exceeds that of the peoples whom we believe to be the flowers of modern civilization. That this fact is a desirable one, few will maintain. It remains, therefore, to briefly consider the probable causes at work to limit the birth-rate. Some of these are, probably, purely selfish, such as a desire for undue gaiety, or luxury, or leisured ease. But there are other causes which cannot be looked on as mere selfishness. Take, for example, the case of a clerk or a superior artisan. He has some sense of culture and refinement, yet his earnings are limited. He contemplates marriage. He has a friend of status similar to his own who has been married for some years. He sees him worried over the heavy expenses of doctor and nurse that attend the birth of each child. He finds him harassed by the growth of the baker's, grocer's,

and butcher's bills, and by the necessity for a larger house. His dress grows increasingly shabby, and his wife loses her good looks through incessantly slaving morning, noon and night in the endeavour to keep the home and children looking, at least, respectable.

And he hears that, despite all his struggles and self-denial, his friend cannot give his elder children the secondary school education that seems so desirable. Can we wonder that our clerk or superior artisan asks himself whether a large family is not more a curse than a blessing? And is he to blame in resolving that if he marries, his wife shall not be a mere house slave, and that if they have children they should not have so many that they cannot afford to educate them as they think desirable? Who shall say whether he is right or wrong? And yet the State needs the children, and it needs them in abundance. But it only requires those that are well and healthily born, well nourished and well educated. How can this pressing need of the State be met? It is argued that children are the State's most valuable asset, and therefore whatever conditions tend towards benefiting children will benefit the State. Recently a proposal came from the (then) Minister of Health to the effect that the Government should pay a small sum towards the expenses of the birth of each child born in the St. Helen's Maternity Hospitals. The sum proposed was not only totally inadequate, but the proposal conveyed no recognition of the fact that the expense incurred at the birth of the child was only the first of a long series of expenses.

However, the proposal was at least a recognition of the fact that the State has a financial obligation towards those who are responsible for its future citizens. It seems to me that this question is worthy of our consideration and study during the coming year.

Equal pay for equal work

In dealing with the question of Education, I referred to the unfairness of the inequality of payment between men and women teachers. But this inequality is the rule in almost all State, professional and industrial positions. Were wage-earning men wiser, they would strongly urge equality of payment, which would not only remove women from unfair competition with them, which they seem to fear, but save their own wage-earning women relations from being exploited for economic reasons. Should the State lead the way in this reform it would help greatly in this eminently just movement.

Economic equality

The Economic Equality of husband and wife has been urged by women's societies for many years. The present position of the law is barbarous. Under it a woman can claim little more than can a slave. Under it, it was ruled by a Wellington Magistrate that a member of the New Zealand House of Representatives need not pay for a pair of boots for his wife. 'Boots,' said the Magistrate, 'are not a necessity, therefore the defendant (husband) is not obliged to pay for them.' That the justice of most husbands is better than the law is a most excellent reason for a reform in the legal status of their wives.

Women Police, Justices of the Peace and Jurors

The addition of women to the Police Force which has been so satisfactory in those places where it has been established has been resisted by both of the late Ministers of Justice in this Dominion. The late Minister of Health has, in connection with his own Department, appointed women patrols, two for each of the four large towns. Probably this was all that the Minister could do, and credit should be given to him. But it is no credit to those who have been responsible for the Department of Justice that they have blocked this necessary reform. There is a distinct need for Women Police for the prevention of minor and juvenile crime by women. But while prevention is their aim, they should have power of police constables, and be responsible to the Chief-of-Police in each centre. Women Police have done good service in London and other large towns in England, as well as in the United States and in Australia, and the experience in those countries should be some guide as to what might be useful in the prevention of crime in New Zealand. I trust that our women will not cease to press this matter on the Government.

The appointment of Women Justices of the Peace has also been neglected by our Government. In dealing with wrong-doers who are young women or children, Women Magistrates, assisted by Women Police, would be much more useful in prevention and reform than the average man who acts as an unpaid magistrate.

It may be mentioned here that the House of Lords has passed a Bill to enable women to be Justices of the Peace.

The making women eligible as jurors is another reform so obviously fair that it should appeal to all.

Social hygiene

It would be sheer cowardice were I to refrain from touching on the delicate but serious subject of social disease. Venereal Diseases are probably the greatest menace to the public health that exists, as they are fraught with terrible consequences, not only to their generation, but also to succeeding ones. They afford an illustration of how the sins of the parents may become a dreadful visitation on the children.

In the discussion on the health of the soldiers at the Conference of the Returned Soldiers' Association, it was stated that women were opposed to notification of Venereal Disease. The Social Hygiene Society of Christchurch, which is doing splendid work in the attempt to deal with the evil, issued a statement giving the position it holds on this question of notification. As its attitude was arrived at after several conferences and the study of the expression of opinions held by the most eminent experts (both lay and medical) in the world on this subject, I cannot do better than quote it here –

'The Society holds that provision should be made for a National scheme of free clinics (bacteriological and other diagnostic tests to be provided free; free drugs, and free treatment; free specially-qualified doctors to be provided) for all sufferers who voluntarily present themselves for treatment. When such provision is made, and only then, doctors should be compelled, under penalty, to notify any case of a sufferer from V.D. who refuses to continue the treatment as long as is necessary, or who exposes to infection any other person, such notification being an entirely conditional one. Members of the Conference protested against a distinction being made between soldiers and civilians, but such distinction is inevitable, since the soldier, being under constant medical supervision, the disease can be immediately detected in his case, and he can be compelled to submit to treatment. Further, the soldier receives medical treatment free of expense, while in the case of civilians the treatment, being prolonged and expensive, is always an obstacle to application for medical aid in the early and most curative stages of the disease, and this is the reason why the Society so strenuously urges the establishment of a system of free treatment for V.D.

'The effect of compulsory notification of all cases has always operated in the direction of preventing many sufferers, especially those who have contracted the disease through no fault of their own, from seeking medical advice. They dread the stigma which naturally attaches to this disease. Under the form of notification advocated by the Social Hygiene Society, the difficulty disappears, and the inducement is to continue treatment.

'Again, we fail to see how compulsory notification can be effected in civilian life, except in the case of those who voluntarily present themselves for treatment, unless examination on suspicion is adopted, and that means the direct enactment of the C.D. Acts and would be operative only in the case of women openly leading an immoral life. It would leave untouched the private prostitute and the diseased man, the latter of whom is the greatest menace to society, and is alone responsible for the spread of the disease amongst innocent women and children.

'The objection to the C.D. Act lies in the facts that –

'1. While under this Act a woman may be detained for treatment for an indefinite time at the public expense, she may be re-infected immediately on her release, and be as great a menace as before her detention and treatment.

'2. The Act is a direct incentive to vice because it creates a false sense of security.

'3. It has been proved beyond all controversy that vice and disease have increased under its operation.

'4. It operates against women only, and under it many innocent women have been subjected to false charges.'

Before leaving this subject I may mention that recent newspapers amply confirm this short statement. As possibly an attempt may be made to quietly facilitate the passage of a similar Act through our local Parliament, it behoves us, if only in the interest of public health, to be alert.

While not purely a woman's question, the alteration of our Electoral laws to allow of Proportional Representation is of great importance. We cannot claim to be a self-governing people while half (and in the present Parliament more than half) of the electors are unrepresented. It has been reported that Mr Massey intends to introduce a Proportional Representation measure to be applied to the city constituencies. But why should the country electors be deprived of its benefits? We should see to it that every honest opinion held by a substantial number of people should be voiced in our Parliament: and that can only be done by Proportional Representation applied to every part of the Dominion.

This address is already of undue length. But I wish to say that to my mind our greatest need is education – education of ourselves and of other women citizens. The most effective method seems to be by enlarging and multiplying our societies, so that the various questions may be studied. An organising secretary would be of great service. A paper of our own (if only a small eight-page one) would help to link the societies together, and affiliation with the International Council of Women would bring us into contact with the women of like minds in other lands.

But I feel deeply that if our work is to prosper we must also enlist the interest of our younger women in Council work. The future is theirs and we shall prosper in our efforts if we have their fresh young ardour and enthusiasm as a driving force.

I regret that I cannot be with you to address you in person. But in heart and soul I am with you, and you have my warmest wishes for a successful meeting.

NCW Session, 1919 (MS Papers 1371, folder 107, ATL)

Chapter 4

What Do Women Want?
1920s and 1930s

The 1920s and 1930s were years of considerable political activity amongst women. However, unlike the earlier phase of franchise agitation, or the later women's liberation movement, interwar activism did not take the form of a feminist movement per se. Rather, it arose in response to the diverse concerns felt by women and was initiated from within a variety of organisations and political parties.

These issues included women's political representation (which gained impetus when women gained the right to stand for Parliament in 1919); the rights of mothers to safe childbirth and a paid allowance; the entitlement of working women to fair pay, conditions and the unemployment benefit; reform of the divorce law; rationalisation of housework; greater access to birth control; and international questions of peace and justice.

Advocacy of women's interests in this period almost wholly took the form of campaigning for particular issues. There was no single cause (like the vote) or organisation that so predominated as to prompt a wider debate about the relative positions of women and men. Questions concerning, for example, women's rights in employment, maternal welfare or the nationality of married women were part of a wide range of issues that were identified within a political context. This was especially so from the late 1920s, when political and economic debate was dominated first by the Great Depression, and later by the growing crisis in Europe. Political ideologies and action were seen as the path to social action and progress.

In its revived form, the NCW took on the role of central, co-ordinating body for women's opinions and organisations. As the number of organisations grew rapidly in the 1920s (including the Women's Division of Federated Farmers, the Country Women's Institute, Townswomen's Guilds, Federation of University Women, and women's clubs), the NCW increasingly acted as the channel through which women's views could be relayed to the government of the day. While it lacked the radical colour of its foundation years, the NCW was, throughout this period, the focus of a good deal of energetic campaigning by and on behalf of women. A new generation, many of them educated and having some professional experience, were drawn to the NCW. Conventional in its tactics, and cautious in its demands, the NCW, nonetheless, acted as a consistent and persistent voice for women.

The NCW's *Bulletin*, from which 'What N.Z. Women Want' (4.1) is drawn, reveals the organisation's range of interests. Preceding this summary of demands were three columns listing 45 measures that had been achieved since 1893. But by 1928, when this piece was published, the NCW had for some years been calling for the appointment of women to positions in the police force, within the prison system, and to service on juries and as justices of the peace. In addition, with the advent of films, they now sought the appointment of women as co-censors. These demands continued the earlier tradition of seeking the removal of women's political and legal disabilities, and their admission to the full range of official and political positions. In these efforts they made little headway, apart from welcoming women JPs in 1926. It was in many ways a period of frustration – the NCW lacked the driving force of political urgency.

New emphasis is apparent in the highlighting of employment concerns (points 2 and 8), seeking improvements in conditions for women teachers and civil servants. This was to become a more prominent subject within the NCW and other women's groups in the 1930s.

International issues also came to have increasing importance in the 1930s. Women's organisations took part in the 1928 Pan Pacific Women's Conference in Hawaii, the first time New Zealand women participated in a regional Pacific rim gathering of women. The NCW made a modest request that one woman be included in the official delegation to the League of Nations. However, they were to become more forthright in championing the cause of women's rights in respect of their nationality.[1] It became a major issue (and one particular to this period). New Zealand women, like women in many other parts of the world, lost their New Zealand citizenship when they married, taking on their husband's nationality. As well as the principle involved (that women and men should have equal entitlements as citizens), the loss of citizenship at marriage could have serious practical implications. In certain circumstances – during wartime, for instance – this could lead to gross injustice, as it had for Miriam Soljak during the First World War, when she was identified and classified as an 'enemy alien'. She had married Peter Soljak, an Austrian. The loss of an independent nationality also restricted a woman's mobility and left her with indeterminate status when a marriage terminated. In addition, it deprived her of guardianship rights to her children. This issue could not be resolved by reforming New Zealand law alone, but had to be pursued at an international level, and New Zealand women were drawn into the campaign along with women in Australia, the United Kingdom and Canada. A pamphlet on the nationality question was published in 1943, as part of the fiftieth anniversary celebrations of women's suffrage.[2]

Parliamentary politics were a focus for women's interest in these decades. In 1919 New Zealand women won the right to stand as candidates and a number did put themselves forward in the 1920s. None were successful until Elizabeth McCombs won the Lyttelton seat in 1933. They were more in evidence at the local body level where a small but steady number of women stood successfully, particularly as members of hospital boards.[3] Ellen Melville, a lawyer and Auckland City Councillor, was the most prominent of these; though when she sought a national parliamentary career she was not successful.[4] There was, then, much interest in and debate about women entering politics, and how they might use the vote they had won in 1893. This was not a debate confined only to 'political' circles. An early issue of the *New Zealand Woman's Weekly* featured an article entitled 'Why Don't the Women Come Forward?' (4.4), which recalled the franchise victory and urged women to become involved. 'Our mothers fought for the franchise and the greater freedom that we enjoy to-day – are we, their daughters, going to allow all that to pass, unheeded, from us?'

During these years women were moving into the mainstream political parties. The parties themselves were becoming more organised than they had been previously, maintaining membership, branches and activities between elections. Women's sections were first formally constituted in the New Zealand Labour Party in the 1920s, and, when the National Party was formed in 1936 from the remnants of the old Reform and United Parties, a women's division was incorporated in the Party's constitution.

Women active in political groups made special appeals to other women to become involved or at least to support their party. Edna Macky's[5] 1928 pamphlet, *Why All Women Should Support Labour* (4.2), is a classic example. Here she asserts that 'Woman's cause and Labour's cause are one and the same'. Both represent the interests of groups who have been submissive and long suffering, and who deserve redress. The relationship between Labour and women is not, however, quite as straightforward as this. Later Macky explains that it 'is to provide food and shelter for their wives and children that men labour, so whatever affects the cause of Labour affects also the economic position of women.' Such a view, which saw women's interests as benefiting only indirectly from the elevation of men by Labour's policies, was to be the source of later conflicts and limitations in government policy towards women.

Edna Macky, and later Elizabeth McCombs, in her 1933 pamphlet *Women and the Labour Movement* (4.3), emphasised the New Zealand Labour Party's policy for the advancement of women. The removal of all political disabilities, the granting of equal pay and equal guardianship rights, and the endowment of motherhood were all part of Labour's programme. Supporting Labour was, they argued, supporting women's rights. There was a strong belief amongst many women at this time that political action was the way to achieve social change. This belief in the political process is a distinguishing feature of the 1920s and 1930s.

As the economic situation worsened in the late 1920s, and the country sank into depression in 1929, the tenor of political debate sharpened and the positions between groups in society diverged. Organisations of unemployed workers formed in various parts of the country, and more people adopted political allegiances they had previously regarded as extreme. Out of this grew the Working Women's Movement, and the New Zealand Communist Party's paper, the *Working Woman*. The movement's objects are set out in an article in the *Working Woman*, November 1935 (4.6). Not surprisingly, economic issues were to the fore. The article discussed the situation of unemployed single women, who were ineligible for unemployment relief, but could receive an 'allowance' for 'training' (4.8), while the entitlement of married women to employment was the subject of another article (4.9). The second was prompted by the experience of married women teachers who were denied jobs during the Depression. Similarly, the particular problems of Maori women (4.5), domestic workers (4.10), and housewives were discussed in other numbers of the paper. The *Working Woman* was a radical paper, and was at times critical of other women's groups, for example, when discussing the composition of Women's Unemployment Committees (4.8). But on some questions it did take the same stance as other groups that claimed to represent women generally. The article on married women teachers was the text of an address given by Miss C. E. Kirk to the NCW.

Domestic labour formed a key part of women's economic debates in the interwar decades. Every woman was responsible, to some degree or another, for the work of running a home. A little less than a third of the female workforce was still employed as domestic servants in private households and the circumstances in which they worked were often far from satisfactory (4.10).[6] The Working Women's Movement endeavoured to form unions amongst domestic workers, while the NCW and other women's groups that were more concerned with the interests of employers lobbied the government to provide training as servants for unemployed girls Until the late 1920s they supported continued assistance for young women to emigrate from the United Kingdom to New Zealand to work as domestic servants.

Other solutions were also sought to relieve women of their domestic burden. Elizabeth Kelso (4.15) asked why there was not a Minister of Domestic Labour and suggested that domestic appliances should be categorised as essential equipment akin to that used in hospital surgeries. Mary Barkas also focused attention on the plight of the housewife, burdened by an unceasing round of domestic work, and she emphasised the economic powerlessness of wives. 'Our men hope to abolish wage-slavery,' she concluded, 'let us resolve to abolish also the wageless slavery of the housewife.' An allowance for mothers – or motherhood endowment – received much support in the 1920s. An extremely modest child benefit was introduced by the Massey Government in 1926 but it was a very limited measure compared to the universal family benefit introduced by the Labour Government.

The problem of domestic work and the calls for the national endowment of motherhood were central features of what women were seeking in this period: economic citizenship. The state came to be seen as the agency through which women could achieve economic independence. Increasing numbers of New Zealanders were coming into a direct economic relationship with the state – especially after the advent of social security. Women had been arguing for a relationship of this sort by emphasising the social, economic and political value of the work they did for the nation as mothers and homemakers. In the later 1930s, such a relationship became conceivable rather than simply idealistic. The claim to political citizenship, which had been made in the 1890s, was expanded to a claim for economic citizenship a generation later. No challenge had been made to the sexual division of responsibilities between women and men in respect of home and family or income earning (though women had pressed for greater access to the latter), but in the later period women's family and domestic responsibilities were seen to have a direct economic value for which recognition should be given.

Women entered a direct relationship with the state as recipients of social security from 1938. But there was a more significant and detrimental change in their economic status when they became defined as *dependents* of male breadwinners whose minimum wage rates were determined by what was sufficient to keep a man, his wife and three dependent children. This social component was specified in the Industrial Conciliation and Arbitration Amendment Act, 1936. Although the first Labour Government's innovative programme of social reform radically transformed the shape of New Zealand life, it was at heart socially conservative. In order to maintain the 'traditional' institutions of home and family the male breadwinner was awarded a wage sufficient to support a dependent wife and children.

Maternity and motherhood were also prominent issues throughout these two decades. New Zealand's Pakeha birth rate began to decline in the late 1870s and continued to fall after the First World War. Motherhood came to have a political and even an economic significance with the close linking of population growth and national well-being. In the early 1920s, political anxiety over the falling birth rate was expressed in concern over levels of maternal mortality, and sparked off a lengthy and often highly charged debate between the Health Department and the medical profession over the management of childirth.[7] In the crossfire, the positions of midwives and, most of all, the interests of women giving birth, were sidelined. Occasional attempts were made to voice disagreement – as when Dunedin women organised a protest against the use of their St Helen's Hospital as a teaching hospital in the late 1920s.[8] Nevertheless, the experience of women giving birth did change fundamentally. By the mid-1930s, most Pakeha women were having their babies in hospitals with a doctor in attendance (and, increasingly, with the use of pain-killing drugs) – a direct contrast with the cottage hospital, midwife-assisted births which predominated at the end of the First World War.

The birth rate showed a marked drop in the depression years. Safer and apparently 'better' conditions in which to give birth were not encouraging New Zealand women to have more children and, as other causes of maternal mortality were addressed, abortion was identified as a significant contributor to the country's maternal death rate. Economic desperation was widely suspected as a cause. The problem of women resorting to (unsafe) backstreet abortions was more commonly seen as a reflection of their economic plight, which made it impossible to cope with the burdens of motherhood, rather than a straight disinclination to continue having large families.

In 1936 abortion and birth control were the subject of a major Committee of Inquiry.[9] Not all women's groups (or even the majority) who gave evidence to this Committee supported the availability of birth control, even on a limited scale, or abortion. But some did, notably the Sex Hygiene and Birth Regulation Society which sought outright to promote birth control. The objects of the Society are discussed by Elsie Freeman (later Locke) in the first issue of *Woman Today* under the heading 'Happier Parenthood' (4.12). Here she emphasises the lack of attention paid to conception compared with maternity and child welfare. Freeman advocates freely available birth control, noting especially the greater difficulty working people had in gaining access to reliable methods. She concludes her case by reassuring the public that the overall aim 'does not mean that our population will be reduced, but that children will be born under the very best conditions possible.'

Woman Today was founded in 1937 by Elsie Freeman (previously editor of the *Working Woman*), with a group of women of diverse political and feminist interests. The magazine stood 'for Peace, Freedom and Progress' and was designed to bring political and social issues to a wider public of women than party papers such as the *Working Woman*. It also sought to provide a wider forum for the discussion of issues of particular relevance to women than did the radical *Tomorrow* magazine.[10] *Woman Today* lasted for three years. Like many magazines of its kind it struggled to find subscribers in sufficient numbers, and was underfinanced from the beginning. Political tensions within the editorial group exacerbated these difficulties, which revolved around Elsie Freeman's membership of the New Zealand Communist Party. Nevertheless, the quality of articles in *Woman Today* during its three years is enormously impresssive. Robin Hyde was a contributor, as was Jessie Mackay. The selection here gives only a hint of the breadth of subjects covered.

Peace was also an international issue of increasing urgency in the late 1930s. Women's groups world-wide had taken a particular interest in the peace negotiated at the end of the First World War, and watched with dismay as the world became divided into antagonistic blocks in the 1930s. Miriam Soljak's article (4.17) in one of the last issues of *Woman Today* was a vital call for women to unite for peace.

The language in which issues were discussed in this period is distinctly different from that used either before or after. Terms like 'women's rights', and the language of the late nineteenth century, which referred to women's 'special nature' or 'special mission', are almost completely absent. Writers tended to be more pragmatic, concerned with the objects of campaigns and details of issues. The idea of equality between women and men was more in evidence.

1. Dorothy Page, 'Women and Nationality', in Barbara Brookes, Charlotte Macdonald and Margaret Tennant (eds), Women in History, Wellington, 1986, pp.157-175
2. ibid.
3. Jean Drage, 'The Invisible Representatives', Research paper in Politics, Victoria University of Wellington, 1992
4. Sandra Coney, 'Ellen Melville', BNZW, pp.435-442
5. Edna Macky (d.1971) came to New Zealand from the United States in 1913. She became the first Auckland secretary of the Howard League for Penal Reform and founded the Fabian Club. Later she founded both the New Zealand Travel Club movement and the Penwomen's Club. (ATL 'Biographies', 1971, vol. 2, p.117)
6. Mary Findlay, Tooth and Nail, Wellington, 1974 and Auckland, 1989
7. Phillippa Mein Smith, Maternity in Dispute, Wellington, 1986
8. Charlotte Parkes, 'The Impact of the Medicalisation of New Zealand's Maternity Services on Women's Experience of Childbirth, 1904–1937, in Linda Bryder (ed.), A Healthy Country, Wellington, 1991, pp.165–180
9. Barbara Brookes, 'Reproductive Rights', in Barbara Brookes, Charlotte Macdonald and Margaret Tennant (eds), Women in History, Wellington, 1986, pp.119–136
10. Andrew Cutler, 'Tomorrow Magazine and New Zealand Politics, 1934–1940', New Zealand Journal of History, vol. 24, no. 1 (April 1990), pp.22–44

Sources and Further Reading

Barrowman, Rachel. *A Popular Culture: the arts and the Left in New Zealand, 1930-1950*, Wellington, 1991
Brookes, Barbara. 'Reproductive Rights: the debate over abortion and birth control in the 1930s',

in Barbara Brookes, Charlotte Macdonald and Margaret Tennant (eds), *Women in History*, Wellington, 1986, pp.119-136

Cutler, Andrew. '*Tomorrow* Magazine and New Zealand Politics, 1934-1940', *New Zealand Journal of History*, vol.24, no.1 (April 1990), pp.22-44

Drage, Jean. 'The Invisible Representatives: Women members of Hospital/Area Health Boards', Research paper in Politics, Victoria University of Wellington, 1992

Ehrhardt, Penny. 'Women for "Peace, Freedom and Progress": *Woman Today* magazine, 1937-39', Honours research essay, Victoria University of Wellington, 1990

Findlay, Mary. *Tooth and Nail*, Wellington, 1974, and Auckland, 1989

Hyde, Robin. *Disputed Ground*. Introduced and selected by Gillian Boddy & Jacqueline Matthews, Wellington, 1991

Kuitert, Veronica. 'Ellen Melville, 1882-1946', MA research essay, Auckland University, 1986

Page, Dorothy. 'Women and Nationality: Feminist organisations in the interwar period', in Barbara Brookes, Charlotte Macdonald and Margaret Tennant (eds), *Women in History*, Wellington, 1986, pp.157-175

Parkes, Charlotte. 'The Impact of the Medicalisation of New Zealand's Maternity Services on Women's Experience of Childbirth, 1904-1937', in Linda Bryder (ed.), *A Healthy Country? Essays on the social history of medicine in New Zealand*, Wellington, 1991, pp.165-180

Sanderson, Kay. 'Mary Barkas', *BNZW*, pp.45-47

Smith, Phillipa Mein. *Maternity in Dispute: New Zealand, 1920-1939*, Wellington, 1986

Smith, Philippa Mein. 'Mortality in Childbirth in the 1920s and 1930s', in Barbara Brookes, Charlotte Macdonald and Margaret Tennant (eds), *Women in History*, Wellington, 1986, pp.137-155

Woman Today, (1937-39) (available for purchase on microfiche from ATL)

4.1.   What N.Z. Women Want
National Council of Women Bulletin (1928)

New Zealand women are working for:

(1) Women Police (long promised, but promise still unfulfilled).

(2) Non-differentiation between men and women teachers with regard to status and salary.

(3) Women on juries.

(4) Woman as co-censor of films.

(5) Women on the Prisons Board.

(6) Farm colony for sexual offenders.

(7) Separation of Child Welfare Branch from Education Department, but under the same Ministry.

(8) Removal of sex disqualification in regard to the Civil Service.

(9) Urging the government to send the full delegation to the League of Nations Assembly, one member to be a woman.

(10) General improvement of conditions for school children, such as smaller classes, better buildings, etc.

National Council of Women Bulletin, vol. 1, no. 4 (October 1928), p.[3]

4.2.   Why All Women Should Support Labour
by Edna Graham Macky (1928)

Woman's cause and Labour's cause are one and the same. For centuries women have brought children into the world at great cost to themselves, physically and economically, making untold sacrifices that their little ones might grow to maturity. Up to the present they have been given no security as to the continued welfare of these products of their love and care, nor have they been given any say in the direction of their affairs after they have gone out into the world. War, starvation and cruelty have been meted out to them. Labouring men like the women, have borne the burden of the day, toiling and sweating that the necessities of life might be produced and their families fed, but they have had no say as to what is to be the ultimate use of their productions, nor in the economic affairs of the community.

Women and Labour have been submissive and long suffering. They have been told that their lot is to obey and not direct. However, with the education of women and the enlightenment of Labour, these two great portions of humanity have begun to question why they have been kept under and made use of for so long. The more they question the more they find that the interests of women and Labour are inseparable. They both work on the constructive principle, and consequently abhor waste and destruction. It is to provide food and shelter for their wives and children that men labour, so whatever affects the cause of Labour affects also the economic position of women.

Labour's platform

The New Zealand Labour Party has recognised this great partnership by including in its published Objective and Platform the following articles, specially designed for the benefit of all women:

1. The removal of the political disabilities of women.
2. Free medical, dental and maternity attention. (Many women are invalids for life for the lack of proper medical attention at childbirth, not being able to afford the present high medical fees.)
3. The establishment of a State Housing Department for the purpose of providing better homes for the people and at less cost by the elimination of private profit. (Women benefit particularly by decent home conditions at moderate rents.)
4. The extension of the pension to include all widows and incapacitated citizens (usually looked after and supported by women).
5. Perfect equality between the sexes in all departments of life, with equal rights of the parents to the children, unless proved to be unfit. (At present the father of the child has prior claim.)
6. The National Endowment of Motherhood.
7. Equal pay for equal work for both sexes in all departments of commercial, industrial and professional employment. (Underpayment of women results in 'sweating' and immorality.)

Labour's idealism

All fair-minded women will admit that these objectives of the Labour Party come under the heading of advanced feminist ideals and reveal idealism, consideration and forethought beyond the conservative policies of other political parties.

All conservative Governments (and Reform is decidedly conservative in spite of its name) stand for the continuation of the present capitalistic system, with extremes of wealth and greed on one hand and cringing poverty and underpaid labour on the other. Labour Governments (and all of them are more or less Socialistic) stand for a more even distribution of wealth, a right to work and a fair return for that work, favouring at the same time humane and progressive legislation.

Conservative Governments have always been militaristic, for ill-gotten gains need to be protected by armed force on account of the greed and envy and desperation which is the natural result of such a system. Labour and Socialist Governments favour productive and constructive principles, a friendly and peaceful relationship between all peoples, and are therefore opposed to war and all the waste and destruction that it entails. Between these two systems of government a choice must be made, and the choice will be put before all citizens of the Dominion at the next election, when Labour and Reform contend for supremacy.

It was not just 'pig-headedness' and old-fashioned ideas that caused the conservative Governments of the world to fight against the franchise of women. No, indeed! The military-minded men among the capitalists who use the political machine to further their ends, knew instinctively that women, once awakened, would not countenance the false values that have been imposed upon the world. Every true woman would rather have love than wealth, and would place life before property, for she knows the preciousness of the life that she brings into the world.

Trade competition main cause of war

When women realise that the foundation cause of all the wars of the past century is the fight for trade between the nations, then they will refuse to become parties to such crimes. The greed for gain has taken investors and traders into foreign lands, and to protect those interests the political leaders, who owe their power and positions to vested interests, will go to any extreme, even to the extent of war, with its consequent sacrifice, i.e. of millions of innocent lives. The South African war was in the beginning a dispute with the Dutch over the rich trade of South Africa. One of the main causes of the late war was the desire of the European countries for supremacy in the world markets for raw materials and sale of manufactured goods, and the jealousies engendered by the competition. The assassination of the Serbian Archduke and other dramatic incidents were merely surface events capitalised for the purpose of propaganda. The recent trouble with China had to do with financial interests in the Orient involving practically all the trading nations. It is really wonderful how wealthy politicians and incidentally owners of newspapers can work upon the patriotism of the populace to arouse feelings of hatred towards the people of any country with which they at the moment happen to be in commercial conflict. An important feature of the Labour Party's platform is a direct bid for the peace of the world. Not only does it aim at the repeal of the Military Service Act and the Defence Act, Acts whereby the manpower of the nation can be conscripted at a moment's notice and without the consent of the parties concerned, but it also guarantees wholehearted support of all efforts to secure disarmament by agreement amongst the nations. The Labour Party's manifesto regarding international peace and fraternity displays the highest idealism that the mind of man can conceive. Labour supporters are pledged to work for:

1. The industrial and political unity of the workers of all countries for the purpose of superseding capitalism by an industrial democracy under which each country will make its contribution to world progress through a league of all the peoples.

2. The unity of all workers in all countries in a world federation of peoples for the purpose of peacefully organising all the resources of the world for the peoples of the world, and thus ending the exploitation by private capitalism. Affirmation of the principle of self-determination to be applied to all races for the purpose of terminating the ruthless plundering of nations by modern imperialists.

Financial gain and its resultant power is the dominant factor in the present world of politics, and if women of all lands do not insist on a reversal of this situation, the world will be faced with the most terrible war ever imagined by the old Hebrew prophets. Air bombs and poison gas will bring extinction to the human race and our present civilisation. Students of political economy and world affairs mark the Pacific for the scene of conflict. European trade is pretty well stable and satisfied, but it is to the teeming East that the great trading nations are looking for profit. We haven't voted a million pounds towards the Singapore Base for nothing!

Women must throw their weight on the side of Peace, and at once.

The failure of the Reform Party

Turning our attention from the big international questions to the particular problems of the Dominion and reviewing the present situation, what do we find?

For sixteen years the Conservative Party has been in power in New Zealand, and with big stick methods, and Orders-in-Council it has had every opportunity of carrying out its policy. Yet we have distress and unemployment on all sides.

There is surely something wrong with our economic system and Government when a country like New Zealand, beautifully situated, with healthful climate, 98 per cent British stock, with plenty of land and labour available for the production of food, should still be subject to unnecessary suffering, distress and unemployment with its consequent poverty. An up-to-date British-American trade journal quotes New Zealand as being the richest country in the world per capita, with Switzerland second, and the USA third. In spite of the reputed wealth of the individual citizen and ideal conditions for food production, distress and unemployment is more acute to-day than it has ever been in the history of the Dominion.

Labour's fight for progress

It is easily seen that the regime of these sixteen years has not advanced the welfare of the Dominion as a whole. New Zealand once led the world in advanced legislation, but that was in the time of the Seddon Liberal-Labour Government. Franchise for women came in during that period, also old age pensions. Any recent reforms in the way of humane or progressive legislation have been due in the most part to the work of the Labour members: for instance, pensions for the blind and improved care of prisoners were accomplished owing to the persistent agitation of the Labour members.

The Labour Party's proposal for payment of an allowance to mothers sufficient to provide the necessities for each child was whittled down to the absurdly inadequate sum of two shillings per week. Other legislation directly due to the work of the Labour members is the improved payments under the Workers' Compensation Act, the increase in the old age pensions, the provision of houses, the Rent Restriction Act, and practically all the legislation introduced for the lifting of the standard of life – and particularly that of the women and children – has been due to the humanitarian foundation of Labour's policy, so ably advocated by the Labour members of Parliament.

Misapplication of resources diverting money into non-productive channels, and the wrong attitude of Reform political leaders towards the people as a whole, is the cause of most of our troubles. Crime and immorality would greatly decline if the importance of the conditions of life of the people were recognised, and extreme wealth and extreme poverty abolished by the reorganisation of our production and distribution system so that the wealth would be paid to all in proportion to their service. It is high time the economic conditions in New Zealand were changed. Remember, the women are always the greatest sufferers under these conditions.

Labour, constructive not destructive

The Labour Party is attracting to its ranks some of New Zealand's deepest thinkers and economists who are bent upon solving the problems that confront the nation. Land policies, insurance schemes covering unemployment, banking and industrial adjustments, constructive social service methods (in place of the present degenerating charity), are all being carefully and earnestly studied with a view to improving the general living conditions of the people. There is no problem on earth that is not FIRST AND FOREMOST woman's problem, for she is the mother of men , and what happens to men in any department of life is her undying concern. Women have been sidetracked from taking an interest in politics because they do not realise that it is upon POLITICS THAT SOCIAL WELFARE HINGES, that it is upon POLITICS THAT INTERNATIONAL PEACE HINGES. If legislation dealing with production, trade, land values and wages is not sound, then the home life of the individual is affected. If our industrial and political relationship with other nations is not right, then war and dissension are inevitable, though we women as individuals shout until we are hoarse in protest. Women must work with men, and political machinery is absolutely necessary. The Labour Party championing Peace, does not favour wars and revolutions by political force, but aims by inspiration, legislation and conversion of public opinion to bring about 'the conquest of political power, local and national, the extension of the organisation of the workers in industry together with the co-operation of all who render social service, to the end that society may be controlled in the interests of all the people.' (Quoted from the official Objective and Platform of the Labour Party of New Zealand, dated Napier, April 18-19-20, 1927.)

Woman's cause and Labour's cause are inseparable, and in this great partnership lies the hope of the world.

It is every woman's duty to support the Labour Party in this their great fight for the new order that must in time supersede the old.

Why All Women Should Support Labour: Identical interests of women and Labour, *Wellington, 1928*

4.3. Women and the Labour Movement
by Elizabeth R. McCombs (1933)

It is now forty years since women were granted the franchise in New Zealand. Ours was the first of the British-speaking countries to give women the right to take part in the election of Parliamentary representatives.

In his book *State Experiments in New Zealand,* one of New Zealand's statesmen, the Hon W. P. Reeves, said: 'So one fine morning the women of New Zealand woke up and found themselves enfranchised'. That sounds very well, but in actual fact the gaining of the franchise was not so easy.

True, the women of New Zealand were not asleep. Those of them who settled early in New Zealand were inspired by the same high ideals as many of the men whom they accompanied to these shores.

The early laws of this country were designed to give protection from many of the abuses that had grown up in older lands. Responsibility for this was not confined to the men. The women also had high ideals. Desiring a greater freedom than they had known in older lands, they wished to help make the laws that governed this young country, and the movement for women's franchise was early afoot. A petition signed by many thousands was presented to Parliament, and the franchise was actually granted in 1893. It was not until fourteen years ago, however, that women were granted the right of election to Parliament, and now in 1933 the first woman has been admitted to the councils of the nation; but New Zealand is far behind many other countries in utilising

the services of women to assist in the government of the country. Even to-day here, women are not yet eligible to sit as members of the Upper House. It was left to the Legislative Council to decide whether they should become eligible for nomination, and the members of that august assembly decided, in their wisdom, that this privilege should not be granted until our 'House of Lords' became elective. Can anything more illogical be imagined? Surely if the electors should have the sole right to say whether women may become members of the Council, it is logical that they should now decide what men may sit there also. The Labour Party will settle that matter when it comes into power by abolishing the nominated Chamber altogether. Meanwhile it should not be within the power of any non-elective body to veto the decisions of the people's representatives. The power of veto should reside in the hands of the people themselves, and this could be accomplished by means of a general referendum law giving 10 per cent of the people the right to demand a plebiscite vote on any proposed legislation, or the right to initiate legislation.

At the present time there are many electors who hold strong views regarding certain public questions; many who are taking an interest in economic reform. Take, for instance, the students of the Douglas Social Credit Scheme. Under such a law as the Labour Party proposes, the students of that system would be able to demand that Parliament should debate that subject on the Floor of the House. Or when the Government took power to extend the life of Parliament, under the Labour Party's proposed law the people could have insisted that Parliament take a vote of the people before it extended its own life for a year.

The Labour Party stands for a scientific system of election. Under Proportional Representation, such as is now on the Labour Party's platform, women will be able to secure the representation they desire. Parliament will become what it is claimed to be – representative of the whole of the people.

I am sometimes asked by women why I joined the Labour Party. My experience in public life has taught me that if one wishes to get things done it is necessary to co-operate with others. It is ineffectual to work alone. The Labour Party stands for many of the reforms in which I am interested. It is the only Party that is out to make more people happy, and happy in a better way while preserving what is good in the existing order. The Labour Party is trying to bring about a better order of society in which the good things of life shall be enjoyed by all who render social service.

Many of the reforms for which the women's societies are working are already written into the Platform of the Labour Party. The Labour Party stands for:

1 The removal of the political disabilities of women.
2 The extension of pensions to include all widows and incapacitated persons.
3 Perfect equality between the sexes in all departments of life, with equal rights of both parents, unless proved unfit, to the guardianship of the children.
4 The national endowment of motherhood.
5 Equal pay for equal work for both sexes.
6 Wholehearted support for all efforts to secure disarmament by agreement between the nations.

These are matters of general principle.

The Labour Party offers practical solutions of many problems now confronting the Dominion. Take, for instance, the problem of unemployment. Does anyone really think that in New Zealand that problem has been dealt with scientifically or satisfactorily? The lack of commonsense in dealing with the whole matter is almost unbelievable. When I think of the present Government and unemployment, I am reminded that there are ten Ministers of the Crown, each of them with twelve thousand million brain cells – all unemployed.

The downright injustice of the Government's attitude in taxing women to the extent of £750,000, and at the same time taking up an attitude of indifference towards unemployed women and girls, is nothing short of a scandal. The fact that the Government has been so callous in its attitude towards unemployed women has aroused the indignation of all thinking women in the Dominion, including members of the Government's own party.

Every little working girl earning ten shillings per week is taxed on her wages. If she gets board as well as wages she is taxed also on the amount assessed for board. If she is a restaurant worker and is given meals, the meals are assessed at 1/- each, and she is taxed on that.

In one case where the meals were sold to customers at 9d, the proprietor stated that the meals supplied to the waitresses were not worth so much because the girls partook of what remained after the customers were served, yet those meals are assessed at 1/- and the girls are taxed accordingly.

Hospital nurses working six and even seven days of 8½ hours a week are taxed on their wages and on their board. In some cases junior nurses are getting only 7/3 weekly. When these girls are unemployed, in some centres they are given two weeks' work at 5/- weekly and then stood down for two weeks. Some of them are assisted also with meals and something towards room rent in stand-down weeks. Is it any wonder that many of these girls are driven to the point of desperation under such conditions?

Another aspect of the unemployment problem that calls for the sympathy of women is the fact that no provision whatever is made for youths over sixteen and under twenty. All boys are taxed upon their earnings. If they are given board in addition to their wages, they are taxed upon that also. If they are given board and no wages, they are taxed on the board. If they have incomes they are taxed on their incomes. Yet boys between sixteen and twenty get no assistance whatever from the Unemployment Board.

Until a boy reaches the age of sixteen, his father, if he is a relief worker, is given work in respect of that boy; but directly the boy reaches the age of sixteen, that work ceases. Yet no work is found for the boy. The result of this neglect on the part of the Government is that the boy is thrown on his own resources. From the Government's point of view he practically ceases to exist. Since educational facilities have also been reduced, and many of the sons of working people have been thereby deprived of secondary education, a serious position has arisen. To meet this, voluntary organisations of business men have undertaken to provide recreation and other means of keeping these boys off the streets. Of course there are large numbers who, by their parents' efforts and even by their own, are making good in spite of adverse conditions; but there is no doubt that some of these lads are falling into evil ways.

With regard to the problem as it affects the whole community, we have been watching over again the application of the old remedy of placing an ambulance down in the valley instead of a fence at the top of the precipice, and a very inadequate ambulance it has been.

The fact that the depression as it developed in New Zealand was aggravated unnecessarily by the mistaken methods adopted to deal with certain phases of it, is one on which some of us hold strong views. Take, for instance, the wage-reduction policy which brought about further huge curtailment of purchasing power. In a country already suffering from that very cause this was disastrous. It is estimated that the total loss in buying capacity occasioned by the wage and salary reductions was not less than £12,000,000.

The cessation of many necessary public works drove numbers of men out of employment. To take men off necessary and reproductive public works and put them on to unnecessary and unproductive works seems little short of madness.

The Government's ill-advised attempts to assist certain wealthy classes of the community have also increased our difficulties. The main fact that confronts us now, however, is that this country is passing through the worst period of its history, and it is imperative that some action be taken in the immediate future to bring New Zealand out of her difficulties.

The Labour Party has a constructive plan which provides assistance to primary and secondary industries and includes all the useful people of the community.

There are at present, according to the latest figures, 80,000 unemployed in New Zealand. This number does not include women and girls, nor does it include boys under 20, for whom no provision is made.

It has been estimated that the actual number of persons unemployed in the Dominion, if we include women and youths, is nearly double the official figures. Added to these there are a very large number of men and women who are working part time or half time. These are earning in many cases no more than relief rates of pay.

This group of workers working part time probably equals or exceeds the number of totally unemployed. Is it any wonder that the business of the country suffers when nearly a quarter of its adult population with all their dependants are deprived of the means of purchasing sufficient of even the bare necessaries of life?

Private citizens in every city and town are trying to mitigate the sufferings of those in desperate circumstances. Relief depots and soup kitchens are everywhere. The people generally are now protesting against the continual appeals made for private charity.

Under the Labour Party's plan real work for real wages would take the place of charity. You know the story of the tramp who was asked if he had never been offered work. He said, 'Only once. Apart from that I've met nothing but kindness.' Well, kindness is what the unemployed are getting. It is true that they are getting plenty of it; but what they want is real work and real wages to vary the monotony.

I cannot believe that the people of New Zealand are willing to tolerate these conditions of poverty and charity much longer. We have traditions of independence, initiative and resourcefulness, and we can alter our conditions without waiting for the world to recover. It has been amply demonstrated that measures such as wage reductions, high exchange, and sales tax have served only to increase the difficulties for most sections of the people.

So far as this country is concerned, Empire Conferences and discussions have borne no fruit.

We want a new outlook. There must be no repetition of past mistakes. Inaction cannot be tolerated. If we are to wait for better conditions in New Zealand until there is world recovery, then we must make up our minds to a long siege.

There is an old proverb which says that a journey of a thousand miles begins with one step. The Labour Party says, 'Let us take that step even if we don't go the full distance.'

The Labour Party has repeatedly asserted that the way to restore normal conditions is to build up the buying power of the mass of the people. As a matter of fact, we have precedent to guide us. Forty years ago John Ballance and Richard Seddon in somewhat similar circumstances lifted this country out of the depression through which it was then passing. They put in hand a programme of public works and land settlement, and so gave work and

adequate wages to large numbers of the people. Under their administration many progressive measures were placed upon the Statute Books which ensured to this country a long period of prosperity.

New Zealand led the way in progressive legislation. Let us regain our ideal of an educated and enlightened democracy living under conditions worthy of the people of God's Own Country.

The New Zealand Labour Party's plan includes a scheme for stabilised prices for primary producers. It includes the fostering and building up of secondary industries now in existence, and the establishment of further industries suitable to the country. It includes the assurance of adequate wages for all classes of workers to provide a reasonable standard of life and the enjoyment of the advantages of the age in which we live.

I think I need hardly say that I think it entirely fitting that the first woman elected to the New Zealand Parliament should be a member of the Labour Party, because I have shown that the Labour Party stands for justice for women, equality between the sexes, and also for most, if not all, of the humanitarian ideals of women.

The women of New Zealand generally believe in enlightened humanitarianism and commonsense in government, and I confidently depend upon their co-operation with the Labour Party's efforts to restore peace and prosperity to our much loved land.

Women and the Labour Movement, *Auckland, 1933, pp.4–7*

4.4. Why Don't the Women Come Forward?
New Zealand Woman's Weekly (1934)

Why haven't we more than one woman in Parliament? There are a myriad matters that need the urgent attention of women – matters which men cannot fully comprehend or understand, and which, consequently, do not interest them. Yet, with all our large feminine population, we have so little support of our own sex that we can number only one woman Parliamentarian to represent the whole of New Zealand's womanhood! In our clubs and other social gatherings, we talk glibly of feminine emancipation, of feminine equality, of feminine freedom – but what is the use of it all, if there is no support, no co-operation, no encourage-

ment, from our own sex? Are New Zealand women prepared to remain in the rut that they are in? Are they prepared to see themselves – and their daughters – pushed farther and farther back into nonentity? Are they prepared to sacrifice the hard-won emancipation of their mothers, allowing themselves to be overruled and swamped by men alone? And yet, this is what is already beginning to happen – there is a big impetus overseas for men to take more and more this attitude – if women do not take the initiative and make a firm stand for their own rights in life. If life is worth living at all, is it not worth fighting for? And, when there are women who are disinterested and unselfish enough to sacrifice their own pleasures of social whirl and pleasantry to devote themselves instead to the welfare of their lesser favoured sisters – and to that of their children – do they not deserve all the support and encouragement that can be given by their own sex – the sex for whom they are fighting?

It is only natural that a section of the community should be most interested in those matters which directly affect them, and that they should, therefore, strive to improve all conditions connected with and affecting those matters. And who should be better fitted to ameliorate and advance the conditions of feminine welfare than women themselves? Yet not every woman is either capable or has the necessary time to devote to such affairs; but every woman can do her 'bit' to help; and the greatest way in which any woman can help – other than by practical participation – is by giving her wholehearted support. Conditions affecting women are in no way so perfect that they need no further attention; they are so much the reverse that they need the attention of every woman.

The conditions governing women in industry and in the commercial world are anything but satisfactory Because women have, throughout the ages, until the beginning of this century, been the mere chattel of man and considered as his inferior in every way, they are still penalised through their sex – and consequently they and their children suffer. No matter how capable and how efficient a woman worker may be, because she is a woman she receives a much lower wage than men doing the same work; while sometimes she is even prohibited from earning her living at all in certain spheres. It is only in very recent times that there were any regulations affecting humane conditions for women workers – and for child workers, too; nowadays, in this Dominion no girl can be employed in a factory unless she has attained the age of sixteen. Fifty years ago, women, and children of ten and twelve, worked from ten to sixteen hours daily in large, densely packed, dark factories, for mere pittances that scarcely kept body and soul together. To-day, there is almost as much exploitation of child and female labour, and, owing to the world-wide depression, a far greater advantage has been taken of it. At any time, when there is a surplus of labour on the markets, wages drop accordingly, but, as the cost of living, relatively speaking, has not dropped there is still existent much hardship. In all the big cities female labour has, to some extent, taken the place of male labour – for, with the vast numbers of women and girls, who have been forced to earn their own living owing to the changed conditions of their parents, employers have been able to obtain cheaper labour. In the commercial world this is especially noticeable: men have been dismissed from their positions and girls taken in their place – not because they are more efficient, but simply because the employers have considered they can exploit them by cutting their wages: so that one may find, for instance, many a girl doing clerical work for anything from fifteen to thirty shillings weekly, for which, if a man were employed, he would receive treble that amount.

Yet, the employers are not wholly to blame in the matter; it is only human nature that overhead expenses be curtailed as much as possible; rather is it the fault of the women themselves – the disinterest they show in all conditions affecting women generally. Remuneration should not be governed by sex, but by efficiency – as in America; there the employer considers only whether the applicant is a good worker worthy of the wages he is offering, irrespective of sex. But, so long as New Zealand women are prepared to sit back and take little or no interest in conditions directly affecting themselves, so long will the penalisation of sex in industry continue.

What is more important still, these conditions will continue while the present apathy of New Zealand women continues, so that the existent state of affairs to-day will react directly on our children, penalising them through their mothers; and, what affects the children, affects the whole nation – for the children of to-day are the parents and the citizens of to-morrow. The longer feminine apathy continues, the longer will it be before any changes are effected – and the more difficult it will be to put anything into effect.

In New Zealand to-day there are small bands of women with vision and capability, who, realising that the present state of affairs will become more and more detrimental to their sex if allowed to continue unchecked, are devoting themselves to the amelioration of conditions adversely affecting both women and children. But – they cannot work without support; and the only concerted support they are likely to obtain will be from those directly affected by changed conditions – from the women voters themselves. Our mothers fought for the franchise and the greater freedom that we enjoy to-day – are we, their daughters, going to allow all that to pass, unheeded, from us? Are we going to permit a return of the industrial, economic and social conditions of fifty years ago? Are we going to allow the Parliamentarians of our country – all men except for one powerless woman (for what can one woman do when pitted against such overwhelming odds?) – gradually to put into force the degradatory legislation that is influencing both Italy and Germany, wherein women are being forced out of all practical work back into the precinct of the home? – where they become powerless, domestic prisoners, nonentities – while their children (both girls and boys), are reared according to man's ideas, and totally irrespective of what the mothers who created them might think.

'Why don't the women come forward?'

New Zealand Woman's Weekly, *29 March 1934, p.3*

4.5. Maori Women Enthusiastic
Working Woman (1934)

Seventeen Maori women and five men gathered in the Mormon Hall, Huntly West, on September 6th and listened with great interest while Comrades Elsie Farrelly and Mrs Baldwin told them of the forthcoming National Conference of working women.

There is great hardship among the Maoris owing to the 'stand down week'. One comrade said that forty adults in their home had to live on the son's relief wages of 26/- per week for three weeks.

However, they realised the value of the Conference in fighting for better conditions and elected a delegate for the Conference; they also formed themselves into a Committee which will meet weekly, Mrs Baldwin to assist them on behalf of the Huntly Committee. At a later meeting it was decided to send two delegates.

The Pakeha Committee of Huntly and the Maori Committee are co-operating in running dances to raise the necessary cash to send delegates from both Committees.

Mrs Baldwin is assisting in sewing and knitting classes to assist the Maori women.

Working Woman, *vol.1, no.8 (October 1934), p.3*

4.6. What is the Working Women's Movement?
by Elsie Freeman (1935)

The Working Women's Movement is a broad non-Party organisation founded at the first National Conference of Working Women in October 1934. We interest ourselves in all matters of concern to working women and welcome membership or assistance from any women willing to co-operate for even one of these ends. We support this paper because of its lead to the working class and this page has been set aside for our own use. The Secretary will welcome correspondence, questions or contributions for this page from any reader of the *Working Woman*.

Our national conference

Do you want to see our movement grow? Do you want to see it become a strong national body and extend to all towns, your own included?

If so, you will be interested in our National Conference, and the first thing you will do will be to write to the Secretary and ask for fuller particulars.

We want delegates not only from our own locals, but from other organisations interested, and from towns where there is as yet no organisation, but a few women who are willing to send someone to learn how to start.

The time will be New Year and the agenda will include discussion on the work of the past year and the plans for the future, work among women in industry, building the movement, the fight against fascism and war, amendments to the programme and election of the new National Committee.

Any suggestions for improvement will be welcomed. It is hoped that the conference will be followed by a training camp at a pleasure resort where we can form friendships in the Movement and have friendly discussions. This depends on our securing suitable accommodation.

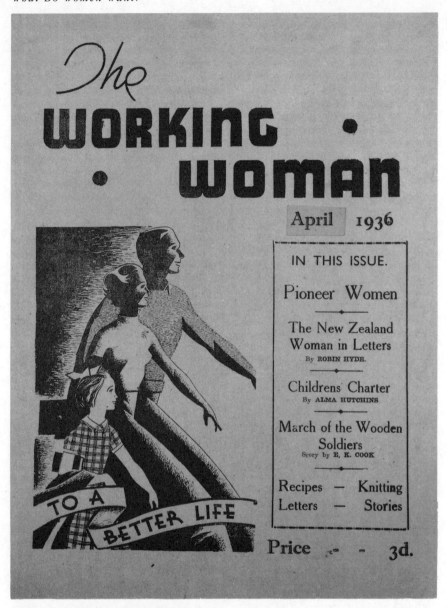

The Working Woman

April 1936

IN THIS ISSUE.

Pioneer Women

The New Zealand
Woman in Letters
By ROBIN HYDE.

Childrens Charter
By ALMA HUTCHINS

March of the Wooden
Soldiers
Story by E. K. COOK

Recipes — Knitting
Letters — Stories

TO A BETTER LIFE

Price - - 3d.

Early cover of the *Working Woman*, Elsie Freeman's paper produced during the early 1930s in conjunction with the Working Women's Movement. *Private Collection*

In order to finance the Conference and Camp we are organising a competition with excellent prizes: First, a Christmas Hamper; Second, a turkey and a ham; Third, a Xmas cake; and four consolation prizes of chickens. Tickets at 3d are available, and you can help by taking a book and getting a few donations. Competition closes on December 7th and decision given on December 15th.

This Conference should be a milestone in the history of the working women. Join in the good work!

Working Women's Movement
OUR GUIDE TO ACTION
Against Fascism and War.
For a Women's Delegation to the Soviet Union.
Equal Pay for Equal Work.

No Discrimination against Married or Single Women in Employment Relief.
Support the N.U.W.M. Demands for the Unemployed.
Free Medical, Dental, Surgical and Maternity Attention.
Equal Facilities for Education in Town and Country and Provision of Books, Uniforms and Meals for School Children.
No Discrimination Between Maori and Pakeha.
Free Dissemination of Birth Control Knowledge and the Legalisation of Abortion.
Social Insurance for all Workers at the expense of the State and Employers.

Working Woman, vol.3, no.1 (November 1935), p.8

4.7. High Prices and Why
Working Woman (1935)

Twenty years ago prices were rising. The cost of foodstuffs added another burden to the housewife already suffering heavily from the war. It was not enough that her menfolk should be taken thousands of miles overseas to offer their lives in order to 'protect the home' – she too had to fight for her home, against the profiteers who endeavoured to place the necessities of life beyond her reach.

Such necessities as sugar, butter, meat, clothing, and boots were sold at extortionate prices. In England necessities were rationed. In Germany and Central Europe, the population went hungry. It was the toll of war.

The wealth of the world, over which a mere handful had control, was utilised for the sole purpose of carrying on the slaughter by which alone they could maintain their profits. A war to save democracy they called it, while the grip of capitalism was being more firmly fixed on to the workers and colonial peoples of almost every country in the world. And against this ring of imperialist plunderers the housewife had to fight for the maintenance of her home. To-day, once again, prices are rising. 'Potatoes, meat, butter, cheese, sugar, soap, all cost more dearly, yet there is no increase in the money coming into the home. Economy of necessities is no solution. Prices must be reduced. How?

As during the war years, prices are rising for a reason. Butter and meat are dear, we are told because of the high exchange – a contrivance which does not really benefit the farmer at all, but which does benefit the financial and marketing monopolies, which are interested in the maintenance of the present order of capitalism. War threatens – the supplies of butter from European sources, such as Denmark, are rushed to the possible belligerents, where better profits are promised. Up goes New Zealand butter. The marketing concerns pocket nine-tenths of the increase, the small rise the farmer gets is delivered to the mortgagee and the housewife searches for a way of keeping down the cost of running her home.

Perhaps more significant is the increase in the price of soap. All fats are needed for maintenance of troops and are stored for this purpose. Glycerine, the other principal ingredient of soap, is essential both for the manufacture of explosives and for tempering steel.

These high prices are indirectly filling the pockets of the manufacturers and distributors and enabling them to extend their profits still further. Indirectly they are assisting in the preparation of a new world war by which alone such profits can be maintained.

By uniting against high prices, by showing how they are connected with war preparations, by rousing greater and greater numbers to fight for a better standard of living, we are making it possible to organise the struggle against war. Indirectly, by taking back for ourselves some of the wealth which the working class have created, we are lessening the wealth of those who would utilise it for war purposes.

Much can be done. We can refuse to buy from those firms which expect impossible prices. We can make agreements with storekeepers who are prepared to assist the fight for such reductions. We can use them to force the monopolist trading concerns to reduce their profits.

Already in Wellington a beginning has been made. It is our task to extend this battle not only for our homes but for world peace.

Working Woman, vol.3, no.2 (December 1935), p.3

4.8. Unemployed Single Women by M. Foskett (1935)

Especially significant in New Zealand at the present time is the number of women and girls out of employment. This problem continues to grow but has so far been kept in the background. Through lack of publicity and actual information the public is scarcely aware that a relief scheme in respect of unemployed women and girls exists. An occasional paragraph in the social notes of the daily press regarding a meeting of the Women's Unemployment Committee is their only guide and many people regard it as a civic enterprise and do not know that it is just a side line of the Government's instituted from the goodness of their heart.

While men's unemployment relief schemes come under the direct supervision of the Unemployment Board, the granting of relief to women and girls is done through the medium of Women's Unemployment Committees. As a guide to its policy on this question the Board relies solely on the advice of a Woman's Advisory Committee of three. This Committee works nationally and from time to time makes a detailed investigation of the position. In this connection a few months ago a member of this committee toured the Dominion advocating a reduction in relief from 7/6 to 5/- a week in an endeavour to effect a saving in relief expenditure. Some members of the Christchurch Women's Unemployment Committee were in favour of this reduction, one member stating that the rate of 7/6 per week made relief 'too attractive' for the girls, as it lessened their incentive to find work.

Figures speak

The only facts available as to the number of registered unemployed girls are contained in the reports submitted to Parliament by the Minister of Employment, and no figures of registration were published. In 1933 the grant was £15,279 10s 9d, and registrations on the 31st July totalled 975. The following year the grant was reduced to £11,410, there being 478 registrations on 30th April.

The grant for the year ending 31st March 1935 was £10,497. A summary of the registrations of the month of March is as follows:

Previous occupations	Registrations
Office	14
Shop	20
Factory	50
Dressmakers and Tailoresses	19
Trained Nurse	7
Cook General	15
Housemaid and waitress	18
Milliner	4
Domestic duties	182
Total	329

Age Groups	
16 to 20 years	131
21 to 25 years	45
26 to 30 years	33
31 to 41 years	44
Over 40	76
Total	329

A study of the above figures shows that the bulk of the registered unemployed women and girls consist of factory workers and domestics – unskilled workers. Recently a Trades Union official stated that skilled workers (belonging to his Union and others) would not register for fear of being placed in domestic work, thus lessening the chances of obtaining work at their own trades.

The Women's Advisory Committee, acting nationally, was appointed by the Unemployment Board. The Women's Unemployment Committees were mostly set up by public meetings called by the various Mayors, and are not subject to recall. They do not exist in every town, but only 'where they are needed'. In some towns apparently, there is no need for assistance.

Relief Committees are functioning in Auckland, Wellington, Christchurch, Dunedin, Lyttelton, Timaru, Invercargill, Hastings, Palmerston North and Napier, but none is operating in other large towns such as Hamilton, Gisborne or Greymouth. The smaller centres, however, do not act as work centres, but as employment bureaux, giving assistance also to those who need it.

The relief rate of 7s 6d a week is universal, but the relief committees contend that the amount paid must not be regarded as 'wages' as the girls do not do 'relief work' at the bureaux. They are given an allowance to tide them over a difficult period, and, in order to make it possible for them to be found a position, they have to attend the bureau at certain times each day, when they are given occupations in the form of sewing or knitting, or receive training in cookery which will later be useful to them in obtaining employment.

Local conditions vary

The conditions under which relief is administered in the four main centres as far as facts ares available, are briefly as follows:

AUCKLAND. Formerly the girls received 7/6 a week, hot midday meal and morning and afternoon tea. There was a stand-down week if work was not obtained within three months. A cheap room was found if necessary, and if a girl arrived at the bureau destitute immediate financial assistance was given. Since last year, however, the Auckland centre has not been open for relief work as this is only permitted where 25 girls are registered. It operates as an employment bureau, but without any relief work to rely on the girls are not given very much choice of their employment. If no work can be found after a week or two they are made a charge on the Hospital and Charitable Aid Board. It is very doubtful whether this centre will again operate as relief work.

WELLINGTON. The girls work 5½ days a week. They receive 7/6 and all meals, including week-end meals. Girls living at home get only 5/- but no tram fares, the Committee contending that they will not take resident positions in housework and also have no room rent to pay. The result is that very few girls with homes register, for it means that their 5/- mostly goes in fares. Assistance is

given to necessitous cases in the form of clothing, and shoe repairs, and occasionally free picture passes are given.The Bureau is very efficient in finding positions for the girls (not very suitable as a rule) but it is noticeable that race discrimination plays a large part in their distribution. Maori girls have been at the Bureau for as long as seven months. A white girl, if she is at all competent, is sent out to a job the first week, and even a poor worker is found a position within six or seven weeks. The only permanents are old ladies who are really not fit for employment.

DUNEDIN. The only information available is that the girls receive 7/6 a week plus a hot meal.

CHRISTCHURCH. 7/6 a week. Meals and week-end rations are provided, and 3/- room rent for those living in rooms. In the cookery centre the girls undergo three months' training under the supervision of a university-trained domestic science expert and are then submitted to a Technical College examination. They stay in the centre until positions are found for them, when, if wages are deemed insufficient, the committee subsidises what the employer can pay. Clothes are provided where necessary. An article in the *Sun-Star* of 6/7/35 states that 15,367 women and girls have been placed in paid positions by the Committee since it began operations in 1931.

New proposals

At present the position here differs slightly from that in the other centres as the Committee is re-organising. It is understood that its policy is now to endeavour to change its basis to one of assisting girls into suitable vocations. The Women's Unemployment Committee and the Girls' Vocational Guidance Committee have amalgamated into the Women's Employment Committee, its members being representatives for both the two previous committees. Its objective is to find positions for girls and also to assist those who are in unsuitable work to obtain positions more suited to them, and especially to assist girls leaving school.

The unemployed girls were not affected by the bonuses or increases that were recently made to the men. It is difficult to create interest in wages or working conditions at the bureaux because the girls know that before any improvement could be made they will be placed in a position. Also the idea of being placed on the same basis as the single men has little appeal for them.

From these facts it is apparent that the position of the unemployed girl is both serious and urgent. It is one which has many aspects and is rather difficult to approach. However, we look to the National Working Women's Movement to define their attitude and to give us leadership.

Working Woman, vol. 3, no.2 (December 1935), pp.10–11

4.9. Married Women at Work
Working Woman (1936)

What attitude do the women's organisations take to the employment of married women in industry and the professions? In her presidential address to the Dominion Conference of the National Council of Women last year, Miss C. E. Kirk, J.P., voiced an emphatic opinion which was endorsed by the general feeling of the conference. The National Council believes that women have the right to enter any sphere of work and any attempt to prevent, for instance, married women teachers from holding a position, is an attack upon women's rights. The following passages from her address are reprinted by kind permission of Miss Kirk.

'Equality' Speaks Out

A married woman earning her own living . . . leaving her home every day, the same way as her husband, to carry on her chosen career . . . finding it preferable to have someone else to mind her home, or to do it in her spare time, to being bound there herself all day . . .

This is still a horrible picture to many men and women, who only see married women as housekeepers and minders of children, and to whom the duties of motherhood consist of feeding and clothing the young rather than giving them intelligent companionship and guidance.

The right to take her place in industry and in the professions on equal terms with men – regardless of marriage – has been steadily worked for by women all over the world for the past century. Social equality is impossible without this right. Without it women cannot develop their talents to the full or give their best to the community.

This right has been fought for against prejudice and petty argument of the worst kind. Men have clung tightly to their privileges. Commercial groupings and public bodies have placed every obstacle in the way of the women. The cry of 'Women's place is in the home' has been parroted back and forth and repeated by many wives who have not had the opportunity to see further than their kitchen walls, whose own vision has been stunted by the system they uphold. Both men and single women have cried that the married women are keeping them out of jobs.

Not one of these arguments will hold water. Women have proved they can carry out their work with equal ability. They have proved too that their homes do not suffer. A study of human psychology has shown that it is harmful for children to be trained by mothers who are deeply, if unconsciously, dissatisfied with the life of a housewife, and that they would receive better care from a mother who has spent her working hours with some task more congenial than washing clothes or scrubbing floors. And one thought of the drudgery of housekeeping will prove that a mother employed elsewhere for her eight hours per day has actually more time to devote to her children than the harassed mother in the home.

As for the cry of wages, it is an utter fallacy, though more difficult to detect, that married women are depriving others of a living. Since the growth of industry women have always been paid less than the men. Their unequal social position has made this possible. But who will deny that the masses of women working for a lower wage than men are undercutting the wage rate of both men and women, and preventing united action for higher wages?

It has been said that the married woman worker blocks the way of promotion for the young girl worker. If this is true, it is also true of the older single woman or the man worker. It has been said that it is unjust for a woman with no dependents and a husband to keep her, to 'create a double income'. The same might be said of two girl friends, or two young men, or a father and daughter, who are sharing a home.

No, there is no evil result, taking it broadly, to the employment of married women in any industry or profession. The establishment of this principle, in practice as well as in theory, will bring greater benefits to men and women workers, to mother and to children, to the home and to the community.

Woman and her place

There is no doubt that most of us will agree with the average man who says 'a woman's place is in her home', but what we do not agree with is the full stop at 'home'. If a woman is a possessor of a home, that home is certainly her place, but not her only place. It is the centre in which she works and takes an interest in what is going on in the world. It is not instead of these other interests that she has a home, but rather as a foundation in the interests of humanity.

What would be the opinion of a man if women were silly enough to say to him, 'Now you have a business; you are a butcher. Your job is to attend to your business. Twenty-four hours out of the twenty-four you must be within the four walls of the building where it is conducted.' He would immediately say, 'I could not be there all the time. I must have some recreation.' And we, being very sensible people,

would agree with him, although we might perhaps wonder whether the sauce served to the goose could not be profitably served to the gander . . .

There is of course, the much vexed question of a married woman holding a position. Many women have expressed the opinion that married women should not hold a paid position except under special circumstances. Surely we have not fought all these years for woman's economic independence just to cast it aside directly it does not suit everyone in the same fashion that we would cast aside a shoe that pinches. Personally, I should be very glad, if in these times of unemployment and real distress the married women whose husbands were earning, had been sufficiently gracious and generous to make way for their distressed sisters, but I fully realise that every woman has a right to choose for herself and that in retaining her position the married woman is well within her 'rights'.

Working Woman, vol.3, no.6 (April 1936), p.6

4.10. The Position of the Domestic Worker by Emily Gibson (1936)

The domestic servant question, like the poor, is always with us and always will be until it has been tackled boldly by the Legislature as it never has been so far in any part of the British Empire. Why this is so is a mystery. We have laws, awards, basic wages, etc., in every other vocation that asks for them, but not for the girls and women who make our homes comfortable and relieve the housewife from the hardest burden of her household cares. Do the people of New Zealand realise that there is not one single law on the Statute Book in connection with the treatment, conditions or wages paid to this class of worker?

Nor is it the fault of the women of the Dominion. As far back as the late nineties of last century the then National Council of Women interested itself in the matter, asking that a weekly half-holiday should be made compulsory. A Bill was introduced by, I believe, Mr Field, year after year, but the House of Representatives would have nothing to do with it. It was only the action of the girls themselves who flatly refused to accept a position where this was not conceded that have made it customary. It is not law yet.

Again, the late Mrs Tasker, of Wellington, a

vice-president of the National Council and a strong Labour woman, formed a union, drew up a list of all rules and demands, but when an application was made to the then Arbitration officials for registration it was refused on the ground that domestic servants were not kept for 'hire or profit', therefore could not receive the benefits of the Act.

Other women have tried since then, always to receive the same answer. The workers in hotels and boarding-houses could not be kept out on those grounds, they come under the hotel employees award and have their wages and hours fixed satisfactorily. It is not to be wondered at, therefore that domestic service in private homes is the most unpopular vocation in the Dominion.

Just look at the position from the point of view of a girl, who, upon leaving school, finds it necessary to earn her own living. She looks around and sees, as I have said, the workers in every other occupation protected by the law or an award. By the united determination and the scarcity of domestics in the past a weekly half-holiday, a day off once a fortnight and perhaps half-a-day on alternate Sundays has been gained.

Apart from these occasions she is not supposed to go over the doorstep without the mistress' permission. It is true that the latter (not being of stone) will generally give the permission, but it is always a favour – never a right. Moreover it is dependent on whether the girl's services are required in the house at that particular time; that is always the first consideration. All the time she is in the house she is liable to be called upon to do something or other for some of the inmates. Then, as most of the housewives out here only keep one maid, there is the terrible loneliness and isolation unless she is fortunate enough to get with extra kindly people. She has her meal in solitary grandeur in the kitchen.

What girl in her senses would choose such a life when she can go to a shop or a factory and be free as air at five o'clock and noon on Saturdays to say nothing of the companionship of all the other girls? But some of the women who call themselves progressive can only groan at the refusal of the girls to enter this occupation and talk of establishing training institutions. The girls do not want to be trained, they want to be treated like human beings, not like slaves.

Some months ago when the Arbitration Amendment Act was introduced by the Minister of Labour and the evil old clause banning those not employed for pecuniary gain from its benefits was deleted, our hopes were raised and we actually had grounds for believing that it would be possible to form a union for domestic workers, and put them on a level with the workers in other occupation. But those hopes were quickly dispelled when the Minister of Labour allowed the Legislative Council to mutilate the Bill and practically restore the clause. Mr Armstrong upon being asked to explain blamed the Council, but we all know that the Bills are always sent back to the House of Representatives in order that the amendments made by the council will be approved or otherwise. This Bill came back in the usual way, but there was no sign, so far as we know, that any one of the eighty M.P.s had a single word of condemnation for the action of the Council or a word in defence of the most overworked and underpaid section of the women workers of the Dominion. The Minister talks of doing something for them later on, 'when the rush of work is over', but that is cold comfort. Consequently the girls who had been preparing to form unions in many centres were once more disappointed.

What most people refuse to realise is that the old system is completely out of date and must be revolutionised. I should begin by forming a union to be called the Home Assistants' Union (in order to distinguish it from the Hotel Employees' Union). The term mistress and maid or servant would be consigned to Limbo and the parties simply employer and employee. Forty-four hours a week should be the limit, eight hours a day for five days, four hours for Saturday and Sundays free. If Sunday work were absolutely necessary, as in the case of sick people, etc., then the maid should have a day off in the middle of the week as is the case with the tram and railwaymen and the girls at the infirmaries and hospitals. For the others, those who call themselves Christians should remember the fourth commandment and keep it in connection with 'thy maidservant and the stranger within thy gates'. A nice cold dinner would not harm anyone, and the lads and lasses who go bathing and picnicking on Sundays seem to revel in boiling billies and making their own beds for once. Therefore no hardship would be entailed by deleting Sunday work from the domestic's routine. Also I would advocate that wherever possible the girls should sleep out, but whether they did or not their time over and above the eight hours should be their own to go out or stay in as they pleased. Any other time worked should be paid for as overtime.

The wages of factory employees, shop assistants, and other working girls have been fixed by the Government to begin at 15/- per week, and there is no reason why these girls should not be paid the same. I may be reminded that they have board. Even so it must be remembered that we are trying to make this calling popular, consequently some inducements must be held out. The second year the wages should be £1, the third and over 25/-. That naturally would only be the minimum, so that housewives of limited means could afford help. Those who required first-class cooks or housekeepers could always pay more, as they do at present.

One more grievance, though a minor one. Some girls object to being called by their Christian names by everyone in the house. When we remember that they may, perhaps, have gone to school with some of the members of the family whom they have to address now as Miss it is rather galling. This, it seems to me, could be surmounted very easily by adopting a more general term. In the hospitals all the attendants are 'nurse' or 'sister'; in the schools the assistants are 'teacher ' to all the children. Would it not be possible to call the maids 'friend' or its equivalent in french, 'ami'? A good servant is a very real friend though everyone does not realise it.

I have remarked upon the fact that the Legislative Council and the House of Representative have let the domestic workers down. But I am not down-hearted, because I remember, as you may all remember, that in one of the first speeches made by Mr Savage after attaining the rank of Prime Minister he said he would see that everyone in the Dominion who worked, male or female, would have a living wage and maximum hours or work laid down by law. The shop, office and factory employees have been attended to already. It is now the turn of the domestic worker, and I am quite sure that we can rely upon Mr Savage to keep his word.

Working Woman, vol. 3, no. 9 (July 1936), pp. 3–4

4.11. The United Council of Working Women: What it stands for
by Lola Scholtz (1936)

Readers of the *Working Woman* who have read our notes month by month may often have wondered just what the United Council of Working Women is. We are glad to have this opportunity of explaining.

The United Council is a national body which links together a number of local working women's organisations in various centres, and individual women in scattered districts. These groups may have different objectives and opinions and do not necessarily have to subscribe to the whole of our *Guide to Action*. Acceptance of one point only is sufficient to enable us to work in common.

The *Guide to Action* was approved by the Second National Conference of Working Women last January, when the present Council was set up with Mrs E. McGowan as President.

A number of important questions have been taken up this year. Adequate sustenance for single women, widows and separated wives was the subject of a number of meetings and demonstrations in Auckland; the Christchurch women also took this up and finally were able to send representatives to the local Women's Employment Committee. Early this year an increase of 2/6 weekly and an allowance for rent was granted the girls.

The Gisborne Women's Branch of the National Unemployed Workers' Movement has been keenly alive to questions of local interest, including rent and fuel allowances, eviction cases, free dental clinics for children, employment of youths, and housing. Similar local activities have been conducted in other centres.

The problem of the domestic worker has also received attention. Domestic Workers' Unions have been everywhere supported, the Dunedin Working Women's Movement being particularly active in this respect.

Improved rations and other assistance for recipients of charitable aid, increased pensions for widows (even after the children have passed the age of fifteen) and for the aged have been the aim of work done in Auckland, Wellington and elsewhere.

Discussions of educational value are carried on in all movements attached to the Council. These discussions tend to follow the most important topics of the time. At present, for instance, birth control and the Government inquiry into the causes of septic abortion are being considered.

The working women's organisations are also vitally concerned with international problems. We stand firmly for peace, and besides educating our own members, we are anxious to co-operate with any other peace movement. The People's Peace Mandate was actively supported, and today we are distributing postcards against military training issued by the No More War Movement. The Wellington Working Women's Club has collected financial assistance for the Spanish women and children who are fighting for peace and freedom. They are also giving their support to the National Peace Conference Committee.

New members welcome
Any woman who agrees with at least one point in our *Guide to Action* is welcome to link up with the Council. If there is no organisation in your district a letter will put you in touch with us. Programme cards are issued for the price of threepence.

In every locality there are urgent questions about which women are becoming more and more concerned. There is only one way to achieve your objective – organisation. Organisation is our keynote and we are pleased to be able to help those who are making a beginning.

From December onwards the Council intends to issue a small monthly bulletin, *Women in Action.* This will be supplied to applicants for a penny a copy, and will contain news of the movement.

The United Council has already assisted in many movements for the advancement of women. In the future, as in the past, we will continue to render service to the community in proportion to the support given us throughout the country.

Guide to action

(Adopted by Second National Conference of Working Women)
For Peace and Democratic Rights.
Equal Pay for Equal Work.
Right of Married Women to Work.
Adequate Pensions for the Aged, Disabled and Widows.
Free Dental, Medical, Surgical and Maternity Attention.
Improved Conditions of Education and establishment of Free State Kindergartens.
No Discrimination Between Maori and Pakeha.
Free Birth Control Clinics.

Working Woman, vol.3, no.13 (November 1936), p.4

4.12. Towards Happier Parenthood by Elsie Freeman (1937)

New Zealand prides herself on her care of mother and child. In particular, the assistance given by the Plunket Society to young mothers has contributed to reducing our infant mortality to a point envied by many of the 'more advanced' countries of the world. Strangely enough, there is one aspect of maternal and general health for which the State makes no provision. Once a new life has begun its journey to the world there are many people ready to assist it; but the conception of that life is left to chance. Sometimes the birth takes place under conditions which are anything but beneficial to the parents the child and the community.

It may be that the mother is afflicted with some serious disease which will endanger her life during pregnancy, or which will start her child in life with some physical defect. It may be that she is already worn out from bearing too many children, or tired from a recent pregnancy. It may be that the finances of the household will not stand the extra expense without taking necessities from the other children or that the wife is still of necessity herself a wage-earner, unable to run the risk of losing her employment.

Bringing children into the world under such conditions only tends to undermine the health of the people and to make the mother in particular incapable of contributing her best to society.

In practice women to-day are realising more and more strongly the need for planned parenthood. Modern conditions make this

necessary for successful family life.

How, then, can parenthood be controlled?

Medical science has evolved methods of contraception which, although not 'foolproof', are almost completely safe, harmless and efficient. Such methods do not interfere with the normal course of married life, but rather tend to make the relations between husband and wife happier by removing the continual tension which overshadows so many homes – the fear of another child which they cannot support.

The essential point to understand about the best methods is that they are useless unless prescribed by a competent doctor after individual examination. Only a medical expert can judge the correct contraceptive, its size and method of fitting, and correctly instruct his patient.

People of means and social position have for years past been able to make use of medical knowledge. Working people, however, seldom have a family doctor with whom such matters can be discussed, and as very little has been written or spoken about birth control in this country, many do not realise the importance of using only the best means of contraception.

What is the result?

When people feel they cannot rear a child they resort to undesirable methods of family limitation. At a conservative estimate, 90 per cent of New Zealanders using contraceptives are following methods inefficient, damaging to health or psychologically harmful. When these means fail, there are two alternatives – to bring the unwanted child into the world, or to procure a miscarriage.

That the latter step is only too often resorted to is shown by the official figures of the Department of Health. 109 women died in four years (1931–35), leaving 338 children motherless, and many more were maimed for life. Our death-rate from septic abortions is far higher than that of other British nations and the U.S.A., although our total maternal death-rate is the lowest of them all! So great is this evil that last year the Government had to appoint a Committee to inquire into the whole matter. At the time of writing its report is not available.

Failures to convict in recent trials show how futile are the legal steps taken to prevent this evil. The only course is to make it unnecessary for women to risk their lives.

Lord Horder, the King's Physician and President of the British National Birth Control Association, said recently that the time has come for birth control 'to take its place, quite definitely and systematically, amongst the health services of this country'. Many local health authorities in England give advice to women whose health does not warrant another pregnancy, and clinics in almost every town assist the poorer mother.

In New Zealand there is no legal barrier to birth control advice being given, but it is difficult for ordinary people to have access to it. The ideal thing, of course, would be for the government to open clinics in connection with the hospitals. At the present time, however, they do not appear willing to do so and indeed cannot be expected to unless the people

clearly show their desire for such services.

An alternative way is for a section of the community to take steps to make advice available. This is now being done by the Sex Hygiene and Birth Regulation Society, which was formed in Wellington last November, and which aims at providing facilities for birth control advice as well as educating the public in a sound outlook on sex matters. The co-operation of the medical profession is shown by two medical men accepting office as Vice-Presidents. At the present time the Society is able to put women seeking advice in touch with suitable doctors who will advise them at a small fee and provide the correct appliances.

Many of the readers of *Woman Today* will no doubt raise objections to birth control services. I have not the space in this issue to answer such objections, but would be pleased to see the correspondence columns opened to the subject and would also be willing privately to answer any inquiries.

It is the profound belief of the Society that New Zealand must fall in line with the international movement for birth control, which is sweeping every country in the world (except the fascist countries), and incorporate birth control advice in our health services.

This does not mean that our population will be reduced, but that children will be born under the very best conditions possible. It is in the interests of the coming generations, and of the parents of to-day, that we appeal for public co-operation.

Woman Today, *vol.1 no.1 (March 1937), p.10*

4.13. Wages for Wives
by Mary Barkas (1937)

New Zealand is forging ahead towards socialist ideals of comfort, leisure, economic security and adequate remuneration for all workers; yet one large and not unimportant section of these is still labouring under a burden of excessive and incessant toil – the housewife.

For her no 40 hour week, but 24 hours a day and seven days a week, and her rare holidays too often mean the same drudgery; she must be economist and organiser, expending the family income to the best advantage, and at the same time cook–general, char and often laundress, nursery maid and governess, seamstress – skilled and unskilled worker in one, and all this without regular hours of work, without leisure

for pursuits beyond the home, and without any financial independence or remuneration for her ceaseless work. Yet the housewife labours on with her round of never-ending toil, removing the ever-recurring dirt, preparing and clearing up the ever-recurring meals, and attending to the wants of the not quite so ever-recurring children – seldom able to get or afford help to give her a brief spell of freedom and leisure, and without pay for her work. Truly one may marvel that she seldom goes on strike, but even shoulders extra burdens in the milking-shed, fowl-house or piggery, and all this as a labour of love – work without a wage.

Is this the best we can do – we who pride

ourselves on having had the parliamentary franchise earlier than most women? Is this drudgery inevitable, and need it be unpaid? The man who has no female relative to keep his house manages to pay a housekeeper. Why should he not also give some remuneration to the housekeeper in his family, so that she too may feel her labours are duly valued and that she can have some degree of economic independence?

We are not suggesting that New Zealand men are mean or grudging about money; many hand over the bulk of their earnings to the home economist to be expended at her discretion. But this is by no means the same thing for her as having, quite apart from the family budget, some money wholly her own to be spent or saved at her whim, the product of her own earning. Some women do not feel this difference acutely, but to many it is a source of humiliation far greater than is often realized by men. The woman who before marriage had free control of her own earnings finds it irksome and humiliating to have to ask her husband for money for her own personal needs, and to explain and justify her expenditure. Moreover some men, perhaps unconsciously, enjoy the sense of power or generosity which such financial control gives them, and some even exercise it with real harshness and brutality. I have known the wife of an extremely wealthy farmer who had to ask each time for a sixpenny bus fare and never possessed even a few shillings cash, though she could run up accounts for large sums.

We believe that the status of the home worker would be raised and her position one of greater dignity and freedom if this condition of things were altered. The service rendered by the housewife to the community deserves respect and remuneration, while the rigours of its conditions might be mitigated by intelligent planning and co-operative effort. Can we not set our wits to work to discover remedies for this state of things, and, if our law-makers cannot find a solution for us, get busy ourselves to use our constructive imaginations to better the drudgery of the home?

The first difficulty to be solved is – where shall the money come from. Is the payment of the housekeeper, be she wife, sister, mother or daughter of the wage-earner, to be a charge on the family budget just as if she were not a relative? Our readers might give us their view. If the standard of wages is at a high level, this is a possibility without endangering the standard of living, but the tendency of women to self-sacrifice may lead to the housewife still regarding her wages as part of the household allowance rather than as her private income. Another possibility is that the State should recognise the importance of her services to the community and pay her directly for those services. If this were done some of the women who leave home to enter paid employment might prefer to remain at home and regard domestic work as a profession no less dignified than others.

Hours of work are another difficult problem, but could surely be solved by co-operative effort and organisation. Children would certainly benefit if more of their time in the earliest years could be spent among others of their own age, and away from the constant care of parents and relatives whom their activities soon fatigue. Nursery schools and creches could be far more numerous and more used, with benefit to child and housewife alike. Housing schemes for towns could be planned on the lines of service flats, grouped round restaurants from which meals could be supplied to separate homes as well as to those coming to a central dining room.

Some hindrance there must be in our minds to account for the fact that we have not yet done so. Are we too conservative? Surely not! Can we not co-operate? The success of many co-operative activities proves that we can. Can we not plan and express our view? This journal gives us a medium in which we can discuss them together. Let us, the women of New Zealand, determine that we have a world to win, and that we can and shall win it. Our men hope to abolish wage-slavery; let us resolve to abolish also the wageless slavery of the housewife.

Woman Today, vol.1, no.1 (March 1937), p.22

4.14. Women and Divorce Reform – An Opportunity for Feminists
by 'Alexa' (1937)

The feminist world was greatly cheered when at the National Conference of the N.Z. Labour Party held at Wellington at Easter, the remit asking for Divorce Reform sent down by the Auckland Women's Branch, emerged from its committee ordeal endorsed with a statement that the Committee recommended it be referred to the National Executive for favourable consideration. Further, that when the remit came before Conference, the general tone was friendly.

The exact wording of the now famous remit was 'That the law relating to divorce be simplified and made less expensive; that cruelty without drunkenness be made ground for divorce; and that the period for divorce by mutual consent or for desertion be reduced from three years to one year.'

Feminists must often have asked themselves why we have so long kept intact such a carelessly drafted, materialistic section of legislation, which has reduced many an unfortunate woman petitioner to the verge of collapse by its intricacy, expense and delays, long before she got to the point of discussing the often sordid details of a wrecked marriage before complete strangers in the murder-trial saturated atmosphere of a Supreme Court.

The whole structure of domestic legislation in N.Z. is long overdue for an overhaul, and it is confidently hoped that this will be accorded when the forthcoming legislation of national health insurance, superannuation and motherhood endowment has been passed. The effects of these steps towards the economic independence of women can, however, be fairly accurately envisaged by any who have studied our social structure and the place of marriage in it. Let us be quite candid with ourselves and own up that in four out of five marriages where the wife had no private income and could not continue her pre-marital occupation, in wage-earning homes her position as a wife and mother was little more than slavery. She had the discomfort and risk of child-bearing, especially if her husband was averse to scientific birth-control; she had the fear of death, sickness or unemployment of the bread-winner always hanging over her and her children; driven by the never-ending responsibilities and labours of housewife and mother,

she knew that she must try to keep her husband faithful to her and the home, for if he could be attracted outside the home it not only meant humiliation and one more variety of nervous strain for her, but it meant that he might spend some of the carefully budgeted income outside the family.

There are four types of marriage which have everything to gain and nothing to lose by divorce law reform. These are: (1) The Happy Marriage; (2) The Unhappy Marriage; (3) The Fruitful Marriage; and (4) The Childless Marriage.

The happy marriage will look after itself without support or coercion from law or church. It has nothing to lose and easier divorce merely gives the parties the moral satisfaction of knowing that misfit couples can speedily be set free to seek elsewhere the ideal happiness which they themselves know is possible in marriage.

The fruitful marriage will, when each person in the family circle is made a complete independent entity, have nothing to fear from easier divorce. A family will be a miniature commonwealth, and will be set free to live instead of dragging along in mediocrity and in the atmosphere of irritation and frustration which penury so often imposes.

The childless marriage, if it is happy, will look after itself; if it fails (as luckily for the State it often does), speedy freedom often results in two fruitful re-marriages instead of the original childless one.

The unhappy marriage, which is often the result of the husband's lack of chivalry through faulty upbringing, or the interference of relatives, or of incompatibility of tastes and principles, cannot too soon be dissolved. When the parties to an unhappy marriage finally separate, in most cases they have been spiritually and physically apart – although living in the same home – for a long period. The wife in most cases has been through an agonising experience, for the average woman does enter upon marriage with love and idealism. Sometimes in her time of trouble she meets someone who can give her the chance of becoming a happy, wanted wife instead of an unloved one. Yet if the parties wish to obtain divorce by mutual consent for separation because of the failure of the marriage, they at present have to wait three years before they can even begin to petition for divorce, and it may take some months after that before a decree absolute is pronounced. For the whole of that time, as has been so graphically said, a woman is neither maid, wife, nor widow. Her economic position is precarious. Certain legalities still tie her to the husband although they may be at opposite sides of the world. She cannot marry, and motherhood is denied to her. For women in middle age, whose desire for children has come in maturity, the long waiting-time for a divorce other than by criminal charge, may mean that the last of the child-bearing years pass in loneliness and futility.

These are only a small part of the total indictment against our present domestic laws. Of course, the actual status of women and their nominal present legal status are two quite different things, as every social worker knows. The mass of Victorian statutory rigmarole which we have so long outgrown should be studied carefully by women. They should realise that now is their chance to speed and to help by their expressed support, the task of reconstruction.

Woman Today, *vol.1 no.3 (June 1937), p.62*

4.15. Do You Stoke or Switch?
by Elizabeth Kelso (1938)

Why have we no Minister of Domestic Labour? Who are doing the brute-labour in New Zealand now? Who are still using the most primitive tools? Women. What is the power used to operate those tools? Woman-power.

And nobody says anything about it – except visitors from England, Canada, South Africa, and America, who are horrified to find that slavery and drudgery still go merrily on in God's Own Country.

I am not a feminist. But after a walk through the streets looking at shop-windows, filled with the most beautiful labour-saving tools safely tucked away beyond the reach of the average woman, I feel in the grandest mood to pull off the gloves and call on all-comers: the inventor first. What are they doing? Making lovely toys for show? In the beginning the motive may have been to ease the work in the home but by the time the machine leaves the factory there does not seem to be much of that high-souled motive left.

Our legislators may be raising wages, but the housewife has no wages. She is economically dependent on the generosity of her husband and washing-machines are expensive. So are motor-cars, radios, tractors, separators, motor-boats, yachts, racehorses, stud-sheep and pedigree bulls. What are the power boards, the Chamber of Commerce, the Engineering and Electrical Societies doing about it? It cannot be said that they are making the machine available to women.

The whole world looks on when the woman with the basket puts her purse on the counter – but what about the woman with the child – and no purse? Is no one interested in her? Is she not worth preserving if not for her own sake then for the sake of the child?

We had a fine furore after the release of the report of the committee set up to enquire into the incidence of abortion in New Zealand. We were shocked to learn of the long working hours of the woman on the farm and the dearth of domestic help. Resolutions are still being passed – most of them of the unconstructive and pious nature. Schemes and plans for training domestic helpers have been sent forward by several women's organisations. Meanwhile, woman labours on, bending over the steaming tub, straining her back lifting heavy wet clothes and turning a wringer, standing for hours ironing, sweeping and beating and in the summer, fighting an endless battle protecting food from flies. And all the machinery, invented to do this for her stands idle in the stores, available only to the well-to-do.

The Minister of Transport made history when he replaced wheelbarrows with tractors. Women have no Minister to protect them and they must go on with their long day, their primitive tools, their aching backs and broken nerves.

One reply to my questions will be: 'You can't legislate for the housewife.' Why not? Because she is not a member of a Union? There are one or two countries where she has economic equality with the husband. There are building laws. Can they not be extended to include the machinery of the home? Another answer I expect is: 'If the economic status of the man is improved the woman will benefit.' And my reply is that we cannot be certain of that.

Modernist cover of *Woman Today*, February 1938 issue, the magazine 'for peace, freedom and progress'.
Private Collection

There are many rich men's wives who envy the freedom of the dock-labourer's wife.

The truth is that women in New Zealand badly need someone to speak for them in high places. It is not sufficient that they should have to trust to getting a sort of backwash of whatever legislation is passed, good or bad. The woman's mental and physical health and strength should be safe-guarded for the sake of the race and therefore the conditions under which she works must be modernised.

A small Parliamentary Committee set up by the Prime Minister might answer the need. Such a committee would advise the Government on Legislation necessary for the well-being of the home and would also receive and co-ordinate information from the voluntary women's organisations which are doing a great deal to mitigate the monotony of the housewife's life as well as helping to broaden it. Were such a committee in existence, I should like to suggest, in view of the dearth of domestic help, that labour-saving machines – especially washing machines – be regarded as necessities in the home and that they be classed with certain surgical instruments and educational material and allowed into the Dominion duty-free.

Woman Today, *vol.1, no.12 (March 1938), p.275*

4.16. The World Demand for Sex Equality
Woman Today (1938)

'As long as law and custom treat women as one race and men as another there will remain a woman question, and not until men and women equal and united side by side, work together free and untrammelled, will the women's movement be a thing of the past.' (Principles of Equal Rights International, with Headquarters in London and Switzerland).

The Women's Movement or as it is sometimes termed, the 'Feminist' movement in New Zealand is not an isolated national phenomenon; it is part of a world movement. Always in the history of the human race, in one civilisation or another on the earth's surface, women have had an aspiration and striving towards better material conditions, and intellectual and spiritual freedom. The movement has had many setbacks, and there have been periods within historical record when women had no more political or social rights than if they had been animals in the fields.

Women have always had to fight for recognition as independent human beings and citizens, man, so determined to claim legal tangible rights for himself, has been quite content to allow the other half of the human race to enjoy rights merely sentimental and intangible, not enforceable in the law courts like this. Women must be suppliants and dependants, not fellow-citizens and fellow-voters.

Some women have maintained that were it not for the coming of the industrial era, and the consequent economic problems caused by women's entry into industrialism or by the dragging weight which ill-fed, uneducated, unskilled women and children were to men caught in the competitive conditions of the labour market, the fight to get first the franchise and later to win a higher standard of home life and labour conditions, would have been even more bitter than it was. It was however quickly seen that the benefits for organisation such as unionism and the co-operative movement in health, housing, and food-supplies, were lost almost as soon as won if unorganised women's labour could be used to under-cut organised man's labour, and if voteless, economically helpless girls and women could be forced into working a sixteen or twelve-hour day while men were fighting first for a ten, then for an eight-hour one.

Still later it was realised that women could make a contribution to society through their children, and that their homes could be steadily radiating centres of progressive thought and culture. For the first time it was admitted that woman – as woman – had a contribution to make to the world's thought and progress. Without women's contribution that progress would be lop-sided, would move in a curve which ultimately would bring mankind back to the starting point, or even lower. With men and women equally free to express their distinctive outlook, working side by side, the progress would be straight ahead with no deflection. **No permanent improvement in the world's condition, either spiritual, pacific, or industrial, is possible unless there is equality of status regardless of caste, creed, colour, race and sex; and also equality of opportunity.**

In the meantime, women to-day are questioning many things which they have till now been forced to accept, and are organising for the better obtaining of their objectives, chiefly by the exercise of their power through the franchise. The consensus of opinion of the great majority of women leaders and feminist organisations throughout the world is towards the following ideals:

(1) **Economic Independence.** Envisaging the ideal of equal pay for equal work, and the right of a woman, married or single, to work outside of the home if she wishes in her chosen profession or occupation. The recognition none-the-less of motherhood as women's highest profession as well as one of the most arduous and highly-skilled, and the consequent claiming of motherhood endowment to ensure that women carrying on the race are not penalised compared to other workers. Women ask for recognition of the economic value of home-craft and mother-craft.

(2) **Legal and Political Equality.** The removal of all statutory and customary disabilities and the recognition of the right of women to follow any profession or to hold any social or political position or appointment, including the highest in the State.

(3) **Personal Freedom.** The right of women to own their own persons, which includes the right to be freed speedily from domestic conditions which are intolerable and degrading, or which limit or bar their right to motherhood. Conversely that no woman should bear children against her will; motherhood must be voluntary and not enforced. Actual facts prove that when there is economic security, good housing, and a mutual desire for parenthood and its responsibilities, women are willing to bear children.

WOMAN TODAY heartily recommends every New Zealand woman to study her citizen status as compared with that of the women of other countries, in order that she may estimate in what relation she stands to the ideal for which the World Women's Movement is steadily working. We must learn, and we must actively contribute our share to the good of our fellow men and women.

Woman Today, vol. 2, no. 6 (September 1938), p. 1

4.17. Women and War: the case for militancy by M.B. Soljak (1939)

'Woman, the creator of life, has the profoundest horror of war. It is flesh of her flesh that is sacrificed on the fields of battle. Woman can and must be the best worker in the cause of Peace'.

The above quotation, culled from a collection of similar timely expressions of opinion from *A Manuel [sic] of Peace*, by Suzanne Bouillet, one of France's leading peace protagonists, raises the question – Is woman opposed to war on general principles, or is her horror of it based on the sacrifice it demands of her as an individual?

I have always doubted the truth of the oft-repeated statement that women as a sex are against war: one has only to cast her mind back as far as the Great War to realise that most of us glorified that sanguinary conflict as a means to national aggrandisement, or satisfaction for personal loss. I would like to forget that section of women who, false to human instincts, utilised the war for the purposes of spurious patriotism or material gain, and counted the widespread sorrow and destruction as merely incidental to something that reacted to their benefit. The memory of their victory jubilations, their white-feather giving, their singing of such songs as *We Don't Want to Lose You* remain with an abiding sense of shame for my sex. It is the ordinary, well-intentioned woman whom we have to consider in weighing the merits of our sex as a factor against war.

Too few women have any conception of Peace as something to be won through struggle and aggression: the reality of the phrase 'Fighting for Peace' made manifest during the last war by conscientious objectors and other war resisters in every belligerent country, including our own, found no echo in the hearts and minds of average womankind.

It is a sign of progress that this militant spirit should have found expression in the emergency resolution moved by Mrs Linda Littlejohn on behalf of the Australian Federation of Women Voters at the 1937 Conference of the British Commonwealth League, which I attended while visiting London. The resolution reads, 'That the women of the British Commonwealth League, desiring the preservation of Peace, should not be satisfied to voice a sentimental opposition to war, but, recognising that the matter is one of life and death not only for the individual, but for the race, they should undertake a serious study of the factors making for war, the armaments race, and the political alignments taking place today and ensure that study is made the basis of determined action in the cause of peace.'

There we have it – the stressing of the need of planned activity against this evil which endangers and destroys so much of vital importance to women. No mere emotional reaction to present-day trends towards war, but 'determined action', based on knowledge of all the factors which make for war. This implies struggle and a facing up to all the implications of the huge development of the war machine in recent times. Casting out fear, prejudice, National hatreds, and traditional alignments, we must prepare to sacrifice much that we have learned to accept as essential to our well-being. We must substitute reason for sentiment, and tauten mind and body for action, for in the coming conflict none will be passive observers, and women will be called on to do more than weep, wait, watch and pray.

Prayer and pacificism not enough.

As to those who hope to see peace dropping like the gentle rain from heaven in answer to prayer, they are doomed to disappointment: for while they pray the war-makers are steadily piling up armaments and intensifying through Press, radio and every method at their disposal, the psychology which will bring war to destroy all that the supplicants hold dear. We learn from history that such calamities as war were never averted by pious hopes or appeal. In the middle ages when the Church was all-powerful and kings sought the advice and did the bidding of ecclesiastical counsellor, religion held sway and prayer was the hourly comfort and stay of every man, woman and child. Peace was then a blessing to be sought after as it is to-day and we may assume that women busy in their homes – whether palaces or cottages – were anxious to attain and preserve it. Yet we know that cruel and bloody battles – internecine and international – were constantly being waged, wiping out alike the work of women's hands and the flesh of their flesh.

And to come down to recent times we saw during the Great War that appeals for Divine aid from each side of the battle front were fruitless, and that victory went to those who could hold out the longest or were least scrupulous in their methods. Unfortunately for hopes of the pious and well-meaning, those who set out to attain their ambitions of power and prestige through human sacrifice deal in hard material factors against which prayer is but a vulnerable shield and pacifism a poor weapon.

To-day, faced with the imminent danger of a mass plunge into war – the logical sequence of all this intense pre-occupation of the leading nations with armaments and all that makes for warfare – women must assume responsibilities and duties never before contemplated, for the next war if and when it comes, will not be one in which we can choose whether or no we become participants. Willy-nilly we shall all be in it some way or other, and the end may be worse than the alternative to Allied victory so often stressed during 1914-18. Our task is to oppose war in the making and the time to begin is NOW.

It is deplorable that in the whole length and breadth of New Zealand there is not one women's organisation devoted to this object – the active opposition to war and its twin brother, Fascism. We are in danger of being shocked into the realisation that we have waited too long while the war-mongers have not ceased for a day to prepare for carnage and destruction. We want in the time left to us – perhaps all too short – more of the frank facing up to this evil thing and those who deal in it rather than hiding from it in the mists of unreality, for there will be no escape when it starts. All this may read like the prognostications of a 20th century Jeremiah, but the times call for plain and emphatic speaking. We need stirring to action not lulling into futile contemplation. And to find a fitting final message I turn again to my *Manuel of Peace* and choose from the writings of Suzanne Bouillet herself this, 'If women expended on Peace the thousandth part of efforts that men expend on war, it would not be long before this scourge ceased to exist.'

Woman Today, vol.2 no.11 (February 1939), p.16

Chapter 5

Mid-century Rumblings
1940s and 1950s

The years from about 1945 through the 1950s were relatively placid compared with the preceding decade of depression, insecurity and war. Politically, the innovations of the late 1930s had been absorbed and a consensus between Labour and National had emerged. The end of the long period of Labour government in 1949 was not marked by a radical shift in political direction. Socially, the overwhelming desire, shared by the vast majority of people was to establish a stable life based on secure employment. Prosperous economic conditions creating full employment, affordable mortgages and a boom in home building brought security to a large number of New Zealanders.

The years immediately following World War Two are often referred to as a time when women 'returned to their homes and families'. Their brief wartime forays into factories, farms and shops as members of the paid workforce had been brought to an abrupt halt, either by the machinations of a patriarchal government, or as the result of a 'natural' process by which society reverted to its pre-war 'normality'. Neither of these accounts does justice to the historical reality.

To begin with, it is important to put women's wartime employment in perspective. In New Zealand only a relatively small number of women were directed into the paid workforce during the Second World War.[1] They were chiefly young single women or married women without children. The number of women subject to manpower orders represented a relatively small proportion of the total adult female population. Of those who were conscripted, most were directed to work in hospitals, shops and factories, in jobs such as cleaning, packing, serving or office work: all traditional areas of women's employment. The number of women who took on the conventionally male jobs – truck driving, labouring, etc. – was small. Contrast this with both the extent and nature of women's wartime work in Britain, where the proportion of women directed into work was much higher, as was the consequent social disruption.

Women's involvement in the paid workforce was, however, increasing throughout this period. The number of women in jobs (and the proportion of the female population in the workforce) was higher in the late 1940s than it had been in the late 1930s. The war certainly accelerated the movement of some women into the workforce, and – very significantly – brought Maori women from rural areas into urban wage employment. In doing so, however, it was advancing an existing trend rather than initiating a new one. Similarly, at the end of the war, while a number of women gave up their jobs (the majority of which were low-paid and monotonous), there was not a major slowing down of the overall movement of women into the paid workforce.

The war was significant, however, in making women's position in the workforce more conspicuous, and certain key groups of women, especially those in the Public Service, in railways and tramways, found themselves in anomalous situations. They were left in temporary, subordinate positions, earning less than the men whose jobs they were filling or alongside whom they were working. The unions made the question of equal pay an industrial issue – would men come back to inherit women's unequal pay?

Not surprisingly then, it was employment issues that provoked the organised voice of women most often in this period. The experience of women during the war, limited though it was, brought the issue of equal pay to the forefront. Equal pay was not a new issue – it had been discussed in the 1890s, campaigned for by the Women Teachers' Association in the early twentieth century and debated hotly amongst post office workers in the *Katipo* (their union magazine) in the 1920s.[2] But the clear inequality in the status and conditions, as well as the pay, of temporary workers in the wartime Public Service (together with the sheer number of women now in the paid workforce) provided the catalyst for agitation.

The initiative was taken by a group of women in the Public Service who, in 1943, formed a women's sub-committee (known generally as the Women's Committee) within the Wellington section of the Public Service Association.[3] Over the following year they publicised the equal pay issue – as in Kathleen Ross's article (5.2) 'Are They 80% Efficient?', highlighting the position of women working in the railways. At the end of that year the Women's Committee made their first breakthrough in gaining agreement to the establishment of a Consultative Committee to formulate new salary scales. The Committee was made up of equal numbers of representatives from the Public Service Association and the Public Service Commission (forerunner of the State Services Commission, the main employing body within the public service). The case put to this Committee early in 1944 by the Women's Committee is included as 5.1. In making their submission, the women were supported by the NCW and the Business and Professional Women's Association.

The case was prepared carefully, after extensive canvassing of women in the Public Service, and research on the situation of women employees internationally. The case submitted that 'the salary scale for females is based rather on sex discrimination than on any genuine attempt to assess the relative efficiency and productivity of female employees.' Mary Boyd presented the case on behalf of the Committee. Equal pay was accepted 'in principle' by the Consultative Committee, but it was to take a determined campaign through the 1950s for this to be translated into action.

As in earlier campaigns, the arguments raised in opposition to a seemingly straightforward plea for justice provoked wider questions on the relative positions and responsibilities of women and men in society. Some of these arguments were addressed in Mrs Caroline Webb's speech to a meeting of Wellington women, sponsored by the Wellington Women's Committee of the Public Service Association in conjunction with the Business and Professional Women's Club, and reproduced in the *Public Service Journal* in January 1946 (5.3). Caroline Webb recalled the historical antecedents in the struggle for women's legal and political equality before commenting on the current campaign for economic equality. 'Not many people advocate in itself the subjection of women, but I think we are all familiar with the technique of refusing to take them seriously, and of completely ignoring their demands.' Women's demands now, she explained, were for economic equality – in the form of equal pay and equal opportunity. This was a simple question of justice, but was also related to the wider goal of elevating women's status within society. Achieving equal pay, it was hoped, would eliminate the lower social status that women's lower pay denoted.

The social dimensions of the claim for equal pay were exemplified the following year in Caroline Webb's article in the *New Zealand Listener* (5.4). It was the text of a radio programme discussing the contemporary position of women under the heading 'Social Evolution and Its Effects on Women'. In the 1940s, and increasingly in the 1950s, 'social evolution' came to be seen in terms of women's paid work vis-à-vis marriage, and, indirectly, it involved the social responsibilities of men as breadwinners. Attempts were made to reformulate the differing demands and character of private households and workplaces, and how women might or should relate to each of these. The situation of mothers in the home was, at times, considered in industrial terms. Interestingly also, in discussing the circumstances of women in employment, Webb makes a clear distinction between the situation and interests of 'career women' and 'married women who work'. And feminist issues such as this did not win much credibility among progressive circles on the left at this time. Marxist analyses tended to relegate 'the position of women' to the periphery as a bourgeois concern, a side issue from the real cause.

In the debate over equal pay, glaring contradictions emerged as the 'ideal' of female economic dependence collided with the reality of women's presence in the paid workforce. The welfare and wages policy instituted by the first Labour Government as part of its welfare state was based on the assumption that male wage- and salary-earners should earn enough to support a man, his wife and two dependent children. Women were thus placed in a situation of economic dependence, and had no claim to equal consideration as members of the paid workforce. In the 1950s, such a situation became increasingly intolerable, as more women moved into the workforce in response to the growing demand for their services. The model of the male as sole household breadwinner was increasingly inaccurate. Many women were of course breadwinners or contributed significantly to a household income, while not all men were breadwinners, nor did they all have dependents. But wage policy had evolved on these assumptions, and was the basis for the structure of wages, salaries, promotion and employment.

Over a decade later, the limitations of domestic life were pressing more closely. The ideals of motherhood and domestic life were often at variance with reality. Margot Roth's hilarious 1957 piece, 'More Mums for the Olympics' (5.5), was written in the wake of the sports frenzy engendered by both the Melbourne Olympic Games and the 1956 Springbok Tour of New Zealand. But it was her 'Point of View' radio talk two years later that sparked a nationwide debate on the position of women. Roth's arguments were taken up much more emphatically in the 1960s, but in 1959 hers was an isolated voice. In 'Housewives or Human

Beings?' (5.6), Roth seeks a rationale for the differences in society's expectations of boys and girls. She condemns the forces that have contributed to a belief – held even by women themselves – in women's inferiority, and denounces the 'overworked housewife' as the creation of a 'homemakers' cult'. She exhorts women to put domesticity into perspective and to develop more satisfying activities.

The editor of the *Listener*, Monte Holcroft, responded negatively to Roth's call in his editorial (5.7). 'A regiment of women, marching behind banners with social slogans,' he deplores, 'is a horrid conception.' It is 'the nature of women to love individuals first and last, and society would be ill indeed if too many of them sought tasks that could only be compensations for what has been missed or lost in the home,' Holcroft concludes. Such sentiments were to come under increasing attack in succeeding decades.

1. *Deborah Montgomerie, 'War and Women',* Women's Studies Journal, *vol. 3, no. 2 (March 1988), pp.3–16; 'The Limitations of Wartime Change',* NZJH, *vol. 23, no. 1 (April 1989), pp.68–86; 'Man-powering Women',* in Barbara Brooks, Charlotte Macdonald and Margaret Tennant (eds), *Women in History 2,* Wellington, *1992, pp.184–204*
2. *Megan Cook and Jackie Matthews, 'Separate Spheres',* Women's Studies Journal, *vol. 6 (1990), pp.168–193*
3. *Margaret Corner,* No Easy Victory, *Wellington, 1988, p.22*

Sources and Further Reading

Cook, Megan and Jackie Matthews. 'Separate Spheres: Ideology at work in 1920s New Zealand. Letters to the Katipo, 1923-1924', *Women's Studies Journal*, vol.6 (1990), pp.168–193

Corner, Margaret. *No Easy Victory: Towards equal pay for women in the government service, 1890-1960*, Wellington, 1988

May, Helen. *Minding Children, Managing Men: Conflict and compromise in the lives of postwar Pakeha women*, Wellington, 1992

Montgomerie, Deborah. 'War and Women: Work and motherhood', *Women's Studies Journal*, vol.3, no.2 (March 1988), pp.3–16

Montgomerie, Deborah. 'The Limitations of Wartime Change: Women war workers in New Zealand', *New Zealand Journal of History*, vol.23, no.1 (April 1989), pp.68–86

Montgomerie, Deborah. 'Man-powering Women: Industrial conscription during the Second World War', in Barbara Brookes, Charlotte Macdonald and Margaret Tennant (eds), *Women in History 2*, Wellington, 1992, pp.184–204

Nicholls, Roberta 'The PSC and the Equal Pay Campaign', in Alan Henderson, *The Quest for Efficiency: the origins of the State Services Commission*, Wellington, 1990, pp.247–279

Taylor, Nancy M. *The Home Front*, Wellington, 1986

5.1. The Case for Equal Pay for Equal Work (1944)

Part 1
The present remuneration of women in the New Zealand Public Service as compared with that of men

Through almost the entire history of the employment of women in the Public Service in New Zealand, they have received a considerably lower scale of remuneration than men.

This position, however, was alleviated for a short time, from 1919 to 1921, when women cadets were taken on to the permanent staff, and successfully lodged appeals against the differential salaries they received as a result of sex discrimination. After hearing these cases, the Public Service Appeal Board ruled that female clerks must be paid equal salaries to males, provided that their work was 'equal in quantity and quality' to that of male clerks.

This decision was short-lived. In 1921 the Public Service Commissioner, supported by the government, ruled that as a matter of policy, no female clerical cadets were to be appointed in future. Female shorthand writers and typists were to be appointed to the temporary staff only, and a new class of female clerical worker was created, which was called the 'Office Assistant' class.

The shorthand writers, typists, and female office assistants were placed on a salary scale independent of that for male employees, and considerably lower than that of either the Clerical Division or the temporary male employees.

The work of the Office Assistant was segregated from that of the male clerical workers, and was limited to routine clerical duties. Thus the differential salary scale was based officially on an assessment of the functional duties performed by the female office assistants, shorthand writers, and typists, but it was also obviously the result of sex discrimination.

In actual fact, the distinction between the so-called subclerical work of the office assistant and the work of the Class VII male in the Clerical Division was proved an artificial one, and since the outbreak of War in 1939, the female office assistant has taken over many of the duties performed by men at the top of Class VII, and in Class VI. The Higher Duties allowance has in no way placed their salaries on a comparable basis with those of their male predecessors, even if the comparative efficiency and years of service of the male and female officers are taken into account.

In recent years, women have been absorbed into many specialist and social service positions in the Public Service, where they are expected to have the same qualifications and ability as men, yet in all cases they have been placed on a lower salary scale hardly differentiated from that of the Office Assistant. Little attempt has been made to grade such positions on a functional basis, or to fix salaries on job content.

The huge increase in the female staff of the Public Service since 1939, together with the absence of any detailed classification system of positions held by females, has accentuated the injustices created by such a system of wage fixing. Discontent with the prevailing conditions of employment and remuneration has become almost universal among the female employees, and the relatively higher wages paid to women outside the Public Service has aggravated this discontent. It is obvious that, but for Manpower direction, a large percentage of the female office assistants and shorthand writers and typists would seek positions outside the Service.

Despite the fact that it has been the official policy of the Public Service Association that the

principle of equal pay for equal work should be accepted throughout the Service, the salary increases so far won for the female groups have only dealt with the fringe of the problem.

The comparative salaries of male and female employees given in the appendix to this report illustrate the fact that the salary scale for females is based rather on sex discrimination than on any genuine attempt to assess the relative efficiency and productivity of female employees. The ratio between the two is a haphazard one, which ranges from 60-80 per cent, and shows that no uniformity exists in the fixation of salaries for the various types of work undertaken by females. This applies not only to wartime positions, but to all positions which have been filled on a temporary permanent basis, since 1921.

In New Zealand, women receive a more marked wage differential in comparison with men, than in almost any comparable country. Great Britain, Canada, Australia, the United States of America, the South American Republics, the USSR and many of the smaller European nations, are years ahead of New Zealand in this respect. The present situation is only comparable to that which existed in Australia prior to the coming into power of the Curtin Government, and the passing of the Women's Employment Act in 1942. As regards status, New Zealand stands almost alone in debarring women from a permanent place in the Public Service. This is an anomaly in a country which has prided itself on its social, political and economic advancement.

The recent activities of the women members of the Public Service Association are indicative of the growing dissatisfaction of female employees regarding the prevailing conditions. At a General meeting of over 200 Public Service women held in Wellington last month, a motion was passed expressing unanimous approval of the Association's policy of equal pay, while in the questionnaires filled in by over one thousand women in Government Departments during the last six months, 81 per cent supported the principle of equal pay. (14 per cent did not reply , and 5 per cent were not in favour).

Outside the Public Service, the Trade Unions are translating their theoretical acceptance of the principle of equal pay into fact. In the Retail Shop Assistants' Union, and N.Z. Chemist's Assistants' Union, certain groups of women are already receiving wages nearly as high as those of the men. Clause 10 of the Shop

Assistants' award states that 'Any female who is employed wholly or substantially in woollen dress, manchester, furnishing, drapery, men's and boys' clothing, mercery, men's hats, men's hosiery, carpets, linos, bedding, furniture, builders' ironmongery, and men's boots departments, shall be paid one half more than wages herein prescribed for females.'

The New Zealand Tramways Authorities Employees' Industrial Union of Workers succeeded in their representations that women should be employed under award conditions including full award pay.

The Medical Profession, the Legal Professions, and the Universities have always fixed salaries on a functional basis, and refused to make any discrimination on the grounds of sex.

Women's organisations, such as the Business and Professional Women's Clubs, and the National Council of Women, are advocating the nation wide adoption of the principle of equal pay.

The Government and Public Service Commissioner should regard it as a duty to both the community and their female employees, to set an example to other employers, by raising the wages of their women employees to the level of those of men, where equal work is done, and admitting men and women into the Public Service on the principle of 'a fair field and no favour.'

. . . .

Part III
The principle of equal pay for equal work

I.   The objections usually raised against the principle:

In New Zealand, as overseas, while much lip service has been paid to the principle of equal pay for equal work, many objections have been raised against its adoption. Overseas countries, however, such as the United States, Canada, and Australia, show that these objections are more apparent than real.

(1) In the first place, there is the problem of avoiding inter-sex competition on the labour market. As was explained by Sir Stafford Cripps, in a speech to the British Federation of Business and Professional Women in February 1943, this can only be done 'by making the field wide enough for all to enjoy'.

To state that money must be taken indirectly from men in order to pay women, when a policy of equal pay is adopted, is a fallacious argument founded on a theory of classical economics, which is to-day no longer accepted by leading economists in Great Britain or America. Instead, the answer to this problem lies in the application of our wartime experience of a policy of full employment to peace conditions.

This is a question of vast economic importance to the world as a whole. At present, a great reservoir of labour is being utilized for the ends of war, and has already achieved a production of materials and services of war in abundance. Most of these materials are for destruction, but at the end of the war the purposes of destruction will have been served, and then many fear that this labour power called into existence by the war, and then suddenly released, will work disastrous results, particularly to males, who fear the loss of their place in industry. But in a well ordered State productive capacity should not be an evil; it should be a factor whereby higher standards of living, greater culture, and more leisure may be achieved. 'It is certain,' said Sir Stafford Cripps, 'that we shall only be able to provide a decent standard for the people of this country if we can employ not only all the men, but a very large proportion of the women as well, after the war.'

During the post-war depression years in Great Britain, it was found that, because women were paid lower wages than men, employers continued to engage them in preference to men, and that consequently women, youths and girls often became the breadwinners for the family. A repetition of this must be avoided.

If such countries as the United States, Canada and Australia, the South American Republics and the USSR can afford equal pay, then surely so can New Zealand, where the proportion of women seeking employment is lower.

(2) It has been maintained that equal work for equal pay cannot be adopted until a universal system of family allowances has been instituted. The Government's proposal to introduce a Minimum Family Income Bill next session should remove all opposition on these grounds. If children are ultimately to be provided for by the State, the classical argument against the principle of equal pay loses all validity.

Opposition to equal pay has been

founded on the supposition that women do not have to support families. Yet in Great Britain and Australia, where the argument has been used recently, investigation has proved it to be a fallacy. In England, it was estimated that 60 per cent of the members of the Business and Professional Women's Clubs had dependents in 1944. In Australia, one third of the women employed in 1944 had dependents, while one third of employed men were not married. In the absence of any statistics regarding New Zealand women and single men, we can only assume that similar conditions prevail, alleviated to a certain extent by the Social Security Act, and a higher standard of living. This conclusion is borne out in the evidence obtained through a questionnaire filled in recently by over one thousand women in the New Zealand Public Service. A large number of these were wartime temporaries who are married women without dependents so that the number would be greater in normal times. This illustrated that approximately eight per cent had dependents or partial dependents.

If wage rates are to be determined by job content, the justification of a lower salary scale for women, in the absence of a universal scheme for family allowances, is illogical.

We consider that it is both practicable and equitable that the principle of equal pay should be introduced immediately in New Zealand. As its logical outcome, this would result in increased support for a scheme of family allowances. That such a scheme is practicable is obvious from the circumstances, already quoted, which surrounded the acceptance to equal pay in the Federal Service of the United States in 1923, and in the Dominion Civil Service in Canada, regulated by the Civil Service Act of 1927. In the United States there are no provisions for any type of family allowance, while in Canada universal family allowances were not introduced until 1944.

(3) In New Zealand, there have been several statements recently in official circles to the effect that women employees are not as capable as men, and that therefore the wage they are at present receiving is adequate. In the absence of any detailed investigations, these accusations are unfounded.

Although it is inevitable that, as a result of wartime conditions the Public Service

should have been forced to employ unqualified and inefficient servants, there are many women who have carried on as efficiently as their male predecessors. It is unfair that these women should be penalised, and that democratic principles and economic principles be disregarded.

Detailed investigations into the comparative capabilities of men and women, in the United States of America and in Great Britain and Australia, have proved that these charges of incapability are false.

The Women's Employment Board in Australia found that in some cases where there was evidence of a comparatively low rate of female productivity, the fault lay not with the female workers, but with the employer, who failed to achieve the maximum output for various reasons which became obvious on investigation. These included poor supervision, bad surroundings, poor organisation, and the failure to utilise intelligently the females in their most efficient capacity, to provide adequate and proper conveniences, amenities, and rest periods, or to provide properly for psychological factors which make so pronounced a difference, not only in the well-being of female staff, but in their productivity.

Where congenial working conditions and adequate remuneration have been provided, it has been found that women prove equal in capability to men.

(4) It has been stated that men object to female controlling officers, and that the adoption of a policy of equal pay for equal work would open the way for women to assume senior positions, with consequent dissatisfaction among the male staff.

In occupations where equal pay has been adopted, however, it has been found that men and women work much better together, and that the men do not object to able and efficient women as controlling officers.

(5) The objection has been raised, that if women receive pay equal to that of men, they will be tempted to sacrifice marriage and/or motherhood to a career.

In fact, it has been shown that men and women have been forced to marry late in life because of inadequate wages, and that many women are forced to continue working in order to supplement the family income. If women are freed from the economic bondage which the fulfilment of motherhood at present entails, few would be tempted in preference to choose a career. In the U.S.S.R. where there is no discrimination in the wages paid to men and women, there is the highest birth rate in the world, and prostitution is practically non-existent.

II. The reasons for the application of the principle of equal pay.

(1) Equal pay for equal work is an abstract principle of justice. We assert that it is in the best interests of the community that, in addition to full political and civil rights, and full opportunity for education, women should have the full right and opportunity to employment on equal terms with men, and should receive remuneration without discrimination because of sex or marital status.

(2) If women are a cheaper labour commodity than men, they will undercut men's salaries, depress wages all round, and ultimately reduce the standard of living. The fact that women undercut men is particularly relevant in jobs created by new developments in industry and State enterprise, which will be continued after the war, and in which Occupational Re-establishment Regulations do not make it imperative for the positions to be relinquished to men returning to their civilian occupations. It is this aspect of the policy of equal pay for equal work which has led many Trade Unions to insist that where women are replacing men they should do so at the male rate of pay.

Positions in the Public Service should therefore be graded, and salaries fixed according to the job content, regardless of the sex of the person appointed to the position. This would do away with the alleged designation of subclerical work, which is at present being carried out by the 'office assistant' on a lower salary scale than that of men doing comparable work in the Clerical Division, and would prevent the office assistant from being a permanent feature of the Public Service.

(3) Women's wage rates should not be fixed on a productivity basis – i.e. as a percentage of those paid to men engaged on comparable work, according to their relative efficiency as compared to men. As Dr Sutch pointed out in his dissenting report to the Government Railways Industrial Tribunal, this method of 'trying to fix rates on a so-called productivity basis is very open to question.

All men working at one job are entitled to the same rate of pay, irrespective of variations in their individual productivity.' It is a basic Trade Union principle in wage negotiations that the merit of the individual worker must not entitle him to a margin over his fellows. The Public Service pays men salaries calculated according to grade, irrespective of variations in their individual ability and efficiency; and it is only fair and democratic that women should be treated likewise.

(4) The adoption of the policy of equal pay for equal work would ensure the recognition of the principle, 'a fair field and no favour', laid down by the Royal Commission in Great Britain in 1929. Women as workers would then be placed on equal terms with men in the field of common employment, and artificial barriers to appointment in the Public Service would be removed. This would open the Public Service as a career to qualified women in New Zealand, and ensure that the person who is best qualified to fill the job would be appointed regardless of sex.

(5) The adoption of the 'merit principle' would mean the appointment of the most able persons, regardless of sex, and the entry of women into the field of employment on equal terms with men would raise the standard of work by increased competition. This would be to the benefit of the Public Service, and the community as a whole.

(6) Up to the present time, women have been working under certain disadvantages. An adoption of the principle of equal pay for equal work would benefit them as follows:

(a) Single women, with their standard of living raised to that of single men, would have opportunities for educational and cultural development at present denied them, because they cannot afford to pay for them. In addition there is every reason to believe that women, as well as men, do save to provide for a future home and children and if both parties can manage to save, earlier marriages can take place.

(b) Opportunities of specialised training for higher positions in the Public Service would be opened.

(c) Women with dependents would have their standard of living raised above the bread-line.

(d) Women with ability and high qualifications, at present seeking employment in outside fields of labour because of the poor prospects and low salaries offered within the Public Service, would be prepared to make a career within the Service.

(e) Women are more prepared to accept responsibility and more suited to wield authority, if they are placed on an equal economic footing with men. Women have a sense of inferiority, which is at least partly due to their inferior economic status, as well as a sense of frustration where they are doing work comparable to that of men, and receive no recognition.

Recommendations

On behalf of the women of the New Zealand Public Service, we therefore recommend, that in view of the social and political changes at home and overseas during recent years, and the fact that women civil servants have suffered from special forms of exploitation and discrimination in the past, there is an urgent need to re-examine their general position and salary scales.

In view of the way in which women, for patriotic reasons or by direction have come forward in war-time and taken the place of men in the Armed Forces, we ask that they too should be given immediate consideration. We therefore advocate the immediate adoption of the following policy with regard to the employment of women in the New Zealand Public Service:

(1) That the principle that men and women should receive equal remuneration for work of equal value be observed throughout the New Zealand Public Service.

(2) That all the positions in the Public Service be classified on a functional basis; that a rate of pay be fixed for the job regardless of who performs it; and that men and women be given an equal opportunity of applying for jobs.

(3) That where women are employed as wartime temporaries taking the place of men in the Armed Forces, they should receive male rates of pay.

Appendix

The following cases have been included in this Report to illustrate the comparative levels of male and female salary scales. They are by no means exhaustive as more detailed examples will be given when the group cases of the female office assistants are presented.

1 a. Shorthand typists doing reporting work.

Female shorthand typists reporting on Royal Commissions, Committees of Enquiry etc where verbatim evidence is taken over long periods:

Maximum salary under PSC £245 (old scale)

Hansard Reporters who are often employed to do the same work:

Salaries range from £425 – £615 (old scale)

The females are engaged on reporting work on a maximum salary that is approximately 57% of the male's minimum rate.

N.B. Women are debarred from becoming Hansard Reporters because it is alleged that they could not work the long hours that are necessary. In fact the daily average of the sitting hours of the House during 1943 Session was 5 hr. 40 min. and there were 8 Hansard Reporters to divide the work taking only 5 min. at a time. This means that the Reporters have time to type back what they have taken before their next spell.

Women reporting commissions, etc. do at least 6 hr of actual note taking per day. The work is divided between 3 or even 2 working half an hour at a time. This does not give them sufficient time to complete typing their previous hour's notes before the next spell.

1 b. Shorthand typist.

Male £265 (new scale)

Female £215 i.e. 81% of male rate.

2. Sorters.

Maximum for male £295 (new scale)

Maximum for female £215 (new scale) i.e. 72% of male rate.

3. General clerical.

a. Case of male and female in the same Department doing the same routine account work where both have had 2 years previous experience

Male £165 (old scale)

Female £115 (old scale) i.e. 69% of male rate.

b. Assessments work

Normal maximum for male £340 (old scale)

Normal maximum for female £205 (old scale) i.e. 60% of male rate.

c. Department would be prepared to replace in routine accounts work

Female £215 (new scale)

by Male £305 (new scale)

i.e. female rate 70% male rate.

d. Senior accounts work – Department would be prepared to replace

Female £235 (new scale)

by Male £340 (new scale)

i.e. female rate 69% male rate.

4. Special group of office assistants.

a. Accounts clerk
Normal maximum for females £260 (old scale)
Normal maximum for males £335 (old scale)
i.e. female rate 77% male rate.

b. Records Clerk.
Female £205 + £20 allowance (old scale)
Male predecessors on £325 and £365
i.e. female rate 69% and 61% of male rate.

c. Staff Clerk.
(1) Female £275 + £10 allowance (new scale)
Male predecessor a Class VI officer on £380
i.e. female rate 75% of male rate.
N.B. The male had one or two assistants, while female has no assistants, yet volume of work has increased as a result of war
(2) Female £295 + £20 allowance (new scale)
Male predecessor £435
i.e. female rate 72% of male rate.
N.B. Volume of work increased as result of war.

(3) Male 1941 £380 (old scale)
Female 1941 replacing him £225 + £20 allowance.
i.e. 73% of male rate.
N.B. Female's duties exactly the same as male's plus the stress of war years and the expansion of the Department from 983 to nearly 2000 from 1941 to 1944.

d. Senior Physical Welfare Officer
Male £425 (old scale)
Female £320
i.e. 75% of male rate.

5. Adult minimum wage
Male £225 (new scale)
Female £175
i.e. 77.7% of male rate.

The Case for Equal Pay for Equal Work Presented on Behalf of the Women of the New Zealand Public Service to the Consultative Committee, 4 April 1944, *pp.1–4, 11–21, (MS Papers 1371, folder 246, ATL)*

5.2.   Are They 80% Efficient?
by Kathleen Ross (1944)

We are glad to say that the Public Service is not the only State organisation fighting for equal pay for equal work; and readers of the local newspapers may have been interested recently to see a report of the struggles of the railway servants to bring about this desirable end.

The Amalgamated Society of Railway Servants (we print the name in full, because Sandy Powell's well-known record has nothing on the initials of industrial organisations) – the A.S.R.S., then, has committed itself to the principle of equal pay, and has just taken the matter to the G.R.I.T. (**That** means Government Railways Industrial Tribunal). The result is not yet known, but since what affects one State service must ultimately affect others, we are printing below some details of the Railways case, and of the present situation of the girls who collect tickets, trundle luggage, and work in the stores, all jobs originally done by men.

Though the basic rate for men is £4/13/4, the girls are paid £3 and £3/5/-, the Department's attitude being that about eighty per cent efficiency is all that can be expected from the girls, and certainly all that should be paid for.

The men are not satisfied
So the A.S.R.S. passed their remit about equal pay, and took the matter to the Minister of

Railways, who, in recognition of the girls' good work, gave them a slight increase – to 1s. 10d. and 2s. an hour while on a 40-hour week. This, while it was certainly an improvement, had nothing to do with the idea of equal pay for equal work, and the General Secretary, Mr McIlvride, and the Executive Council, not having received an acknowledgement of the basic principle involved, took the matter further, to the Tribunal. This body, which has been set up recently by Act of Parliament, consists of Mr Stilwell, S.M., Mr E.C. Casey, representing the Government, and Dr Sutch, representing the various Societies' organisations.

Women fill the breeches
The case which Mr McIlvride prepared is as follows: 'As we all know, our women have been prepared to supply labour power wherever possible, in order to release men for military service, and it is a matter of deep regret that no provision has been made to give them the same status and rights accorded the men whose places they fill. We all admit that equal pay for equal work is a fair principle, and, after all, what does it matter whether the person doing the work wears a skirt or a pair of trousers, so long as the work is done?

December, 1944. The Public Service Journal. 505

Women's Page

By Kathleen Ross

Are They 80% Efficient?

WE are glad to say that the Public Service is not the only State organisation fighting for equal pay for equal work; and readers of the local newspapers may have been interested recently to see a report of the struggles of the railway servants to bring about this desirable end.

"*Girls Who Trundle Luggage.*"

The Amalgamated Society of Railway Servants (we print the name in full, because Sandy Powell's well-known record has nothing on the initials of industrial organisations)— the A.S.R.S., then, has committed itself to the principle of equal pay, and has just taken the matter to the G.R.I.T. (That means Government Railways Industrial Tribunal.) The result is not yet known, but since what affects one State service must ultimately affect others, we are printing below some details of the Railways case, and of the present situation of the girls who collect tickets, trundle luggage, and work in the stores, all jobs originally done by men.

Though the basic rate for men is £4/13/4, the girls are paid £3 and £3/5/-, the Department's attitude being that about eighty per cent. efficiency is all that can be expected from the girls, and certainly all that should be paid for.

THE MEN ARE NOT SATISFIED

So the A.S.R.S. passed their remit about equal pay, and took the matter to the Minister of Railways, who, in recognition of the girls' good work, gave them a slight increase—to 1s. 10d. and 2s. an hour on a 40-hour week. This, while it was certainly an improvement, had nothing to do with the idea of equal pay for equal work, and the General Secretary, Mr. McIlvride; and the Executive Council, not having received an acknowledgment of the basic principle involved, took the matter further, to the Tribunal. This body, which has been set up recently by Act of Parliament, consists of Mr. Stilwell, S.M., Mr. E. C. Casey, representing the Government, and Dr. Sutch, representing the various Societies' organisations.

WOMEN FILL THE BREECHES

The case which Mr. McIlvride prepared is as follows:—

"As we all know, our women have been prepared to supply labour power wherever possible, in order to release men for military service, and it is a matter of deep regret that no provision has been made to give them the same status and rights accorded the men whose places they fill. We all admit that equal pay for equal work is a fair principle, and, after all, what does it matter whether the person doing the work wears a skirt or a pair of trousers, so long as the work is done?

"The Department's contention is that equal work is not being done by these women, and it is because we cannot subscribe to this contention that we are appealing to you. The President and myself, while visiting different parts of the country, have made it our business to investigate the position.

"We have watched the women at work and discussed it with them. We have satisfied ourselves that in many positions they are doing exactly the same work as the men who performed it before being called to the colours. We have interviewed their supervisors and the men working alongside of them, the former expressing satisfaction with their work and the latter maintaining that the women were doing exactly the same work as them.

"As a matter of fact, at one place we were informed that the women had not only proved that they were the equals of the men replaced, but they had proved that they were able to do more and better work than the men. We watched a porter and porteress handling heavy luggage on one station, and the woman handled case for case and kit bag for kit bag with the man.

NO LILIES THEY

"In the Wellington Station luggage room now porteresses are doing a full-sized man's job, that of receiving, checking, stacking and delivering luggage—no light task. Against this the Department argues that the women must be placed in selected positions because their services cannot be utilised to the same extent as those of the men. For example, a woman cannot be sent out to pilot an engine or work in a shunting yard. That

"*A Full-sized Man's Job.*"

Kathleen Ross's 1944 challenge to her Public Service colleagues, 'Are they 80% efficient?', in *The Public Service Journal*, December 1944. *Alexander Turnbull Library*

'The Department's contention is that equal work is not being done by these women, and it is because we cannot subscribe to this contention that we are appealing to you. The President and myself, while visiting different parts of the country, have made it our business to investigate the position.

'We have watched the women at work and discussed it with them. We have satisfied ourselves that in many positions they are doing exactly the same work as the men who performed it before being called to the colours. We have interviewed their supervisors and the men working alongside of them, the former expressing satisfaction with their work and the latter maintaining that the women were doing exactly the same work as them.

'As a matter of fact, at one place we were informed that the women had not only proved that they were the equals of the men replaced, but they had proved that they were able to do more and better work than the men. We watched a porter and porteress handling heavy luggage on one station, and the woman handled case for case and kit bag for kit bag with the man.

No lilies they

'In the Wellington Station luggage room now porteresses are doing a full-sized man's job, that of receiving, checking, stacking and delivering luggage – no light task. Against this the Department argues that the women must be placed in selected positions because their services cannot be utilised to the same extent as those of the men. For example, a woman cannot be sent out to pilot an engine or work in a shunting yard. That may be so, but that is not the point.

'The point is that men have always been employed in the luggage room, and if in normal times a man was sent into the yard, another man took his place in the room. Now men are not available, women have been substituted; they are doing men's work and should be paid the same rate as the men.

Women in the stores

'Another case in point is that of the women employed in the stores department at the Hutt Workshops. The management readily agreed to our request to be allowed to investigate the position, and we did.

'We learned from the supervisors that the work of the women was highly satisfactory, and

later verified the statement of our members that in the receiving, issuing, dispatching and stationery departments the work being done by the women was in no way different from that performed by the men.

'Everywhere we went, everything we saw convinced us that the claim for equal pay for the women was fully justified.

'These women unload material from lorries on to barrows and then push the barrows laden with heavy material into the store, where they again unload it into the different bins. I made way for one woman with her barrow and noticed included in the load a heavy coil of machine belting and trays of $^7/_8$ in. bolts. All material received, issued or set away is entered by these women on cards from which departmental records are compiled, which means that the complete circle of work in the store is started and finished by them, just as it was by the men whose work they carry on.

Are they flexible?

'Here also, however, the Department holds that the women lack the flexibility and versatility of men, stating that they cannot be sent to work in the yard or at the iron rack.

'Our answer is that men have been transferred to this section and have worked there for years without being sent once to the yard or rack, but no one ever thought of paying them less on that account. We found that these women were doing a man's job and we ask that they be paid a man's wage.

'In the stationery section no one could point to a single job formerly done by men that the women cannot do or are not doing. It is work for which the women are admirably suited. They are deft, painstaking and accurate, and earn every penny of the man's rate.

'We were informed that prior to engaging female labour in these sections the work was behind. Now it is up to date and the stores cleaner than they have been for many a long day.

In future?

'This is a question involving extremely wide ramifications and touching also upon our struggles for a new world order. Within us all is the spiritual urge for higher achievement and a higher and more equitable standard of life; but our struggles will have been in vain if we have to tell the men and women who return from the war that while they have saved the world for a new order our only offering in return for their sacrifice is a continuation of the old, with its recurring unemployment and constant under-payment.

'We trust that you will see the justice of our claim and grant our request for equal pay for equal work.'

Public Service Journal, *December 1944*, *pp. 505–506*

5.3. Social Aspects of Equal Pay by Caroline Webb (1946)

In conjunction with the Business and Professional Women's Club, the Wellington Women's Committee recently sponsored two meetings on the subject of equal pay for equal work. The speakers were Mrs Leicester [Caroline] Webb, who dealt with the social aspects of the problem, and Mr R.L. Meek, who covered the economic angle. We are printing below part of Mrs Webb's address, which is of general interest to women, and hope at some future date to be able to give some extracts form Mr Meek's, which dealt with some very involved matters in a particularly lucid manner.

The status of women in English-speaking countries has improved tremendously during the last hundred years, but we are still a long way from possessing equality. It was the generation of our grandmothers who won for us legal equality, or at any rate, laid the foundations of equality in the Marriage and Divorce Laws and the Married Women Equality Acts. Then our mothers' generation won political equality for us, in winning the right to vote. But it still remains for us to complete their work by winning economic equality.

The natural order

The general criticism of those who advocate improvement in the status of women is that it is altering the natural order of things. To those people I would say: What order? Is it the order of things one hundred years ago that they wish to preserve, when women had no legal existence at all, but were merely the property of their fathers before they were married, their husbands after they were married, or else they became a burden on their nearest male relative if they did not marry? These women had no claim even to their own children: the father of a family could remove the children from the home and forbid his wife to see them, and the wife had no redress. And a married woman had no right to her own money; the man could claim his wife's money whether she possessed it before or after she was married. You may remember the famous case of the woman, Caroline Norton, who won for herself a place in history. After she was deserted by her husband, with considerable difficulty she earned enough to support herself. Her husband claimed her money, and the law courts upheld his claim. That was the status of women in the beginning of the nineteenth century.

We have come a long way from this, but the idea of women as something less than full human beings has not entirely disappeared yet. Ghosts of these old ideas still linger in odd corners. Not many people advocate in itself the subjection of women, but I think we are all familiar with the technique of refusing to take them seriously, and of completely ignoring their demands. You remember the lengths to which the suffragettes had to go in England to have their ideas taken seriously. The story of the suffragettes has not received sufficient attention in the history books, possibly because they are mostly written by men. And there seems every reason why the story should make a good moving picture. The scorn with which all the people regarded the antics of the suffragettes is well known, but as I grew older I began to find that all the intelligent and thinking people had supported the suffragettes, because they realized that what were called their antics – the mass meetings, the demonstrations, the marches on Parliament, the hunger strikes – had been made necessary because of the refusal by the men in power to consider their claims and to take them seriously. In New Zealand women did not have to go to such lengths before they were given the privilege of voting. But they worked hard, organizing meetings, writing articles, canvassing Members of Parliament, getting up monster petitions, and we will have to be no less resolute and determined in our demands if we are not just to rest content with what our forebears have won for us, but to complete their work by winning for the women of New Zealand economic equality with men.

Economic equality

Perhaps I had better explain what it is that I mean by economic equality. I mean two things:

equal pay and equal opportunity. About equal pay, I should like first to say this: it is not just a demand for more money on the part of women, in fact the amount of money they receive, I think I am right in saying, is much less important to us than the value that is placed on the work we do. At present, because women are paid less their work is generally valued less, and their standing in the community generally is lowered by this fact of low pay. Those of you who have read Virginia Woolf's books will know what I mean. Virginia Woolf was anything but a rabid feminist – she would probably have disclaimed the title – but she realized very clearly a hundred and one ways in which the low pay of women affects their influence in society. Independent opinions, she said, to be effective must be based on independent income, and she argues that the number of women whose incomes are sufficient to make their opinions effective is so small that the world is still run by masculine opinions and masculine standards of value. That is worth thinking about, and her books are well worth reading on that subject.

A step towards a new standard of values has been achieved recently in the universal family allowances. Besides recognizing the work of the mothers in the community, it does away with the justification for the payment of higher wages to men than to women. The contention that women can be paid less than men because they do not have to support a family, can no longer be maintained, now that the principle of paying women for the support of each child has been adopted. Of course there is room for the extension of this principle, particularly by benefits in kind. We already have such benefits in kind in free education of children, free dental service, and so forth. We could well have free school dinners and perhaps also the system which is in operation in Sweden, where the rent of State and municipal houses is reduced by 10 percent for each child in the family. Such things would extend the principle. But the important thing is that we now have this principle accepted, which means that the old assumption that a man must be paid more than a woman, because of the dependents he has to support, can be discontinued.

Payment for the job

Now, as to what we mean by the demand for equality. We mean payment for the job, irrespective of the person who does it, whether it is a man or woman. It should not be possible for a job to be advertised as it is in the teaching profession at one salary for a man, and at another salary for a woman. Nor should the award rates contain two scales of pay, one masculine and one feminine, for similar work. The clerical award rate rises to a maximum of £6/11/- for men, and only £4/1/4 for women. Even more unequal is the basic wage set by the Arbitration court in 1936 – £3/16/- for men and £1/16/- for women. The assumption was that the average wage of women was just about half the average wage of men. And yet it costs women just as much to live as it costs men. They do not get their houses or their food or lighting or travel or entertainment any cheaper, and they have to pay taxes at the same rate. Why should they receive so much lower wages? Payment should be for the work done, and not according to the kind of person who does it. You do not differentiate according to the height of people, their nationality or their religion. Why, then, should we differentiate according to their sex?

At present, women form a pool of cheap labour, and there is a constant danger of their keeping men from jobs just because they are cheaper to employ, particularly in times of unemployment. In old-established industries, men have guarded against this eventuality by erecting barriers around all the best paid and responsible jobs to keep cheap women's labour out. We all know instances of that. But many of the new industries are being based on women's labour just because it is cheaper and efficient. If equal pay were to open all this field of women's work to men by insisting that women should be paid men's wages, then men would have the advantage of a whole new field of opportunity before them. And this would be a great advantage at this time when thousands of men are being rehabilitated into civil life.

Women, we declare, should hold their jobs because they are efficient, and on no other basis. They should not hold their jobs just because they are lower paid than men. They should prove their efficiency in an open field. This is the case in the professions – women doctors and accountants are paid the same as men and have the same opportunities as men. In the Tramways, the decision to pay women conductors at a men's rate was not done out of kindness to women. It was done in the interests of men, so that if women conductors should prove as efficient as men the Board would not continue to employ women merely for the sake of economy.

Equal opportunity

This leads us to the second point in the demand for economic equality. The first is equal pay, the second is equal opportunity. As I have said, the effect of cheap women's labour has led to an artificial division of labour between men and women. The work of the community is not divided between men and women according to what they can each do best, but it is divided according first of all to the reluctance of men to allow cheap women's labour into many of their occupations, and on the other hand, by the desire of employers to employ cheap women's labour as far as possible. So the counterpart of joining women's work to men's by paying a man's wage for it would be to admit women to any occupation, to give women the same opportunities as men, the same opportunities of advancement, and the same opportunities to enter apprenticeships and to rise to the top in industry or the professions. The only apprenticeships to which women are admitted are chemistry and upholstering. They are not even admitted to the window-dressing trade, which obviously is one in which women would be very useful and successful. Our demand is for a fair field and no favour.

Now that family allowances have removed the basic reason for the difference in pay between men and women, now that the war has given women the opportunity to prove their ability in every field of work, and now that the United Nations have reaffirmed in their Charter the equal rights of men and women, now is the time to press our demand for economic equality, and so complete equal status for men and women.

Mrs Leicester Webb, 'Social Aspects of Equal Pay', Public Service Journal, January 1946, pp.13–14.

5.4. Mothers Can't Form a Pressure Group by Caroline Webb (1947)

Would you agree that the present is a particularly significant and difficult time for women? I think it is, for this reason that the conditions in which we live have changed so much since the beginning of the century and are still changing rapidly. This means that we can't just live our lives as our mothers and grandmothers lived theirs. Instead of following a pattern already laid down we have to draft a new pattern to fit the different conditions in which we live.

As I see it there are two major changes particularly affecting women. First of all there is the change to a one-class society. As far back as history goes there has been a working class and a leisured class, with varying gradations between these two groups. Now we are approaching a one-class society, and New Zealand has gone as far as any country in this direction. New Zealand mothers, at any rate, are all working class – that is, we all do our own work. Fortunately we don't have to work outside as well as inside the home. If any of you have been to Oriental countries and seen, as I have seen, women working in factories with their babies lying underneath the loom or the machine, you will realise the significance of this. The working woman who, in older countries, is forced by poverty and expected by custom to work in a factory and bring up a family at the same time does not exist in New Zealand. Neither does the lady of leisure. Any girl who has been brought up, as the saying goes, without doing a hand's turn for herself is faced with as much hard work as any other woman when she becomes a mother.

I wonder if you have read Olive Schreiner's book *Women and Labour.* I sometimes think of it with amusement when I am hectically busy. Her thesis was that Western civilisation was on the verge of collapse because educated women did not have enough to occupy them. She wrote at the end of last century when all these women had a large staff of servants to run their houses and bring up their children, and she felt that unless women were admitted to all the professions and occupations they would degenerate into idle drones and become a demoralising influence on society. She brought half a lifetime of research to bear on this thesis – but how differently things have turned out! However, it is quite a tonic to remember how narrowly, in Olive Schreiner's opinion at any rate, we escaped the danger of becoming demoralising drones.

But there are other dangers I am not so sure we have escaped. Worst of all is the danger that life for mothers will become a mere struggle for existence and that graciousness, beauty and hospitality in the home will be lost. It is to preserve these values that a new pattern of living is needed. It will have to be a pattern that concentrates on the essentials and cuts out the frills, that preserves the worthwhile things in life and discards the merely conventional. Already our rooms have achieved an almost Japanese simplicity compared with the over-furnishing of our grandmother's time. Wash-stands in the bedroom, the bedroom fire, and the bath that was pulled out from under the bed have all gone. We take turns in the bathroom and use an electric heater. Our clothes, too, especially children's clothes, are much simpler than the starched frills I was accustomed to in my childhood. But things have to go still further in this direction if life is not to be a mere hand-to-mouth existence for parents.

And here I must pay a tribute to the New Zealand father. He is wonderful in the way he does the washing at the week-ends, and can even cook the Sunday dinner. But surely parents should not have to spend every minute slaving after their children. They should some-times have leisure to be men and women as well as parents, to keep up with what is going on in sport and to entertain like other people.

The family allowances, tax reductions, and maternity benefits have of course relieved the financial strain on parents very much. I think, however, that further development along these lines should take the form of assistance in kind rather than in money. There are so many things that money can't buy nowadays. School dinners, such as are provided in the primary schools in England, would be worth far more to busy mothers than the cost of them. So would permanent play-centres for pre-school children, larger houses for families, and help in the home for sick or expectant mothers.

Some attempts have been made by groups of women to organise these services for them-selves and they have done most valuable experimental work. But I do not think it would be possible for volunteers from among already over-worked mothers to provide such things on a nation-wide scale. Mothers could be relied on to help at play-centres and with cooking dinners, but I think either the State or local authorities would need to pay the overhead costs and employ the permanent staffs.

Unfortunately, mothers are not in a good position to urge these things for themselves. They don't form a pressure group in any way comparable with the average trade union. Having nothing to sell they can't even stage a strike. And this is a serious state of affairs at a time when people are tending more and more to divide into occupational groups engaged in

securing advantages for their members.

So far I have dealt entirely with the effect of the one-class society on the woman in the home. But there is, of course, a very large group of women who work outside the home – the women who hold jobs, career women. In Olive Schreiner's day the interests of the two groups clashed. They clash still to some extent in many countries. The married woman worker wants protection from the double burden of work – work inside and work outside the home. She wants shorter hours than male workers and special protection to safeguard her health when she is having children. The career woman, on the other hand, wishes to be allowed to com-pete with men on terms of equality and objects to any differences in conditions of work or pay between the sexes. In New Zealand there are so few women with young families in industry that the interests of these two groups, though different, are not opposed. As a result they could, if they would, support each other's interests; the career women backing measures to make the life of the mother less burdensome and the mothers joining forces with the wage-earners in their demand for equality between the sexes.

In Russia, I gather, there is practically no distinction between the two groups, the child-bearers and the wage-earning women. Most women work outside the home whether they have families or not and discrimination be-tween the sexes seems to have been practically eliminated. This, I take it, though I may be wrong, is more the result of conditions in Russia than of principle. Because the demand for labour is very urgent all women are encouraged to work and special institutions are provided to care for children outside the home. It remains to be seen how this system works out. Personally I would not be surprised, when the tremendous demand for labour slackens, if the Russians did not change their minds about the mothers of young children working, just as they have changed many of their ideas about education. It is at any rate interesting to find a different solution to these problems in another country; and it will be interesting to see, as the century goes on, whether we adopt the Russian system or they adopt ours, or whether we continue to differ.

Now, I said at the beginning of this talk that there were two major changes affecting the lives of women to-day. The first is the change to a one-class society, which I have been talking about. The other great change is the development of equality between the sexes. Our grandmothers' generation won us legal equality – or at any rate laid the foundations of it. Our mothers' generation won us political equality and now we are feeling our way towards economic equality. I can't say of this change, as I did of the other, that we in New Zealand have gone as far as any other country.

In fact we tend to lag behind other English-speaking countries. Women in the British Civil Service, for instance, have better status and opportunities than women in the New Zealand Public Service; and there is a greater difference between men's and women's rates of pay here than in the Australian Commonwealth Public Service. How the able and energetic American

women hold their own with men in all sorts of activities is well known, and in the American Federal Civil Service men and women have had the same rates of pay since 1923. This is also usual in the various State Civil Services, while six states, including New York and Washington, have even passed Equal Pay Acts prohibiting discrimination between the sexes in paying wages. Here in New Zealand, though women may have the same training as men and the same qualifications, jobs in which they receive the same pay and the same opportunities for advancement are rare.

New Zealand Listener, 7 March 1947, pp.10–11

5.5. More Mums for the Olympics by Margot Roth (1957)

The tumult and the shouting of the Olympic Games is now dying away, with only a sporadic outburst of recrimination and, for me, the stains on the carpet to recall those two weeks when everyone followed Father into the living-room to eat their dinner by the radio. However, one impression has lingered with me. It is that the newspaper and radio reports all showed a rather unpractical approach in their attitude towards those married women with children who were successful competitors. This 'even though she has had children' touch is reminiscent of a butcher's words to me some time ago. I asked him what kind of mutton it was that his city shop sold so much more cheaply than mutton in other shops.

'Well Miss,' he said with flattering inaccuracy as he leaned confidentially over the counter at me, 'I don't want to put you off, but you must have noticed for yourself that once a woman's had a baby, she's never quite as good again. That's what this mutton is.' My feelings, as I moved the baby over to make room in the pram parked outside the shop for my large hunk of not-so-good mutton were a mixture of indignant sympathy for the maligned ewes and a certain amount of complacency that I had, momentarily anyway, given the impression of being stamped with the red line instead of the second-grade blue.

I remember that when Mrs Fanny Blankers-Koen was breaking records at the Olympics four years ago there was always that undercurrent of 'Well, fancy, her with two children and all.' Now honestly, when one comes to

consider carefully, is it not more likely that a woman who has been trained by a couple of normal toddlers can jump over a few obstacles like hurdles at a greater speed than one who has merely jogged round an uneventful training track? Take any mother of young children who, for the first time in months or even years, really looks closely at herself in an evening dress. Where are those softly rounded arms, those smooth shoulders of her lost youth (the one that meanly got away by winning a scholarship that took him overseas)? Through the bumps and grinds of shoving prams and push-chairs, of slinging children into crowded vehicles with that cheap slab of mutton oozing on the other hip, they have been dissipated into rippling muscles that could put a shot or throw a discus with extraordinary power.

For speed records to break all records, I suggest lining up some mothers with a few toddlers enclosed 100 metres away. Simultaneously with the starting gun the toddlers could be released and a car or a few large dogs could be driven towards them. The Olympic torch would send up sparks from the rush past. Of course some more refined method would probably have to be introduced to pacify those dog lovers who objected for humane reasons – perhaps something similar to decoy ducks.

Nobody unfortunately had the presence of mind to time me, but I feel I can make a modest claim to one record. It happened one afternoon when I was in the local grocer's shop, filled with people on their way home. I suddenly realised that my three-year-old was with me but my one-year-old had vanished. There were plenty of people about; he could only just walk, and current road repairs meant that there was a huge drop from the footpath to the gutter, so he couldn't get far. I comforted myself as I All Blacked out of the shop. A tram was moving off from the terminus with the conductor and the motorman deep in conversation on the front platform. There was only one passenger and he had obviously just managed to clamber on to the back platform before the tram went, and was busily engaged in making his way inside on all fours. Never have I pursued a tram gathering speed with so fleet a foot. What's more it wasn't Betty Cuthbert, the new Australian champion, who was the first to run a race with her mouth open. It was me, because I happened to be calling on the tram driver to stop at the time. Not only did I break a record, but I didn't finish my run by relaxing all over a tape. I made a magnificent leap to grab my highly indignant son and I feel that a simple Olympic hurdle that wasn't swaying along tram lines in disrepair would be nothing to it.

Now this experience of mine, in different form, could be multiplied dozens of times by dozens of women, especially those who are blessed with climbers in the family. Is there anything more athletic, I have been forced to ask myself, than an emphatically pregnant woman climbing a tree after a mountaineer who is paralysed by the fly-past of what he swears is a vulture?

The field of sport is not the only one where solid experience has been overlooked by the experts. First Mt Everest, now the Antarctic make claim to our national pride of achievement. Much of the organisation for these expeditions has revolved round working out supplies and equipment. Just look at the beaches during the summer months when they are covered by women, who, very often at the short notice provided by the weather, have masterfully assembled supplies and equipment to cater for a varied range of ages, tastes and food requirements, including Teddy and that tip-truck acquired at Christmas and enough clothes to cover all unthinkable emergencies, all assembled within the compass laid down by hand transport. In fact if the day's exercise includes a pre-pre-schooler, one might just as well be going to the Antarctic anyway.

This is election year, the heady though short-lived period when housewives and mothers hit the headlines and lip service is paid to their sterling qualities by hopeful vote-seekers. Now is the time to write to your M.P. and urge him to press for More Mums At The Olympics. After all, think of the financial saving in training such a team when any woman – especially if she is fortunate enough not to live on a flat section – going about her normal pursuits can Do It Herself at home. See you in Rome in 1960?

New Zealand Parent & Child, *June 1957, pp.11–12*

5.6. Housewives or Human Beings?
by Margot Roth (1959)

A friend of mine has a large and highly intelligent family. When she went along to enrol her eldest daughter at secondary school, the headmistress said yes, the child's record definitely showed she should join the top third form. Very gratifying. But Mother's pride soon changed to fury. The headmistress added that there must be a lot of chores falling to the eldest girl in such a big family, so she'd place the child in the second stream in case she couldn't keep up. Fortunately for this pupil, her mother's indignation at the idea of school work having to take second place won the day. But this is the point. Can you imagine a head*master* of a boy's secondary school putting a child into the second stream because of all the lawns he had to mow? No, of course you can't. And neither can I. What's the reason for this shattering

distinction between what's expected for boys and what for girls? Why have so many of our Kiwi males got the same attitude towards women as my son at the age of three? He remarked: 'We like Mummy because she makes our food and looks after us.' Well, fair enough at three, but it jars twenty or thirty years later. Could it be that many Kiwi females don't deserve more than this? I think for the answer we've go to delve into our past. The idea of men's role in society being of primary importance, with women as contributing subordinates rather than partners, isn't it simply a hangover from out-of-date British working-class customs?

But today in our mainly middle-class lives, these old distinctions are out-of-date and meaningless. We no longer need to build Father up to withstand the strains of being overworked and underpaid. These adjectives though, do describe many mothers with small children. They're the ones who most emphatically need half an hour or so of oblivion behind the evening paper at six o'clock. In spite of this, we – and I do mean women as well as men – go on thinking and behaving in the same old way, preserving the same stale old distinctions and taboos. Listen to this. Its' s the testimony of an English visitor, Amabel Williams Ellis. She says: 'I can still hear in my mind the gentle, rather weary voice of a young suburban mother in New Zealand whose four-year-old son was playing near by. "You don't want to play with dolls,' said the tired voice. 'Dolls are for girls! You play with your nice engine . . . No Ronnie, not that . . . You don't want to play with dolls".'

You know, I don't think it's odd that New Zealand's two international contributions to women's welfare are the Plunket system and marching girls. The Truby King system of mothercraft – what was it but an authority encouraging women to be manly? It's sissy to play with dolls is it? All right, we'll show you. Our babies are going to be little engines that keep to the rails. The railway timetable rules of the early Plunket days were really a negation of motherhood. In the same way, I feel, marching girls are a negation of femininity. Women are a different shape from men, if you've noticed, and all that masculine vigour simply develops the wrong muscles. Anyway, what's the point of marching like men? I know that marching teams give girls a chance of fun with others of their own age; they get gay uniforms and rhythmical exercise in the open air. These are all normal needs. But our society's way of filling them is an *ab*normal travesty of men being drilled for war.

Quite obviously, our society's out of plumb somewhere. And I'm suggesting that one way of helping to correct it is to get nearly half of it – the women – out of the mould of inferiority in which they're settling themselves more and more firmly. And again I'd like to stress that it's something which is largely their own fault. You see, over the years I believe we have been busily cultivating a myth – the myth of the over-worked housewife. Like most myths, it has a definite basis of fact.

Looking backwards again, our pioneer women coped with conditions we just can't picture. Although the majority of the earliest assisted immigrants were classified as servants, such a label didn't necessarily mean that they had any clues about dealing with what they found here. As for the women who weren't herded into the steerage with the lower orders on the way out, some of them were even more helpless . . . So housework came hard to a great number. It was a sort of moral challenge, met, we can proudly say, with courage and ingenuity . . .

But once again, times have changed, and once again our attitudes haven't changed with them. Today the hard-worked housewife stuff is propped up by the Homemakers' cult. We make a virtue of necessity and cling to our housework like a miser to his gold. Ours being a competitive society, we're encouraged to buy lots of labour-saving devices. Not to save our labour, but as ends in themselves – to keep up with the Joneses and to put money in advertisers' pockets. If we're honest, though, we must admit that housework, or homemaking as some advertisers prefer to call it, produces nothing that is directly useful to society. It opens no door to the future. Domestic chores should take their proper place as a background necessity, like brushing our teeth. This happens only if the person doing them is a creative worker of some kind, or making some contribution to society.

But all the forces in our lives bring pressure to bear to cast a false glamour over what's called 'the creative role of wife and mother'. Of course I know it is creative up to a point, and certainly it may be emotionally satisfying. But the *permanent* company of children and the kitchen sink is hardly stimulating mentally. True creative work implies a steady development. And you can't tell me anybody's developing if all she ever thinks about is food for the family and her resentment at their lack of appreciation for her often self-imposed drudgery. It seems to me utterly fantastic that our children should grow up with the belief that women fall into two classes. The married, despised for their intensely personal, housebound preoccupations, and the unmarried, despised because they lack that magic gold band that immediately transforms women into superior beings with no effort on their part. Oh yes, there are plenty of women who *do* realise that just being their mother's daughter, or a Married Woman – in capital letters – doesn't provide them with instinctive knowledge. So they go in hordes to learn about arranging flowers or cooking or sewing or child development. But – and this is a very big but – such studies too quickly become an end in themselves instead of forming just one part in an all-round development of the personality. We don't take ourselves seriously because we're so conditioned to the idea that domesticity comes first, last and all the time – the one really important thing in our lives. And this in turn leads straight to the old, old story that women, as such, aren't capable of really extending themselves individually.

Actually we do have another, better tradition, which stems from the old liberal *middle*-class in New Zealand. We used to have leisured women from this class who took their community responsibilities seriously. As well as other social reformers, they worked like beavers all over the country to get the vote for women in 1893. This in spite of opposition from their husbands, other women, Richard Seddon and the brewers. Most of these women came from families who could afford education . . . Until the last war, anyway, New Zealand has always had such a leisured minority.

And today? Well, the point I want to make is that today it's no longer a *small* minority. Growing numbers of women have, or could have, the leisure to devote to activities which benefit the whole community. This isn't because we can employ help, but because of our generally smaller families, our better health, longer lives and high standard of living. Yet our false commercialised picture of the Little Homemaker means that, with few exceptions, all this spare time hasn't led to wide social or cultural reforms. What it *has* led to is a woman's organisation at every lamp-post. And if the majority of them were laid end to end round our coastline they wouldn't be much loss. Why? Because most women's organisations, if you come to grips with them, devote their time to organising their organisations. They elect officers, frame constitutions, argue among themselves and battle with their rival associations for prestige. But when you get down to it, you find that few of their members are anxious to do away with injustices and abuses, which would make their association unnecessary.

For instance, there are several hardworking organisations catering for mothers and children. I've benefited from them myself. But generally speaking they're slaving so hard to organise a ball that's to be a highlight of the social season, or rehearsing for a concert, or arranging lectures to tell us where we're going wrong in bringing up our children, that they've overlooked the *basic* need of many mothers with babies. I mean relief from social isolation and the physical and mental exhaustion caused by a 24-hour day. Surely more mothers would

be helped and more babies saved from the effects of Mum's fatigue, if some of this time were spent in hanging out washing for tired young mothers, or baby-sitting while they went out with their husbands leaving the dishes in the sink. And with all our chatter about children's welfare, it takes a newspaper scandal to bring day nurseries into the limelight. Yet in our community there are always children who need special care because their mothers are widowed or divorced or supporting invalid husbands, and so have to go out to work. Women like this deserve the public support of proper day nurseries for their children. But no. Our social code says a mother must stay at home, regardless. Overseas studies bear out my own observation that good and bad parents are distributed equally among mothers who go out to work and those who don't. If a mother doesn't think it's important to be home after school, she won't be there whether she's at work, at a meeting or a golf tournament.

It seems to me we have such a one-eyed outlook. The effort to overcome it, and to train our sons and daughters to overcome it, is a major challenge of our time and community. I would argue that it's sensible to urge our daughters to regard their adult lives as being divided broadly into three phases.

Firstly, they train for or work at a job. Then, if they marry, there comes the period when their children need them most of the time. With luck, after that they should reach a third phase when they can devote some time – quite a lot of time – to work outside the home, whether it's for money or to further their interests and education. Of course, it isn't always easy to do this. But if we're determined enough we'll learn to concentrate and work solidly after keeping eyes and ears for so long on ten activities at once. That's why mothers should be enabled to have time off just to practise finishing a thought without interruption, or to keep their hands in at some outside activity. What a relief for our families too. And let's be honest with ourselves about the housework that's really necessary and what we do just to sustain our busy legend. Let's discriminate between well-earned leisure and mere timefilling.

I've been talking mainly about mothers with children. But of course lots of women don't marry or have children. And here again I think we've developed a wrong attitude. For far too many women marriage has become the essential goal in life, and I'm sure that this over-emphasis on the necessity for getting married has cheapened the whole institution There are worse states than being unmarried and obviously for some people being married is one of them – one out of ten New Zealand marriages ends in divorce. Quite apart from that, today's most popular age for marrying is 21. On the average, this gives a bride another fifty years of life, and statistics show that she's likely to outlive her husband. Can we truthfully say that domesticity – which is what we mean when we talk of marriage as a career – can keep her usefully occupied all that time? I don't believe it for a moment.

Now all these out-of-date attitudes and assumptions that I've mentioned – really, you know, women are quite as much to blame for them as men. They're so often content to be regarded as second-class citizens. Their energies are dissipated in the trivial and the superficial. They don't make the effort needed to get below the surface. I'll give you an example of what I mean. One of the occupational hazards of motherhood is frequent attendance at meetings involved with children. Over the years I've never been to one where the air hasn't been beaten with the parrot-cry of 'Discipline! We want the kids to have more of it.' Yet we don't dream of disciplining ourselves to look a little deeper and press for small classes and better working conditions for teachers. Have you seen some of those dreary cupboards labelled staff-room? If all those women muttering the word discipline really banded together what mightn't they get done. It was unity, after all, that got us the vote.

The point is that whether women go in for birdwatching or Highland dancing or promoting equal pay, it shouldn't be just because they have the time to meet such nice people. It should also be because they want to extend themselves in some way, to learn from and contribute to our society. Isn't that asking rather a lot? Of course it is. According to public opinion, a woman who devotes herself wholeheartedly to something simply can't win. If she's single, you'll hear people say, 'It's all very well for her – she hasn't got anything better to do', in spite of the fact that she may be holding down a job equal in responsibility if not in pay to that of many men. If she's married, the line is, 'It's all very well for her, but you should see her house.' Well, these are the bad old attitudes, and it's high time we discarded them and began to instil some better ones into our children. It's in the home that we should start – that's where they learn most. If we go about it with vigour and good sense, they'll grow up with the knowledge that women are people too, and once that idea begins gaining ground we'll be well on the way to a juster and happier society.

New Zealand Listener, 20 November 1959, pp.6–7

5.7. Women Behind Banners
by M.H.H. (Monte Holcroft) (1959)

When a woman speaks sharply to other women, and urges them to be more active in building a better society, wise men step softly to the sidelines. Yet few of us are wise, and the opinions of Mrs Margot Roth (printed on page 6) are too enticing to be left entirely to a female counter-attack. Her argument seems to depend on the following points: (1) Women in New Zealand are too often 'contributing subordinates rather than partners', a condition seen as 'a hangover from out-of-date British working class customs'. (2) A resulting sense of inferiority brings one of two reactions, an attempt to be more like men – producing such oddities as marching girls and regimented babies – or a retreat into a false glamour around 'the creative role of wife and mother'. (3) Nowadays women have more leisure, and should use it to escape from their 'mould of inferiority', especially by devoting themselves 'to activities which benefit

the whole community'. (4) But women are said to misuse their opportunity. Even when they join organisations they bring about no social reforms: they are too much concerned with protocol and tea-cups. (5) What women do outside the home should be done 'because they want to extend themselves in some way, to learn from and contribute to our society'.

If some women feel inferior to men (instead of merely different), they should not blame the accidents of our short history. The uneven relationship of man and wife has been noticed in other parts of the world, and in cultures quite different from our own. It may be true that our environment, still too masculine, makes women react more strongly – or at least more vocally, though neither an emulative 'manliness' nor a recessive femininity could be described as distinctively New Zealand attitudes: they are merely human, and have no geographical significance. What *is* New Zealand, however, is Mrs Roth's belief that women should snap out of it and do something useful for 'Society'.

Fortunately, women are in general too busy to organise themselves for a march to better things. It is true that 'family planning' has made the reproductive function less demanding than it used to be; but the function is still there, and even two or three children must – or should – keep a mother engaged at home while her husband is earning his place outside. Later, when the family is growing up, a woman has more leisure; but the special experience of wife and mother does not always equip her for competition or partnership with men in fields that require a different sort of training. Some women are natural managers who turn eagerly to wider interests as soon as they are free to do so – sometimes, perhaps to the relief of husbands who have been managed almost beyond endurance. But it is not a fault in woman if she prefers to stay out of the forum.

When leisure comes, there are interests which can still be centred on the home. A woman who loves her garden, who likes to read good books without interruption, and to listen to music, is 'extending' herself in ways that suit her best, and by so doing is making her contribution to society. But why on earth should this business of 'contributing to our society' be regarded as an end in itself, an end which too many women are unwilling to pursue? A regiment of women, marching behind banners

with social slogans, is a horrid conception – on a different level, not unlike the marching girls of whom Mrs Roth understandably disapproves. How many male citizens move outside the narrow range of work and home? Thousands of them are doing work as monotonous as a housewife's and in their leisure they seek nothing more elevating than a weekend in the garden and a game of golf or bowls. Are they to be blamed because they feel no reforming zeal? Social action is in the hands of a creative minority, men and women; but the absentees are neither drones nor slackers.

Mrs Roth seems to have taken no notice of personal relationships, surely the heart and core of the matter. Companionship between man and woman, and between parent and child, gives life its central richness. The strength of these relationships means more to society than a thousand programmes for reform. What, after all, *is* society if it is not the larger family, held together by men and women who are learning to live with one another? Whatever may be said about the 'false glamour' of the home-maker, it is still true that 'the creative role of wife and mother' offers women the best work and the deepest satisfactions. Noble women have loved mankind, and worked for it; but it is the nature of woman to love individuals first and last, and society would be ill indeed if too many of them sought tasks that could only be compensations for what has been missed or lost in the home.

New Zealand Listener, *20 November 1959, p.10*

Chapter 6

The Changing Role of Women
1960s

The questions posed in the 1950s concerning the responsibilities of women in marriage were more widely aired in the 1960s. The relationship between employment and marriage continued to be discussed, but the second element was no longer considered unproblematic. The satisfactions derived from devotion to husbands, children and home-making began to be questioned. The experience of nearly two decades of suburban living was beginning to tell on large numbers of New Zealand women. The impetus for change in the 1960s came from Linden, Johnsonville and Otara, rather than from the city centres where paid workers spent their days.

The pace of social change was quickening. The contraceptive pill became available to New Zealand women in 1962, and, as fast as it began to be used (a higher percentage of New Zealand women were taking the pill than British or American women by 1966[1]), became the focus for intense debate, especially amongst Roman Catholics. Social divisions, highlighted with the advent of the 'permissive society', were evident also in New Zealanders' reactions to the sex-segregated screening of the film *Ulysses*, and in their attitudes toward mixed flatting by university students. Codes of sexual behaviour were under challenge. The generation of people reaching adulthood in the 1960s were not as accepting of the suburban ideal as their parents had been. Generational conflict was evident in popular styles of music and dress, and served partly to fuel the Vietnam protests.

The nature of debate in the 1960s was much broader in scope than it had been for some decades, focusing more on women's position 'at home' and 'in society' than on a particular issue such as equal pay. This was soon thought of in terms of women's 'changing roles'. 'The changing role of women' became the title for a number of lectures, adult education courses, group discussions, seminars and publications. One of the most celebrated of these was the lecture series organised by the Linden Play Centre in 1966. The texts of the talks were subsequently published and two of them – Beverley Morris's 'Women's Role in Perspective' and W.B. Sutch's 'Women's Contribution to Society, II' are reproduced here (6.1 and 6.2).

In her address, Morris (an adult education lecturer who had been active in the Playcentre movement) points to the multiple roles women were already performing as wives and mothers. She suggests, gently but persuasively, that these roles need not necessarily be rejected, but might be expanded – and this could benefit not only women but also the men and children with whom they shared their lives. She acknowledges the pressures of looking after small children and of always being at the beck and call of children's needs – the legacy of a generation of Pakeha women raised on the ideology of Drs Spock and Bowlby and their ideas of maternal deprivation. Morris puts her analysis of women's position in New Zealand society within a broader context – citing Ibsen, Woolf, Friedan, and researcher on Australian women, Norman McKenzie – in describing 'the New Zealand problem that has no name'.

Sutch, speaking as an economist, was more programmatic and uncompromising in his commentary. Women in New Zealand, he argued, occupied a very low status, 'they can be compared with the Maori in this country'. To remedy this he advocated better education – including a ban on the teaching of pre-vocational subjects (shorthand and book-keeping) in schools – equal pay, and a rethinking of domestic work, as women increasingly took up part-time paid employment. He also criticised the New Zealand housing patterns that contributed to loneliness and isolation amongst women.

Two years later, Dr Fraser McDonald set the debate alight by describing women as the 'Negroes of New Zealand society', when he drew attention to the high incidence of depression amongst suburban women. This theme was taken up in the first issue of *Thursday* magazine in October 1968 (6.4 and 6.5). Refusing to categorise its potential readership, because of the 'sheer impossibility of defining women and womanhood within a few simple, well-chosen words', *Thursday* pursued these controversial topics under the editorship of Marcia Russell.

Kathleen Macdonald continued the debate in January 1969 in a personal opinion (6.5) as a British immigrant of three years' standing. She saw the sexual demarcation in New Zealand society as very sharp, and put part of the blame on 'Mrs New Zealand', who 'seems only too happy with life on the wrong side of the beer keg.' She decried women's lack of involvement in serious debate, and believed that New Zealand society, because of its sex patterns, was in danger of becoming a museum in which women were the fossils.

The language used in the 1960s debate is significant – in Morris's piece the child is still 'he', but in *Thursday* Diana Rigg is deliberately 'a modern woman (not a 'girl'), and women *are* women (not 'womankind', or simply 'woman' – a term that has implications of a singular identity and commonality of interests).

In many ways sociological and psychological concepts and ideas held more appeal for people coming to adulthood in the 1950s and 1960s than did political theories or positions. Terminology derived from social and educational theory predominates in much of the writing and discussion of men's and women's positions from this point on.

The small number of items included in this section belies the very widespread interest which existed in the situation of women at the time. Magazines such as *Thursday* had a large popular circulation, so that small articles like those selected here had a wider influence than did a longer article in *Woman Today* in the 1930s. Similarly, the Linden series of lectures, *The Changing Role of Women*, was attended by several hundred people, and the ensuing publication read by many more.

Even so, these ideas did not give rise to a single campaign, or to a new expression of organised feminism, but the 'problems' of women began to be identified and articulated. Betty Friedan's *Feminine Mystique* was read in New Zealand. 'The problem that has no name' was recognised by a number of New Zealand women. Broadcasters and journalists, including Cherry Raymond and many of the women who hosted the National Programme's 'Feminine Viewpoint', were themselves casting out in new directions and provided a more satisfying diet of current affairs, intellectual debate, etc. than the popular media had generally offered in the 1950s, when the focus was on royalty, recipes and knitting patterns.[2]

1. *Sandra Coney, 'The Pill', Sunday Times, 6 August 1989, p.7*
2. See, for example, *Julie Glamuzina, 'Prudence Gregory', BNZW, pp.251–253*

Sources and Further Reading

The Changing Role of Women: Lecture course held by the Linden Play Centre, 1966. 2nd. ed. [Wellington, 1968]

The Changing Role of Women [Waikato Branch of the Society for Research on Women with the Extension Committee of the University of Waikato], Hamilton, [1968?]

The Changing Role of Women: a series of lectures organised by the Department of University Extension [Auckland] in association with the Society for Research on Women, Auckland, 1968

Dunstall, Graeme. 'The Social Pattern', in W.H. Oliver with B. R. Williams (eds), *The Oxford History of New Zealand*, Wellington, 1981, pp.396–429

May, Helen. *Minding Children, Managing Men: Conflict and compromise in the lives of postwar Pakeha women*, Wellington, 1992

Society for Research on Women. *Urban Women*, Johnsonville, 1972

6.1.   Women's Role in Perspective
by Beverley Morris (1966)

I find that the Oxford Dictionary defines 'role' as: 'one's function, what one is appointed or expected or has undertaken to do.' Thinking of ourselves as women, our main function is that of child-bearing and child-rearing. Since that which is appointed, or expected or undertaken depends mainly on the society into which we are born, we can expect to have many conflicting roles because we live in a complex society.

In all societies in the world, women's role varies tremendously, and historically has done so as far back as the ice-age. Women in New Zealand settings can change from mother to any one of the following in a matter of minutes: dressmaker, cook, gardener, chauffeur, teacher, nurse.

Women seem to be required to play the greatest number of roles, though men and children have roles too. Children slip in and out of roles frequently during imaginative play. We have only to speak to our child's teacher to realise that the role which he exhibits at school is often different from his home role. Men as they leave home in the morning are father and husband, but during the day are neighbour,

commuter, professional worker, tradesman, boss or hireling. Alice Rossi, contributing to the publication *Daedalus* writes, 'human beings have a greater tolerance for sharp contrasts in role demands than social scientists give them credit for.'

For modern women, however, the great difficulty lies in the multiple choice of roles. Some thirty years ago, the common pattern in New Zealand was, the woman was regarded as the home-maker and she did not work unless she had no means of support economically, or occasionally if she maintained her professional job, although married. Today there are a number of new occupations because of technological advances and at the same time more labour-saving devices are available to reduce the amount of time necessary for running a household. There are also more jobs than there are workers, so that there is some pressure from industry for women to enter the labour market. Changing conditions lead to confusion in many women about their true roles.

Sometimes women play what I shall call 'counterfeit' roles. Instead of living lives that pertain to themselves, they are living through

145

their husbands or children, enjoying life at secondhand. Oliver Wendell Holmes once said, 'Washington is full of interesting men and the women they married when young.' A woman can become too absorbed in the role of supporting her husband and providing the needs of her children, but in the process her own personality is negated.

It is valuable for a woman to see her life as a series of changing roles from dependent child to college pupil, to wage-earner, to being an engaged person, then a marriage partner and parent. She is conscious of change because of her monthly rhythm, and the effort that is sometimes required to maintain her current role. However, mothers of pre-school children often feel that they have acquired a role that will last forever. They cannot imagine a time when they will have finished with bottles and napkins and everlasting demands upon their time and attention as the pre-schooler tries to learn about his world.

This role is a fatiguing one, particularly because the manner in which our society is organised cuts off the mother from the support and hope that she could have expected in a larger household containing grandmother, sisters, aunts or cousins. She misses the rational conversation of adults. A modern mother cooped up in a small house listening to childish prattle for twelve hours a day can find the situation a burden on her nervous system. Some community organizations such as Parent Centre, Plunket, Play Centre and Kindergarten can help to alleviate this difficulty but many mothers do not perceive their problem, let alone seek a remedy. It is a little help if a woman can be made to realize that this is only one role among many, and that sooner than she thinks she will be facing the position of having all the children at school, later at college and finally there will be the 'empty nest' stage.

That we are becoming more aware of change is apparent in the wide response to this course. We are able to gather facts together and draw conclusions about them in regard to the changing role of women. This objectivity is in accord with the scientific bias of our times. Comparing the roles of women in other countries will show just how vastly women's roles can differ. In some Central African tribes, the women constitute the major agricultural labour force, since the belief is that men are not suited by nature to soil their hands. In Iran the women are expected to be practical, cool and calculating while the men are expected to show

emotion and sensitivity, preferring poetry above logic. The women of the Kibbutz of Israel have equal civic and educational rights with the men and are conscripted with them into the Army. If there are children, they are raised in the children's house and can see their parents for three hours daily and at the weekend. Child-rearing there is shared by the State authorities to a high degree. Equal status is accorded to women and educational opportunities have increased so that many doctors, scientists and technicians are women, whose children have special care in creches and day nurseries. In America, one-third of all married women work, and more than half of all women between 18 and 55 are working outside the home. The statistics for England and Australia are similar.

Is there any reality behind the axiom 'the woman's place is in the home'? In New Zealand 26% of the female population is working, mostly in industry or in offices. Though we have had equal rights in voting since 1893 (the first in the world except for one small state in America) and certain property rights within marriage, women have not reached the positions of responsibility that could be expected. In relation to the men, there are few women in the professions in this country.

Historically woman's role has been a changing one, very much dependent on the economic and social forces permeating the level of society into which she was born or married. Under Roman law, women held equal status with men, yet in Saxon times, they were regarded as chattels and their husband's property. The Norman barons of the Middle Ages had rights to the bride over the bridegroom on the wedding night. It was held in these times that sexual guilt lay with women who tempted their menfolk who were otherwise pure! A husband was permitted by law to thrash his spouse with a cudgel but not to knock her down with an iron bar.

In the Georgian era, there was no satisfactory mode of existence open to the woman who wished to support herself at a professional level except by being a courtesan. Gradually in the late eighteenth century with the Romantic Revival arose the idea that marriage should be based on mutual love with equal rights and respect on either side. The Victorian attitude towards middle-class women was similar to that of medieval times. Submission, modesty and hard work were the virtues sought, with visits to the poor for relaxation. Any reference to childbirth or other feminine matters was strictly taboo and any condition between neck and knee was known as a 'liver'.

Simon Yudkin in his book about working wives points out that working class women have always worked. Around 1850 because more girl babies survived than boys and because many men were migrating to the colonies, there was a shortage of men, leaving large numbers of unmarried women whose only occupations were being governess to other people's children or needlework. These were the women who pioneered the attack on the male monopoly of middle-class jobs. Long before this, women laboured beside their menfolk at industry in the homes and later in tremendous, ill-equipped factories, to eke out a miserable salary for maintaining their families. The fact that children existed was of no importance – they fitted in where they could, entering the labour force themselves at an early age. Each war has encouraged more women to take up employment outside the home, till now one economist claims that if all working wives gave up their jobs, there would be a major economic disaster.

When we look at the many roles of modern woman, we are impressed by her improved social, economic and legal status. This is reflected by the balance in the husband-wife relationship. Whereas in the nineteenth century the male was the dominant partner, it is more usual in western societies now to find responsibility equally divided.

Regarding marriage as an institution, we note that it has become more popular, so that there are fewer unmarried members of the community. Both men and women tend to marry at an earlier age. The average age for marrying in New Zealand is 22. The average size of family is much lower than in Victorian days, due to better methods of birth-control. Another factor affecting the role of women is that their families are completed earlier, which reduces the number of years in which the woman is deeply involved in child-rearing. Some women feel unfulfilled unless they are bearing children for this gives them status, but many are content to do their best for three or four children.

At the other end of the scale, due to better living conditions and the conquering of many diseases, the expectation of life for New Zealand women has been raised to 75 years. Formerly it was 45, synchronising with the end of the child-bearing years. In present circumstances a woman has as long after menopause as her adult life preceding it.

Immediately there is a decision to be made – how to 'make use of' (in the best terms) or 'fill in' (in the worst terms) this section of life, when one is physically capable of many accomplishments?

Another consequence of increased life expectancy is that if one marries early, the marriage may last over 50 years. Perhaps this puts extra strain on the marriage relationship, requiring more give and take. Perhaps it is extremely important to make the right choice of marriage partner in the first place. Certainly the task of arriving at compromises must be worked at.

New Zealand men nowadays tend to help with household chores without feeling a loss in masculinity. Such prejudice is dying out, as your husbands realize that many hands are needed to cope with babies and toddlers. Their necessary assistance is one way of cutting down on the number of demands upon the young mother. We should avoid allowing this domesticity in the male to go too far – the balance depends upon one's style of living.

How is the woman of today educated for her many roles? Certainly she can be the recipient of a very good education if she has been well-advised. Many occupations and professions are open to her and her expectation is that on leaving high school she will embark on a career. Some will find deep satisfactions in their job, others will tolerate repetitive and uninteresting work as a stop-gap until marriage intervenes. What many fail to realize is the necessity for keeping sights on what will be required should they return to the working field after the children have grown up. (Certainly there is very little preparation in our education system for running a home economically or in child-rearing).

When a family is established, a kind of isolation can occur, even in a crowded neighbourhood. The woman becomes centred upon her children and feel lonely for adult company. This is the time when she may become a 'vegetable' if she is not using her mind for things other than the household and family requirements. In some ways, new emphasis on the needs of the child has swung too far, thus leaving no room for the needs of the mother. Pioneer women worked with their neighbours and the children helped where they could. There was not time to become worried or bored. But alone in a house with small children, a mother can become anxious about what effect her continuous nagging will have upon them.

More is known today of the psychological make-up of male and female. It is not so much the differences between the sexes that are surprising, as the similarity in temperament, traits and intelligence. The same range of intelligence potential is present in both male and female but opportunities to show superiority in scientific subjects, mathematics, etc., have been insufficient as yet.

Better methods (more reliable, that is) of contraception are changing women's role. 40% of New Zealand women are using the contraceptive pill, thus being able to determine the size and spacing of their families. A certain amount of Puritanism underlies our attitudes towards sex and sensuality. Both this and a deep abyss of ignorance about the emotional side of human behaviour, menstrual disorders and the mental illnesses that can follow childbirth, hinder our understanding of women's role. We should also need to know more about how the hormonal system affects a woman's body and mind at the different stages of her life.

Now a woman can choose what to do with the extra time on her hands when her children are at school. She may find creative work about the house, undertake some art or craft work, do voluntary community work or take on full or part time jobs. The question is summed up neatly – 'a middle-aged woman with children at school is like a child at an ultra-free school who asks, "do I have to do what I want to do again today?" ' Too much freedom is as limiting as too little. Some feel guilty if they go to work, thus neglecting the children. On the other hand, social workers in the south of London found that mothers who did *not* go to work were considered neglectful because they were not earning money to raise their family's standard of living.

Many women have training and latent skills which could be put to community use, if some encouragement is given. Regarding work, Edna Roston writes in *Daedalus*: 'Both men and women have a need to work as a means of absorbing aggressive energy and directing it from destructive and hostile acts into deeds and

objects of value, thus at the one and same time serving the economy of the society and the individual personality.' When the satisfactions of motherhood are diminishing, something must take its place.

The woman's need to fulfil her personality potential are represented in literature by Ibsen's play, *The Doll's House*, in which his main character, missing the maturing years between childhood and motherhood, wonders at her dissatisfaction with life. Another cry from the heart is heard in·Virginia Woolf's *A Room of One's Own*. She gives examples of women writers who could only succeed when they were economically secure and had a room in which to write. She deplored many wasted talents. Betty Friedan in *The Feminine Mystique* develops the theme that women have been encouraged to return to household tasks by an affluent society but she maintains that this fate does not extend the intellectual powers of the majority, who have a hunger for something more. Norman McKenzie, a political correspondent with the *New Statesman*, visited Australia for a year and collected much data on the women's place in Australian society. He was impressed by one fact above all: the gap between their potential and their achievement.

We have a duty to show our daughters the many roles of modern woman, so that they will not have such a difficult choice when they grow up. Let us see that both boys and girls receive the best education possible. Let us stress to our educationalists that there have been changes in everyday living, that more changes are coming and that we want our children educated to become adaptable to future changes. As John Stuart Mill writes: 'Books, institutions, education, society, all go on training human beings for the old long after the new has come. Much more is coming and the true virtue of human beings is to live together as equals, claiming for themselves nothing but what they freely concede to anyone else.'

The Changing Role of Women: Lecture course held by the Linden Play Centre, 1966. *2nd ed. [Wellington, 1968] pp. 2–8*

6.2. Women's Contribution to Society, II
by W.B. Sutch (1966)

I am speaking to you primarily as an economist – i.e. one who is interested in getting more out of a country than at present and trying to

maximise its wealth. An economist is interested also in improving the quality of what is produced and the quality of the producers.

First, I will say I agree with all that Mrs Gilson has said and on reading her lecture, you will find how true and how deep are some of the remarks she has made. Now I will continue with some suggestions as to how women may contribute to society to achieve equality. Compared with other countries in the world in which I have lived, the status of women in New Zealand is very low. When we see the menial tasks they are expected to do, the jobs they are kept out of, the pay they get, they can be compared with the Maori in this country. Consideration is not given to them in the business world and this is amazing in a country that can read and write, but it is true and something must be done about it.

Let us start with the schools, where we find more boys get University Entrance than girls. There is something wrong with that. It is immediately starting the slippery slope backwards. The girls do not take advantage of the education opportunities that are there. At the University in 1893, when women got the vote, there were more women than men attending. Today at the University, for every three men there is one woman. Women have a very subordinate place in the University. When we look at the kind of education, semi-education or pseudo-education that girls get at our secondary schools, we realise too how further backward they are getting themselves by accepting the kind of curriculum that is handed out to them. What do I mean? Young girls in forms three and four, instead of getting an education are taking silly subjects like book-keeping and shorthand and wasting their time. When this is happening you can see immediately that these young people have had their education partly thrown away in the third form.

Most educators agree that education consists of studying those subjects that have the most links with other things. These subjects have been defined in New Zealand as English, Social Studies (History and Geography), Mathematics, General Science, Art and Physical Education. These things are all so important that to drop any one of them means that we drop a part of our education. Because the world is going to be so complex in the future, we have to go on longer. In my day I could leave school after four years of secondary education, today I might need six years. It is this sort of comparison that we need for our children. Instead of giving youngsters a secondary education we are trying to cheat a little by putting into the curriculum vocational subjects.

You will know that a girl can learn shorthand, book-keeping or typing in a very short time if she has an education. If she has not she can take years over it and still never learn. One of the things we do in this country is occupy a girl's time at secondary school with a lot of these pre-vocational subjects instead of giving them an education. This is committing them to an inferior position for the rest of their lives.

Girls are getting married younger now. A girl leaves school at 16; in three or four years time she is married. In those years she takes some sort of job, some part-time job, some job that is a dead end with no future. Many girls think it does not matter what they do because the end result is marriage. Now the true result is: the last child goes to school when the woman is 33 to 35 years of age, and she then realises there is another forty years of life to live after that. This is a social revolution in our country. It did not happen in my mother's time. The expectation of life then was about 52 years of age and now it is 75. There are forty years after the last child has gone to school. When you realise that, you realise how much an education is going to matter. Not education for the three or four years after the child leaves school, but education that will take them right through their thirties, forties, fifties and sixties. It is this period of time that matters.

The education children get at school must be such as to take them through a life when they may perhaps have to take up a new occupation, and you cannot take up a new study unless you have got a deep and wide education first. The big thing to give to any girl is a wide education. Then when she becomes a mother, first of all she will have education to pass on to her children, and this is the greatest responsibility a woman can have. But for her own sake, after that she will need a good education to go on with the job that almost inevitably she will take up when the children go to school. The majority of them will, as is happening in Denmark and other countries.

This is what I stress so much in secondary schools. Any girl who is going to secondary school and taking a thing called homecraft or clothing or stitchery is taking a subject which is cutting into her education. Those subjects, valuable as they may be, should be taken after you have your education. Not instead of.

The first thing that we can do to help on the status of women is to make sure they get an education at secondary school and allow no child to take a pre-vocational subject until that child has had about four years' education. No child, boy or girl. This means insisting that at secondary school your child does not take a commercial course; that your child takes a commercial course at the right time, in a tertiary institution provided for studying and quickly attaining a particular skill. This is what is meant by getting equality of status: an education first and studying later for the specialty, whatever it may be, hairdressing, photography etc.

Now you may argue that these institutions do not exist. It is your duty to make them exist. Your first job is to eliminate from secondary schools all those subjects which are pre-vocational and put them into tertiary schools. So when you have a vote, talk or argument about this kind of thing it is your job to say that no child should take these pre-vocational subjects, especially if the excuse is that the youngster is going to be married, therefore she doesn't need an education. You know that you can learn to make marmalade very easily without going to secondary school, and you also know that when a woman is working she may not want to make marmalade.

Summing up then, do not let any child give up their broad secondary education; eliminate, if you can, all those subjects alleged to be of use in their chosen occupation; press for a higher leaving age. You should not condemn any child to leave school at the age of 15. You must try to get the child as far through schooling as you can, and if there are some who want to leave at 15, make it illegal. I know that four-fifths of them go until they are 16 now, but it is that one-fifth that do not that are important. These are the ones who have to go through and get a better education – it is their life that is at stake.

Another thing we must press for is equal pay. Equal pay for equal jobs. In this country of all countries, it is so easy to justify it. We have the Family Benefit, which is a payment for each child. We have the age benefit at 60 years, and in some cases earlier. This means that these areas are more or less cared for and it means that you cannot readily use the excuse that somebody has to pay for the children and somebody has to pay for the old people. You cannot use these arguments as much as you can in other countries. Even if you do use them, you ought to know that a woman's responsibility for looking after old people and relatives is the same as a man's responsibility for looking after these people. So do not be put aside by any arguments about differences in responsibility. The rate for the job is the thing to aim for,

and then women will not be doing menial jobs, the low paid jobs, unskilled jobs, the jobs they tend to be doing at present, according to Mrs Gilson. They will be doing jobs that their capacity warrants their doing, and the level at which the job will be done will be better. We will be choosing the people from 100% of the population instead of 50% and the standard must increase. At the present time we are not using the ability of 50% of our people, the women. This is broadly speaking, of course, as we have the exceptions of nursing and teaching. We would have a better country if we could choose from trained women but we cannot choose from trained women until they are available for these jobs.

The next step is to see that there are jobs. It is a new thing in our country to have jobs, at least to me it is. I was brought up in the times when there were thousands unemployed, when, if a married woman went to work she was looked at askance because she was taking a single woman's job who was unemployed. The situation we have had in the last fifteen – twenty years of full employment is the key thing that is giving women jobs and offering women scope in all sorts of occupations they would not have been offered in the days of the depression. In those days, a married woman teacher would be asked to give up her job to a single woman. Now we are struggling to get married women for jobs in teaching. So another thing you must fight for always is full employment. Do not ever advocate unemployment as a cure for anything in the economic system. This is a much broader thing than just agitating or talking about jobs for women.

We are cutting into a broader field still. I have talked of full employment, but how can we have full employment in a country such as ours when we have got such a low level of manufacturing occupations? In Denmark, which is a small country, you find a multitude of factories and multitude of occupations that men and women can go to. In our country we have only just started to get manufacturing, we have only just started to do some of the skilled things that other countries have done, because we thought that all we needed to do was to grow the grass and the grass could be sent abroad and we could sell it in the shape of meat and wool etc, and we could get back what we wanted. This has been one of the faults in this country, thinking we could live on the product of the grass. If we did that it would mean there would be no jobs, except growing grass and things to do with farming.

This means your minds must broaden out into a wider field still – thinking of the economic system with manufacturing and service jobs of all kinds which must be promoted. This not only gives more jobs for people but it enriches their lives. If you live in a colonial economy, as we have for many years, and there are not a variety of jobs, your own minds and lives are constricted by the lack of variety if there is only one kind of job to do. After full employment comes variety of jobs, which means promoting the industrial development of this country. This then becomes a woman's concern as well as a man's.

The chief problem in this country is not that women have babies and have to look after them. It is the antiquated attitude that we have to women's role in the community. This is as Mrs Gilson remarked. If we had a different attitude to women's role, we would not have to wonder and ponder about whether a woman should be going out to work. We would be taking all that for granted and organising how it could be done for the good of the community, family and children.

But we have not got that far in this country, we are still debating whether women should be in the economic system. So the main thing to remove is this attitude that there are jobs that are done by women and jobs that are done by men. This is all designed by us. In some communities women do all the donkey work; they do most of it here, but it is not paid for. In some countries there is an entirely different disposition of men's and women's work. I have been to international conferences of an economic nature where the Minister of Finance of the country may be a woman. The Minister of Economic Affairs might be a woman. Women are very good at accountancy. This is expected in a Scandinavian country, or in the United States. So this idea of particular roles for men and women has to be thought about very seriously indeed.

If you believe that men and women are equal, and this of course is a very big if, then start behaving and thinking that way. You do not bring up your boys and girls to have a feeling that this is done by boys and this is done by girls. You do not let your boy drop his shirt on the floor for somebody else to pick up. That boy then thinks the woman is the servant around the house and may take this as a pattern for his future life. These attitudes are developed from babyhood.

On the other hand, if you give a girl the idea that all she has got to do is get a man and look forward to the wedding day, you are doing something very wrong. That girl has got a long life ahead of her. She is going to be a mother, the most important thing in her life and you cannot exclude that girl from getting the best education there is in this world in order that she be a good mother.

Think of the things that are in the home that are laying down a pattern of behaviour for boys and girls. I know young boys who come home, go to their drawer and expect to pull out a shirt, ironed. Somebody did it for them. Immediately you are setting the pattern, a pattern which has to change if you are going to leave your home and go out to work, whether it is half- or full-time. You will not be able to do all the housework my mother did. Mother made soap, because in my mother's day that was one of the jobs that women did. I wonder how many of you are ironing sheets? How many are ironing pillow cases? Are you thinking about these household tasks that are kept on because you may as well keep them on as they are traditionally women's work?

A woman going out to work has to alter her ways. I mentioned marmalade just now. I can make marmalade, but I have not the time. This has to be the attitude. Have I the time if I am working to do all the things I did before, or must I just buy it in packet, tin or bottle? These are the things that you have to think about when you are thinking about going to work. You think of a different kind of home, you think of a kind of home which does not involve you in too much work.

I know men who, when looking for sections, say 'I'm not having that one, look at the size of the garden', or 'I'm going to put it down in concrete so I won't have to mow the lawn'. Now these men are thinking about the work around the house. This is one of the things that women have to think of too. How do we organise a woman's life in the home to get the work done? Because you have got a vacuum cleaner, you do not have to cover the place with carpet. Do I have carpet to keep warm or because the neighbour has it? Do I have venetian blinds to look through or because the neighbour has it? I was brought up with venetian blinds and I had to dust them, and this is something to know about when you are advising your sons and daughters about their future home. Think of the things you can eliminate from the daily drudgery.

After all, the drudgery had to be done because it was the way of life, but now we can live differently. The fact that you can now go out and buy some frozen peas means that you do not have to preserve peas yourself. All that can go. I am not saying it must go – it is fun doing it – but I am saying we must decide one way or the other. Do not try to think you can carry on the old ways of life if you have got a part- or full-time job.

One of the tremendous strains on the women in this country is trying to keep up a house, be the lady of it, and do all this Victorian work too. I do not mean that the place should not be kept clean, but it is the man's job to keep the place clean as well as the woman's.

It is not just a matter of thinking the Government should do something or the local bodies should do something or the manufacturers. We should do something ourselves. What should we do to organise our lives so that we can get out when we want to? I am not saying that because a woman has got her child off to school she should immediately walk out into a job. What is the step to take at this stage? Work on ways of having jobs so that when the children come home from school there is somebody there to look after them. This means a part-time job. This means instead of saying 'There are no part-time jobs and they are difficult to get', work to get part-time jobs. Organise yourselves to get part-time jobs. Try to get the manufacturers and the service people to give part-time jobs. Join in the movement, organise all over New Zealand. Part-time jobs are one of the essential things in order to give women equality.

This is what you do, you do not just wait, you join a movement to try to get part-time jobs, or you join a movement which says 'In our area we could have an arrangement so that after school there is some place where the children can go.' In Denmark and Switzerland they have places where, after school, children can go. We will work out ways of doing it our way, but somehow or other these are the things that are going to have to happen. We will have to change our ways. Kindergartens, nurseries and play centres are all part of the development that women must press for. Why not men? Men too, but as women are the ones who are trying to be emancipated, trying to be equal, perhaps they might try a bit harder. So we have got to think then of all the ways of organising life so that women can work part-time.

Also we have to think of altering conditions

so that women can work the whole of their life if they want to, and have babies. This happens in many countries. Some women prefer to organise their lives in such a way that at a certain stage of their pregnancy they get leave from their jobs and perhaps six months later they return and life is organised for looking after the children. It is possible for married women to work and have children, and it is done in some countries with proper social security payments for the times before and after the birth. Study how this is done, what is happening in other countries, how could we achieve it here? You study it in conjunction with women's and men's groups, and if you come to certain conclusions you want to advocate them and press for them.

You might press for a creche, which is a type of kindergarten at a factory. My mother, who I have quoted several times, came from Lancashire, a cotton spinning and weaving place. She used to tell me of the places where you took your baby when you went to the factory to work. There was a creche with a nurse in charge and the baby was fed or you could go and breast or bottle feed it yourself if you wished, and this was sixty or more years ago. I have seen factories in New Zealand where women can take their youngsters of three or four years to the nursery, where a trained staff looks after forty or fifty children. In the afternoons they have their sleep and something to eat and then mother comes and picks them up. Now this is happening and this is the sort of thing to press for.

We are a kind of antiquated society and have got our ways firmly fixed from a time when women did menial work and were supposed to stay in the home and it was a man's job to keep up the standard of living. This time has gone, but we are not organised properly to see that women can create and be creative in jobs. Mrs Gilson mentioned this. 'Women need to feel creative and women do not have to be alone.' I know that you have had a talk on suburban neurosis and I know that this is a real thing which comes about largely because of this business of not being with other people. I believe that we all like to work, that we all want to work and that we all want to express ourselves in working positively for something. I believe that we are wasting humanity if we are not allowed to work. It must be a part of this that some women feel in the home, when the children are away at school and the housework is done by 10 a.m. and all they have to do is go down to the butcher and have a yarn. That is fine, there is a little bit of socialising in going down and talking to the man or woman at the dairy. In the old days this used to be done by the people who washed their clothes at the village pump and all the women would meet together and have a talk.

This being together is very necessary in our lives. Men get it at the office, pub or in the bus. If you are at home, when do you get this feeling of being with people? It used to be Saturday night at the pictures, but I suppose it is around the television now. In many other countries people often live close together, in blocks of flats and apartments with playing areas around them so they are close to people all the time.

In our country we like to have our little house with a piece of land around it and be alone. These houses stretch for miles. This has its effect on us as persons. There are desirable things about this, but the loneliness that comes out of it is a thing we have to think about a great deal. So I believe that we should be very open minded about the kind of house we live in. You might find that for a big portion of your life it might be useful to live in a flat with less housework and closer ties with other people, and a lot of your work done for you. I lived in New York for six years of my life and I found that all the nappy washing was done by some central organisation. In Sweden I found that you could get soluble baby napkins, perhaps you do here – all ways of handling life more simply that would improve the freedom of the women in the home.

So what I am saying is: try to keep an open mind about these things because even if you are happy where you are and you do not want to change we have an obligation to allow other people to get their freedom. Now this obli-gation is on all of us, both men and women. Even if we are perfectly content where we are and we can read and ring up on the phone and talk to people and we do not feel this worry about having to get out – we should know that other people are worried. We should know that others want to get out. We should *never* say 'that woman is working and she should be looking after her children'. What we should say is 'how can we improve our community to see that the children are looked after better'. This is the positive approach, not just sitting and criticising somebody else. We have to free our minds and try and help the other woman who is trying to do something else. Trying to help somebody, that other woman, is a very important thing for us to do.

Now, briefly, what have I said:

Do not let anybody in secondary school take a pre-vocational course especially if that course is homecraft or clothing, or commercial.

Raise the school-leaving age.

Keep your youngsters at school for four or five years.

Take advantage of every educational oppor-tunity there is after secondary schooling; the Polytechnic, hairdressing schools, typing schools and universities.

Agitate for full employment.

Work hard for industrial development.

Make quite sure that equal pay is an issue – wherever it is an issue that you fight on the right side for it.

Above all, work with other groups to find what can be done to ease the lot of women who want to work part-time or full-time and need something organised to be able to.

The Changing Role of Women: Lecture course held by the Linden Play Centre, 1966. *2nd ed.* *[Wellington, 1968] pp. 54–64*

6.3. Memo from the Editor
by Marcia Russell (1968)

It seems this is the age of labels when the new game among the trendsetters is to find a phenomenon and turn it into a generalisation.

We have 'executive living' which offers the privilege of paying twice as much as would be reasonable for your section because all your neighbours will earn $4000 a year or more and their houses will look just as nice and just the same as yours. There are 'Twiggy looks', result-ing from starvation diets, and 'significant films' which contain at least a dozen scenes between male and female which take place in, around or on a bed.

'Jet sets' are people with his and hers aeroplanes and private yachts whose divorces make headlines and whose clothes qualify them for the best-dressed lists, while 'gracious living' means ikebana flower arrangements done personally and asparagus tongs on the dinner table.

'Culture' is the word for anything that you can't understand but you feel sure must be good, 'peasants' are average people with average tastes, moderate habits and usually common sense, and 'cabbages' are now housewives who are being told to stop being what they are by people who ought to know better.

But try as they may, the word spinners (or all those people who used to be called 'Madison Ave ad-execs' – and we gather that's old hat now too) have not been able to put an overall label on womanhood and make it stick.

As *Thursday* is a magazine for women (although we wouldn't be at all surprised if you have to toss him for it now and again) we are opposed to any sort of label that ties us down.

And when somebody comes along and says 'Please define your policy' – we answer blandly, 'Our policy is to please our readers' – and they go away looking mystified and slightly hurt because they cannot label us.

The point is we're women too and we can't think of anything less likely to succeed than a magazine that lumps women into one basket and gives it a label. Quite frankly, we wouldn't dare.

The sheer impossibility of defining women and womanhood within a few simple and well-chosen words came into sharp focus when we began researching the cover story for this, the first issue of *Thursday*.

We took a simple but outrageous statement – made by Dr Fraser McDonald, of Kingseat Hospital and widely reported in the press: 'Women are the Negroes of New Zealand Society', and set out to investigate it.

And, as we progressed, it became increasingly evident that the phrase was a sweeping statement of the most immense proportions.

Dr McDonald agreed. He intended, he said, to stir up a storm. And good for him, because the problem of depressions in the suburbs is very real. The point is, what's wrong with our society when things like this happen?

Our research led us to the mythical cabbage patch, to the aridity of the 'Otara syndrome', to the socio-economic ramifications of suburban neuroses, to battered babies, to the effects of town planning, to the responsibility of men in marriage, to the responsibility of parents who rear daughters on suffocating neo-Victorian myths about love, sex and marriage, to the social problem engendered by status seeking, sexual ignorance and insufficient or inadequate education.

Whew! No wonder staff writer Bernadette Noble looked increasingly wild-eyed as she raced from area to area while her simple story about New Zealand women being Negroes grew into a magnum opus of such proportions that even Simone de Beauvoir could be excused for quailing at its enormity.

So without labels – without making any attempt to identify, classify or categorise – we introduce *Thursday* – the magazine for younger women.

And in this issue: Diana Rigg, who we feel is a pretty good example of modern woman (and we say woman as opposed to girl), talks about sex, marriage and non-marriage, and seven gorgeous men give their views on what makes a woman fascinating – for them.

We have a story about kids on the campus – university mums and how they are coping with children and lectures. There's an unexpected visitor – whose face and figure at one time adorned (we suppose that's the word) the front pages of practically every newspaper in the world – Christine Keeler.

There's fashion of course – that elusive, fascinating ever-changing aspect of modern living which no woman worth her mascara can afford to ignore, and the first chapter of an exciting new novel by British authoress Margaret Forster.

Geoffrey Lee Martin begins the first of a series about a European holiday in summer – and 'Our Girl Thursday' Gwen Skinner, on board the yacht Swanhilde, begins her story of adventures encountered on the first part of a round the world voyage.

Look for Our Man Thursday – whose real identity must remain a secret for his own protection – and see what he has to say about the sorry state of all us poor New Zealand women. You'll be amused or mad – either way we feel you won't be unaffected by what he has to say.

We don't expect you to like everything in Thursday magazine. But if it makes you think, makes you laugh, makes you happy, or makes you furious – then we'll feel we're doing our job. And we'll be delighted if you're so enraged or so pleased with something that you just have to put pen to paper and tell us about it.

Enjoy yourselves.

Thursday, *3 October 1968, p.3*

6.4. Who Says I'm a Cabbage?
by Bernadette Noble (1968)

Women, the 'other half', have been lumped together and labelled since time began – the fairer, the weaker, the gentler sex; a man's inspiration and his ruin; hags, nags and bores; illogical and cunning. But now, in a rage of controversy, indignation and feminist banner-waving, it is the 'Negroes of Society', 'Slobs in Slippers', 'Second-class Citizens' and finally 'Cabbages' . . .

A new social disease, the 'cabbage patch' syndrome, we are told, is filling our mental hospitals with depressed young women, no longer able to find a reason for living. New housing areas are described as 'cultural deserts' and we get yet another new phrase, 'the Otara neurosis.'

A society is set up for research on women; the subject is on everybody's lips, from MPs to young mothers. So I went to look at the cabbage patch myself.

I couldn't find it.

A cross-section of women from various suburban areas all claimed that they were not really good examples to interview. They all said they had neighbours who were cabbages but that they themselves kept from vegetating by attending – or teaching – night classes, by taking in work at home (everything from hairdressing to dressmaking), by joining Plunket mothers or kindergarten committees, or by helping with the local amateur drama club or art society, or church, or school.

Where then are all the cabbages? Is there a season? Or does the cabbage patch only exist in the minds of the poor little petunias who fear they are in it?

Real or imagined, is the cabbage patch a matter of town planning or education? Economics or philosophy? Emmeline Pankhurst or Brave New World?

If the cabbage patch was hard to find, the answers were impossible.

But I did find intelligent people, intelligently concerned.

Everywhere I went I encountered men and women, many socially and economically removed from the area of this problem who held strong and often explosive views.

Dr Fraser McDonald, medical superintendent of Kingseat Hospital, coiner of phrases now synonymous with the present chapter in the 'woman question' was emphatic.

'Our sacred institution of marriage needs drastic revision,' he said. 'It is a man's world and this problem will get worse until something is done about it – legal and financial equality in marriage would be a good start.'

He, perhaps better than anyone, can describe the disaster of so many young housewives. They queue in his waiting room day after day. He has treated, literally, whole streets of women for the same illness: depression, feelings of uselessness, a lack of hope.

Not all come from the much-publicised areas like Otara: the majority of them have reasonable homes, refrigerators, wall-to-wall carpets and good husbands.

'If you can call a husband 'good' when he has an into-bed-or-nothing-at-all attitude,' he said.

Childbearing is lessening in importance, the world has too many children already, and Dr McDonald is assured of a full waiting room until women are treated less as homemakers and more as human beings.

In the meantime he advises women to go to work – even if they earn only enough to pay for a babysitter.

'It works,' he said, 'until social pressures from husbands, neighbours and mothers-in-law supply the ingredients for a guilt complex.'

Professor Muriel Lloyd Prichard, associate professor of economic history at Auckland University, spoke of the new place of women in society as a resuming role, of working women as natural.

Her views are well founded. Until the eighteenth century and the great changes that took place in industry at that time, women were involved in every possible occupation, she said, from spinning and weaving to silversmithery. It was possible because manufacture was carried out in the home.

'Housewives are doing just as good and important a job in the economy of the country as they did then,' she said, 'but now they receive no credit for it – their part is not recognised.'

She would have a greater sharing of the family income, and greater financial security for women from the State. Her views are feminist orientated – though she deplores that label.

'Women must insist on equality,' she said, 'it will never be given to them. They don't push enough, neither themselves, nor other women.'

Who says I'm

a cabbage?

WOMEN, the "other half", have been lumped together and labelled since time began—the fairer, the weaker, the gentler sex; a man's inspiration and his ruin; nags, nags and bores; illogical and cunning. But now, in a rage of controversy, indignation and feminist banner-waving, it is the "Negroes of Society," "Slobs in Slippers," "Second-class Citizens," and finally "Cabbages" . . .

A new social disease, the "cabbage patch" syndrome, we are told, is filling our mental hospitals with depressed young women, no longer able to find a reason for living. New housing areas are described as "cultural deserts" and we get yet another new phrase, "the Otara neurosis."

A society is set up for research on women; the subject is on everybody's lips, from MPs to young mothers.

So I went to look at the cabbage patch myself.

I couldn't find it.

A cross-section of women from various suburban areas all claimed that they were not really good examples to interview. They all said they had neighbours who were cabbages but that they themselves kept from vegetating by attending—or teaching—night classes, by taking in work at home (everything from hairdressing to dressmaking), by joining Plunket mothers or kindergarten committees, or by helping with the local amateur drama club or art society, or church, or school.

Where then are all the cabbages? Is there a season? Or does the cabbage patch only exist in the minds of the poor little petunias who fear they are in it?

Real or imagined, is the cabbage patch a matter of town planning or education? Economics or philosophy? Emmeline Pankhurst or Brave New World?

If the cabbage patch was hard to find, the answers were impossible.

But I did find intelligent people, intelligently concerned.

Everywhere I went I encountered men and women, many socially and economically removed from the area of this problem who held strong and often explosive views.

Dr Fraser McDonald, medical superintendent of Kingseat Hospital, coiner of phrases now synonomous with the present chapter in the "woman question" was emphatic.

Staff writer BERNADETTE NOBLE went looking for the suburban "cabbage patch". But the only one she found was the market garden of the Connell Bros. at Avondale. One of their prizes appears on the cover (the object with all the green leaves described by the Oxford dictionary as "a kind of cultivated vegetable with a round head or heart"). Here is Bernadette's report on the mysterious syndrome which everyone else but the people she spoke to apparently suffer from — life in the "cabbage patch".

28

The first issue of *Thursday* magazine, October 1968, 'the magazine for the younger woman', ran Bernadette Noble's article, 'Who says I'm a cabbage?'. *Alexander Turnbull Library*

Unequal rates of pay, unequal opportunity, and too often, unequal education are all matters for her concern.

'I suggest that women straighten their backs,' she said. 'There are many, many competent women who should be directors in hospitals, broadcasting, education. There are heaps of spheres in which women can shine.'

Her ideal is for women to work when their families allow them the time. She considers it right and proper for women to devote themselves to children when they are small, but for those who do not want to stay at home there should be creches provided by employers.

The husband who feels slurred when his wife goes to work, she calls ridiculous.

'Did he ever object to his wife doing menial and manual work at home?' she asks.

Miss C. Wynne, president of the women's organisation Zonta, and the technical librarian at New Zealand Forest Products, waves a slightly paler feminist flag.

She sees New Zealand women as being treated, and often feeling like 'second-class citizens'.

Women,' she said, 'want nothing more than to be treated as people – but a special kind of people – complementary to men, but sharing equally in privileges and responsibilities.'

The working woman, either unmarried or without a family, faces much discrimination, she said. No woman is likely to get anywhere near equal opportunity with men, no matter how well she is trained.

'This frustration eventually leads to a lessening of ability.'

The problems so many young married women with children are facing, she feels, is largely the fault of their parents.

'They are not trained in any way for marriage,' she said. 'Young girls think that a ring on their fingers is the be-all and ultimate.

'Before they know where they are they are thrown into a maelstrom of wailing children, dirty washing and financial deprivation.'

But Miss Wynne keeps her opinion of the majority of New Zealand women as hard-working and well-adjusted people.

'They were the first in the world to get the vote,' she said, 'and they are rather slow in developing it – which is their own fault. Women,' she said, 'should support one another.

'And women should place more emphasis on education,' she added, 'in all fields. They must cultivate a pride in their womanhood.'

Dr Margaret Liley has five small children, and a successful career in medicine. She would appear to have managed the best of both worlds, and I expected another determined deluge of battle cries for the advancement of female equality.

I was surprised.

Perched on a sunny windowsill in the office she shares with her husband at the National Women's Hospital, she informed me, in no uncertain terms, of her view on the equality of men and women.

'That,' she said , 'is a ridiculous equation! Such a sum is simply not valid – and a sterile and extremely dangerous thing to try and do.

'One half of all grown women are ashamed of themselves for not being men,' she exclaimed, 'and that is what the suffragettes of this world have done. They undermine a woman's confidence in her sex.

'The whole function of reproduction is an important part of womanhood, but all the time I am dealing with women who don't want to see pregnancy as a woman's function at all . . . they would rather be a "good guy with the boys."

'Disturbed sexual behaviour in men is a crime,' she said, 'but there is no law against women rejecting their sex, although it is much more common.'

Dr Liley sees a mass of women who can't recognise the satisfaction and fulfilment which is theirs by nature as many men who do not appreciate women are incapable of forming a 'love relationship'. But the women who do find delight and fulfilment in having and raising children also have a problem. To be thoroughly satisfied with a life at home they need to have a large family – and this is often impossible.

Dr Liley's answer is to give them something to do outside the home once the children are at school. To make this a practical and smooth-running proposition she envisages the introduction of sessional employment in all fields of female occupation.

Sessional employment is a system which divides the working week into tenths, or sessions, each remunerated separately at the rate of one tenth of what would be paid for the whole job.

It is a system which would enable women to work just as much as they are able at any time, throughout their lives.

'The arguments for it are multiple,' said Dr Liley, who operates under this scheme herself. 'It ensures "pay for the job," continuity of employment and does away with the need for retraining women after their children have grown, because they are able to keep in touch with new innovations.

'This is what women should be pressing for,' she said, 'instead of outmoded "equality."' '

Another professional woman with a large family – six children, the youngest just four months old – held surprisingly similar views to Dr Liley, and was impressed by her 'sessional employment'.

She is Mrs N. Tollemache, a lecturer in the Law School of the University of Auckland. She resents men and women being divided into those groups. It is an 'incidental division.' They are all people and complementary to one another.

'Women who have been trained in a profession,' said Mrs Tollemache, 'will work because no matter how they love their children and home it is not a totally fulfilling role, they will feel a gap in their lives.

'Cabbages,' she said, 'are really few and far between in New Zealand.'

But she does feel that New Zealand women are pressurised into marriage too soon, and that once settled into a domestic role they work unnecessarily hard.

'All this bottling and baking,' she said, 'is of no virtue if it is done just because the neighbours do it. And women take too much responsibility for the upbringing of the children. Too often Father leaves her all the decisions and just agrees.

'The battle of feminism,' she said, 'was behind us long ago. Now it is up to the individual.'

'If the individual woman is awake to it,' said Mrs Barbara Penberthy of Babs Radon, the women's fashion manufacturers, 'she will find that the world is her oyster. It is without doubt a woman's world – if she chooses it to be that way.'

Mrs Penberthy, who has been in business for 11 years since her youngest child was 18 months old, is sure that being a woman holds no uncertain advantages in the business world.

'I have never had any trouble at all,' she said, 'men go out of their way to help.

'Women,' she said, 'are treated as they want to be treated – if they put more in they get more out. It is like an end-of-the-year dividend. Some people will be cabbages no matter how they are prodded, and the others will be doing things, being what they want to be.'

Another married woman, with no children, whose interests range from visual arts to opera,

and whose talents are in writing and public relations as well as voluntary social work, would agree.

Horizons, she believes, can be broadened in the simplest ways, sometimes by not even leaving the house. She herself recently found a new joy in life through acquiring a stereogram. Now she can indulge in her love of opera by buying records and, going even further, researching the histories of the composers who interest her the most.

'It has led me into a whole new dimension,' she said, 'and I don't even have to leave my house to do this.'

This woman does not believe that going out to work is a blanket solution for the problems of suburban neuroses among women. It works for some and not for others, she claims. On the possible ego-destruction engendered by a career wife on a not-so-successful husband, however, she has this to say:

'I think it is a Victorian myth that men resent women who earn good money and who hold down good jobs. A sense of status and ability is something that comes from within and if everything is shared, from decisions to money, then there should be no clashes of this nature . . . at least, not with people who are prepared to nut things out and put them in perspective.'

A young mother living in a fairly new housing area in a pleasant, though outlying, Auckland suburb had the last say. Her environment is no different from that of thousands of other young women.

She is firm in her conviction that her present state of being tied down by two young children is purely a phase: as soon as possible she intends to return to work. Her reasons vary but most of all she misses adult company.

She would also like the extra money.

She finds her boredom is manifested less in depression than in frustrated anger, and when this happens she does a job she absolutely loathes – like weeding the garden or window cleaning.

Her job, before marriage, was that of private secretary to the managing director of a large company. Her big love and most active interest at one stage of her life was amateur theatre.

Now there is no real time for amateur theatre, baby sitters are a difficulty.

'I can see how easy it would be simply to vegetate and not care any more,' she said. 'I do know women like this. But I don't think there is any need to turn into a slattern. If you are made that way you will be that way. But most women are aware of this danger and try not to let it happen.

'If you make an effort,' she said, 'there is no need at all to become a housewife recluse alone with slippers and hair curlers and children. Added to this, there is a tremendous sense of learning from watching children grow and develop. I learn something every day. When they are older and all the novelty and newness wears off, then it'll be the time for me to take off and grow some more in a different direction . . . All this is purely temporary.'

And that was precisely as close as I came to the cabbage patch. I had found instead a lot of interested and interesting women, more advanced in their thinking than ever before, and certainly aware of the potential of their world.

They are asking for a new look at marriage, a new role for women. They want equal opportunity and 'pay for the job.' They suggest that husbands and men in general take a new look at women and they agitate for new concepts such as sessional employment.

Some of them feel that women have got the vote, but somehow, missed the boat. Others have no complaint, and have made a success in the world as it is. Many have said, 'It is up to the individual.'

And with the individual the problem must lie.

If you are crying against a life in the cabbage patch, I suggest you are in no danger. 'Cabbages' are probably happy creatures; while you are protesting you can't possibly be a cabbage. It is the awareness that counts.

Thursday, 3 October 1968, pp. 28–31

6.5. Opinion
by Kathleen Macdonald (1969)

One of the most quoted comments of 1968 was Dr Fraser McDonald's reference to New Zealand women as the Negroes of their society. Lively reactions all round suggest that this touched some deep chord in this nation's vision of itself.

Dr McDonald had a point. In a heavily masculine society women are the outsiders. They have their place and are expected to stay in it. Men – the whites of this divided community – are apt to find the presence of women rather an embarrassment.

Just as in some relatively liberal circles in America the Negro is permitted to speak, so in some sections of New Zealand society women will get a hearing.

Predominantly male committees will co-opt a woman to 'get the woman's angle.' But nobody will suggest that women are just as likely to be as useful as men. And it is unthinkable that they might have an individual point of view and should be allowed to air it.

It would not be too far-fetched to suggest that there is in New Zealand a whole feminine subculture centred in the home and spreading outward into the community. There exist vast ramifications of domestically oriented activities that are virtually unknown outside the world of women.

Dr McDonald's analogy, however, breaks down on one essential point. Whereas the Negro is already rebelling against his second-class status, Mrs New Zealand seems only too happy with life on the wrong side of the beer keg. (The Iron Curtain is a gossamer veil compared to the impenetrability of the imaginary line drawn around that wretched keg at most New Zealand parties.)

The average New Zealand woman accepts as her total lot in life the domestic routine – home-making, child rearing and so on. And when she does move out into the community she almost invariably plumps for some activity that is merely an extension of her home life – kindergarten committees, sewing and cooking bees . . . If she goes to evening classes it is to learn about beauty-care or flower arranging.

Before I am buried under an avalanche of flower vases, scones and pavlova cake, let me emphasise that she does many of these things superlatively well. She works extremely hard – much harder than her English counterpart. (She has to, of course, in a country where hired labour is ruinously expensive.)

In fact, Mrs N.Z. works far *too* hard. She is obsessed with keeping her cake and biscuit tins filled, her larder shelves stocked with preserve jars and her deepfreeze bursting at the seams. She is intent on making work for all those labour-saving devices that bedeck her spotless kitchen.

One does get the feeling that somewhere deep inside the Mini-driving, gadget-happy New Zealand woman of the sixties is a pioneer woman struggling to get out. Or possibly she has simply forgotten how to adapt herself to the security and prosperity of post-Depression New Zealand.

She is still busy holding her family together with her housewifely skills – as though the whole structure might collapse should she relax for one second.

It is tragically true that families did disintegrate during the Depression, but times have changed. Today different pressures threaten family life and managing the household budget is only part of the answer.

New Zealand women also seem to have a deep-seated emotional antagonism toward men in the role of drinking cobbers. She dislikes and distrusts the pub and the masculine mateship of the pub.

Admittedly, there was a time – and Mrs NZ has ossified in it – when depressed, workless men had to be kept away from the pub by their women. But surely the New Zealand woman of today must realise that the happy home isn't going to be broken up by a few beers.

Her tradition, then, and her picture of her role in society, stem from harder, harsher times than these. In the bad old days she did what she thought was right and nobody questions the virtue of that.

And what of Mr New Zealand? One can see why he has an interest in maintaining the status quo. It's probably great to be treated as a mixture of master and mischievous small boy to be humoured and indulged. His immediate needs are attended to (these rarely seem to include intelligent conversation) and he's satisfied.

One might hope that by 1968 the average New Zealand woman would be anxious to throw off the shackles and leap beyond the petty confinement of her life. But still she clings to her sewing machine and batches of scones.

Why? Possibly because she is in her own home very much the boss, the matriarch. And, knowing little of any other way of life, she settles for the power and title of Queen of No.1 Average Avenue.

What, then, should she do? Well, she might at least start to feel herself part of the bigger community outside the home. It's not so much a question of hurling herself into all sorts of hitherto alien activities but rather of involving herself in the world which at present her men have largely to themselves.

After all, shouldn't any mature, emancipated being be as interested in social and political goals as in personal ones?

New Zealand was once called the social laboratory of the world. It would be a great pity if it were to turn into a social museum – with its women as the fossils.

Thursday, *23 January 1969, p.41*

Chapter 7

Women's Liberation
1970s

The 'second wave' of active feminism burst suddenly on New Zealand in 1970-71. Groups of women began to meet during these years, adopting the name Women's Liberation, and circulating books, articles and ideas from the United Kingdom and America. From the outset it was clear that theirs was a radical agenda, distinct in its form, style and concerns from existing women's organisations.

Women's Liberation groups formed in Auckland and Wellington in 1970 and in another four centres in 1971.¹ The ideas had an immediate appeal to existing circles of women, most of whom were already involved in left-wing groups in the universities (7.1 and 7.2).

The first issues to be articulated by Women's Liberation groups were equal pay, the restrictive effects of social stereotyping, the objectification of women's bodies, and the exploitation of female sexuality for commercial gain. Protests were organised against beauty contests, advertising, and other activities where women were being used 'as sex objects' (see 7.3 and 7.8). Women's Liberation also demanded the right to control fertility and the right to twenty-four-hour child care. These women strongly rejected the double standard apparent in 'the sexual revolution'.

The double standard was not confined only to sex but was also implicit in the way women were designated according to their marital status. Whereas men's marital (and thereby sexual) status or experience could not be distinguished by the term Mr, feminists made a great deal of the fact that women were either Miss or Mrs. The campaign against honorifics and in support of Ms was an early focus of feminist attention. Newspapers and many other institutions refused simply to use women's names, but insisted on using Miss or Mrs. The alternative, Ms, while not embraced by all women, was a symbol of freedom – freedom from the public declaration of a relationship to a man (father or husband) implied by the Mrs/Miss distinction. This campaign, already being waged overseas, was taken up in New Zealand (7.9).

Women's Liberation also directed criticism at the lowly status accorded to housework, to child care and to the people who performed these duties. In addition they launched a scorching condemnation of the sexual division of labour in the home: men going to work to earn the money, while women (wives) stayed at home, responsible for the unceasing tasks of child minding, cooking, house cleaning, shopping, etc., while remaining economically dependent. Groups formed to analyse the position of housewives and to assert their value against the pervasive low esteem evident in the apologetic manner in which many women introduced themselves: 'only a housewife', 'just a housewife' (7.5 and 7.11). As 'housewives' they were married as much to their houses as to their husbands.

Some of the issues identified by Women's Liberation groups were simply more radical statements of concerns that had been discussed in the 1960s and earlier. The difference lay in the overall context in which the issues were placed. Changing the position of women was no longer simply a matter of changing attitudes, of resolving the tension between marriage and a career, or of finding satisfying creative occupations – it was a question of 'liberation'. Women were described as being oppressed by a harsh and unyielding regime.

The language (and analysis) came from the liberation struggles that arose as part of decolonisation in Africa, South America and Asia, and from the civil rights movement in the United States, where the human rights term 'discrimination' originated. The language of Women's Liberation couched women's plight in more dramatic terms than ever before. The power suggested by the word 'liberation' was of much greater dimensions. It encompassed the anger women felt against the limitations and constraints that bound them, as well as the personal sense of frustration and hurt that they experienced on an individual level. Women's Liberation released an equally strong expression of creative energy and potential – liberation was taken literally, and was expressed in appearance, behaviour, language, song, exuberance, initiative, etc.

Women's Liberation, and the broader movement it gave rise to (in which the radical section was only the most conspicuous part), grew very rapidly. *Broadsheet* began publication in 1972 and quickly expanded its readership from an Auckland to a national one. Germaine Greer's visit in 1972 gave the movement an enormous boost in publicity. In her person and speech (and in her subsequent court appearance on a charge of using obscene language), Greer represented the spirit of Women's Liberation in its initial phase – freedom, outspokenness, strength and a defiant sexuality.

In the same year (1972), the first National Women's Liberation Conference was held in Auckland (7.4), and the following year the first large-scale gathering of the movement was convened in Auckland by Toni Church (7.6 and 7.7). This first United Women's Convention was important in two respects. It acted as a channel for the diverse initiatives underway all around the country, and it was the first significant occasion on which the new 'liberation' movement came into contact, on a national level, with an older generation of women's organisations and activists, including the women whose ideas about themselves had been altered by 'the changing role of women' debates in the 1960s. A national set of priorities was canvassed.

Differences of direction were also apparent at this first national gathering. The most significant break came over the issue of fertility control, and, in particular, over the right to abortion. Connie Purdue, a long-time union activist for women, led a small group out of the conference in protest at the stand taken by the rest of the convention in support of women's right to make a choice on abortion. The feminist movement was, from its beginning, a loose movement rather than a centrally organised campaign. In these first large gatherings it was defining itself in terms of what it was not, as well as what it was. The right to control fertility became a central tenet of the new, or liberation, feminism. Whatever other differences there might be among feminisms and feminists, the defining issue of 'second wave' feminism was its support for abortion as a matter of choice for the woman alone.

In 1973 the Domestic Purposes Benefit was introduced. It was little noticed at the time, but quickly became a major issue for feminists, and the focus for much of the social and political unease stirred up by the changes in marriage and family patterns, and the challenges which women were increasingly making to traditional expectations of themselves as wives and mothers. The third Labour Government (1972-75) commissioned a Select Committee to investigate the role of women in New Zealand society. This type of initiative was met with considerable scepticism and outright disregard by the radical Women's Liberation Movement, which saw parliamentary politics as irrelevant and outmoded (a gathering of fusty men – the epitome of patriarchal power and preoccupation); however, the final report was used to some effect by incoming, younger, radical MP, Marilyn Waring, herself sympathetic to the Women's Liberation Movement.

In the meantime, the second United Women's Convention was held in Wellington over Queen's Birthday Weekend, 1975 (7.14). Margaret Mead was the principal speaker, and the huge and uncomfortable venue of the Winter Show Buildings was completely mobbed by women from all over the country. As in 1973, but on a much larger scale, the United Women's Convention acted as a meeting point for all kinds of individuals, issues, and ideas, ranging from radical women's liberationists to traditional women's groups. All identified themselves as having some common interest in the advancement of women, and this was pursued at many levels – from comparing individual experience in small groups (the core of feminist awareness and knowledge), to discussion of social theories and policies.

In the later 1970s the political situation became more difficult for women and for the women's movement – as it did also for Maori activist groups and the campaign against sporting contacts with South Africa (these three were undoubtedly the most prominent protest movements in New Zealand at that time). For women, the crackdowns on Domestic Purposes beneficiaries in 1976 and 1977 and on abortion clinics were the most serious. Pacific Island and Maori women were also subject to direct action in the form of the raids on overstayers and the actions taken against protesters at Raglan and Bastion Point. The Royal Commission on Contraception, Sterilisation, and Abortion, established in 1975, continued to receive submissions during 1976, and resulting legislation was passed the following year. From then on access to abortion became extremely difficult. For a time New Zealand women had to fly to Australia to obtain abortions. Access to abortion services has been vulnerable and tenuous, unevenly available across the country since then.

Further United Women's Conventions were held in Christchurch in 1977 (7.15), and Hamilton in 1979. On each occasion the gatherings became larger and more complex. The task of organisation became monumental. Growth in the movement also brought more divisions. And, while there were certainly challenges at a political level, feminism, as a living movement, continued to affect the lives and attitudes of people throughout New Zealand.

Legislative reform with far-reaching effects on women's constitutional, legal and material status was also being implemented. The Equal Pay Act (1972) brought equal pay policy into the private sector. The Human Rights Commission Act (1977) outlawed discrimination on the basis of sex, race and religion. Its most obvious impact was seen when job advertisements in daily newspapers could no longer specify jobs for men and women, thereby making one chink in what had been – and continues to be – a sharply divided workforce.

The Matrimonial Property Act (1976) made a key change to the material basis of marriage by giving effective recognition to the contributions made by a non-earning spouse (most commonly the wife) in raising children, maintaining a household, etc. This gave women some financial stake within marriage and a financial basis on which to consider a future should the marriage end. This measure had a direct continuity with the concern of nineteenth-century feminists for the economic independence of married women and for legal equality in marriage.

Similarly, the Evidence Amendment Act (1977) outlawed the questioning of rape victims about their sexual history. The trial was to be a trial of the accused rather than a public humiliation of the defendant. The fear of rape contributed to women's continued dependence on men. This was a central issue within liberation feminism. Rape crisis telephone lines and centres, 'reclaim the night' marches, and self-defence courses were all aimed at providing women with independence and freedom. Legislative reform was an important part of the overall campaign and provided continuity with preceding generations of feminists, who had sought change in the law to enhance women's equality. In the 1970s, however, the challenge offered by women was not confined to one sphere. Changes in attitudes, behaviour, language and the structure of society were tackled simultaneously.

1. Christine Dann, Up from Under, *Wellington, 1985, pp. 5–8*

Sources and Further Reading

Aitken, Judith. *A Woman's Place? A study of the changing role of women in New Zealand*, Auckland, 1975
Bunkle, Phillida and Beryl Hughes (eds). *Women in New Zealand Society*, Auckland, 1980
Dann, Christine. *Up from Under: Women and liberation in New Zealand, 1970-1985*, Wellington, 1985
Dann, Christine and Maud Cahill (eds). *Changing Our Lives: Women working in the Women's Liberation Movement, 1970-1990*, Wellington, 1991
Kedgley, Susan and Sharyn Cederman (eds). *Sexist Society*, Wellington, 1972
Sutch, W.B. *Women with a Cause*, Wellington, 1973
Te Awekotuku, Ngahuia. *Mana Wahine Maori: Selected writings on Maori women's art, culture and politics*, Auckland, 1991

7.1.   Women's Liberation: an introduction to the aims and ideas of the Women's Liberation Movement in Auckland (1971?)

Women's Liberation is a movement for human equality, a movement aimed to liberate women from the deeply embedded image of their own inferiority. It is a movement aimed to liberate women from narrow, limiting social roles, so that women in New Zealand can grow up facing an open future with many and varied opportunities for development and fulfilment. It is a movement aimed to liberate persons, both men and women from stultifying social roles and stereotypes, in order that men and women may be fairly assessed as PERSONS. It is a movement aimed to encourage more honest and realistic relationships between men and women. It is a movement aimed to improve the quality of life of men, women and children in New Zealand. We see this as possible only through the improvement of the position of women in our society.

We aim to change:

The stereotype role

To be a 'success' as a woman in our society one is expected to be 'feminine', that is, to be a passive, servile, submissive sex object existing mainly to make men happy. The woman is forced to live vicariously through her husband and children as she has few outlets of her own to express her individuality. Her appearance becomes very important as a means to impress prospective husbands or to impress other women with the economic success of her husband.

The image of women in the media

The media perpetuate the stereotype of women with their glossy, flawless, unattainable image held as an ideal to aspire to. The natural, vulnerable women with her imperfections feels insecure and inadequate when she can't match up. We believe that women should be free from societal pressures to choose their own directions in which to develop. They should be accepted as a person on their own terms not on the terms of society's idealised version of women.

The structure of marriage

All too often when a woman finally 'catches her man' and marries him she becomes his legal, economic and probably psychological dependent symbolically taking on his name and his ring. Once married she is a housewife; if she has outside employment this merely means that she has two jobs, one paid, the other not. When children arrive and she is forced to give up her paid job she becomes even more dependent on her husband. Should her husband die or divorce her she is treated as an incapacitated person to be supported thereafter by the State or her ex-husband. With increased life spans, lowered marriage ages, contraceptive tech-

niques, and smaller families the modern New Zealand mother usually has her last child in school by the time she reaches her early thirties. She then has forty years to look forward to. Our present society presents few opportunities for meaningful fulfilment of these years.

We believe that a union between free and equal beings is the only 'marriage' worth having. We believe that the chores and joys of housekeeping, child rearing and outside employment should be shared either equally by both partners, or on a mutually agreeable basis not determined only by sex.

Because we believe every person has a right to be free and equal, to pursue their own fulfilment and enjoyment to the best of their own capacity and talents without limited choice or hindrance through discrimination based on mere genital differences,

We demand:

Free contraception

Free, easily available contraception would reduce unwanted pregnancies, abortions and increase women's control over their own actions and thus their freedom of choice.

24 hour child care centres

These are essential for mothers whether working or not. No mother should be tied to a child all the time. The centres should be staffed equally by fully trained men and women and should be Government subsidized to be within the means of all.

Abortion on demand

Abortion should not be a matter for the law, but purely and simply a matter for the conscience of the woman. Repeal, not just reform of the abortion laws is needed. Women are responsible enough to decide what they want to do with their own bodies. They should not be forced into unwanted pregnancies or dangerous and illegal abortions.

Equal pay and opportunity

The concept of equal pay for equal work is agreed to be fair and just. However the Stabilisation of Remuneration Act prevents equal pay from being introduced into private industry. To prevent the situation where only one sex performs a job because of the pay rate (e.g. general nursing, typing) we suggest that there should be a 'rate for the job' to be dependent upon the experience, qualifications and skills required and the responsibility of the job. The family situation of the person should not determine

WOMEN'S LIBERATION

An introduction to the aims
and ideas of the Womens
Liberation Movement in
Auckland.

Manifesto of the Auckland Women's Liberation Movement, 1971, with the symbol that was to characterise the movement. *Ephemera Collection, Alexander Turnbull Library (Ephemera A Women 1971?)*

the reward for his/her labour nor should it determine the level of advancement. Discrimination against women in employment based on the claim of insecurity of tenure is unfounded and unjust.

Legislation to make sexual discrimination in any area illegal is needed.

Non-discriminatory education

The education system in New Zealand reinforces the traditional sex roles from the time the child first starts school. Primary schools use books showing independent, active boys, passive girls, working dads and stay-at-home mums. Intermediate and secondary schools segregate the pupils into male manual skills of woodwork and metal work and female manual skills of cooking, sewing and typing. All pupils would benefit from learning all the skills. At the universities the majority of women take the Arts courses and emerge wondering why the job opportunities are so limited for BA graduates.

Vocational Guidance services also channel girls into the traditional service type jobs as secretaries, clerks, etc. The community is denying itself a wide range of much needed skills as well as limiting the choice of women.

Suggested further reading

Betty Friedan, *The Feminine Mystique*
Germaine Greer, *The Female Eunuch*
Kate Millet, *Sexual Politics*
Robin Morgan, *Sisterhood is Powerful*
Leslie Tanner, *Voices from Women's Liberation*
Shulamith Firestone, *The Dialectic of Sex*
Simone de Beauvoir, *The Second Sex; The Nature of the Second Sex; Women's Liberation – A blueprint for the future.*

For further information contact: Women's Liberation, P.O. Box 5341, Wellesley Street, AUCKLAND.

Leaflet (Ephemera A Women 1971? ATL)

7.2.   An Introduction to the Wellington Women's Liberation Movement (1971?)

WE BELIEVE
– that women are discriminated against and treated as second-class citizens – as less than human beings.
– that women must be guaranteed the right and the ability to make *real* choices about their lives and not be streamed into narrow, subordinate roles which limit their potential.
Therefore WE DEMAND
– the repeal of abortion laws. Abortion is an essential part of birth control. Contraception without the right of abortion means that the state, in effect, controls our bodies if we become pregnant unwillingly. We say that only women have the right to decide whether or not they have an abortion; the right to choose.
– freely available contraception. More education on contraception is needed at an early age and for this to be effective, contraceptives should be easily available and free, on social security. Doctors should not have the right to refuse contraceptives on their own moral grounds. They have a duty to serve their patients.
– free, 24 hour, community-controlled child care centres. The government should provide full child care facilities of a high quality throughout New Zealand. These should be free and staffed by qualified people, men and

women. The centres must be under the control of those who use them, to prevent bureaucratic 'baby-dumps' developing. Women should not have to bear individual responsibility for the care of children. They need relief from this heavy task. Children need to be able to mix socially at an early age and will have more equal opportunity if they have access to the facilities a good child care centre would provide.
– equal pay and opportunity NOW. Employers have no right to pay women less than men, or to keep women in menial jobs. The government must act to correct this injustice to women, by making it illegal for employers to discriminate against them. To enable women to have really equal opportunity, all schools must stop streaming women into 'service' jobs and eliminate all sexual bias in curricula. The education system must play a large part in undoing the conditioning of women to accept an inferior role, by encouraging women to assert themselves in all fields.
We also want:
An end to beauty contests and advertising which exploits women.
An end to the oppression of lesbian women who are ridiculed for their rejection of the traditional sexual role.
Our goal is the total liberation of woman-

kind, so that we can be free to determine our own futures, and realise our potential.

The Wellington Women's Liberation Movement believes that by united action, we can achieve our aims. We also see the necessity for raising the consciousness of women about their situation, and hold regular discussion meetings which help to do this.

We produce *Up from Under*, a women's liberation paper which has done a great deal to spread feminist ideas in new Zealand.

We do not have men at our regular meetings because we have found, through experience, that we can build the women's movement better without men. We do hold occasional mixed meetings of a teach-in nature.

All women are welcome to come to our meetings, whether they are financial members or not. If you are curious about women's liberation, come along and meet us, ask us questions, add your views, laugh with us, argue with us or just watch and listen and see what you think.

Our meetings are held every Monday at 7.30 pm, usually in the Lounge, first floor, Student Union Building, Victoria University.

Our membership fee is $1.00 per year which includes payment for our regular newsletter. You can be on the mailing list for this whether you participate in the group or not. If you are interested in the Wellington Women's Liberation Movement and its aims, fill out the form below and send it in.

Leaflet (Ephemera B women WWLM 1971? ATL)

7.3. The Synthetic Woman in a Plastic World by Christine Wren (1972)

Little girls are made of sugar and spice and all things nice.

What then are women made of? Women are made of dreams, hopes and illusions. Wherever they go they are followed by sweet wafting perfumes which whisper of moonbeams and dewdrops. Their skins are radiant behind the pure silky foundations, blended with transparent blushers and subtle faceshapers; all set in place with shimmering translucent powders. Lips are painted glossy and moist. Eyes are made bold and beautiful with shadows, liners and false lashes. In this way their faces can be anything the women desire. If all these magic aids fail then plastic surgery may be the answer. Their bodies are moulded by diets, exercises, yoga, sauna baths, exercise belts, corsets and foundation garments. The body is then fitted into trendy clothing, poor-wearing pantihose and uncomfortable, distorting shoes. The whole masterpiece is then crowned by a glowing, cascading halo encrusted with hairspray, conditioners, colourings and clips.

This then is the woman who stares hypnotically from billboards, glossy photographic paper, posters, and TV and film screens. The dream which is mirrored in their eyes is to be every woman's reality. These women are passive, weak, frivolous and incapable of opening doors, always waiting for their knight in shining armour. They are intuitive, childlike, conniving and the 'power behind the throne'. Their role is to serve and to raise children.

But these are not real women, they are the synthetic women created by the mass media and the mass education system. They are des-tined to live in an unreal plastic world of romance and child-rearing. The creating of this synthetic woman is extremely profitable for those who provide the props, scenery and gilding.

Real women are human beings made of skin, bone, tissues, nerves, fingernails and hair. Their brains are no less effective than those belonging to men. Their fingers, arms, legs and feet enable them to be perfectly capable of opening doors and standing. Their physical structure no more suits them to washing floors, cooking, cleaning toilets or for that matter looking after children than the equivalent parts of the male.

So why then are women so terribly afraid of admitting what they are? Why do they live in the twilight world of suburbia, sheltering behind mass hairstyles, clothes and striving for a standardized face created from cosmetics? Why are they afraid of realising their true potential or even admitting their full capacities or allowing others to do so without subjecting them to criticism and prejudice?

The obvious answer is that they do all these things to get their man who will provide for them and their children. To find out why this is at all necessary one must look at the forces which mould the synthetic woman and cause her to act in this manner.

The first area to look at is the physical appearance of the synthetic woman. A number of features are held by society (and most importantly) by women themselves to be essential. The most important of these is YOUTH. This creates a large market for products which will produce this illusion such as hair colouring, moisturisers, skincare and covering products as well as plastic surgery and foundation garments. Another striking feature is that the synthetic woman NEVER smells as this will repel men. The aids for this are soap, toothpaste, deodorants and clothes-washing agents. The synthetic woman is always slim and uses special slimmer's foods, diets, pills and doubtful miracle methods to reduce weight and to remain that way. In lesser demand are methods for increasing weight. Most of this fanaticism is centred on increasing the bustline so as to become 'sexier'. A more recent requirement is a tanned skin acquired from the numerous tanning agents or sitting for hours in the hot sun to become burnt, blistered and headachy. But the most important requirement of all is that she is BEAUTIFUL. She is what all women want to be like and aspire to become. She is what men think women should be like and this in turn governs how they react to all women judging them as successes or failures to the extent they measure up to the synthetic woman. To fail to comply with that image is to fail as a woman. This is no wonder when considering the tremendous resources which have gone into the creation of the synthetic woman. She appears everywhere we look constantly being drilled into our subconscious.

The perpetuation of this image is extremely profitable (not to forget the time and effort required by each individual woman to acquire it). According to VOGUE (April '71) £235,000,000 (UK) is spent every year on cosmetics. (This includes lips £8m; eyes £5.7m; hair products £140m; and complexion £15m.) In 1967 U.S. women bought 960,000,000 pairs of pantihose.

The more frequently the fashions change, and women feel inadequate without window dressing, the more profitable it is. In this light it is no wonder that there is no one constant feature which is, at all times throughout history, considered beautiful. The idea is to encourage women to disguise what they already have by superimposing something else.

What advertising defines as beautiful is usually extreme so that not many women start out with the necessary attributes. All these factors become obvious when looking at old, out-of-date films and magazines. The women all look ugly and artificial wearing shoulder pads, bright red lipstick and stark eyebrows.

The average woman, having been brainwashed into wishing she was identical with the artificially created beauty-norm (set up by the advertising) is offered a fake solution. She can attain the magic standards, the advertisers tell her, if she purchases all kinds of magic products offered to her[. These do not] actually, singly or taken together, make her into the 'ideal' but she feels compelled to go on and on buying the products. Some of them even impair the natural beauty she started out with (e.g. skin lotions that leave the texture of the skin impaired).

The magic image justifies or persuades the payment of high prices when the same ingredients could be obtained more cheaply without the mystique generated by advertising, packaging, displays and purchasing of strategic counter space.

The tremendous range of products available (often manufactured by the same firm) creates confusion as to their use. Wastage arises from buying makeup for the wrong skin type or colour. Young girls experimenting with these products for the first time experience frustration, disappointment, not to mention loss of their time and money.

Even when she has used all the products the advertisers offer, an individual woman will not be able to conform to the current image. This causes in her a great sense of failure and unhappiness. Women often blame themselves and not the fact that they have been misled. They do not see the fact that they cannot change their basic physical shape. They often see the answer as being the purchase of another, different product. By wearing makeup a woman feels she can hide and submerge her feelings of inadequacy and insecurity. In this way she can avoid being a positive person naturally any different from others.

It is very profitable for manufacturers of magic products to get women to want to change themselves and believe that the synthetic is better than the real thing. 'Woman' has become synonymous with beauty as created by makeup. Because these views are so widely accepted, if a woman is to get a good job she must wear certain types of clothes, hairstyles and makeup. Some jobs are concerned primarily with appearance (modelling, air hostesses, receptionists). In most other jobs physical appearance is advantageous. Many newspaper advertisements specify 'attractive young lady' when it has no actual bearing on the service to be performed. One never sees an advertisement for 'good looking young man'.

The main reason women comply with these demands is to 'get a man'. For men have been conditioned by advertising to expect women to come packaged in this manner.

Very powerful influences are at work to

condition the attitudes and mind of the synthetic woman so that she will fit into the way of like demanded by the plastic world. It is estimated that it will cost $85m to institute equal pay in New Zealand and this shows how profitable it is to get women to accept they are inferior. In the past many women have accepted unequal pay in industry and business because they are expected to do unpaid work in the home and any reward, no matter how unjust, seems to her to be better than house-bound serfdom.

A mass of male chauvinist lies, legends, myths and 'put downs' together with actual discriminations (over abortion, equal pay, matrimonial property, etc.) create in many women an acceptance of a subordinate status, her fitting in to the role of mother and domestic servant. She sees this condition as her 'natural destiny'. Because of this a vicious circle is created. Myths which arise due to this situation are taken to justify the situation itself. Women are told at every possible opportunity that they are illogical, intuitive, impractical and unintelligent. Her mind is constantly cluttered with trivia, frills and flowers. Because of this natural state, her life is to be one of serving. She is not as intelligent as men and, as she is going to get married anyway, it is naturally not worth bothering with too much education. As a result, she gets dull, poorly-paid jobs serving and flattering the ego of her male boss until she marries. The rest of her life is spent in her house in the suburbs; decorating her nest, having children as well as cooking, sewing and knitting for the family.

On this level women are subject to a barrage of advertisements because they make 75% of consumer decisions. There is never a shortage of housewives to testify how satisfying it is having a daily confrontation with dirt and germs. She spends her day keeping her washing whiter than the neighbour's, having gleaming pots and pans and stain-free baths, and using refrigerators and washing machines. The manufacturers' products are her means to succeeding in keeping her gleaming house in order and thus succeeding in marriage. Because she has a vagina this is her natural place in life. Everywhere she looks psychologists, doctors, anthropologists, acquaintances and the media attest the truth of this. It is inevitable and she will never be happier than doing the never-ending, rewardless, time consuming housework only to get up the next morning to start again.

At times this circle may become tedious but it is all made worthwhile because she possesses a MAN who comes home to her every night. Her whole life is for others and through others as this will fulfil her creative urges.

How is this situation perpetrated? The round starts when children are fed fairytales ending in marriage and happiness. While little girls are helping mother make beds, lay tables, wash dishes and make dolls' clothes their brothers play adventurous games (such as being spacemen). At school, girls aspire to being mothers and the education they wish to get need only be used for fill-in jobs. A class of 12-year olds were asked what they would do when they left school. All the girls in the class replied they would marry in their early 20s filling in time with jobs like nursing, teaching, child minding, acting, air hostessing, hairdressing and secretarial work. Of the boys only three wished to marry. One of these said he would have no children, another said he would have one son which his wife would stay home and look after. They aspired to becoming pilots, sea captains, surveyors, hunters, whalers, farm advisers, All Blacks and being very rich by winning the jackpot. Because of the channelling by parents and schools, as well as the girls' own limited ambitions, they end up taking homecraft, typing, biology and languages to equip them for being office workers, teachers, nurses or getting B.A.s in relatively useless subjects. These are all jobs which are poorly paid with limited opportunities for advancement but their ultimate aim is to become wives and mothers. Society makes marriage inevitable, and very easy. Compare the time and ease it takes to get married with the time, trouble and expense it takes to get a divorce. These girls fail to take account of the future working life they will have when their children grow up, or the strong possibility that their marriage will not last.

It is highly likely a married woman will need to work to earn enough money for the family to live on. At the present time she will be at a disadvantage because of the lack of equal pay, education and opportunities. As well as this she will be subjected to all the old wives' tales which say a woman's place is in the home. In addition to her job she will be expected to do the housework and care for her children and husband, unaided.

If she should decide not to marry she will be subjected to all the tiresome rubbish about her natural destiny. Everyday she will be immersed in images of childlike figures of trendy teenagers or bubbling housewives being held up as ideals for her to emulate. She will be isolated from other women as most of her contemporaries will be men who will be scornful and critical of her. Primarily she will come up against unequal pay and opportunity justified because she 'may' get married. Marriage for her will not provide her with someone who will stay home and care for her so that she may concentrate on her job.

Yet as men do not think solely in terms of marriage or work why should women? Marriage for both should be part of life not life itself. The ideal situation would seem to be a sharing of housework, child minding and money-raising. This could be achieved by both spouses working half a day or alternate weeks. This would be especially beneficial to children who would see the parents equally.

The emphasis should be on CHOICE. If women wish to stay in the home they should be able to. At the present time if they don't wish to they are severely handicapped because there are no 24-hour day care centres and, while their children are young, they are financially dependent on their husbands. At the moment there is no completely effective way of controlling their fertility so as a result everything is uncertain for them.

The first step towards recreating women as people is to change the attitudes towards them. Women's Liberation has been defined as the freeing of women from the myths which confine her in her own mind and in the minds of others. The hardest task will be to change the image of the synthetic woman in her plastic unreal world which is drilled into her own head from birth. It will be necessary to eliminate all kinds of engendered differences. Why, for example, should little girls be dressed in pink frills to mention a very minor point. The belief that women are best suited to menial, non-thinking, repetitive, supervised tasks because they have a womb must be ended. They should be encouraged to participate in society as human beings and not live vicariously. This will involve a change in the steering which schools give. All schools must be co-educational. Women should make up 50% of those entering university instead of the present 25%. The subjects they take should not channel them away from meaningful careers when they have the potential.

Why can't the media show women as real people travelling, experiencing new, exciting events and discoveries instead of living in a half world as appendages? Songs, films, books and satires should be about female people, not women as the suffering heroine concerned solely with herself as subservient to the needs of others. TV should stop portraying women as idiots. Women should be writing, directing films, editing women's magazines (they buy over 50m a month), newspapers, reading the news and directing policy equally with men. While women are young they should be enjoying their freedom, greater wealth and lack of responsibilities, meeting many different people, experiencing numerous situations instead of spending their time and energies on getting one solitary man. They should stop men telling them what they are like and need and find out for themselves.

In fields participated in largely by women (such as the quality of purchases they make) women hold little sway and are dictated to by men. Women should be taking their place in society as human beings. They should take control of their own lives and live them as they feel they should, not as others tell them. They should make up 50% of Parliament and participate in the decision-making which decides their lives. They should constitute 50% of lawyers, magistrates and judges who represent and judge them as people. They should participate more in careers like engineering, architecture and medicine. In other words women should start participating in a full balanced life.

Why can't real flesh and blood women participate in life fully and equally with men instead of disguising themselves and their abilities and wishing they were different? They should be able to accept their bodies as they are without guilt.

BOOK NO. 2
Published by
Wellington Organisation for Women,
P.O. Box 662,
Wellington.
February, 1972

see also –
BOOK NO. 1
Women's Liberation: Are N.Z. women ready to examine the case?

The Synthetic Woman in a Plastic World, *Wellington, 1971 (Ephemera A Women 1972, ATL)*

7.4. Reports from the National Women's Liberation Conference (1972)

Abortion

Convenor: Claudia Mason.

Proposals adopted:

1. That the women's liberation movement nationally support International Abortion Action Week, May 1-6; that we organise marches and other activities in each centre on Friday, May 5, around the demands:

REPEAL ALL ANTI-ABORTION LAWS
'ABORTION – A WOMAN'S RIGHT TO CHOOSE'

with the following corollary demands:
Free and easily available contraception
Voluntary sterilisation.

2. That more research be done on developing an effective contraceptive for both women and men.

3. That the law against giving contraceptive advice and instruction to those under sixteen be repealed.

4. That realistic sex education be given at all levels at school (primary and secondary).

5. That sterilisation should be freely available to both men and women.

6. That we invite those women who have had abortions to come forward and declare this during Abortion Action Week.

7. That this National Women's Liberation Conference demands the repeal of all anti-abortion laws. (This came from the floor at the plenary session and was carried unanimously.)

Equal pay

Convenor: Ann Ruth.

Proposals adopted:
We demand equal rates for the job and equal opportunities in training and education, and that a law be passed making it illegal to discriminate in employment on the basis of sex.

In addition we demand:

1. An equal minimum living wage for all workers.

2. That part-time workers be paid in accordance with their qualifications.

3. Greater flexibility in hours and job structure.

4. That subsidiary benefits such as transfer allowances and paid leave to care for sick dependents be extended to women workers on the same basis as men.

5. That discrimination in tax exemptions (women supporting a husband get less tax exemption than men supporting wives) be ended.

6. That paid maternity (and/or paternity) leave be instituted in all jobs.

7. That education authorities be instructed to alter curricula to eliminate educational separatism.

8. We demand an end to the family wage with the eventual probability of every person over school leaving age being paid for the work or study in which they are engaged – this would include persons involved in housework & childrearing.

We urge women to take the following actions:

1. To organise seminars for women in employment to discuss their status at work and the unions. This could be done by women's liberation groups in close contact with union officials.

2. That we set up a referral service for women who have been victims of sexual discrimination in any area of employment.

3. That we exhort the Federation of Labour to follow up its initial support for the basic right of women workers by actions on our further demands forthwith. We suggest that they ratify these demands in their 1972 conference.

4. That we should send a copy of these demands to unions, the government, political parties, educational institutions and all other relevant bodies.

5. (From the floor) That women's liberation groups should actively support women when they strike for equal pay and better working conditions.

Child care

Convenor: Belinda Gillespie. (Sonja Davies gave report.)

Recognising the need for greatly increased numbers of child care centres this Conference recommends that:

1. A national campaign of awareness followed by a petition which would be organised by Women's Liberation groups throughout the country, such a petition to provide the means of educating the public and convincing politicians.

2. This Conference urges all Women's Liber-

ation members to join the New Zealand Association of Child Care Centres as associate members, both in groups and as individuals and to support the aims of that body.

3. That as soon as practicable no child care centre should operate without at least one member of the staff holding an approved training qualification.

4. That in drawing up standards for Child Care Centres, the government be asked to give careful attention to the developmental needs of children.

Gay liberation
Convenor: Ngahuia Volkerling.

One cannot love another until one first loves oneself. Given this state, one then has the right to decide, in whatever context, how one will express love for others.

We demand social respect, not tolerance.
We demand the right to sexual self-determination.
We demand the right to choose the loving expression of that sexuality we prefer.
We demand a rational clarification of the lesbian issue within the context of individual women's liberation groups.
We move that this Conference openly supports the rights of lesbian women.
(Carried enthusiastically.)

Legal rights
Convenor: Joan Rotherham.

Suggestions made included:
(a) the establishment of a Legal Advice Bureau in centres, similar to the Bureau operating at present in Porirua. Groups could perhaps write to district Law Societies to interest sympathetic solicitors.
(b) That a pamphlet *Women's Legal Rights on Dissolution of Marriage* be prepared for distribution possibly through Group mailing lists and enclosed in all correspondence going out from Groups.
(c) That groups approach local branches of Society for Protection of Home and Family to interest the society in a plan for a referral/publicity venture. Cost of proposed pamphlet and its contents could be a shared effort between Society and Group.

Area workshops

Student women
Convenor: Carole Ferrier.

Most problems of women students are those of women in general. Most women students have a small bursary but are dependent either upon poorly-paid part-time or temporary work, or else upon a man – father, husband or lover – for an adequate income.

It was suggested that students might be paid a wage to study (as with the proposal for pay for housepeople, men and women) but this raises the problem that the government might demand much more control over the university if subsidising them to this extent. Students could organise more of their own services (baby-sitting, food communes) to save money, but the point was made that it was valuable for students to work in the community for a time. The position of women in student politics also seemed to reflect their position in national politics – there has been only one woman president of the NZ University Students Association, but that was during the war.

Resolutions: to be actioned by university women's liberation groups.

1. To initiate discussion in all the universities of the possibilities of introduction of a women's studies programme, either in the form of papers within existing disciplines, or as a separate department. Lecturers should be approached about this, and it would result in the employment of more women lecturers.

2. Students should concern themselves with the position of women workers in the university – cleaners, cafeteria workers, etc., and support their rights.

3. A study of the financial position of women students should be made, with a view to increasing their bursaries.

Report adopted.

High school women
Convenor: Sue Kedgley.

Recommendations:
1. That segregation in co-educational schools should cease. (At present many secondary schools segregate classrooms, playgrounds, assemblies, etc.)
2. That single-sex state schools merge with other high schools to become co-educational.
3. That existing segregation in vocational guidance literature be stopped. (At present there are brochures for girls, and separate ones for boys, which serve to restrict the vocational choices of students.)
4. That vocational guidance commence at the third and fourth forms, instead of at present, in the fifth, sixth and seventh forms only, and that

vocational guidance facilities in schools be expanded to enable all pupils to receive adequate assistance.

5. That sex education – including instruction on contraceptive techniques – be a compulsory subject in schools, preferably commencing in primary schools.

6. That contraceptive advice and contraceptive measures be made available to persons requiring them under the age of sixteen and that the law of consent be abolished, if necessary, to make this possible.

Report adopted.

Working women

Convenors: Robin Scholes and Janet Bogle. (2 workshops)

Employers use women's child bearing function as a basis for discrimination, exploitation and oppression. To counteract this, the Working Women's workshops recommended the following:

1. That employers provide full pay for an expectant mother for one month prior to confinement and five months following the birth (a reasonable period of leave without pay to follow this).

2. That child care facilities should be provided at places of employment of either parent wherever there are a sufficient number of parents employed. In the cities these should be provided at times and places convenient for working parents and at no cost (the workshop thought that any compulsion on employers of working mothers only to provide child care centres could lead to discrimination against women, and that this would be based on the erroneous assumption that they alone are responsible for the children.)

3. That re-employment together with retraining schemes should be made more available for mothers following pregnancy and child rearing (it was noted that the Labour Department's present plans include such provisions).

4. That working adults should have a provision of leave to care for a sick family member over and above their own personal sick leave. This would allow either a father or mother to care for a sick child, and would allow husbands and wives to care for each other when sick.

5. There should be community provision of inexpensive laundries open 24 hours a day.

6. Apartment blocks, state housing areas, community centres and schools should henceforth be built with special after-school rooms for children of working parents.

7. There should be community provision of good, moderately-priced facilities for families to eat out.

The Workshop also recommended that all working women should be adequately covered by a union. It was noted that there are many women not in unions and that those already in unions often do not take a full part. This is often due as much to the difficulties encountered by women in attending union meetings, as to any lack of interest on their part. Unions often unintentionally contributed to this state of affairs by not realising the importance of having meetings within working hours or providing creches for union meetings so that women could attend. Unions were urged to give thought to such positive measures to encourage women's involvement.

The Federation of Labour was urged to investigate the situation of working women both inside and outside the unions and to act upon its findings.

The Labour Dept is currently doing a survey on Women in Employment and has apparently passed a resolution to increase facilities for retraining women re-entering the workforce after their children are at school. There is already a course at the Wgton Polytechnic and the workshop urged all groups to enquire about the creation of such schemes from their local Labour Dept. They should stress in addition the need to improve job expectancy amongst women and to teach Industrial Relations and Trade Union history in Social Studies and Liberal Studies at primary and secondary school levels.

Report adopted.

Housewives' workshop

Convenor: Julie Cameron.

There was a frank and honest discussion among the housewives about the problems and tensions we face in our daily lives. We found that the problems and frustrations listed below were common to us all, despite our obvious personality and emotional differences and the type of man we are married to. We then suggested possible solutions.

Causes of frustration.

1. **Economic dependence** on our husbands which, in this materialistic society where people are valued according to their contributions to the economy or the amount of money they earn, means that we as a group

have little social esteem.

2. Our artificial sex roles. Because we are female we are expected to be cooks, housemaids, child-minders, laundresses, general serving maids, and mistresses – and like it! – despite our aptitudes, personalities and interests.

3. The emotional drag of children, who are utterly dependent on us in their early years is exhausting as well as being rewarding, no matter how much we love them.

4. Isolation from the outside world because of our roles as mothers and housewives which keep us mainly within the home and do not leave us sufficient time to pursue our own interests and to grow as whole, individual people.

5. Our lack of identity as individuals. It is usual for a wife to be identified by her relationship to her husband. For example, a wife will probably be introduced as Mary, Tom Brown the butcher's wife.

Solutions for frustrations

1. Increase in the family benefit, which should be made payable to the wife, to include a housewife's allowance in order to decrease our economic dependence on our husbands. This could possibly be obtained by applying political pressure on the government.

2. Education of men and boys about their role as 'house-husbands' who should be prepared to help with housework and child-minding so that their wives are freed to pursue their rights as people to interests outside the home.

3. The establishment of Child Care Centres so that mothers are freed from the emotional drag of children for a few hours during the day each week.

4. The establishment of a Housewives Union, both to help prevent the feeling of isolation and suburban neurosis, and to achieve recognition of our contribution to the economy of our society. Such a group could also help us to grow as individuals by providing for outside interests.

5. Education of girls into what marriage entails to counteract the prevailing view of white wedding dresses, a sparkling home, a loving and unselfish husband who is also a companion and Prince Charming, and the other myths with which our society brainwashes its female population.

6. Payment during retraining courses once the housewife is free to re-enter employment.

Report adopted.

'Issues Workshops' from Reports of the National Women's Liberation Conference, 1–2 April 1972, *Wellington, 1972*

7.5. Homemakers away to a Good Start
by A.B. (1972)

Since Julie Cameron suggested, at the women's liberation conference at Easter, that there was a place and a need for a union for housewives (later changed to homemakers, so that men could be included in the membership) her mailbox has had a steady stream of replies. Membership is now over the 300 mark and plans are in hand for a conference to be held in Wellington in November.

There is nothing phenomenal about the birth of a new club or group. We must be among the most group-minded people in the world – great joiners, committee-attenders, club-goers. One wonders whether all this joining isn't because we are basically a lonely, inarticulate community which needs to join things so that we can feel less alone. Isolation, loneliness, being apart – these are very real problems which shouldn't exist in a small country like ours where we still pay lip service to the idea that no better place than New Zealand exists.

But the choice, by Julie Cameron, of the word union, instead of club, group, association or movement, was quite deliberate.

'A union is,' she says, 'any society . . . lawfully associated for the purpose of protecting or furthering the interests of workers engaged in any specific industry or related industries.'

Homemaking, says Julie, is an industry which is unrecognised and underprivileged. She cites as one of the examples of how little recognition there is of the work of homemakers the Woodhouse Report, which excludes compensation for accidents that happen within the home. After all, being a housewife is a job, which like any other can be done badly or well, depending on the individual.

There are three basic aims for the Homemaker's Union:

• To protect and further the interests of homemakers as a group
• To achieve recognition of the contribution

by homemakers to the economy.

• To help prevent feelings of isolation and loneliness occurring among homemakers and to help them develop more fully as individuals.

The union intends to achieve these aims by working on several levels. At one level will be the working committees – the pressure groups of the union. They will work in with any other existing groups to achieve a desired result – whether that be bulk buying on one level or working with Carp at another to help stop rising prices. Different groups in different areas are interested in specific projects. The Auckland group is particularly keen on family planning clinics, in Wellington it's child care centres, in Gisborne open drains. In the Wairarapa the group hopes to open a homecraft shop and serve coffee, so that people will have a place to go.

On another level, there are chapters. These operate specifically to help prevent those feelings of loneliness. Members of the union within any area meet and form interest groups, which may include lectures on topics of interest, child-minding or home-help service, or simply getting together over coffee and talking to each other.

Julie says that because church membership has fallen off so much, people who could once have turned to a minister in the times of stress no longer have anyone to talk to. She hopes that the chapters will be able to alleviate some of these difficulties.

The Homemaker's Union is not especially for the educated, the intellectual, the articulate. 'It is for the next layer down – those who can't express themselves, the old, the ordinary housewife who simply does not understand what women's lib is all about, but who still experiences the same feelings as her more educated sisters.'

There is a basic need at the moment for more leaders – those women who are quite naturally thrown forward because of their natural abilities of leadership. But if H.U. members are from the group which Julie maintains really need it, then the leaders are not as likely to emerge.

Having everyone acting, at the chapter level and perhaps even on the working committees, on their own initiative, brings multiple problems of too many generals and not enough soldiers. But Julie says that her ideas are only a starting point for the union. Eventually the members themselves will change her ideas and start running it in their own way.

I wondered whether the Homemaker's Union didn't already duplicate some of the aims of existing groups. Julie feels that the major difference is that the union treats its members like people and not just as mothers like Plunket, or farmers' wives like WDFF or gardeners like the gardening circle.

Obviously if such a union was going to start it had to be begun by someone intelligent, but somehow Julie Cameron is the antithesis of the ideal member one might imagine.

She's attractive and bright, in that flinty way that some women are, she has an MA in English and is studying so that she can set up a farm accounting business.

She's on the Wairarapa Hospital Board, and for a farmer's wife she has to be considered radical.

And that's another thing. Julie is not a typical farming wife. While she helps her husband on his 2000-acre farm, while she farmhouse bakes and freezes, looks after her pre-school son, John, in a curious way she doesn't really look as if she belongs on a farm. She hasn't settled down to a rural existence. And certainly she hasn't stopped thinking. Perhaps it is the area in which she lives – 23 miles from Featherston above Lake Onoke, a windswept region in which many women would feel stranded and abandoned – that has made her aware enough of other people's needs to start the Homemaker's Union.

Anyone interested should write to Sharon Stapleton, 2 Roband Rd, Glenfield, Auckland; Robin Hayes, 590 Wainui Rd, Gisborne; Leith Holland, 54 Oxley Avenue, Christchurch; Jan Taylor, 164 Miromiro Road, Normandale, Wellington; or Julie Cameron, R.D.3, Featherston.

Thursday, 12 October 1972, pp. 76–77

7.6. Areas of Discrimination
by Margaret Wilson (1973)

The Universal Declaration of Human Rights states that: 'All human beings are born free and equal in dignity and rights'. While few people would disagree with the truth expressed in these dozen words, women today are still struggling for equal rights. They may have thought in 1893, when they were granted the right to vote, that their struggle was partly over. As time has shown them, however, it was only the beginning of a long campaign for recognition. It is shameful when you realise that it has taken nearly 80 years, since women were given the right to vote, for women to be given equal pay for equal work: and they will have to wait four years before even this basic right is fully implemented. It would be a mistake for women to think that, just because we now have equal pay in New Zealand, all discrimination against women on grounds of sex will disappear. Discrimination against women does exist in New Zealand, and it will continue to exist unless women unite together to prevent it.

Before women can meet the challenge of preventing discrimination however, it is essential that they recognise the form in which it exists in New Zealand today. Most men would strenuously deny that they discriminate against women. It is true that there are few laws that discriminate against women. Those that do exist relate mainly to the area of employment. They were originally enacted to protect women, and as such at that time may have fulfilled a social need. Today however, even these protective laws are discriminatory in that they prevent women from pursuing spheres of employment of their own choice.

While, then, there may be little in the way of legal discrimination, it does exist in a far more subtle and invidious form. It operates when a woman may wish to enter a particular type of employment that has previously been considered 'men's work'. It operates when a woman seeks promotion or advancement in her employment. It operates when she tries to raise finance to buy a home for herself and her children. It operates in the bureaucracy of organisations that require a woman's honesty and reliability to be vouched for by a male. It operates in all aspects of a woman's economic, political and social life. Why is it then that women are treated differently just because of their sex? Why does a woman have to prove herself more qualified, more competent and more capable than a male in our society today? The answer is not simply that men and women are different. This fact cannot be denied, just as it cannot be denied that all men are not the same. They are individuals, just as all women are individuals and as such should be accorded equal dignity and rights.

The answer lies in the fact that it is assumed women have a predetermined role to play in our society, just as men have an assigned role in society. To put it very simply, it is the role of the man to work and the role of the woman to remain at home and raise the children. This concept of the roles of the sexes in our society has gradually been eroded, until today it is no longer valid to assume that all women will want to remain at home and devote their full time and energies to raising a family. In fact in many instances today it is an economic necessity that women find employment. What has happened then, is that there is no longer an accepted and defined role for either sex in our society. If this is the situation, then recognition must be given to the fact that women must have the freedom and the right to choose whatever activity they wish to pursue. A woman cannot, however, have this freedom if she is discriminated against by laws, conventions and practices, both written and unwritten, that at present exist.

In what way, then, is a woman discriminated against and thus prevented from achieving this freedom of choice? It is pointless to list endlessly individual instances of discriminatory practices. We have probably all experienced them in one form or another, whether it be a denial of promotion, or having to obtain a husband's signature before your electricity is connected. In many situations also it is difficult to prove whether in fact you were discriminated against on the grounds of your sex alone. It is frequently argued that an employer has a right to decide whom he shall employ or grant promotion to, or that a company has a right to refuse an application for a mortgage from any person. If the situation was any different then we would be interfering with the employer's or the company's rights of freedom of choice. What we have to decide is whether or not one's sex alone is a sufficient ground upon which to discriminate against an individual. If a decision in the cases I have just mentioned was based on the ground of merit of the person involved, there would be little argument, but frequently a woman in such a situation is at a disadvantage and cannot be treated on the same footing as a man. It is essential then that women be in such a position that they are able to compete equally with men, if they so wish.

This brings me to a consideration of an area of discrimination that is at the root of many other forms of discrimination, that is, that in New Zealand, a woman is economically discriminated against. Because of the present structure of our society, if a woman is to achieve equality and assume equal responsibility, she must be economically secure and independent.

It is perhaps in the area of employment that women are most blatantly discriminated against. There is an increasing number of women entering the work-force. This increase is particularly noticeable amongst married women who are re-entering the work-force once their children have entered school. In 1936 the percentage of married women in the female work-force was 8.5%. In 1966 this figure had risen to 41.5% and today it is probably even greater. When we talk of women in employment then, we are talking of a considerable proportion of New Zealand's work-force. What are we doing, then, to prepare women for employment, so they can take advantage of the opportunities available? A survey conducted by the Advisory Council on Educational Planning found that secondary school girls, in part, see employment as a premarital activity, and as such tended to follow traditional patterns in their education and sought jobs with pre-conceived ideas of what is women's work. By following this pattern, they frequently find, when they wish to re-enter the work-force, that they are ill-equipped to do so. There is perhaps nothing obviously discriminatory about the courses at school offered to girls, but what should be done is to make girls aware of the possibilities of employment outside the traditional women's work areas, and to make them aware of the fact that there is a strong possibility that in the future they may wish to continue in employment, or in fact be forced to re-enter the work-force through economic necessity.

Statistics show that the majority of the female work-force is concentrated in clerical occupations (57.86% of persons employed in this area are females), as saleswomen and shop assistants, in the clothing industry, as teachers and nurses and in service industries. It is perhaps significant that with the exception of teachers, these occupations tend to be amongst the lowest paid occupations in New Zealand. There are a growing number of women entering the professions and into managerial and executive positions, but their percentage is still relatively low at the moment, for example, only 11.95% of persons in administrative, executive and managerial positions are females.

Why women do not enter employment in areas outside the traditional women's work areas and do not advance to positions of responsibility is due to a number of factors. The first, of course, is due to lack of educational qualifications, that have already been men-

tioned. Another factor is that in some instances women are prevented from pursuing certain types of employment by provisions in the award that govern their conditions of employment. These provisions prevent women from obtaining the more highly paid jobs, and in some cases are a barrier to promotion, for example, under the Air New Zealand Stewards' and Hostesses' Industrial Agreement, it is impossible for a woman to hold the responsible position of purser, because the award specifies such person in this position must be a male. Restrictions as to age and hours of employment have also been placed upon women; for example, in general, women under 25 years cannot be employed in hotel bars, also, until the recent announcement of the Minister of Transport, women could not drive taxis during the night. Also the Factories Act states that women may not be employed after 11 p.m. and before 7 a.m. These provisions and others are justified on the grounds that they are protecting women, yet this protection does appear to be rather selective when 17-year-old girls can perform as strippers into the early hours.

Discrimination also exists in the retirement policies practised by many companies. There appears to be no logical reason why women should be forced to retire, in some cases, ten years before men. Such discrimination, again, only serves to place women at an economic disadvantage, thus preventing them from participating in society on an equal footing with men.

Many of the instances of discrimination in employment may be related to the fact that the majority of awards and agreements are negotiated by men, who naturally have a vested interest in protecting their own jobs and economic status. It is time the trade unions assumed their responsibilities towards their female membership. Also it is time women themselves became involved in the activities of trade unions. These organisations exist to protect workers, and this includes female workers. In 1971 it was estimated that there were 322,200 females in the work-force, the vast majority of whom are members of a trade union or employed in the public service, and thus having an opportunity to join the Public Service Association. The vehicles exist to a certain extent, then, to overcome some of the discrimination in the employment area. If women would only unite and interest themselves in these areas then such matters as maternity leave, child care centres, and allowances payable to married men but not married women, could become a reality, instead of a pious hope for the future.

It is the lack of such things as maternity leave and adequate inexpensive child care centres that prevent women from either taking the employment of their choice or advancing in their chosen occupations. In effect then, just because a woman performs a vital role in our society in becoming a mother, she is discriminated against.

It is also interesting to note that many of the instances of discrimination that occur apply particularly to married women. By assuming the status of wife and mother, frequently her status as an individual is denigrated. Suddenly she becomes a bad employment risk, because she now has family responsibilities. yet when a man becomes a father he is congratulated and is now considered a good employment risk because he has 'settled down'. Once married, also, a woman who remains at home and cares for her family frequently finds the economic value of this service she is performing not only for her family but also for the community at large, is not recognised. An anomalous situation also arises in the case of the married woman who is working and is either supporting her husband, or who finds she must work in order that the family has an adequate income. Allowances granted to married men are frequently not payable to a married woman. There appears to be no logical reason for this

situation, except perhaps the irrational attitude that women do not really have to work and that they do so only to supplement the family income and to provide themselves with extra money.

It is time then that the whole attitude towards women in employment is reviewed. If the traditional organisations that are responsible for the protection of the rights of women are not performing their duty, then women must look elsewhere. New Zealand women are particularly fortunate in that they will be given the opportunity next year to make submissions before a select committee of Parliament that has been set up to look at the whole question of discrimination against women on the grounds of sex, with a view to bringing down legislation. This is an important step towards women attaining equal rights. It does mean, however, that women themselves must now come forward on their own behalf to ensure that their case is properly and responsibly presented. It also means that women themselves must start reconsidering their role in society. It is often said that women are their own worst enemies. Now is our opportunity to prove this is not true. We have the opportunity to attain equality in law and to show we are able to assume the responsibilities associated with equality.

United Women's Convention, 1973: Report, *edited by Sandra Coney, assisted by Anne Parsons and others, Auckland, 1973, pp.18–20*

7.7. Maori Women in Pakeha Society by Mira Szaszy (1973)

Seen through the liberation conscious eyes of women today, the position of the Maori woman in pre-European society seems inferior and lacking in status.

It is true that pre-European Maori women did not enjoy all the privileges of their Maori male counterparts. Although tribal history teems with references to women of outstanding ability, who exerted considerable influence behind the scenes and performed feats of great daring and physical endurance, seldom were they able to express their opinions openly in the public forum – the marae.

As in Western societies prior to Women's Suffrage, Maori women were barred from entering the Highest Houses of Learning, professions and training in specific skills, and therefore restricted from becoming warriors,

priests, orators, historians, astrologers, philosophers, carvers, carpenters or tattooists – all high status roles in Maori society. However, except for warfare, few common men could aspire to these professions either, or gain entry into the Houses of Learning. Eligibility was exclusively for the sons of chiefs and priests (Tohunga). Yet some high-born women were admitted to the Whare Wananga (House of Learning). Indeed, several women of chiefly, or Ariki rank reigned as queens in their tribes (Hine Matioro of Ngati Porou and Mahinarangi of Kahungunu for example) and were borne upon litters, so sacred were their persons. Others challenged men of lower rank, even on their most sacred courtyard. This they were able to do by virtue of their nobility.

As in all primitive societies and peasant

communities, division of labour between the sexes was necessary for the protection and survival of that social group. Hence the learning of such skills as cooking, weaving and plaiting by women, and fighting, canoe and house building and so forth by men. But the skills and activities of weavers, cooks and mat-makers were as highly respected as those of the hunter, the fisherman or the husbandman. Thus, when choosing a wife or husband, both men and women looked for such characteristics as, not only beauty, but acquired skills and industry. It is important to note that these qualities were sought for in all grades of Maori society. Therefore, both men and women of chiefly rank participated in all but the most menial of tasks, which were performed by slaves and captives of both sexes, and not relegated to the female of the species. Work, generally, was in no way considered demeaning – industry and service were encouraged in both sexes.

Although prohibitions were placed on women during the performance of certain sacred rituals and activities (as in the Christian Church even today), their very non-sacredness made women indispensable during the opening ceremonies of important or sacred buildings in the community. It would appear that the development of the oppressive aspects of Maori society on its female sector stemmed from religious origins, once again in line with Christian and other societies – Adam's rib and his downfall through Eve's evil ways and thus Man's eventual destruction through Women. Yet, this simplistic view of the Maori women of old is a distortion of their place and status in their society. In looking backwards, especially by way of mythology and time, is it not easy to see only those features in a society for which one is looking and to fail to perceive the quality of life and the essence of personality produced by that society and which produced that society? The very structure of pre-European Maori society, based as it was on kinship groups, with the basic unit being the extended family (whanau), largely diluted the oppressive effects of an otherwise sexist society.

The life of the Maori woman was not based on the concepts of 'Motherhood' and 'Homemaker'. The fact that three terms – whaea, whaena and koka – are used by different tribes indicates that a specific term for 'mother' is comparatively recent. The woman who bore a child was a lover, or a means of procreation ensuring tribal continuity, but never quite the 'mother of children' as seen through the eyes

of the child today. Actually, the Maori child was cared for by all the relations and had many mothers with equal rights over him or her.

The duties of a Maori woman – mother, wife or sweetheart – went beyond her own family and were primarily those of fulfilling the needs of the whole extended family group and often those of the sub-tribe and the tribe during family crises. She was a community worker and a community hostess. Her pride and dignity, and that of her family and tribe, demanded that she maintain a full larder at all times so that all requirements of hospitality were fully observed. The qualities basic to this role were generosity, kindness, hospitality, love, grace and dignity, and the instilling of such qualities was fundamental to her early training – and this was the province of grandmothers. In this context, then, despite the prohibitions placed upon her because of her sex, the pre-European Maori woman was an extremely graceful, dignified and serene human being.

According to Professor James Ritchie, a male Pakeha psychologist, whose views are supported by Dr Pat Hohepa, the status of pre-European Maori women was far from inferior. He states:

'In this kind of cultural climate, it might seem at first that women would be subordinate. This was by no means the case. Property and status could be inherited from the female side . . . Through women men are born; women ensure inheritance. Women had their place, usually behind men, yet in all but pre-emptive status, they were equals in dignity, in mana, in power and in influence, and sometimes somewhat more than equal.'

European Cultural Contact

Keeping this picture of pre-European Maori women in mind, let us now look briefly at Maori and Pakeha history and life together, and the effects of culture contact on the Maori people generally, and the Maori women in particular.

According to Dr Joan Metge:

'In the history of contact between Maori and Pakeha, the Maoris have unquestionably yielded, borrowed and changed most.'

The greatest changes were psychological – those which influenced the personality of the Maori. One eminent Maori wrote thus:

'As the result of bewilderment and disillusionment created by the clash both in culture and arms, Maori society broke up, and with it the mind of the people.'

Another Maori, this time a woman, the Hon. Whetu Tirikatene Sullivan, describes this period of Maori life as 'a long history of deprivation and devaluation.'

During the first hundred years of contact, the men of our race appear to have suffered most, partly because of their involvement in three wars and because of loss of life and land, mana, dignity, status and leadership. At first, they adapted quickly to the new life and economy, but this changed after the wars between the two races. The Maoris then retreated to their tribal lands, and this self-imposed separation lasted until the call to arms in 1940. Maoris rallied all over New Zealand and, thus, World War II was the cause, and the beginning, of Maori urban migration.

Urban Migration

Maori men went to war; Maori women moved into the towns and, together with Pakeha women, they manned the industries, serviced trams and buses, eating places, hospitals and schools. Maori women also entered the market-gardens as labourers; those left in the rural areas took over the farms. However, although many had entered the labour force, and some trained as nurses and teachers, the majority stayed at home. Consequently, despite vast social changes – wars, diseases, depopulation, intermarriage and the expansion of Pakeha society – the basic role of Maori women remained the same. However, when the missionaries introduced Western domestic arts and mothercraft, as well as marriage to Europeans, this spelt the beginning of life as a homemaker and housewife for the Maori woman – so she became the modern lady of the house, or drudge, mother to her children as well as being all things to the community. In this new situation, men went out to work and the women were left at home, inevitably awaiting the opportunity for change.

Wairaka of the Mataatu canoe had long ago proved that a woman could do a man's job. Her deed in saving her tribal canoe gave the locality its name – 'Whakatane' (to become a man). Because of her act of bravery, barriers against women in those tribes were lowered. This has opened the way for present day women to demand this right – politicians, teachers, social workers, nurses, students and female elders are respected and listened to but, as yet, not on all maraes. Another great Maori woman of her time was Princess Te Puea Herangi, the power behind the last Maori king. She led her Waikato people out of isolation and tremendous eco-

nomic stress into their present position of status and dignity. Although of noble birth, she preferred to toil in her gardens rather than replace her responsible men in the role of public speaker and leader. Her greatness was in her shrewdness, administrative ability, concern for her people, subtle humour and simplicity.

Despite the leadership of such women, the position of Maori women has generally, in fact, deteriorated. If Pakeha women and Maoris generally are second class citizens, then Maori women are third or, rather, fourth class citizens. The relative situation, according to Elsdon Craig, could be assessed as follows:

'Like many other NZ men, but no doubt to a greater extent, the Maori considers a woman's place to be in the home. Family life is strong, it has not entirely severed its ties with the tribe, and the grandmother is still a major influence in the home. Consequently, the community takes a greater load off the shoulders of the Maori mother than it does off her Pakeha sister. On the other hand, the domestic responsibilities of the Maori mother in a changing society are often beyond her means. Besides childbearing and rearing, cooking and cleaning, she must do most of the gardening and, in the country districts, the milking and even looking after the stock. At the same time, she is expected to maintain her traditional identity with the community, attending the hui and tangi at which she performs a major role in welcoming guests and feeding them. Yet she is prevented from giving the benefit of her experience to the community at large by traditional restrictions applying to her role.'

Maori migration to the cities in the 40s, together with their increasing social and economic problems, finally alerted the powers that be to the recognition that the root causes of Maori problems were centred around the mother, the child and the home. Yet, traditional barriers prevented Maori women from publicly airing their grievances, especially in the newly formed, tribally-based organisations. For a number of years Maori women had been joining Pakeha organisations such as the CWI, WDFF and various church and local organisations, but only those women who were in constant touch with European life and society had the confidence to join such groups. In any case, matters of discussion had little bearing on Maori life, and the majority of Maori women, who were in great need of help, could never be persuaded to join. Hence, there was really no organisation in existence with which Maori women could identify themselves as self-determining individuals, with the right to choose the best course in the ever-changing society in which they found themselves.

A conference of Maori women was called in 1951 from which was born the MWWL (The Maori Women's Welfare League) – the organisation which has given Maori women their greatest liberation, but liberation with a difference. Its basic aims were concerned with fundamental needs – better education, housing and health; freedom from discrimination as well as the right to free speech even whilst promoting Maoritanga – but underlying these aims, and the selection of a Pakeha-style organisation to implement their work, was the principle of self-determination and the demand for racial equality.

The first president, Mrs Whina Cooper, was one of the most outstanding women of her day. Prior to her presidency she had already established other firsts for Maori women – as Chairman of the Northland Division of Federated Farmers and of the Hokianga Rugby Football Club. Throughout her life she has appeared to recognise no barriers, being at ease on the marae as well as taking on Ministers of the Crown. She was seldom challenged. With such a personality at the helm, and the guidance and help of the Controller of Maori Welfare and his field officers, the League came to be the body through which all matters pertaining to Maoridom were directed to Parliament. It became a powerful pressure group and social welfare organisation. Its success prompted a former Minister of Maori Affairs to publicly state that 'the greatest social advancement of the Maori people over the last 10 years was due to the efforts of Maori women themselves, under the Welfare League's inspiration.'

Twenty-two years have passed since the MWWL began, and during this period 70% of the Maori population has moved into the urban area. After 30 years of urban living, it can be assumed that, like many city housewives captured in their urban square boxes and 1/4-acre sections, Maori women are now also exhibiting the same symptoms as their Pakeha sisters. Add to this the total disorientation of rural-born women, the cultural deprivation of the city-born, plus the continuing traditional customs of subordinate status as well as lower socio-economic status, where does this place Maori women in Pakeha society?

If we are to believe the statistics, put out by the Health, Social Welfare and Justice Departments, urban living has taken its toll on Maori women and children. Maori women have the highest rate of mental breakdowns (an affliction also particularly suffered by under-24 Maori youth). Maori infants suffer the highest mortality rates and Polynesian children rank highest in juvenile delinquency and crime. The cause of mental breakdown, according to Dr Fraser MacDonald, is 'suburban neurosis' – whatever that is. For Maori women and children, it is basically socio-economic – poverty, cultural deprivation and poor education.

Professor D. C. Pitt, in a recently published study of NZ society says that:

'Polynesian minorities were caught in a vicious circle of poverty, poor education and low occupational status. The effect of this deprivation on the Polynesian community is to produce a variety of problems such as gangs and mental illness.'

The response of some Maori women is to go out to work, and this has been accelerating considerably in the last two years. A recent survey has disclosed that the majority of Maori women who do work land the most menial of jobs with the lowest pay – predominantly in the $35-40 per week wage bracket. Due to family responsibilities, many married Maori women are forced to take on 'twilight' work. Many Maori women engage in financial 'risk' activities. In many cases, therefore, the gain in spending money in no way compensates for the resulting social implications at home. In fact, it may even aggravate the situation.

Future prospects for young Maori girls appear to be no better. 1970 education statistics reveal that by far the greatest number of Maori girls leaving secondary school are unqualified and destined for factory, domestic and other low status occupations. For example, of 250 entering health services that year, fully 147 were unqualified (without School Certificate) and so must gravitate to the domestic jobs in hospitals.

The pressure and demands upon Maori women in the urban situation are too great. Without the support of their extended family group and, more important still, the support of their men who usually escape to the traditional male leisure pursuits of rugby, racing and beer, Maori women break down. Luckily for most Maoris, they allow themselves pleasurable releases which other groups of equal socio-economic status may not contemplate. Whilst this provides a temporary safety valve, it produces a vicious circle of social ills and, in the end, greater stresses in the family situation, especially on the children.

In summary, therefore, Maori women have been and are a powerful force for social progress in their own society. They are voluntary workers, forever called upon to give such service which, in Pakeha society, is a middle and upper middle class pursuit because of the leisure time available and/or financial resources needed.

They have also been involved to a lesser degree in national and international concerns – at home, with Equal Pay (participating in the very first delegation to Government), Corso national appeals for money and on the World scene, with opposition to the 1970 Rugby Tour to South Africa, nuclear testing in the Pacific (from 1959), close involvement with PPSEAWA and Church conferences, aid to Bangladesh and Hurricane Bebe disasters, as well as sending members to Australia to help with the Play Centre movement among the Aborigines.

The work of Maori women in the future must still be geared to the basic needs of Maoris

and the inequalities existing in our total society, and their aspirations cannot be other than those of the people as a whole. At this stage in our history, it is difficult to inspire women bowed down with misery and insecurity to look upwards at what appears to be middle-class based aspirations of Pakeha women, although many Maori women see the relevance of these to women everywhere.

Of the future, I know not – except to say that if, in your surge towards sex-equality you carry Maori women with you, and uplift their status also – so be it! But remember the crippled boy in the story of the Pied Piper of Hamlin – who only heard of the wondrous life through the Piper's music.

Appropriately then, let this end with a non-sexist Maori quotation, which says:

'Tera te ra kei tua o tawaowao e whiti ana.'

'Beyond yon high mountain top, the sun ever shines.'

United Women's Convention, 1973: Report, edited by Sandra Coney, assisted by Anne Parsons and others, Auckland, 1973, pp.21–24

7.8. Why We Oppose Miss Canterbury (and Any Other Beauty Contest)
Christchurch Women's Liberation Movement (1973?)

'Whenever we treat women's bodies as aesthetic objects without function we deform them and their owners!'

Germaine Greer

We oppose beauty contests because:
Woman was given a mind and a spirit, as well as a body. Yet so far she has chosen (or others have chosen for her) to use only her body as a sex object, a clothes horse, a baby bearer and a household machine. Flesh sags, wrinkles spread, hair goes grey and all the cosmetic artifices in the world can not halt the march of time. To be eligible for the Miss Canterbury contest women must be young and single – that is they must be 'available' (for ogling by thousands of people) and desirable.

Today the emphasis is on **youthful** desirability which is reflected by the baby dollish look of modern cosmetics.

An older woman may be considered attractive but social taboos say she should not be overtly desirable. Hence the 'mutton dressed up as lamb'.

'Miss Canterbury' fosters the image of

Woman as a passive physical object destroyed by time. The contestants concentrate on BEING – being attractive, being charming, being sexy and DOING nothing in particular, refusing to comment on anything vaguely political, intellectual, relevant, or important.

Beauty contests assume that it is both valid and sensible to parade women, stare at them and place them in an order based on genetical accident deciding that one inherited face and figure is superior to another.

It may not be sensible or valid, but it is proving profitable. This contest purposefully uses women as stooges for its advertisers and sponsors. True some of the profits of Miss Canterbury and Miss New Zealand go to charity – but does the end always justify the means?

We believe that the vices of beauty contests far outweigh the benefits. By encouraging society to look at women as purely physical objects they make it difficult for the many to use faculties to gain acceptance and reward. Women predominate in professions where the body is used – acting, modelling, dancing, etc. – but are sadly under-represented in pursuits where the mind predominates – business, engineering, and many other fields, although women have been proven to equal men in intellectual capacity.

Therefore we would be glad to see beauty contests abolished until such time as women, after being given equal pay, equal opportunities, freedom from excessive child bearing and from enforced housework, are actively represented in all fields of endeavour using mind and spirit.

We believe that beauty contests reinforce this tendency to the detriment of all women who are more interested in their work than in their looks.

In short, unlike beauty contest organisers, we believe that women have better things to do than be stared at and judged. And while beauty contests may be trivial things in themselves, in so far as they do influence society's attitude towards women, fostering the belief that WOMAN is primarily flesh and thus her mental and spiritual needs are of secondary consideration, they are harmful to some women in particular and to society in general for this attitude is false.

Therefore we oppose beauty contests and wish to see them abolished.

Christchurch Women's Liberation Movement

If you are interested in this or any other issue that affects women or if you want further information about the Christchurch Women's Liberation movement, please write to 15 Onslow Street, or 88 Abberty Cres, or else phone 557-591.

Leaflet (Ephemera B Women 197–, ATL)

7.9.   Society for the Abolition of 'Miss' (S.A.M.) (1973)

What's all this fuss about Ms instead of Mrs or Miss? Is it being used by a few women who just want to be different, or are there justifiable reasons for reconsidering an old custom?

A form of inequality

Well, just ask your husband or other men how they would feel about spending the rest of their lives wearing a sign saying 'I am married' or 'I am not married and have never been married.' You'd get some very rude replies like: 'Are you crazy? It's nobody's business but my own whether I'm married or not, and I see no reason why I should go around advertising the fact.' And yet this is exactly what women are expected to do. Everywhere we go, everything we do, whether it's enrolling for the vote, opening a bank account, applying for a library card, or just being introduced to new people, we are expected to identify ourselves as married or single. Why, when men do not have to do so, should we? And what does our marital status have to do with most things anyway? Men are always Mr regardless of marital status.

Outmoded reasons

The original reasons for the custom have long since become outmoded, or should have. That is, when women were regarded as possessions of men, they had to use the Mrs to indicate that they were one. Also, men wanted to know whether a woman they encountered was available for 'courtship' or what have you, or whether she belonged to someone else. There were also reasons relating to the fact that a woman had no rights of her own, and was considered an extension of her husband economically, as well as legally and politically. Are these reasons still valid enough to warrant a continuation of this form of inequality between the sexes?

Sweden abolished it

In 1965, this custom was abolished in Sweden, when all the newspapers announced simultaneously that from that time on, all adult women would be called 'Mrs' regardless of marital status.

They gave as their reasons the following:

1. There is no reason to discriminate between married and unmarried women.

2. Older unmarried women feel inferior when addressed as 'Miss'.

3. The title 'Miss' implies innocence, which is no longer the case with most young women today.

4. It would free unmarried mothers and their children from stigma.

5. Increasing numbers of divorced and

separated women feel hypocritical in referring to themselves as Mrs, if it means 'married woman', but if they have children, they cannot easily refer to themselves as 'Miss'.

At the time of this change in Sweden, one editor (male) said: 'It is absurd to label women as married or unmarried. It is an injustice long perpetrated by a man-made society.'

Looking for a mate?
Those looking for a mate need not be concerned; they can still signal their availability by not wearing a ring.

Ms or Mrs for all?
It would seem it is time we eliminated this form of discrimination against women in N.Z. We need a term which just means 'adult female human being'. But which is the best way to do it? Should we call all adult women Ms or Mrs starting about the age when men change from Master to Mr, the voting age? The

advantage of the latter term is that we would not be introducing a new element into the language, and that instead of all women having to make a change, only a small percentage of women would be required to. The advantage of the Ms term is that it is already acquiring some currency, and it is free from the connotation 'married woman' which Mrs will carry for some time. If you agree that this form of discrimination is unfair and outmoded, which in your opinion is the better solution?

How to support S.A.M.
And how do you become a member of S.A.M.? There is nothing to join, no dues to pay, no meetings to attend; you don't have to demonstrate. All you do is wear a button and explain the idea to people when they ask about it. Ultimately only public pressure can effect this change.

Leaflet, Auckland, 1973 (Ephemera B Women UWC 1973, ATL)

7.10. Women's Liberation – a Class Issue!
Auckland District Communist Party (1973)

A United Women's Convention to mark 80 years of women's suffrage is being held in the Y.M.C.A. on 15th and 16th Sept.

At this convention there will be women from all walks of life who are interested in the role of women in society. In N.Z. there have sprung up many different groups, all working in their own way for women's emancipation. These are playing a role in attempting to bring women together for a common cause.

However, we need to see that such unity can only be of a temporary nature, for women in capitalist society form part of the two opposing sections which exist in this society, the ruling class and the working class. Two examples which emphasise this are:

1. This week the owner-Manager of N.Z. Towel Supply Ltd, donated **one million** dollars to the Salvation Army. For this generous act Mr Plowman will receive great praise from the members of his class. On the other hand the workers at the Towel Supply Launderers (a large percentage women) know that it is their labour which made the gift possible, NOT 'the hard work of Mr Plowman.'

2. Recently at Allied Industries, Panmure

nine women clerical workers went out on strike for equal pay. They were backed by 200 men in the plant who went out for 2 days in support. Because of this action they won 60% of the difference between men's and women's pay with the other 40% to be given within the year.

This is a good example of what can be achieved through united action. For the first time in N.Z. history women have gone on strike for equal pay from which direct action the result has been the getting in 12 months what it will take 5 years by being negotiated for by Arbitration.

Today more and more women are going out to work – some because of economic necessity; exorbitant rents; cost of living etc. – others because of the need of not becoming a suburban cabbage. They do this in spite of the fact that they are now doubly exploited – such as being cheap labour; having only limited facilities for child care etc.

Women are needed and do participate in production in a capitalist society but this will only be for so long and under such conditions as the capitalist class lays down – if they are satisfied with lower salary, are young and healthy, etc. and the profits of the ruling class are going up and up. BUT, when capitalism goes through a crisis (as is developing today) when the demand for manpower drops, the first to be thrown out will be the women workers.

LET US BE VERY DEFINITE ABOUT THIS. There can be no solution to women's liberation unless class struggle is seen as the basis. IT IS A POLITICAL QUESTION. Without the participation of the industrial worker, male and female, equality will never be achieved, for under the capitalist system it is impossible to achieve full emancipation as the woman worker, along with her counterpart, the male, is a wage slave.

For many of us not exploited at the point of production, emphasis on class struggle may seem remote, but let us have no illusions. The patching up of a decadent, dying society may afford a little sop here and there where it is in the interest of capitalism, but it will not and cannot provide liberation for we who, as women, are doubly exploited.

The pioneer Communist, Engels, once said that sex equality would come with equal participation in social production. But true equal participation cannot come until the entire working class owns the means of social production.

THIS IS THE NUB OF THE WHOLE MATTER – women's liberation is dependent on working class liberation. For how can the female part of the working class be liberated ahead of the whole class?

By the same token, how can the working class be liberated if one half of it is left out of the struggle by the males?

With proletarian equality in the home (each treating the other as they treat their workmates), both men and women must struggle shoulder to shoulder for working class liberation, for the proletarian revolution.

GO FORWARD TO WOMEN'S LIBERATION THROUGH CLASS STRUGGLE.

The correct 'Women's Lib' slogan should be:

'WORKING MEN AND WOMEN UNITE,
YOU HAVE NOTHING TO LOSE BUT
YOUR CHAINS OF EXPLOITATION AND
OPPRESSION'.

Leaflet (Ephemera B Women 1973, ATL)

7.11. Feminism in Suburbia
National Organisation for Women (Upper Hutt) (1974?)

The purpose of this workshop is to explore some of the physical and social aspects of the suburbs and to examine their impact on the women who live there.

We are employing a feminist approach in our view of suburbia, this being the type of community we are most familiar with, where the most important part of our daily lives is enacted, yet where our shared feminism may have the best chance for bringing about the changes we want for ourselves and our families.

Because of the short time available to discuss a large topic, we have settled on three main areas for discussion, recognising from our own experiences that these are crucial to women. These are:

'Occupation: Married Woman'. The myths that surround this, and women as perpetuators of those myths.

'The Suburban Way of Life – the Consumer and the Consumed'.

'The Child-Care Experience'.

We begin with an **audio-visual display** highlighting some of the sights and sounds directed at the woman who has home and family as her chief responsibilities. This will be followed by a mime depicting some of the values upon which our N.Z. way of life is built. Next, there is an **introductory talk** to illustrate the formation and growth of the suburbs – an historical perspective. Each discussion topic will be preceded by a short talk hopefully providing a basis for our discussion and approximately 25 minutes will be available for all participants to talk together on the sub-heading. We would like each group to appoint a spokesperson to present that group's recommendations to be given in the last 15 minutes of the workshop. The material we are presenting is a small but real part of our experiences typically in suburbia and we hope, above all, that you will feel free to share your own views, feelings and experiences as they relate to the situation of where your life is lived.

1. **'Occupation: Married Woman'**

'Her honour is to be unknown; her glory in
the respect of her husband; her joys in the
happiness of her family' – Rousseau

What did you do today, dear, what did
you do today?
I've been nailing gentle tacks into my
soft coffin
sucking sweet dust in an endless lust
hoovering manoeuvring
weird shrieks out of every room
I pressed out life's creases in your
crumpled clothes
spent two tangible hours with Jimmy
Young
washed sorrow down my gullet with a
long oversweetened draught of song
waited for a vision . . .
when the telly goes wrong, I don't know
what to do
the children accuse me with their violent
eyes for not being you
everywhere I turn
I find
dull unfinished beginnings
of my mind
I've hung listless on an upturned spike
waiting for wind
the world turns in its own breeze
I know nothing of your hurricanes and
worldly tornadoes
my winds are zephyrs
and zephyrs are not winds at all
but promises
of embraces . . .
Yes, but what did you DO today, dear,
what did you DO today?

Pat van Twest

Occupation Married Woman/Housewife
seems to mean being held in low regard by
the community. To a society in which
money determines value, women are a
group who work outside the money economy. Yet society which eulogises the role
of the mother nurturing and caring for
her family fails to give her any real support
in performing this function, penalises her
for the rest of her life for having done it and,
by calling it 'Women's work', implies that it
is not fit work for men.

a) Has your experience of being a Married
Woman lived up to your early expectations
of it?

b) While children may have their rumpus
rooms and husbands may have a den –
where can you go?

c) How have we been enlarged by marriage and how have we been diminished?

Perhaps the following are some of
the personal actions we could take to
give a greater feeling of integrity and
confidence:

• Providing paid Motherhood help
• Employing such symbolic actions as
  dispensing with make-up if we feel
  it is a barrier to confidence in our real
  selves
• Refusing to act out the role of the
  weaker sex
• Describing yourself as 'Mother', 'Unpaid
  Child-minder', etc. instead of Married
  Woman, Housewife, i.e. which doesn't
  merely define you as an appendage of
  a man.
• Dropping such titles as Miss/Mrs
• Dropping of gallantries like door
  opening
• Reverting to one's single name
• Campaigning for more child-care
  provions: more realistic maternity
  leave, etc.
• Realising that sexual, biological differences of our children do not warrant
  the vast difference in social treatment
  they will be accorded
• Protesting against the teaching of sex
  stereotypes
• Insisting that proper Vocational Guidance with accurate lists of careers be
  available, especially to girls
• Joining party branches: framing remits
• Nominating and standing as candidates
  for local bodies, rate-payers and progressive associations.

2. **'The Suburban Way of Life – The**
Consumer and the Consumed'

The suburb has evolved to facilitate
factory production and to consume what is
produced and can therefore be seen as a
sort of game. The factory system needs
dedicated and mobile workers and has
encouraged the evolution of the nuclear
family and neighbourliness and status-
seeking.

Happiness is the accumulation of
material blessings. Advertising has created
the standards to which we aspire. With
increasing complexity, the household

demands full-time administration and this conveniently combined with child care to solve the capitalist society's child-minding problems. Men's family involvement consists of little more than bringing home the pay packet but retains final decision-making power. The housewife can see herself only as a child-minder and housekeeper and as a sucker for marketing techniques. To do what she does well, she must spend money on her family. To get any excitement from life she must spend on herself.

Women at home provide a convenient labour float for the economy. Last in, first out – as the economy expands and contracts.

J. K. Galbraith argues that a woman's primary economic role is managing consumption and offers an explanation for why this is not widely realised. He believes that if this were seen to be so it would soon cease to be the case.

a) If it is a game then is it enough to change the rules of the game or do we need to change the game?

b) Are material possessions sufficient recompense for the loss of full human status?

c) How can women opt out of being 'Consumer Administrators'?

3. 'The Child-Care Experience'
Consider John Bowlby on Fathers:

'In the young child's eyes father plays second fiddle and his value increases only as the child's vulnerability to deprivation decreases. Nevertheless, as the illegitimate child knows, fathers have their uses even in infancy. Not only do they provide for their wives to enable them to devote themselves unrestrictedly to the care of infant and toddler but, by providing love and companionship, they support her emotionally and help her maintain that harmonious contented mood in the aura of which the infant thrives. In what follows, therefore, while continual reference will be made to the mother-child relation, little will be said of the father-child relation; his value as the economic and emotional support of the mother will be assumed.'

and David Cooper:

'We don't need mother and father any more we only need mothering and fathering.'

a) The responsibility for the emphasis on the mother in the childcare experience belongs to John Bowlby. Why have we accepted it so enthusiastically?

b) Can the harassed mother who stays at home out of a sense of duty to her children really promote their well-being?

c) What are the effects on children of fathers who go out to work?

d) Is it love to make ourselves indispensable in the eyes of our children?

e) Is it desirable to grow up to be 'secure and trusting' yet also be rather dull conformists lacking in qualities such as intelligence, curiosity, boldness in questioning and exploring and sensitivity to experience as longitudinal studies on products of the Bowlby school have been shown to be?

On the value of Feminism in Suburbia

We regard our Feelings as our most important source of political understanding. Though we will disagree a lot of the time, we must remember that our basic and most important strategy is **unity** and with it our collective strength numbers half the world's population.

'When the group reaches the point where it realises the problems discussed are not just personal but are imposed by society, then it must use its collective wisdom to look at the basic structures in society such as the family and the economy and decide how they could be changed, the means to use and the ends to be desired.'

Women's Estate by Juliet Mitchell

Reading List

MS Magazine (May, 1974) – 'The Housewife as a Consumer Administrator', J. K. Galbraith
Suburbia, David Thorns (Paladin)
The Death of the Family, David Cooper (Pelican)
The Feminine Mystique, Betty Friedan (Penguin)
Women's Consciousness, Man's World, Sheila Rowbotham (Pelican)
Women with a Cause, Dr. W. B. Sutch (N. Z. University Press, 1973)
The Female Eunuch, Germaine Greer (Macgibbon & Kee)

Women and Madness, Phyllis Chesler
(Avon, 1973)

Urban Woman, (S.R.O.W., 1972)

Maternal Deprivation: a reassessment, Michael
Rutter (Penguin)

Separation, Anxiety and Anger, John Bowlby
(Hogarth Press, 1974).

Workshop programme *(Ephemera B Women 1974?*
ATL)

7.12. Some Ideas for Maori Women
by Ngahuia Te Awekotuku (1978)

Tihei mauri ora. E nga aitua, kua haere ki te po,
e nga tini mate, nga matua wahine, nga kuia ra
hoki, haere, haere, haere.

E nga hau e wha, nga morehu, ko tatou nga toa
wahine, nga wairaka o tenei ao hurihuri tena ra
tatou katoa.

First, I greet the dead – our foremothers,
those from whose wombs we came, through
whose energy, pain and awareness we all
arrived here. Those principally whose achievements, perceptions, and even being, were cast
down by the arrival of an alien missionary and
colonialist ethos. This ethos imposed itself
upon a preliterate society in which I conjecture
the dynamic transition from a matriarchy –
women oriented culture – to a patriarchal
system was in progress. The successful invasion
of Christianity accelerated the change, the
male chiefs greedily and intelligently adopted
those precepts which suited their way . . .
it is significant to note that those tribes,
generally, who maintain the most rigidly
misogynist traditions – Te Arawa, Waikato,
Tuhoe, for example – embraced the new
Religion, blending it over the decades with
spiritual developments of their own.

And yet history, legend, and cosmology all
abound with the mysteries and adventures of
Maori women –
Hine nui te po, the Great Lady of the Night, in
whose massive vulva Maui, the insolent demi-
god, was crushed in his quest for 'Man's Im-
mortality'. Wairaka, whose legendary strength
dragged the voyaging canoe Mataahia up on to
the safety of the Whakatane shore. Materoa, of
Ngati Porou, who led victorious armies into
battle on the coast. Rihi Puhiwahine, whose
poetry celebrating the domains of Waikato and
Tuwharetoa, is chanted to this day.

Thus I invoke a few of our foremothers –
women whom we now remember and celebrate.

In any discussion of Maori women's role, it's
necessary to initially understand the massive
diversities of differing tribal traditions. Despite

contemporary propaganda, the Maori Race is
not one tight homogeneous entity. There are at
least 9 different dialects, and there are as many
different forms of kawa – marae protocol – as
there are tribes. Similarly, there exist many
contrasting attitudes and responses on the
tapu/noa, sacredness/profaneness tradition that
signifies WOMAN.

From this point, I will write as a Maori
woman raised in a traditional marae environment, fed with all the baffling inconsistencies
of being a Te Arawa female. This tribal group
inhabits the area from the Bay of Plenty coast,
to the mountains of the Central North Island,
as the proverb states, 'Maketu ki Tongariro'.

Women – young girls – were programmed
according to a massive catechism of prohibitions – many concerned the perils of menstruation, others the reality of being female. We
were so aware of what we couldn't do – speak
on the marae, carve, sit on tables, walk over
men's legs etc. etc. etc. – that sometimes we had
to be reminded of **what** our privileges were.
These included the Karanga – 'the first voice
heard on Te Arawa-Tuhoe-Waikato marae is
ALWAYS a woman's', and the magical power to
open newly built houses – our very profane-
ness dissipating all that sheer psychic and
dangerous energy, thus rendering the place
safely habitable for the community. For this
ritual, virgins were, and still are, considered the
most effective, blessed, and ideal agents. And
yet these functions, although necessary, were
never considered as privileged or prestigious,
as those duties performed exclusively by men.

This brings me to what I call the Maoritanga
problem – the urge on the part of many Maori
leaders both urban and rural, to freeze the
culture, thus maintaining an impenetrable and
continually reinforced wall of BEING: Maori
being. And with two or three highly notable
exceptions who are totally male oriented
anyway, the voices leading the Maori struggle
in Aotearoa are male voices.

Which are in no way getting to the flax roots

of the conflict – the patriarchal, male directed, and manifest imposition of racism, sexism, and classism. Few Maori male leaders – in fact, I cannot think of even one right now – in the current struggle will concede to a female voice, or female counsel unless she is working within the patriarchal definition of **power over**.

Because Maori society has been defined as hierarchical and stratified, and because the Maori male maintains the visible leadership, what seems to be happening, in the most simplistic terms, is this. The moderates are demanding that the Ruling patriarchy, i.e. white N.Z., accommodates and understands the indigenous patriarchy; while the Radicals are working to undermine, and ideally overthrow the white system, and establish their own cock oriented male alternative – instead of pakeha male power, Maori male power.

But still, MALE POWER.

No reira, kei hea nga wahine Maori?

So, where are Maori women?

The true revolution for me lies in the harnessing and manifestation of women power, women being, women spirituality.

But in the Maori world the most urgent and desperate sense of political commitment is based on a woman's ethnicity, our Maoriness – which distinguishes and isolates us from the white majority – makes us different, even makes us better.

However, within the racially exclusive confines of the marae, we are seen as WOMEN.

We see each other as women – and the men see us as – NOA.

Unclean. Profane. Feared. But always, secondary.

The endeavour to live her Maori being will inevitably lead the Maori woman into compromising her woman being with the demands of what has become, through the last 150 years of cultural redetermination and upheaval, a basically machismo socio-cultural environment.

We cannot go backwards now. We cannot resurrect the finest aspects of long forgotten Oceanic matriarchies. We cannot, as Maori women, sedate ourselves believing, 'our voices come first, so we must have the power'. Because that power comes to us from men. And if we want change, we must seize that power from them. Moving ever onward, we reclaim the mana of Hine nui te po.

For most Maori women that challenge must doubtlessly sound heretically **non** Maori. If we allow Maori-ness, Maoritanga and Maori being

to be defined and described exclusively by male voices and perceptions, as has been done for generations, then such a call can only seem blasphemous and deluded. But, the sorry fact is that in being Maori today, one is being Maori according to a principally male-directed way of being Maori – we can be Maori only the way that they, i.e. Maori **and** pakeha men, want us to be; we have a duty to fulfil their expectations. Choosing to be oneself may cast doubts on one's Maoriness – and few Maori, female or male, will tolerate being called white. Often, Maori women who bravely speak out for themselves have been dismissed thus – 'She does things the pakeha way'. The ultimate put down. Especially if it comes from another Maori woman, which can often occur.

As in the pakeha world, the setting up of woman against woman remains a vital patriarchal strategy in the Maori environment – however, in recent history, Maori women have rallied to unite and counter the ravages of cultural change and economic crisis. Over the last century, some women's groups have sprung up, worked through the hard times, then faded away again; others have continued to function, cushioned within and even subsidized by, government and other paternalistic institutions.

The extent to which these groups have continued to tap the 'flax roots' of the Maori woman's world is debatable – the blatant absence of even obscurely representative Maori submissions to the Royal Commission on Sterilization, Contraception and Abortion last year reveals this. Yet at their inception, most of these groups were deeply involved with meeting the needs of a Maori woman's life.

The groups may have changed, their rationale may have shifted. The realities – the pressures of institutionalized racism, urban living, feelings of cultural and social inadequacy – have remained, worsened, magnified.

Every pakeha, no matter how liberal, well meaning or politically sound, is racist, because white privilege, which is part of the overall scheme of patriarchal oppression, operates **regardless** of gender.

Politically concerned Maori women – even the most sophisticated city dweller – will thus tend to avoid specifically women-oriented actions, and put their time and energy primarily in to the ethnic struggle. As a short term tactic, this is feasible and valid – but I maintain that ultimately, if at all, they move forward with the men on their backs.

Which is hardly moving anywhere, or

anyone, except perhaps male interests.

Ideally, we Maori women should focus on ourselves – demythologize the phallic concepts that have so long disabled us; and recreate our own sense of woman culture from the Richness that is our immediate inheritance. Take for ourselves without guilt these features of Maori being that are beautiful, matriarchal, strong – for there is at least as much to validate our women loving vision, as there is to undermine that white supremacy which our brothers challenge.

For our brothers I say now, let them be. Let them tend to their own problems . . . let the men clean up their own messes for a change. Far away from us.

As long as we continue to allow men, brown or white, to determine our Maori being – which will be directly related to their priorities and selfish needs – we Maori women will stay down. Only by pooling our energies and resources with each other, and then non-Maori women, will we realize our basic rights.

Related to this is an awareness of, and alliance with, the lesbian separatist perspective which questions the origins of patriarchal oppression, refutes the millenia of prick directed programming, and by merely being, threatens to topple that most male supportive institution of all – heterosexism.

Heterosexual Maori women, through the fact of their loyalty to their men, must inevitably place their energies in the ethnic struggle – the Realization of their male defined Maori being, mana Maori motuhake, is the immediate priority. Although perhaps occasionally considered, their womanbeing is examined only as it relates to this primary commitment. It is not an issue in itself, seldom can be when one is constantly meeting the demands of a male partner whom one is traditionally bound to feed, and follow.

Thus the comparative absence of Maori women from this meeting.

The patriarchal inheritance which is power over people instils and ensures the continuing oppression of women. **This happens irrespective of race.**

To change and challenge this inheritance – to denounce it – we women must articulate our own vision. Males have absolutely no part in this process. Because their power, strengthened by the 'divine right of heterosexuality', cuts across all cultural, ethnic, racial and social boundaries.

To counter that, women must cross these boundaries too – with the consciousness, sensitivity and faith in women sharing, and women growing.

Lesbian separatism offers such a vehicle of political exploration and experience. It transcends, and thus discards, those male definitions of the universe which shackle women and keep us powerless.

The Maori woman is in a unique position. Much of her heritage – her matriarchal heritage – persists in the extended family structure, the widening kinship patterns, the secrets of poetry and chant, the rituals of creativity and dance. She has a lot to offer. With this background, and a growing awareness of the inconsistencies of the male defined contemporary Maori scenario, the Maori woman can choose her own world.

Hopefully, she will begin to choose that world which will consider her needs, as a woman, as a Maori.

No reira, tena ra tatou katoa.

Paper read at the Piha Women's Congress, Jan. 1978 (Ephemera B Women 1978, ATL)

7.13. Rape
(1975)

1.   A Member of the New Zealand Homemakers' Union

In the research work for this paper the author received much help from members of the Homemakers' Union; from the following professional women: a lawyer, a police officer, a psychiatrist, a broadcaster, and two social welfare workers; and from a woman marriage guidance counsellor, a woman associated with Halfway House (Auckland), and two male police officers. The legal definition of rape has

been omitted from the paper as it is given in the woman lawyer's paper which immediately follows. Comparisons with the situation in the United States have also been omitted. Deletions are marked by points of omission.

The Incidence of Rape

Many cases of rape are not reported by the victims because of embarrassment, shock, shame, fear of the rapist or of court procedures, or reluctance to face the ordeal of a court case and the thorough medical examination required by the police . . .

Rape

Date	Offences Reported	No. Prosecuted	Cleared by other means than prosecution	Complaints proved groundless
1962	104	50	26	(no figures
1963	95	38	35	given)
1964	103	48	43	
1965	125	45	42	
1966	130	50	39	
1967	131	55	47	
1968	129	52	52	
1969	133	43	63	
1970	170	60	4	87
1971	160	56	1	66
1972	210	68	3	100
1973	251	80	4	126

Causes of Rape

1. Alcohol.
2. The urge of a man with an aggressive personality to overpower and coerce.
3. Resistance to overtures sometimes provokes rape because it arouses excitement.
4. The rapist's poor social adjustment and self-image and his belief that, because he has a poor opinion of himself, other people also have a poor opinion of him. He inclines to violence as a substitute for his inability to form relationships.
5. Jealousy and the wish to retaliate against wife or girl friend.
6. Conscious or unconscious anger against women or society.
7. The perception of women as property or of sex as a commodity.
8. Encouragement by other men.
9. The desire to experiment with forms of perversion.
10. The need to prove virility, especially by getting the victim pregnant.
11. Provocation by women, including walking alone after dark, wearing tight clothing, petting.

Note: 1. The need for sexual satisfaction is often given as a motive but its truth has been disputed – for example, Menachim Amir, in *Patterns of Forcible Rape* (Chicago, University of Chicago Press, 1967), says: 'Sexual satisfaction is not usually the motive, but it is socially accepted and therefore is given . . .'
And Dr Nicholas Groth, Chief Psychologist at the treatment centre for sexual offenders in Massachusetts, says: 'The fallacy about rape is

that it is done for sexual needs. It is done out of aggression.'

Whether one man can rape a woman is a subject frequently discussed. In *Medical Jurisprudence and Toxicology* (Edinburgh, Churchill and Livingstone, 13th edition, 1973) V. Glaister concludes: 'A healthy adult woman can be raped by one man, but careful consideration should be given to the factors of each individual case.'

Characteristics of Rapists

1. In New Zealand 70 per cent of violent offenders are under 25 years of age.
2. They usually do not suffer from impairments to normal sexual relationships . . .
3. Many have a criminal record – for example, Mary Schumacher found that 52 per cent of rapists in New Zealand had previously committed violent offences.
4. Most rapists plan the rape and most of them either live in the same neighbourhood as their victims or know them. In New Zealand 35 per cent of rapists knew their victim.
5. Most are insecure and aggressive. In *Crime and the Mind* (New York, Macmillan, 1965) W. Bromberg says: 'The victim is the source of unconscious gratification for the aggressive sex offender. Quite apart from her value as a sex object the offender satisfies his need for a position of sexual dominance by placing the sex object in an inferior, degrading role through rape or sadistic or perverse acts.'

Effects of Rape on the Victims Problems they Face

1. Group or gang rape often causes more serious injury than rape by one man. The Criminal Injuries Compensation Board statistics for 1963-70 show that 34.6 per cent of victims of the former type of rape and 13.5 per cent of the latter needed hospitalisation.
2. According to the same source, only 35 per cent of cases of rape are accompanied by violence. In the absence of physical evidence of violence it is almost impossible to charge an offender unless there is a corroborating witness.
3. Victims have to undergo a thorough, embarrassing, and sometimes painful medical examination to prove intercourse, and lengthy intimate cross-questioning to establish the offence.

4. There is usually the fear of pregnancy and disease.
5. For a child victim the appearance in court, the examination, and the attitudes of parents and others can result in considerable psychological damage.
6. Because the severity of the penalty is greatly affected by the degree of provocation that can be established, in court the victim is also 'on trial'. Her previous sexual experience is taken into consideration when determining the possible extent of provocation . . . The Criminal Compensation Act (1963) also requires that provocation be considered before any payment is made to the victim . . .
7. Victims feel guilt because: they fear they will be accused of having given provocation, they feel shame at the degradation and embarrassment at the publicity and the personal and intimate details they have to give in court. They are also afraid of their friends', their parents', and their husbands' reactions. Some husbands divorce their raped wives and some men change their attitude towards a woman who has been raped because they suspect her of having either provoked the rape or complied in it.
8. Women are accused of having reported rape only after their sexual indiscretions have been discovered, as an excuse and moral vindication of their behaviour . . .

Assistance Available

1. Medical help for physical injury.
2. At the discretion of the doctor concerned, the 'morning-after' pill can be given. But many doctors refuse to give the pill.
3. Under some legal circumstances an abortion can be obtained.
4. Legal aid and advice.
5. Samaritans and other emergency support and counselling agencies.

2. A Woman Lawyer

Sexual intercourse and rape are defined in and governed by the Crimes Act (1961).

Sexual Intercourse 'Sexual intercourse is complete upon penetration.' It has been held in various cases that 'the least degree' of penetration suffices, no matter how slight. It has been held in one case that 'some part of the male member should be within the female labia' to constitute penetration. Rupture of the hymen is not necessary. On the other hand emission without penetration will not suffice.

Rape   Rape is defined as:
The act of a male person having sexual intercourse with a woman or girl
(a)   Without her consent, or
(b)   With consent extorted by fear of bodily harm or by threats (which must be threats of bodily harm to the woman directly concerned), or
(c)   With consent extorted by fear on reasonable grounds that the refusal of consent would result in the death of, or grievous bodily injury to a third person (an example of 'fear on reasonable grounds' would be obtaining consent from a woman by threatening to grievously injure her husband or mother), or
(d)   With consent obtained by personating her husband (There have been several cases of this, for example, where a man gets into the bed of a sleeping woman. It is not sufficient that the woman believed the man to be her husband; it must be established that the man himself intended to pass himself off as the husband), or
(e)   With consent obtained by a false and fraudulent representation as to the nature and quality of the act. (This refers only to the physical aspect of intercourse – for example, misrepresentation by a doctor that what he was doing was by way of surgical treatment. In one case it was held to be rape when a singing master had sexual intercourse with a pupil while pretending to operate for better voice production.)

Capacity   The Crimes Act says there is no presumption in law that any person is, by reason of his age, incapable of sexual intercourse. For example, a boy aged nine would not, by reason of his age, be deemed incapable of performing the act of intercourse. However, the Crimes Act also provides that children under the age of ten years cannot be convicted for an offence.

Consent   Consent must be given freely from a person of sober and rational mind who understands exactly what she is consenting to – for example, women of feeble intellect may not necessarily be consenting. Also, it is important to distinguish between consent and submission – for example, 'the woman who fails or ceases to resist when resistance or further resistance would be futile is not to be regarded as consenting.' Also, 'consent given at first may be withdrawn' and there would be rape. On the other hand 'if the woman begins by resisting but changes her mind and consents, there is no rape.'

Onus of Proof   Generally speaking, the

burden of proving the offence of rape is upon the Crown, acting on behalf of the complainant. The Crown must prove two elements in order to establish rape: first, the physical act of intercourse without consent; and, secondly, the fact that the man intended to have intercourse without the consent of the woman. The onus is on the Crown to prove to the jury beyond a reasonable doubt that the woman did not consent. If consent is established then the Crown must prove beyond reasonable doubt that it was procured in one of the ways referred to in the definition of rape.

Defence It is a complete defence to a charge of rape that the woman freely consented. It is also a defence if the woman did not consent but the man honestly believed that she did so.

The recent decision of the House of Lords in England on the issue of defence has been given widespread publicity. All that decision has done is to restate the law that, if a man believes that a woman consented to the act of intercourse, then that is a sufficient defence. He is not required to establish grounds for his belief, whether they be reasonable or unreasonable. However, from the tone of the House of Lords decision and from the cases that come before New Zealand courts, it is clear that, if a man was to raise the defence of belief that the woman consented, without giving any evidence to establish grounds for his belief, a jury would most likely disbelieve him and return a verdict of guilty.

The Character of the Woman On a charge of rape the woman's character becomes relevant to her credibility as a witness and to the issue of consent. If consent is in issue, evidence of a general nature is admissible as to her being a woman of loose or unchaste character. If the woman is cross-examined by the defence as to her general bad character and she denies the same, the Crown cannot call evidence to contradict her answers. On the other hand the defence may also cross-examine the woman as to her immoral acts with the accused man, and if she denies them the accused may prove in his defence, by his own evidence or by evidence of other witnesses, of her past conduct with him. (Many people think that a woman should not be subjected to cross-examination of her past sex life unless her conduct relates to her association with the accused man.)

Corroboration It is a practice of our courts for the judge to direct the jury that it is dangerous to convict a man of rape on the uncorroborated evidence of the accuser. The woman therefore usually calls a doctor to give medical evidence that intercourse has occurred and some person to whom she complained of the offence immediately after it occurred.

Suppression of Name It is also a practice of our courts to suppress the name of the woman making the complaint.

Rape of Wife The Crimes Act provides that no man can be convicted of raping his wife 'unless at the time of the intercourse (a) there was in force in respect of the marriage a decree nisi of divorce or nullity, and the parties had not, since the making of the decree', resumed freely living together as man and wife, 'or (b) that there was in force in respect of the marriage a decree of judicial separation or a separation order.'

Parties to the Offence A husband may be found guilty of raping his wife if he aided and abetted another man to rape her. It is also legally possible for a woman to be found guilty of rape if she aids and abets a man to rape another woman.

Punishment A person convicted of rape is liable to imprisonment for a maximum term of fourteen years. For attempted rape the maximum term is ten years.

United Women's Convention, 1975, *ed. by Phoebe Meikle [Wellington, 1976], pp. 45–47*

7.14. Order of Service, Ecumenical Church Service, United Women's Convention (1975)

Leader We meet to worship God.
Welcome, everybody.
All Welcome, everybody!
Let us worship God!
Leader Let's say who we are.

All We are sisters gathered in a Convention which has given us much to share and much to think about.
Leader Why have we gathered together in the act of worship?

All We feel that the things we have been sharing together are relevant to our faith.

We believe that as we share together in worship we will be encouraged by our common faith, we may gain deeper insight, and we will be strengthened in our faith.

We accept that if we are challenged, God will be in that challenge.

Leader Jesus promised that in perfect truth there would be freedom.

All We thank God for the promise of truth in Christ. We pray that we shall be made free.

Leader Perhaps God will speak to us through the words of others. Let us see what they say:

The Apostle Paul: (In Christ) there is no such thing as Jew and Greek, slave and freeman, male and female; for you are all one person in Christ.

Read in Silence Sister Helen Goggin, a Sister of Mercy from Christchurch: We are told that at the last judgment we will be asked whether we responded to Christ's needs in the person of our neighbour.

Men, apparently, will not be judged on the so-called male virtue of courage and steadfastness, and woman on the so-called womanly virtues of meekness and compassion. In the final summing up we will all be treated equally.

Among the neighbours whom we women must feed, clothe and visit is the male. In turn the needy ones the men must feed, clothe and visit are the women.

We are capable of this task only to the extent that we are free human beings who have affectionately integrated our own sexuality, and can approach this neighbour with genuine respect, love and humility.

Women as Christians have the same obligations and rights as men who work for the kingdom of God, to serve and love and change the world.

The Boston Women's Collective: What we want is to reclaim the human qualities culturally labelled 'male' and integrate them with the human qualities that have been seen as 'female' so that we can all be fuller human beings. This should also have the effect of freeing men from the pressure of being masculine at all times – a role equally as limiting as ours has been. We want in short to create a cultural environment where all qualities can come out in all people. In no way do we want to become men. We are women and we are proud of being women.

Leader Jesus gives us hope: In the world you will have trouble. But courage! The victory is mine; I have overcome the world.

All *We shall overcome,*
We shall overcome,
We shall overcome some day.
Oh, deep in my heart, I do believe
We shall overcome some day.
We're on to victory . . .
We'll walk hand in hand . . .
We are not afraid . . .
We are not afraid today
The truth shall make us free . . .
We shall live in peace . . .

Leader Explanation of what is to happen.

All Sing *'Judas and Mary'*

Said Judas to Mary, 'Now what will you do
With your ointment so rich and so rare?'
'I'll pour it all over the feet of the Lord
And I'll wipe it away with my hair,' she said,
'I'll wipe it away with my hair.'

'Oh Mary, oh Mary, oh think of the poor –
This ointment it could have been sold;
And think of the blankets and think of the bread
You could buy with the silver and gold,' he said,
'You could buy with the silver and gold.'

'Tomorrow, tomorrow I'll think of the poor,
Tomorrow,' she said, 'Not today;
Far dearer than all of the poor in the world
Is my love who is going away,' she said,
'My love who is going away.'

Said Jesus to Mary, 'Your love is so deep
Today you may do as you will,
Tomorrow, you say, I am going away,
But my body I leave with you still,' he said,
'My body I leave with you still.'

'The poor of the world are my body,' he said,
'To the end of the world they shall be;
The bread and the blankets you give to the poor
You'll find you have given to me,' he said,
'You'll find you have given to me.'

'My body will hang on the cross of the world
Tomorrow,' he said, 'And today;
And Martha and Mary will find me again,
And wash all my sorrow away,' he said,
'And wash all my sorrow away.'

Movement into groups

In the group you may like to share things that have happened to you at Convention
a dream which has been born or fulfilled

something you are disturbed about
something you have learned
something beautiful which has happened to you.

Share by: talking to someone in your group
telling the whole group
writing it out on paper
offering a prayer.

Leader Brings group sharing to a close.

Leader Reading of selections from Proverbs 31, v.10-31

(SILENCE)

Minister Jesus says, I have come so that you might have life, and have it to the full.
Let us pray.
For our lack of courage to be ourselves,

All Lord have mercy on us.

Minister For our failure to stand against oppression and prejudice,

All Lord have mercy on us.

Minister For our impatience with others' views,

All Lord have mercy on us.

Minister For hurting others, for hating others,

All Lord have mercy on us.

Minister For our lack of faith in your power,

All Lord have mercy on us.

Minister Let us now declare together our sorrow:

All I confess that I have sinned against You, Almighty God, and against you, my sisters, and against my brothers, in thought, word, deed and omission, through my own fault. I ask your forgiveness in the name of Jesus Christ our Lord.

Minister Friends

All We are forgiven!

(SILENCE)

Minister You have called us, O Lord, to life:

Left side groups You have called us out of darkness into light, to become a chosen race, a royal priesthood, a holy nation, Your own people to make the world anew according to Your will.

Right side groups And therefore we proclaim Your good news to the ends of the earth, and join with all who know Your name to sing of Your glory:

All *Holy, Holy, Holy, Lord God of hosts. Your glory fills all heaven and earth Hosanna in the highest.*

Left side groups O Loving Father, You have called us, gathered here in Your name, that this bread and this wine may become for us the body and blood of Your Son, the pledge of eternal life.

Centre groups For He, the night before He suffered, took bread and gave thanks.
He broke the bread, gave it to His disciples and said:

All Take this all of you and eat it:
This is my body which is given for you.

Centre groups When supper was ended, He took the cup.
Again, He gave thanks and praise, and giving the cup to His disciples said:

All Take this, all of you, and drink from it:
This is the cup of the new covenant. It is shed for you and for all people so that sin may be forgiven.
Do this in memory of Me.

DISTRIBUTION IN GROUPS.

(As you pass the bread and wine to each other, you may like to say,
'The body of Christ, broken for you.'
'The blood of Christ, shed for you.')

Minister The peace of the Lord Jesus Christ be with you all.

All Thanks be to God.

Right side groups For freedom Christ has set us free; stand fast, therefore, and do not submit again to a yoke of slavery.

Left side groups For we were called to freedom, sisters.
But let us not use our freedom as an opportunity for self, but through love become servants of one another.

Centre groups For the whole law is fulfilled in one word: 'You shall love your neighbour as yourself.'

All We pray, O God, that love may break the barriers between us all, so that Your daughters and sons may be freed to live in love and joy together.

We thank You that this is happening now, here and everywhere, through the power of Your Spirit.

All SING *'Magnificat Now'*
Sing we a song of high revolt;
Make great the Lord, His name exalt!
Sing we the song that Mary sang
Of God at war with human wrong.

Sing we of Him who deeply cares
And still with us our burden bears.
He who with strength the proud disowns,
Brings down the mighty from their thrones.

By Him the poor are lifted up;
He satisfies with bread and cup
The hungry ones of many lands;
The rich must go with empty hands.

He calls us to revolt and fight
With Him for what is just and right,
To sing and live Magnificat
In crowded street and council flat.

This service was prepared and conducted by Sister Barbara Stephens, Ms Cathy Wilson,

Rev. Sylvia Jenkin.

Music was provided by members of the Home League of the Salvation Army.

Pottery made by Audrey Brodie.

Leaflet (Ephemera A Women 1975, ATL)

7.15. The Politics of Feminism: Radical feminist theory United Women's Convention (1977)

Conveners of the 'Radical Feminist Theory' workshop report that their sessions were aimed at two groups of women: (1) Those who wanted some information, who wanted to know what radical feminism involved, to see where we're going and how we'll get there; and (2) radical feminists from all over the country who wanted to exchange ideas about tactics and plans of action.

'As conveners, we considered this workshop a political action in itself. We did not see our role as being present to provide answers, but rather to share ideas and analyse their effectiveness in explaining the causes of women's oppression, and their possible usefulness as tools for liberating ourselves. We feel that it is important to take the 'heaviness' out of theory before we can assume that a theoretical analysis must precede any action.'

After an initial presentation of poems, theoretical essays and personal statements by the six conveners, participants split into six small groups in which everyone could make herself heard.

'We found that there was a great deal of confusion and curiosity regarding radical feminism. We defined radical feminism in contrast to reformist feminism and the groups discussed its relevance to our daily lives. It was generally agreed that, without losing sight of our revolutionary aims, we had to fight for some reforms which are a prerequisite for a feminist revolution. Such reforms included the eradication of gender roles, equal opportunity as well as equal pay, the fullest participation of women in public life, and change in the abortion law.

'Many women showed an interest in the relation between socialism and feminism. Both share the common goal of creating an egalitarian society, but feminism insists that sexism is as much a part of the structure of society as the economic modes of production. As radical feminists we believe that sexism is the basic

oppression, but we also aim at an economic restructuring of society so that no group exerts power over another. We believe that attitudinal changes go hand in hand with structural changes and that both are essential.

'Abortion was very topical because of the recent publication of the *Report of the Royal Commission on Contraception, Sterilisation and Abortion*. It was foremost in the minds of the many women who saw as basic the need to control their reproduction, and who wanted to take some 'action' promptly, although it was realised that the immediate fight was not for repeal of the law but just the maintenance of the status quo. We found that our workshop gave women of all ages, occupations, geographical areas and political persuasions the opportunity to get together on that one issue, analyse their position and coordinate some action.'

Throughout the convention altogether eighteen groups were formed in the various sessions of the workshop and some of these passed resolutions. Some groups also came up with slogans such as 'Reforms are not Enough', 'The Personal is Political' and 'Sexism is Part of the Structure'.

'The variety of resolutions reflect the wide-ranging concerns of participants, many of whom were encountering radical feminism for the first time,' the conveners point out. 'We found that we all benefited from the exchange of views, from the discussion of ways and means to achieve our feminist goal, and from the communication between women who would seldom otherwise have a chance to meet each other.'

Workshop 35: RADICAL FEMINIST THEORY.
Conveners: Denny Grant, Andree Levesque, Jill Livingstone, Jane McChesney, Edith Mercier, Fern Mercier. Convening organisation: The Theory Group of the Dunedin Collective for Women.

WORKSHOP 35 – RESOLUTIONS

1. That we condemn the whole section referring to abortion in the Report of the Royal Commission on Contraception, Sterilisation and Abortion.
2. That we denounce the conscience votes in Parliament and urge parliamentarians to express the wishes of the women of their electorates regarding abortion.
3. That women's health centres be set up where women themselves control abortion procedures, even at the risk of breaking the law.
4. That given the risk of poor reporting and distortion by leaving the choice of news reporters to the media, and given that this is an all-women convention, we want to exclude the media completely from this and future conventions, and take upon ourselves the responsibility for reporting the convention in our own areas.
5. That every woman assure her MP she will not vote for her/him at the next elections if she/he supports any legislation restricting the availability of abortion.
6. That employers and trade unions make a reality of equal pay and *opportunity*, e.g., by not reclassifying jobs.

Comment

. . . I had come in the hope that my prejudices would be stripped away and that the radical feminists would be able to show me that there is more to them than one learns through the media.

. . . The wailing began – low key and enigmatic. It became increasingly tortured in tone – bitter and tired. It faded away . . . we were to dissipate into smaller groups. My prejudices were still with me.

Then came an amazing revelation. I joined a 'learning' group and learnt indeed! Once I had worked through the confusion which had arisen in my mind between my understanding of 'revolution' and 'anarchism' and their understanding of the words; once I had heard about the Dunedin group's actual and serious attempts to put their ideas into action, I was left feeling much more sympathetic to radical feminists . . .

A Workshop 35 participant
Janine Jeffery

Changes, Chances, Choices: a report on the United Women's Convention, 3–6 June 1977, edited by Joy Browne and others, Christchurch, 1978, p. 79

7.16. NOW: for equality, against discrimination
National Organisation for Women (Auckland) (1978)

'Feminism is believing women are people and that they therefore have at least as much to offer as men; it is against discrimination and oppression, and for equality of opportunity and free choice of life styles.'
UN Status of Women definition.

N.O.W. originated in the U.S.A.

The inaugural meeting for the National Organisation for Women in New Zealand was held in Auckland in February 1972.

We take a positive stand and believe that anything we regard as a just, feminist cause can be backed up by practical and good sociopolitical reasons. As society is in a state of flux, we endeavour to direct it for the benefit of women by acting as catalysts. We work with other organisations to achieve our aims.

Members receive a monthly newsletter. Meetings are held monthly and seminars, often in conjunction with other organisations, at intervals during the year.

Sub-committees work in areas of specific interest, to provide material for the executive and membership.

Representations are made to Commissions, appointed bodies, Government and local authorities where appropriate on matters concerning women.

N.O.W. is also active in:

Whangarei, Upper Hutt, Wellington, Christchurch, Hastings, New Plymouth . . . and other areas as interest grows.

Policy statement decided July 1975

As a basic feminist aim, the National Organisation for Women reaffirms its belief that contraception and contraceptive education should be easily available and free to all, regardless of sex, age or marital status. Furthermore, tubal ligation or vasectomy should be unconditionally available to adults, regardless of marital status.

Because present society does not adequately provide all forms of contraception and contraceptive education, or adequate care, concern or protection for the born child and its mother, N.O.W. believes that such a society has no right to impose its moral views on decisions regarding contraception or abortion. N.O.W. therefore holds that it is a fundamental right of a woman to follow the dictates of her own conscience in making a decision regarding the termination of her pregnancy.

For this to be a realistic choice of conscience, she must be able to expect sympathetic and objective counselling. If she should decide to terminate the pregnancy, abortion should be available at a public hospital clinic or a registered, low-cost, non-profitmaking, day-patient clinic.

Alternatively if she decides to continue with the pregnancy, greater community support and help with the subsequent long-term care of the child must be available. Such a choice will be hers alone.

Equality . . .

1. Achieving full equality before the law in all fields where it does not yet exist.
2. Meeting the health needs of girls and women equally with those of boys and men, which should be recognised as a prerequisite to the promotion of equality between them and to the full participation of both in the development effort.
3. Promoting equality of economic rights, including the right to work and the right to equal pay for work of equal value; non-discrimination in employment opportunities, governmental as well as private, and security of employment after marriage. To recognise the value of the woman at home caring for dependants.
4. Promoting equality of rights and responsibilities in the family and home and creating awareness and recognition that men and women have equal rights and obligations towards themselves as individuals, towards their children as parents, and towards their society as citizens.
5. Ensuring that women as well as men participate fully as equal partners in policy formation and decision-making at the local, national and international levels, including development planning, educational programming and questions of foreign policy, such as disarmament and the strengthening of friendly relations among States.
DEVELOPMENT FOR WOMEN PREVENTS DISCRIMINATION.

6. Improving the awareness of women in the developed countries through effective information and education of the living conditions and problems of women in the developing areas in order to intensify the contribution of the former to international development co-operation.
7. Improving the living and working conditions as well as the status of both men and women throughout the community and expanding freedom of choice for all persons in planning life patterns that permit the development of their potential as individuals. Providing flexible working hours, part-time and shared jobs.
8. Improving the quality of rural life through the provision of cultural, educational and employment opportunities in the rural areas.
9. Ensuring equality of educational opportunities at all levels (including vocational training) and the same choice of curricula for male and female students, preferably in the same schools for boys and girls. To end sex stereotyping in schools.
10. Actively encouraging women to train for and enter non-traditional occupations, providing proper guidance and counselling and expanding co-operative programmes among women of different countries that would contribute to international understanding through shared endeavours.
11. Provide training (including in-service training) for women in all fields, including citizenship and leadership, consumerism, management, and science and technology, keeping in mind the concomitant need to help find employment opportunities for women who complete the training period.
12. Providing social services for health, family planning, childcare, social and community services and health services for the protection of maternity and of the health of the mother and child.
13. Seeking to improve the situation of women in prisons and other places of detention.
14. Combatting exploitation of women and girls through illicit and clandestine trafficking.
15. Recognising the value, for the country's overall development and advancement, of the untapped resources of women to contribute to the national culture, development and spiritual value through their work in voluntary activities as well as in the labour market and home management.

PEACE . . . Women must safeguard peace to promote conditions for the advancement of the status of men and women, by combating colonialism, neo-colonialism, foreign domination, alien subjugation, apartheid, sexual and racial discrimination and realising the principle of the right of people to self-determination.

WITHOUT PEACE WOMEN CANNOT ACHIEVE EQUALITY.

Leaflet (Ephemera A Woman 1978, ATL)

7.17. Bashed Wives Reveal Their Lives of Hidden Suffering
New Zealand Woman's Weekly (1978)

New Zealand needs to know its battered wives

All is peaceful in the home of Joanne M. and her family. Joanne – who works part-time – and her two children have had their evening meal and are just finishing drying the dishes.

Suddenly the peace is shattered.

Husband Dick arrives home in a very bad mood. 'Where's my dinner?' he demands.

Joanne tells him it is keeping warm in the oven. 'I'll just get it.'

But as she reaches for the towel to dry her hands Dick pushes her aside. – 'My dinner!' he shouts.

By this time Joanne is frightened. She grabs the meal from the oven and puts it on the table.

Instead of sitting down, Dick slaps her face, complaining that the dinner has dried up.

In no time at all an ugly argument is in progress.

By the time it is over, Joanne will probably be injured. If she is lucky the injuries will be slight – little more than light bruising.

But she – and the children, too – could just as easily be seriously hurt.

The names of this couple have been changed, but their problem is shockingly real.

In New Zealand the police receive many calls for help during so called 'domestic disputes.' But even so, very little information is available about violence of this sort.

What help?

It is not known, for example, how often the police are called, how often women receive injuries, where they seek help and what type of help they require.

Auckland psychologist Miriam Jackson believes research into the subject of battered wives in New Zealand is urgently needed. The *New Zealand Woman's Weekly* supports this view.

In an effort to gather information Ms Jackson has already interviewed 30 women who have been assaulted by their husbands to find out why they stayed in violent domestic situations. Now she is eager to gather more material.

If YOU have an experience in your life that could be helpful in this research you are invited to fill out the questionnaire on this page (your name is not required) and send it to:
'Questionnaire',
P.O. Box 5799
Wellesley St,
Auckland.

Battered Wife Questionnaire

Age . . . . Man's age . . . .
Occupation . . . . Man's occupation . . . .
Education . . . . Man's education . . . .
Race . . . . Man's race . . . .
Number of children . . . . Ages . . . .
Are they his? . . . . Are you still together? . . . .
How long have you been/were you together? . . . .
Have you ever left/did you ever leave your man temporarily as a result of his violence? . . . .
If so, for how long? . . . .
Why did you return? . . . .
How often does/did your man hit you? . . . .
When did he first hit you? . . . . When did he last hit you? . . . .
What did he do to you when he last hit you? . . . .
What injuries did you receive? . . . .
Who helped you? . . . . How did they help? . . . .

Why do YOU think your man hit you? ....

What was his explanation or apology? ....

Have you ever called/did you call the police? Did they come to your home? ....

How many times did the police come to your home? ....

How did they help? ....

What effects did your being beaten have on your children? ....

Bashed wives reveal their lives of hidden suffering

'On the occasions I consented to go out with my husband to parties (if I did not I was beaten) I usually ended up being beaten, or otherwise dropped off in some remote area in the middle of the night. He would then try to run me down with the car, even driving up on to the footpath to accomplish this . . . '

That's not a character in a television police drama talking.

It is a New Zealand woman – one of 220 *Woman's Weekly* readers from many parts of the country who answered our questionnaire for 'battered wives' published in June.

The half-page questionnaire appeared at the request of Auckland psychologist Miriam Jackson, who is doing research into the hitherto neglected subject of battered wives, with the aim of finding ways to help them.

She intends to present information gathered from the questionnaire to the Parliamentary Select Committee on Violence.

Many readers accompanied their questionnaires with signed letters which together with the answers to the 29 questions paint an appalling picture of hidden violence behind lace curtains and drawn blinds.

It appears that:

* Some New Zealand husbands are committing near murder – and getting away with it.
* Children are suffering shocking emotional injuries.
* Severely beaten wives are too frightened, ashamed and demoralized to seek help.
* Little help is available for many of them, anyway.

The police are reluctant to interfere in so-called domestic disputes and women themselves are often reluctant to see offending husbands charged.

10 times worse

As one victim explained: 'The best the police could have done would be to arrest him. Then some magistrate may have given him a couple of weeks in jail and he'd have been 10 times worse when he came out. It is hard to find a place to hide with two kids and no money.'

Only six of the 220 wife-bashers were charged.

This seems incredible when the extent of the injuries involved are considered.

Several women suffered permanent disabilities such as blindness, loss of a kidney and spinal injuries. More than 40 received broken bones, 46 had cuts and stitches and a further 18 were knocked unconscious. Twenty-two women said that they had been nearly strangled.

One in every seven reported the beatings began while she was pregnant and several women miscarried as a result of their injuries.

One victim was thrown down stairs – with her five-month-old baby in her arms.

Bashed daily

For some, the beatings were isolated instances, but 65 women reported being regularly bashed more than once a week, and for a handful of unfortunates violence was just about a daily occurrence.

Most of the bashers could give no explanation for their actions. Some could not remember afterward what they had done.

Not surprisingly, alcohol played a part in almost half the cases.

A number of readers described their husbands as alcoholics and several deplored the dearth of facilities available to help both the victims of this disease and their families.

Said one: 'I always say you marry two men. One with the booze in and one without the booze.'

According to Miriam Jackson, however, alcohol only acts as a lubricant and lessens a man's control. Therefore, 'other reasons such as general dislike of women seem to be important.'

The victims saw these 'other reasons' mainly in terms of bad temper, jealousy, inability to handle responsibility and stress.

Guilt over excessive drinking, sexual difficulties, or extra-marital affairs – according to our survey – can also drive a man to use his wife as a punching bag.

Some bashers need no more than an overcooked egg or too-strongly-brewed tea to spark them to violence.

Several women commented that their husbands had been 'spoiled' before marriage by doting mothers. Other offenders had come from violent backgrounds. Some, however, had been members of 'quiet, gentle' families.

Answers to the questionnaire would seem to give the lie to the widely-held belief in the relationship between joblessness and wife-beating.

Only seven men were unemployed at the time of the bashings.

By contrast, 18 held professional jobs.

Of the remainder, 82 were described as unskilled workers and the rest were spread across a variety of occupations.

Several respondents pointed to an intellectual difference between themselves and their men – and certainly the women appeared to be better educated, though not necessarily of a higher socio-economic class.

They tended to have slightly more children than the current New Zealand average of 2.4, and in most instances said those children had suffered terribly as a result of violence in the home.

Nervousness, fear, bedwetting, vomiting, emotional withdrawal, bad behaviour and hatred or rejection of the father were common reactions.

Still together

Yet in the face of appalling injuries to themselves and shocking effects on the children, more than one-third of the women who answered our questionnaire were still living with their brutal partners – 30 of them after 20 years or more.

Many of these women had at various times left their husbands temporarily, usually staying away a few days.

Their reasons for returning were varied, the first and most obvious being that they often simply had nowhere else to go!

A woman and four children may be welcomed with open arms by family and friends for a day or two, but after that? If she has no money to pay for accommodation she is trapped.

Miriam Jackson explains: 'These women can only apply for an emergency benefit if they are no longer living under the same roof with the man concerned. But if they've no money to get out it's a catch-22 situation.'

Women wrote also, however, of husbands who promised to reform (they didn't); the shame of marriage failure; reluctance to leave the family home; the fear of not being able to make it as a solo parent – and the 'stigma' of solo parenthood itself.

Said one: 'You would have to know the loneliness and shame that goes with the breakdown of your marriage to understand why a woman "hangs on". One can feel emotionally beaten with that failure, which can be as tortuous as being physically beaten. Until attitudes to those women labelled solo parents change, even the most battered married woman thinks twice about becoming one.'

Some were too frightened of their husbands to leave. They believed that if they did so, the men would track them down and 'get' them.

'Once you've been knocked around a few times you become very low on self-esteem,' Miriam Jackson points out. 'You're depressed, apathetic, and totally exhausted. The constant fear of violence drains you.'

She adds that many women are so ashamed of being punched, kicked, or partially strangled they will not admit even to their doctors how they received their bruises, cuts and other injuries.

Police little help

Although two-thirds of those who answered the questionnaire reported summoning the police at least once, many said they were little help.

Usually the police – who failed to answer one woman's call – talked to the husband, sometimes issuing a warning, or offered advice to the woman, telling her she should leave, see a doctor or lawyer or consider prosecution. But at least one policeman advised against prosecution, saying that the woman's husband would be bound to come back and bash her up.

What help did the women receive? Half of them – none.

A 'lucky' few, however, were able to turn to relatives for financial assistance, accommodation and emotional support, and others got help from doctors and lawyers.

According to Ms Jackson, the first thing a battered wife should do is find (if she can) a sympathetic lawyer who deals in domestic and legal aid cases.

With verification of bruising and other injuries from doctor or lawyer she can then obtain an interim non-molestation order, although if she does so while still at home she faces the problem of getting her husband out of what he regards as his house.

Thus there is an urgent practical need for

alternative, temporary, protective accommodation.

'Preferably, this accommodation should be
large enough for several families,' Ms Jackson
explains. 'When beaten women leave home
they need people around them. They are constantly frightened. And it's got to be free – a
refuge for the woman until she can apply to get
back to the matrimonial home.'

On a more subtle level, a change in attitude
toward sex roles and images (do we equate
manliness with aggression?) is called for.

A battered wife is the innocent party. Yet she
is ashamed. Why?

Miriam Jackson: 'We scapegoat victims because of our own vulnerability. So the battered
wife is accused of being a nagging wife, just as
the rape victim is accused of asking for it.'

Male attitudes
She says the survey indicates that barbaric male
attitudes such as 'a woman should be kept
barefoot and pregnant' and 'she's my wife, I'll
do what I like with her' are still very much alive.

It also indicates just what a trap the 'traditional female role' can spring for some women.

According to Ms Jackson, women are
traditionally conditioned into being emotionally dependent. When it comes to the crunch,
they often fear they would be unable to cope
with children on their own. They have also
been led to believe it is a woman's responsibility
to keep the marriage together.

'We need to encourage women to be independent and confident, to be able to overcome
the rationalizations and conditioning that keep
so many hidebound in domestic situations that
are so damaging to themselves and their
children.'

Terrible sense of shame
These excerpts from battered wives' letters
speak for themselves:
- 'On one occasion I had gone to bed but
  couldn't sleep. I got up and was ironing
  when he came home at approximately 3
  a.m. I began to cry and said nothing, and he
  took to me. I was pregnant.'
- 'The most common feeling of battered
  wives – and I have spoken to a few – is
  shame. This is what I felt. I didn't want anyone to know my husband had beaten me
  up.'
- 'I received various injuries – dislocated jaw;
  cuts to self and baby from rocks thrown at
  us through the window; black eyes; spinal

injury resulting in removal of two discs;
kicks in head and stomach, etc, etc, etc.'
- 'I asked the policeman to speak to my husband, which he did. But the sympathies
  were for my husband and I was treated as a
  hysterical woman.'
- 'He knocked me out for three days. I was in
  hospital. I received a cut head and black
  eye.'
- 'My husband was considered a 'good person' and I don't think anyone would have
  believed me had I told them that he hit me.
  He never hit my face and head, but pum-
  melled my upper arms, and on some occasions my ribs. During the summer I could
  seldom wear sleeveless tops because of the
  bruises.

  'When I was pregnant . . . and almost due
  to give birth he twice hit me on my enlarged
  stomach. It could be thought that the
  unborn child was the aim.'
- 'The police didn't help. They told me it
  would blow over in a couple of days.'
- 'Each time I left him he would come bearing
  expensive gifts, begging and crying how
  much he loved me. I always went back because I did not know how I would manage
  with the children . . . I realise now how
  stupid I was, bowed down with fear, mentally beaten, and the biggest downfall of all
  – pride.'
- 'The Women's Refuge Centre was fantastic.
  Not only did I meet women in a similar
  position (I had blamed myself before), but
  I was helped with every aspect of what one
  goes through after coming out of a dreadful
  marriage.'
- 'The effects on my children were vomiting,
  bedwetting, nail biting – also, lies and
  tantrums.'
- 'I used to be very sore, frightened, suffered
  migraines, couldn't sleep and lived in fear.
  He once strangled the cat and kittens.'
- 'I had seen my mother put up with years of
  abuse from my father (physical and emotional) and was not going to go through the
  same thing. But it seems there is not much
  help for it. If you are middle-aged with no
  children, no job prospects or money, you
  seem to be expendable all round.'
- 'The worst part is having no one to talk to.
  Your horrible story can't be told to anyone
  and you feel ashamed.'

New Zealand Woman's Weekly, *5 June 1978, p.11,
and 23 October 1978, pp.12–13*

7.18. Workshop Programme, New Zealand Men's Conference
Men's Alliance for Liberation and Equality (1978)

Dear People,

I write to inform you that the first New Zealand **Men's Conference** is to be held at Auckland University on the weekend of December 1-3. It promises to be an exciting, explorative, and insightful weekend for all those people (both men and women) who are interested in the emotional, psychological, and sexual liberation of the New Zealand male.

In particular, I believe it will be of real and immediate value to concerned gay men throughout the country. Why? Because I believe that the liberation of **all** men – despite sexual orientation – is inextricably bound to the crippling emotional disease of 'homophobia'. You may not agree! Why not come and discuss our liberation with me (and many others) in the first weekend of December.

Our programme includes film, workshops, speakers, and social evenings. (By the way, it's the same weekend as the Bowie concert.) The major part of the weekend will be spent in Workshops led by experienced and aware men and women on such topics as Consciousness Raising, Sexuality, Men's Bodies, Caring Men, Violence, Gay Rights, and Assertiveness. The Registration Fee of $10.00 provides admission to all events on the programme.

Enclosed, you will find further information and registration forms. I would be grateful if you could distribute this information amongst members of your organisation, and I look forward to your participation in an event of great meaning to us all. Please don't hesitate to contact me for further information.
Yours sincerely
Bobby Pickering.
for the Conference Collective.

Workshops:
Major workshops:
Two sessions.
1. Saturday morning
2. Sunday morning.

1. **Consciousness Raising**.
What are we trying to raise? Who should be doing it? What sorts of things should be experienced? Looking at what we feel and why we deny these feelings in ourselves and in others and why this confusion occurs.

2. **Sexuality**. Is there a difference between love, friendship and sex? What does sex feel like? Do we feel guilty about our fantasies? Do we feel good about our concepts of sensuality and sexuality? Are orgasm and ejaculation the same thing or are they different in a man's sexuality?
3. **Caring Men**. Do men care about themselves and others? What is caring anyway? Are we aware of caring for children? Are we aware of caring for ourselves? What limits us to only really care for one or two other persons?
4. **Men's Bodies**. How do we feel about our bodies? How do we feel about other bodies? How many bodies do we have as a comparison? Do we need to have a comparison at all? Bodily health, massage, various male ailments, all will be approached.

Minor workshops
This is a list of what may be offered in three sessions such that each person can choose and do three separate ones. The final decision depends upon space and facilitators. Minor workshops are looking to what can be done in society, i.e. leading to possible positive action, either in the personal day to day or on a broader political front.
1. **Sexist Roles**. Looking at the roles we all adopt, e.g. straight, gay, children, aged, men, women and the roles we force on others. The ways that these roles are oppressive. How do we feel about free and creative living rather than the rigid stereotyped roles that are the 'norm'? How to respect persons rather than roles.
2. **Gay Men**. What does being gay mean? Who is gay anyway? Do straights see gays as being different? What sorts of social norms cause straight persons to see gays as different? Do we oppress gays and ourselves in order to appear liberal?
3. **Assertiveness**. To obtain and realise our personal freedoms and rights. The rights to opinions and mistakes, to have feelings and self-respect, etc. The difference between aggression and assertion. To have a right to 'I AM. . .' statements.
4. **Violence and Men**. To look at the different types of violence: mental, physical, institutional, etc. To see if aggression, wars, rape and murder are natural. To realise that violence,

even if not realised, is one of the major oppressors in our 'normal' standards.

5. **Oppression of Women.** How do men oppress women? Do women oppress men? Oppression to be seen in two contexts, that of legitimate(?) 'power over' and assertive, personal power. What sorts of activities and word-watching should take place in order to develop this awareness?

6. **Competition and Power.** Is competition doing our personal best or is it winning? Does society see competition as a basic tenet and how does this lead to a hierarchical structure, if in fact it does? Is there such a thing as healthy competition and can there be such a thing in our lives, i.e. in the workplace, sports, etc.? What is power – is it the power the system ekes out to us or is it a personal thing? Can we handle personal power or do we need it legitimised in some way?

7. **Alcohol, Drugs and Escape.** Does alcohol and the use of drugs cause us to shut off and to hide from what is around us? Is their use an illness or not? Is escape bad or is it simply getting in touch with ourselves and realising who we are?

For example, are people simply getting more in touch with that anger we all can feel and expressing it in 'socially defined' ways?

8. **Men and Children.** How do men care for their children? How much time are men *allowed* with their children? Should there be paternity leave from a job? How can men get involved in creche work? How do we go about setting up a creche (i.e. what are the Rules?). Are children persons or are they 'children' until the law deems otherwise?

9. **Racism.** What is race as a concept to us? Does it mean a negative or not? Are we cross-cultural in our friendships or not? What sorts of differences stand between persons of different races relating?

These words are no doubt contentious, or at least raise some questions. The collective have thrashed them out and the point of the workshops is to extend these words into what we actually feel about these topics and what we can do about it.

First New Zealand Men's Conference, *Auckland, 1978 (Pam 893.75 N.Z. Men 1978, ATL)*

Chapter 8

A Place to Stand
1980s and 1990s

The 1980s can be considered the second phase of the contemporary women's movement. The feminist or women's movement, as it came to be termed ('women's liberation' was heard less often), diversified as groups and individuals took up particular causes, and the first flush of political activity and exuberance transformed into more sustained action. The conference at Piha in 1978, and the fourth and final United Women's Convention, held in Hamilton in 1979, demonstrated that the movement had grown too large and too diverse to be contained within single gatherings. From then on national meetings tended to be organised around specific topics and approaches, for example, Women's Studies Conferences (from 1978), the Women's Health Conference, 1982 (8.6), the Women in Recreation and Sport Conference, 1981, and Labour Party Women's Conferences from the mid-1970s.

The very recent past is difficult to bring into focus for a survey history of this kind, as the longer-term results of many of the campaigns and events have yet to be seen. Presented here is a selection of pieces relating to some of the most important issues raised by women in the 1980s and 1990s.

During the initial years of the 1980s, the broad political background was by no means sympathetic to feminism. The adoption of the Working Women's Charter by the major unions and the Federation of Labour was a major triumph. The 1984 election, which ousted the atrophied conservative Government, inaugurated a new climate of hope and change in national politics. For a time, in the mid-1980s, feminism began to exert significant influence on government policy. The most conspicuous sign of this was the establishment by the fourth Labour Government of a Ministry of Women's Affairs. A major episode later in the decade was the challenge made by feminists Phillida Bunkle and Sandra Coney to the medical profession. 'An Unfortunate Experiment', the article they published in 1987, exposed the inadequate treatment of cervical cancer patients at National Women's Hospital, and the powerlessness of women within the health system generally. This article was a major blow made by women against the authority of the professional establishment.

The decade began and ended with working women to the fore. In 1980, the Working Women's Charter (8.1 and 8.2) was adopted by the Federation of Labour after extensive discussion within individual unions. The Charter laid down basic principles of justice for women within the workplace and beyond, including vocational and trade-union education, child care, family and parental leave. It represented a wide-ranging manifesto for reform of the workplace. The Charter encompassed basic feminist goals, such as a woman's right to decide on abortion,

206

which proved to be the most controversial clause (and was the target for the anti-abortion group Feminists for Life). At the end of the decade, an attempt was made to try to bridge the gap between men's and women's earnings. The disparity had persisted, despite equal pay legislation, and a solution was sought through the principle of equal pay for work of equal value – pay equity. The Employment Equity Act was passed in 1990, establishing the mechanisms to compare various types of work and assess rates of pay. The legislation was repealed by the incoming National Government in December 1990 before it had a chance to be tested. Since then, employment conditions have changed radically, with the introduction of employment contracts to replace collective bargaining. The impact of this new arrangement between workers and employers is still being assessed, but it appears to be eroding considerably both pay levels and conditions, particularly among younger and less skilled workers for whom overtime and penal allowances often topped up a low basic wage. However, these allowances are rapidly disappearing from employment contracts. Closing the gap between men's and women's economic status continues to be a central issue for feminists.

The extension of employment opportunities has also been pursued through the 1980s. The provisions of the Human Rights Commission Act (1977), directed primarily at removing the barriers limiting women's entry into jobs and professions, were extended in the 1980s by the inauguration of equal employment opportunity (EEO) programmes within some larger organisations. From 1988, these became a statutory provision within government departments under the State Sector Act (8.16). A thorough assessment has yet to be made of the degree to which these measures have effected significant change within employment practice and broken down the gender divisions that have characterised New Zealand workplaces.

Discussion by feminists in the 1970s about housework and the status of 'housewives' bore fruit in the later 1980s, with some official recognition being given to women's unpaid work. The 1986 census was the first to ask about the amount and variety of voluntary activity done by New Zealanders. The Royal Commission on Social Policy (1986-88) emphasised the value of unpaid work, most of which was performed by women. This subject also received attention in the popular media. Claire Parker's 'Mate's Rates' (8.14), in the *New Zealand Woman's Weekly* (1987), was an attempt to place a monetary value on the variety of activities performed by a mother in the course of a year. The total, calculated on union and professional rates, amounted to a salary of well over $80,000. The question of unpaid work was one of a number of issues that, in the 1970s, had generally been regarded as on the 'fringe' or as representing the views of 'extreme feminists'. By the 1980s, such analyses commonly appeared in the mainstream media, where they were likely to receive serious treatment – proof of the impact of the feminist movement on New Zealand society over ten to twenty years.

Another workplace concern which came to prominence in the early 1980s was sexual harassment. In the early 1980s, efforts were made to institute formal procedures outlawing sexual harassment. Mary Sinclair's article and questionnaire (8.3) were written to raise awareness and to gather information as part of the campaign to make harassment an industrial issue. Grievances that were first identified by women in the 1970s were being taken up in the second phase of the contemporary movement and defined as industrial, educational or political concerns within relevant organisations and structures. The energy that had been sparked by and for women in the 1970s began to be channelled into change in schools, workplaces and churches. Institutional recognition was sought for feminist issues.

Besides sexual harassment, several other issues relating to the dangers of sexuality were highlighted in the 1980s. These included the campaigns against pornography, domestic violence, and sexual abuse. In the 1970s, Women's Liberation encouraged women to express and to celebrate their own sexuality (therefore access to birth control and abortion was of key importance), and opened up the world of intimate love between women. The 1980s, however, were more concerned with the hazards of male sexuality. While opportunities appear to have expanded for women in such areas as education, employment and sport, the continued vulnerability of women to male violence, and particularly sexual violence, was perceived to be anomalous and especially abhorrent. The complexity of sexual desire became the centre of discussion in the later years. At the beginning of the decade, AIDS was unknown; within a few years, it would radically reshape perceptions and expectations of sexual relationships.

Some of the initial targets of feminist protest persisted, as the protest against the 1982 Miss Wellington contest testifies (8.5). However, in the 1980s, the principal focus for campaigns against the sexual exploitation of women was the pornography industry, which blossomed with the advent of home videos. Street protests against video shops were relatively frequent in the mid-1980s (8.10 and 8.11). The campaign quickly gathered momentum, and became a priority for many women's groups – including some traditionally conservative organisations. The question of how to deal with pornography engendered a vigorous debate within the feminist movement, from extremists who sought a ban on all material, to others who did not seek a total ban, but supported some limitations on the industry, based on distinctions between sexually explicit material and sexually degrading and violent pornography (8.11). Other difficult questions were tackled: whether the material viewed on film or video had a direct influence on an individual's behaviour; and how to establish an acceptable system of regulation. Such concerns were finally handed over to the Ministerial Committee of Inquiry into Pornography in 1989. The recommendations of their report have been largely encompassed in the Films, Videos and Publications Classification Bill currently before Parliament. If passed, this will considerably increase the powers of government to limit the sale and distribution of pornography.

The power of 'moral' issues concerning sexual behaviour to polarise public opinion was demonstrated most graphically by the lengthy and much debated Homosexual Law Reform Bill of 1985-86. The Lesbian Coalition's pamphlet (8.12) was one of many pieces of publicity used to draw support for the Bill, and to counter the considerable opposition that had been mobilised against it. The strength of antagonism exposed in the debate served as a reminder of the profoundly conservative body of opinion that persisted in the face of the challenges made by feminists, gays and lesbians to reshape sexual and family relationships and institutions. It exposed the legal and social vulnerability of lesbian and gay New Zealanders. Sexual orientation remains outside the protection afforded by the Human Rights Commission, though this, too, may change in the near future. A bill extending statutory Human Rights Commission protection to include sexual orientation (and age) is currently before Parliament (though the part concerning sexual orientation has been introduced as a private member's bill rather than as a Government measure, unlike the rest of the amending legislation).

Another feature of the development of the feminist movement and of feminist ideas in the 1980s has been the closer examination of feminist politics and feminist theory, and the closer convergence of feminist politics and feminist theory with other political movements. The 1980s have seen continued growth in the strength of Maori activism, and in the challenge made by Maori feminists to the priorities and political agendas of Pakeha feminists. The Waitangi Day protests in the early 1980s were a key issue for many feminists. Donna Awatere's trail-blazing 'Maori Sovereignty' was first published in *Broadsheet*, and sparked an intense debate amongst readers. With the increasing recognition of the Treaty of Waitangi through the 1980s (exemplified in the extension of the Waitangi Tribunal's jurisdiction to hear claims dating back to 1840, and in the incorporation of Treaty principles into state sector activities), the starting point for many feminist groups has become the Treaty of Waitangi.

The anti-nuclear ships movement (8.8), peace and the environment (8.4) have been major issues of the decade in which women have participated very conspicuously. Later in the 1980s the rise of 'new right' policies in business, government and public policy have seemed to threaten the conditions in which women might realise their apparently greater freedom and aspirations. For these reasons feminist debate has, in recent years, tackled some of the wider aspects of Government policy.

In the last two or three years, there have been suggestions that the feminist movement has come to an end; that New Zealand, along with much of the rest of the world, has reached a post-feminist era. There follows the implication that the practices and attitudes of the 1970s and 1980s are no longer appropriate; that any separate or special focus on women is no longer needed. Such suggestions are strenuously denied by many women, who can quickly point to the continuing disparities between women and men in pay, assets, educational qualifications, superannuation, and media profiles (for example, in sport), and to the continuing incidence of male violence towards women. There is some support for the idea that there is currently a 'backlash' against women and that we are in a post-feminist era. This is the theme of Susan Faludi's *Backlash: the undeclared war against women* (London, 1991). The response to her visit in June 1992, when hundreds of women turned up to hear her speak in several centres around the country, would indicate that this idea has support amongst New Zealand women.

The development of feminist ideas in the 1980s has occurred against a background of sustained economic recession, increasing unemployment, and insecurity in many sections of New Zealand society. Over the decade a massive change has occurred in economic and political life. The role of the state and the relationship of individuals to government have changed substantially. Feminists, and women generally, have occupied a number of positions in this process. In many areas – especially since 1984 – women have become involved in policy-making, often bringing with them feminist goals and modes of working. The establishment of the Ministry of Women's Affairs is the most prominent example, but there are many others also. The Ministry's 1986 objectives (8.13), illustrate what enormous expectations there were. In the succeeding Government two women occupied senior positions within Cabinet, but they have not been popular in feminist circles because their policies have not generally been perceived to advance the interests of women. Many more women in the 1980s have found themselves as economic dependents of the state as the number of people on unemployment, domestic purposes and sickness benefits has increased (so too has the number of people receiving government superannuation, the majority of whom are women). Since 1 April 1991 many have had to make do with considerably smaller benefits. Very recently women have had to come to terms with changes in the way education and health services are organised. Here women are the major providers of services, as well as being recipients. There are feminist questions being asked in these areas.

One of the paradoxes of the 1980s and early 1990s is the fact that a number of women's and feminist issues have gained public and official recognition at the same time as real movement towards gender equality has proved elusive. There are codes prohibiting sexual harassment; sexist language is disappearing from television news; women's refuges have become tax-deductible charities (even if domestic violence has not been eliminated). We now have a woman as Governor-General – more than a symbolic gesture – and Kate Sheppard, the first woman other than a reigning monarch, on a banknote. Public recognition and a small amount of public money are supporting Suffrage Centennial Year. These signs of progress are welcomed by feminists and can be seen as representing the successful impact of the feminist movement, but equality has not yet been achieved. And some of these recent events have engendered a considerable degree of controversy. Feminist debate continues in New Zealand in 1993.

Sources and Further Reading

Awatere, Donna. *Maori Sovereignty*, Auckland, 1984
Bunkle, Phillida. *Second Opinion: the politics of women's health in New Zealand*, Auckland, 1988
Coney, Sandra. *Out of the Frying Pan: Inflammatory writings, 1972-89*, Auckland, 1990
Coney, Sandra and Phillida Bunkle. 'An unfortunate experiment at National Women's Hospital', *Metro*, June 1987, pp. 46–65
Dann, Christine and Maud Cahill (eds). *Changing Our Lives*, Wellington, 1992
Guy, Camille, Alison Jones and Gay Simpkin. 'From Piha to Post-feminism . . . ', *Sites*, no 20 (Autumn 1990), pp. 7–19
James, Colin. *New Territory*, Wellington, 1992
Rosier, Pat (ed.). *Been Around for Quite a While: Twenty years of Broadsheet magazine*, Auckland, 1992
Royal Commission on Social Policy. *The April Report: New Zealand today*, Wellington, 1988
Status of New Zealand Women, 1992: Second periodic report on the Convention on the Elimination of All Forms of Discrimination Against Women, Wellington, 1992
Te Awekotuku, Ngahuia. *Mana Wahine Maori: Selected writings on Maori women's art, culture and politics*, Auckland,1991
Waring, Marilyn. *Women, Politics and Power*, Wellington, 1985
Waring, Marilyn. *Counting for Nothing*, Wellington, 1988

8.1.   Working Women's Charter: This document could change your life
by Robyn Welsh (1980)

The Working Women's Charter [for full text see 8.2] will dramatically affect women throughout New Zealand – those in paid employment and those who have chosen to remain at home caring for their children.

But it seems that only minority elements of New Zealand's one million or more women are sufficiently concerned about the charter's implications to get behind moves either to implement it at trade union level or to fight its most controversial clauses.

The charter is a 16-clause statement covering women's issues, including equal opportunity in work and education, the right to work, parental leave, improved working conditions and comprehensive research into women's health matters.

But it is clauses 12 and 15 covering child care, and urging freely available sex education and birth control advice, that are generating the most vocal opposition. Clause 15 also states that legal, financial, social and medical impediments to safe contraception, sterilization and abortion be removed.

Sonja Davies, the sole woman on the Federation of Labour executive, introduced the concept of a charter on her return from an Australian trade union meeting in 1976, the year after she founded the Working Women's Council.

She is not upset by the time it has taken for the FOL to accept the charter overwhelmingly this year because of the widespread discussion this has generated at every level in the community.

Inevitably it has created opposition. 'You can't overlook the opposition to clause 12 but it just wasn't there at the hundreds of meetings I spoke at,' she says.

Now, telephone calls and letters of support to Sonja (who is based in Wellington) are running 10-1 in favour but she acknowledges that the fight for the charter's implementation by the FOL's 431,000 members in 197 affiliated unions is only just beginning.

'I'm a realist and I expect this sort of thing,' she says about the charter's opponents. 'I know where it will come from. I respect people's opposing views and at no time are we seeking to foist anything on people.'

'Nobody is asking anybody to use contra-

ceptives or have an abortion but those women who wish to should have the opportunity. This is vital if women are to join the workforce on the same footing as men.'

Sonja Davies says the most encouraging sign so far is the growing acceptance among men of the value of more women trade unionists.

It is these women at grass roots level whom the FOL is relying on to implement the charter.

As well, a detailed plan of action is to be put to the federation's national council meeting in mid-August. But just what it will entail depends on information Sonja receives from Australia soon on the progress of charter campaign committees there.

She also wants unions to step up discussions with women employers to push charter clauses in their annual awards – a point which several unions have taken up already.

The Working Women's Council's Wellington branch is to draw up a guideline list of claims for unions and it intends setting aside time for a major debate on the charter at the council's annual conference in August.

As well as this Sonja Davies wants nationwide trade union pressure on the international trade union movement for increased World Health Organisation research into safe contraceptives and greater union involvement here in child care, parental leave and after school care provisions.

'It won't be a pushover,' she says simply, 'I wouldn't like to put a time on it but it's the goal to aim for.'

But the chairwoman of *Feminists for Life* Connie Purdue, an Auckland trade unionist, strongly disagrees.

The Auckland-based group says it has been deluged with requests for its *Mothers' Petition* and has extended the closing date to August 30. It has also started a *Concerned Citizens* petition to cope with the people wanting Parliament to hear their objections and their support for 'life and family.'

She describes it as 'a David and Goliath fight' because she says the charter's endorsement by the FOL, the Labour Party and the Public Service Association means that almost every working person is committed to it.

She says many trade unionists have told her that when the charter was put to them they felt they could not oppose the concept of better conditions for women, even though they believed that abortion on demand had no place in trade union affairs.

As national vice-president for the Society for the Protection of the Unborn Child, Connie Purdue says she'll fight to the end.

Once the two petitions have been presented to Parliament she says Feminists for Life intends starting a Charter for the Family, similar to the Maternity Patient's Bill of Rights promoted earlier.

SPUC's national president, Marilyn Pryor, says she supports the organisation's stand and describes the charter as a dangerous document capable of seriously damaging the concept of family life.

Among trade unions already moving on the charter is the New Zealand Meatworkers' Union which intends pushing the child-care clause at industry level this year.

National executive member Ken Findlay says the union has already won the support of one employer.

But he thinks it unlikely that the charter will be taken up at the union's annual award talks because of what he describes as 'other issues which will take precedence, such as technology.'

'Free day care has also been included in claims from the combined unions of four Wellington motor assembly plants and this could pave the way for similar claims elsewhere,' says Graeme Clarke, from the Wellington district Coachworkers' Union.

He says agreements initiating in Wellington are usually the trendsetters but he admits he is not optimistic of total employer support.

The North Island Electrical Workers' Union, however, strongly opposes the charter, although its general secretary, Tony Neary, says the union will still promote issues affecting women members at award talks.

He is a member of the FOL's policy committee and is now well-known for his vocal stands against the charter at the FOL and Labour Party's annual conferences in May.

He describes the charter as 'a step backwards' simply because it is called *The Working Women's Charter*.

He is particularly concerned at clause 15,

which he failed to have amended, but adds: 'The rest of the charter is divisive and discriminatory because what we are doing now is separating males and females from each other.

'The charter is a step backwards, serves no useful purpose whatsoever and I'm prepared to debate that with the people who have been promoting it.'

He is convinced that the charter's promoters have just camouflaged clause 15 to get it through and says the big questions now are how the FOL intends implementing it, whether its funds will be used to push clause 15 and whether it will push the Government for the repeal of the relevant legislation.

To these questions, Sonja Davies says simply this: 'The FOL won't be doing it, it isn't the place. It's just the vehicle through which the policy is formulated and it's the job of the affiliated unions.

'We've had quality child care as our policy for 14 years but nothing has been done about it until the charter,' she says fiercely.

On the other side, the New Zealand Employers' Federation has yet to consolidate its views but its director of advocacy, Max Bradford, thinks the charter is 'unworkable.'

He questions how equal educational opportunity can be obtained in award negotiations, but stresses: 'It's not that we're necessarily against a substantial number of elements of the charter but in many cases they're just unworkable.'

Zonta, which represents professional woman, does not speak collectively, but Marie Keir from the Zonta Club of Wellington says that the charter has already been a success because of the ensuing discussion . . . although some clauses are 'debatable.'

But, she adds: 'It's shocking that such a bill of rights is necessary in the 1980s. If we had the right sort of caring society then it wouldn't be necessary and I admire Sonja Davies for seeing it through.'

The Public Service Association, with its 68,400 members, has endorsed its version of the charter but has yet to take steps to implement it.

New Zealand Woman's Weekly, *28 July 1980, pp. 4–5*

8.2. The Working Women's Charter
Wellington Working Women's Council (1981)

At home and at work, all women need . . .

THE WORKING WOMEN'S CHARTER

The Working Women's Charter is a Bill of Rights for working women.

Women in Australia, Britain and Ireland have endorsed similar charters. In 1977 the N.Z. Working Women's Council convened a gathering of 400 women, who came from all over New Zealand and who represented women at home as well as women in the paid workforce. This convention debated and approved the Working Women's Charter. The Charter was later endorsed by two Annual General Meetings of the Working Women's Councils. Then the Charter was presented to the union movement for discussion. After two years of education and discussion it was endorsed by the 1980 Federation of Labour Annual Conference.

The Charter represents a step forward for New Zealand women. Both working women and working men strongly support it.

This pamphlet prints the full Charter and explains why you should support it too.

THE WORKING WOMEN'S CHARTER

1. The right to work for everyone.
2. The elimination of all discrimination on the basis of sex, race, religion, political belief, marital or parental status, sexuality or age.
3. Equal pay for work of equal value.
4. Equal opportunity of entry into occupations and of promotion regardless of sex, race, religion, political belief, marital or parental status, sexuality or age.
5. Equal education opportunity for all.
6. Union meetings and special trade union education courses for all unionists to be held with paid time off for participants with special attention to gain more active participation of women unionists.
7. Equal access to vocational guidance and training, including on-the-job training, re-training, study, and conference leave for all workers.
8. Introduction of a shorter working week with no loss of pay, flexible working hours, and part-time opportunities for all workers by union agreement.
9. Improved working conditions for all workers. The retention of beneficial provisions which apply to women and extension of these to men. Other benefits to apply equally to women and men.
10. Removal of legal, bureaucratic and other impediments to equality of superannuation, social security benefits, credit, finance, taxation, tenancies, and other related matters.
11. Consultation with and special attention to the needs and requirements of all workers from ethnic communities with special attention to those of women.
12. Wide availability of quality child care with government, employer and community support for all those who need it, including industrial creches, after-school and school holiday care.
13. Introduction of adequate paid parental leave without loss of job security, superannuation or promotion prospects.
14. Availability of paid family leave to enable time off to be taken in cases of family need.
15. Sex education and birth control advice freely available to all people of appropriate age, and legal, financial, social and medical impediments to safe contraception, sterilisation, and abortion to be removed so as to allow the individual concerned to make their own decision.
16. Comprehensive government-funded research into health questions specific to women.

That is the text – what is the message?
- All women are working women. In homes or in factories, in offices or in classrooms – wherever they work and whatever they earn, all women are working women.
- Housewife or teacher, nurse or mother, lawyer or machinist, cleaner or secretary, driver or librarian . . . whatever work a woman does she should have the same rights and opportunities as other workers.
- The Working Women's Charter seeks to ensure that all people, women as well as men, have the same access to suitable and satisfying work, and the same control over pay, hours and conditions of work.

- All women are not yet treated equally and fairly – the Charter sets out the rights which working women need to gain if we are to live in a truly equal and just society.
- The key message of the Charter is choice. Every clause of the Charter deals with a basic right which will allow working women to choose from the same range of options in life that working men take for granted. When these rights are guaranteed, then whether you choose to use them or not is up to you. But remember – unless we have these basic rights, none of us has a real range of choices.

Choice One: The right to work

If you *want* a job, you should *have* a job. No one who is qualified to do a job should be turned away because they are female, or Maori, or married, or a parent – or have anything else about them which has nothing to do with how well they can do the job.

Choice Two: Freedom from discrimination

We have a Human Rights Commission which is supposed to monitor and discourage discrimination. But a Commission can't prevent discrimination – it can only take the worst cases to court. To end discrimination against women and all other groups which have traditionally been discriminated against we all have to get involved, making people more aware of their rights and how they can use them.

Choice Three: Equal pay

Yes, there is an Equal Pay Act – but did you know that women still earn on average only 75% of what men earn?

The Labour Department is still concerned that the Act is not being properly enforced, but in most cases these lower wages are due to women being stuck in jobs which are poorly paid. Which is why we need . . .

Choice Four: Equal opportunities

Picture a typist.

You pictured a woman? Yes – because 99% of typists are women. Picture an engineer. You pictured a man? Yes – because 95% of engineers are men. There are so many, many jobs which are almost entirely men only or women only. This sort of sexual separation represents a frustrating and expensive waste of talents, since both women and men have the same sorts of skills and intelligence. While for

women it often means being stuck in jobs with low pay and low status. But what else can they do? They need . . .

Choice Five: Equal educational opportunities

If women are to have well paid, interesting jobs, they need the right training, the right attitudes and the right assistance. Starting from kindergarten they need to be offered the same chances as boys. To play with building blocks at age 5 and build houses at 50, as well as playing with tea sets at age 5 and keeping house at 50. Girls need to be encouraged to study sciences and mathematics as well as commerce and cooking. In fact they need to be encouraged to stay at school! There are just as many bright girls as boys but only one third of university students are female. A good education is the key to so many life and work opportunities – boys and girls should be given the same options and encouragement right from the start.

Choice Six: Union meetings in work time

Not only are all women working women – most women have two jobs. The unpaid work they do at home and the paid work they do outside. Many women (and more men, as they realise that the home and family is their responsibility too) come home to a 'second shift' of household duties. House workers are often too tired or too busy to put the time into union affairs that they should, if their union is to be truly democratic and representative. Both women and unions would be happier and healthier if union business could be dealt with in work time.

Choice Seven: Equal guidance and training

Even if you get the sort of schooling talked about in Clause 5 of the Charter, you may find you need more education to get on well in your job. Research among teachers has shown that the women don't get as much access to training as the men do. Other women workers report the same problem. Women should be encouraged and assisted to receive as much training and study leave men do.

Choice Eight: Shorter working hours

Male and female workers who have home and family responsibilities need more flexible working hours and a shorter working week. Working fewer hours will ease the unemployment situation as more workers are hired to make up the extra hours. More *permanent* part-time work (where workers have the same protection and benefits as full-time workers) will allow parents to share breadwinning and child care responsibilities more equally, making for more satisfied parents and happier, closer families.

Choice Nine: Improved working conditions

If work is too dirty, dangerous or unhealthy for women then it is too dirty, dangerous or unhealthy for men. Medical studies prove that working late night shifts and broken shifts is bad for all workers, not just women workers. If women are to have the same job opportunities as men then men must have the same protective provisions as women.

Choice Ten: Other equalities

Some bank managers still won't lend money to a woman without a male guarantor, even when she's earning good money of her own. A married woman still isn't entitled to an unemployment benefit, even though she and her family may rely on her income. Some landlords refuse to let their houses to solo parents . . . and so on . . . All this discrimination is based on unthinking prejudice – it's unfair and it's got to go.

Hepanui Tekau Ma Tahi: He kaupapa ki nga hiahia o nga wahine, a, ki nga kaimahi hoki o roto i o tatou iwi Maori, iwi mangumangu.

Ua fou nei le ganga o le Papalagi ia te oe, o ou matua ma le tou aiga e afe maila o tou vāvā ai ma o nofoaga ua malulu ma faigata ona fa'omasani i ai, o lou galuega fo'i ua eseese lava ma o tou galuega i Samoa, ma ua e le masani tele fo'i i uiga ma tulaga o le olaga Papalagi, o osi tama'ita'i i galuega faleoloa ma oaga e pei lava ua faigafie ma masani uma i nei tulaga o le olaga, ae e pei lava ua e le masani tele i ai . . . e faigata tele ona tatou fa'amasani i le olaga Niu Silo i tulaga faigaluega ma tulaga fa'aletama'itai. Awhinatiamai nga wahine nei kia taea ai e ratou te whai te matauranga ki tu tangata ai ratou i roto i te ao pakeha.

Did you understand that? Did you know what languages it was in? It said, 'English is a new language to you, your parents and grandparents are thousands of miles away, the city is cold and confusing, your new job is so different from work back where you came from, you are not familiar with pakeha customs, the other women at work, at the shops and the play-ground all seem to be able to cope better than you . . . It's hard fitting in as a worker and as a woman in New Zealand society. Women from ethnic communities need special assistance if they are to get equal education and opportunities, and achieve equal success.'

* Choice Eleven: Special attention to the needs of workers and women from ethnic communities

Not all New Zealanders come from the white European background most of us take for granted. How would you like to have the problems of the immigrant outlined above? Women and workers from ethnic communities need the right to decide on their own needs and to have those needs met by society as a whole.

Choice Twelve: Quality child care

Ever tried to find a reliable babysitter just after moving to a new home? Ever wished someone would mind the kids for one or two afternoons a week while you go shopping, go to a class, do part-time work, play a sport or just have some time to yourself? Ever dreaded the school holidays because it is so hard to find good care for the kids while you're at work? Ever felt trapped at home, needing and wanting a job but unable to find good care for your child?

At some time or other most parents could use quality child care services. Services which are available 24 hours a day, 365 days a year *not* so that kids can be 'dumped', but to cover all possibilities. The possibility of both parents working outside the home 35 hours a week, or the possibility of sickness in the family, when you'd like the security of knowing that the children are well cared for while you cope with the crisis. The possibility of a child-free afternoon to go shopping, or the possibility of a night out with no worries about whether the teenage babysitter can cope. Lots of different families, lots of different possibilities . . .

A quality child care centre is a warm and exciting place for a child to be. Loved by its parents, stimulated by the variety of playmates, playthings and adult carers at the centre . . . research now tells us that quality child care is not harmful to children and may be very positive for them. Children as well as parents benefit from quality child care.

Choice Thirteen: Parental leave

Perhaps you'd rather look after your child yourself at home. It should be your choice. But children don't stay small forever and you may be wanting your old job back before too long. That's why the Charter stresses parental leave as a choice for parents. Not just maternity leave, because sometimes fathers will want to be the parent at home while the mother is out at work. Some countries now offer generous paid short-term parental leave and unpaid long-term parental leave. It gives you security both as a parent and as a worker, and that's a right worth having.

Choice Fourteen: Family leave
Both parents are at work, the kids are at school, when suddenly DISASTER! Young Sally breaks her collarbone. She'll have to be visited in hospital, then nursed at home. It's no use wishing Mum was at home full time to do all the running around. 50% of the female workforce in New Zealand is married and chances are she's out at work, earning the money to feed and clothe young Sally and pay her doctor's bills. So workers need to be able to take time off to deal with emergencies like these – it's a small additional right like the right to take paid leave yourself when you yourself are sick.

Choice Fifteen: Better birth control
Bringing up children is important and sometimes difficult work. It's a job that all parents do as well as their normal paid work. Until recently the unpaid work of child rearing was women's responsibility, but now more and more women want the recognition, stimulation, independence and essential income that goes with paid work, while more and more men want to play a greater part in family life, to see more of their kids while they are young and actively experience the joys and trials of parenthood.

So whether to have children, or when to have them, is a vital issue to all workers. Vital to the children too – they have a right to be wanted, loved and well cared for.

For workers and children to be secure, potential parents need easy access to safe and effective birth control. Everyone needs to know how bodies work and how to avoid unwanted pregnancy. For most people that means knowing about and using some form of contraception. The choice should be yours and yours alone – it's your body.

Unfortunately, we don't yet have foolproof sex education, foolproof contraception – or foolproof people! To many people (about 5,000 New Zealand women a year) abortion is an acceptable solution to the problem of unwanted pregnancy. Once again the Charter states that the individual should have the *choice*, unrestricted by laws which represent the views of those who say they would make the opposite choice.

If a woman is to control her working life, she must be able to control her fertility. The choices a woman makes in this area will affect all her other life choices, so the rights outlined in Clause 15 are an essential basis for all other women's rights.

Choice Sixteen: Health research
No one needs to be reminded how much our happiness, as workers and women, depends on our health. It is also obvious that women have special health needs because they bear children. Good quality maternity care, safe and effective contraception, a good knowledge of how our bodies work, knowledge of how to stay healthy and how to treat minor disorders should all be our right in this day and age. Filling gaps in our knowledge of women's health should be a priority for society – the health and happiness of half its citizens should be seen as vitally important.

Pamphlet (Ephemera B Women 1981, ATL)

8.3. Sexual Harassment in the Workplace
by Mary Sinclair (1981)

Most women face unwanted sexual attention at work but very few complain about it. This unwanted attention is termed sexual harassment and can range from leering, pinching, patting and other unnecessary physical contact, verbal comments, and subtle pressure for sexual activity, to rape and attempted rape.

All women are vulnerable to sexual harassment, in any occupation and at any level. The sexual harasser may be the boss (controlling officer or section head), a colleague, or a client, and will be found in all types of jobs, from offices to factories to hospitals to building sites, etc.

How much harassment?
Although few statistics are available in New Zealand, the experience of other western

countries like America and Australia suggests that the few cases which are currently being dealt with by PSA and other union officials are merely the tip of the iceberg. In a 1976 survey in *Redbook Magazine* (USA), 88 percent of the 9,000 respondents reported that they had experienced one or more forms of unwanted sexual advances on the job. Some women have taken cases to the anti-discrimination bodies in various Australian states and unions are taking up reports of sexual harassment. In 1979 over 1,000 charges relating to sexual harassment were brought before the American Equal Employment Opportunity Commission. An American women's group Working Women United ran a survey on sexual harassment in 1975 and found that 70 percent of respondents had experienced harassment. Fifty percent of the women who were polled in a United Nations survey by the Ad Hoc Group on Equal Rights for Women in 1976 had either experienced or were aware of sexual harassment in the UN.

Why don't women complain?

A common finding of all surveys was the low complaint level of victims of sexual harassment. Most victims felt that nothing would be done; others felt the problem would be trivialised or they would be ridiculed; and others felt they would be blamed and possibly penalised if they complained.

As with rape, it is often the victim of sexual harassment who pays the greatest price, not the harasser. In most societies, few women report the harassment or complain officially. Those who do are often dismissed, transferred, or given poor work reports or assessments. It is rare for the harasser to be dismissed, transferred or in any way punished.

In our society, where jobs are scarce and equal opportunity has yet to be won, women are particularly vulnerable to the coercive threat of sexual harassment. The status of women in the workplace – lowly paid and in low status occupations – is a major contributing factor in sexual harassment. Most women are economically dependent on their job in a tight job market, and often need the job to maintain emotional and professional confidence in themselves. Women can be particularly at risk when they enter a traditionally male work area, such as construction work or freezing works.* Most women are forced to give up their job to get away from the harassment.

If a woman decides to stay in the job despite the sexual harassment, she then has to deal with the anxiety and fear engendered by the harassment. She may start asking herself: what have I done to deserve this treatment? How can I keep working under these conditions? What can I do about it? Will he ever stop harassing me? She will be placed under severe emotional stress with the double threat of losing her job and sexual assault. This stress can lead to deeper psychological problems or physical illness.

The victim of sexual harassment may find her ability to do a good job curtailed if her harasser has the power to punish her because she will not comply with his demands. He may demote or fire her; he may subject her to increased harassment, give her poor work assignments and reports, sabotage her work, make sarcastic or abusive remarks, have her transferred, or deny her raises, promotions and other benefits normally available to her.

One of the other main reasons for women's silence on sexual advances in the workplace is the prevailing social assumption that women have encouraged the advances, have somehow 'asked for it', or have been a willing party. For some reason men tend to believe that a woman says no and means yes. Male relatives of the victim are often suspicious and accusing rather than supportive. Colleagues will often assume that the woman is 'sleeping around to get promotion' and do not consider the possibility of coercion. The effect of these attitudes can induce quite unjustified guilt in the victim.

Why do men harass?

In recent years the economic climate in New Zealand has worsened. Unemployment has risen and people have less control over their lives. Newspapers are reporting more and more incidents of domestic violence, the other side of sexual harassment in the office or workplace.

As more women enter the paid workforce and compete for jobs in traditionally male areas, some men are beginning to feel very threatened and inadequate. The male-dominated workplace is often the one place where men have some control and importance, as the breadwinner for their families. Women entering these workplaces are seen as intruders and less powerful. Sexual harassment is, therefore, not an expression of sexual frustration or desire, it is simply a means of attacking and establishing power over a woman. Even men at the top of their profession or organisation harass women at work, as a statement of their power and society's scorn for women.

Can the silence be broken?

The first step in breaking the silence is the publication of articles and surveys which can outline the problems and make women aware that they are not alone if they have suffered harassment. Women often fail to recognise that harassment is used as an instrument of power against them, not because of their race or status, but because of their sex.

The sharing of experiences with other women in small groups, either based in the workplace or in speak-outs organised by women's groups is another mechanism which will help women to understand their experiences and act collectively to stop them.

Women have to recognise that if they stay silent about workplace harassment it will continue to be seen as a personal problem rather than as a social issue.

Breaking silence in the workplace may take several forms – talking to female co-workers, union delegates and/or officials, personnel or welfare officers, professional counsellors, or the harasser's superiors.

Legal redress can be hard to achieve as only the most extreme cases of harassment seen by others involving several women would ever get to trial. The Human Rights Commission can give support and assistance but because the complaints service is in its infancy as yet, complaints take some time to process and can provide only minor compensation for the victim.

The union movement is perhaps the best chance for redress for women workers faced with sexual harassment. Several cases of harassment have been handled by the PSA's field staff, with varying degrees of success. Few union officials or members are aware of the extent of sexual harassment on the job.

In co-operation with the Public Service Association, we have taken a first step of including with this article a slightly amended version of a questionnaire first published in *Redbook Magazine* in the USA in 1976. We would also appreciate a brief outline of any problems you may have encountered in your place of employment.

* For a particularly graphic description of a woman's experience in a traditionally male occupation, see *Broadsheet*, No. 85 (Dec. 1980), pp.16-18.

Sexual Harassment Survey
(Reprinted from the *Public Service Journal*)

1. Occupation: ....
   Nationality/Race: ....
   If children, number: .... Ages: ....
   Other dependents: ....

(MARK X IN THE RIGHT SQUARE)

2. What is your age?
   ☐ Under 20
   ☐ 20 to 24
   ☐ 25 to 29
   ☐ 30 to 35
   ☐ Over 35

3. Which of the following have you experienced with male co-workers or supervisors?
   ☐ Leering or ogling
   ☐ Sexual remarks or teasing
   ☐ Subtle sexual hints and pressures
   ☐ Touching, brushing against, grabbing, pinching
   ☐ Invitations to a date with the implication that refusing may count against you
   ☐ Sexual propositions, with the implication that refusing may count against you
   ☐ Sexual relations, with the implication that refusing may count against you
   ☐ Other forms of sexual harassment
   ☐ No sexual harassment at all

4. Which one of the following statements best reflects the way you feel?
   ☐ Sexual tensions between men and women who work together are natural
   ☐ Innocent flirtations make the workday interesting
   ☐ An attractive woman has to expect sexual advances and learn to handle them
   ☐ Encouraging the boss's sexual interest is often a way of getting ahead
   ☐ Women who are bothered by male co-workers are usually asking for it
   ☐ Unwelcome male attentions on the job are offensive

5. If a male co-worker or supervisor has made sexual advances to you, how did you feel about it?
   ☐ It was embarrassing
   ☐ It was demeaning
   ☐ It was intimidating
   ☐ It was flattering
   ☐ It was a way of keeping me, a woman, 'in my place'
   ☐ It was of no consequence
   ☐ Not applicable

6. At work have you ever used your sexual attractiveness for any of the following purposes?
   - [ ] To improve relations with a male supervisor
   - [ ] To catch the attention of higher-ups
   - [ ] To get out of the chores I dislike
   - [ ] To obtain special help from men
   - [ ] To manoeuvre into a better job position
   - [ ] To obtain other advantages
   - [ ] Not applicable

7. What do you think of a woman's using her sexual attractiveness to gain job advantages?
   - [ ] It's only natural – sexual attractiveness is a basic asset meant to be used
   - [ ] It's a woman's answer to the way men gain job advantages (in locker rooms, on the golf course)
   - [ ] It tends to perpetuate a system of sexism
   - [ ] It's her own business and it just has nothing to do with me

8. In getting your job how important do you think your physical attractiveness was?
   - [ ] More important than my other qualifications
   - [ ] Equally important
   - [ ] Less important
   - [ ] Unimportant

9. At work how important is a man's physical attractiveness?
   - [ ] As important as a woman's
   - [ ] Less important
   - [ ] More important
   - [ ] Unimportant

10. If a male co-worker or supervisor has made sexual advances to you, how did you react?
    - [ ] I enjoyed it
    - [ ] I ignored it, hoping it would stop
    - [ ] I worried that if I objected, it would somehow go against me
    - [ ] I played along with it, hoping it would lead to a promotion
    - [ ] I asked the man to stop it
    - [ ] I reported it to a supervisor or a union representative
    - [ ] Not applicable

11. If you were to report a man's unwelcome attention to a supervisor or union representative, what do you think would happen?
    - [ ] Nothing at all
    - [ ] I would be told not to take it so seriously
    - [ ] The man would be asked to stop – or else
    - [ ] I would be labelled a 'troublemaker'
    - [ ] I would be offered a job in another department to help me avoid the man
    - [ ] I would be moved to another department in retaliation
    - [ ] I would be fired

12. How would you feel if you saw sexual advances being made to another woman at work?
    - [ ] I would sympathise with her
    - [ ] I would blame her
    - [ ] I would envy her ability to make sexual attractiveness work for her
    - [ ] I would think nothing of it

13. How do you feel about sexual harassment?
    - [ ] It is a serious problem
    - [ ] It is a minor problem
    - [ ] It is of no importance at all

14. Have you or any woman you know ever —
    - [ ] Left a job because of sexual harassment?
    - [ ] Been fired because of sexual harassment?
    - [ ] Not applicable

15. How do you shield yourself from sexual harassment?
    - [ ] I pretend not to notice
    - [ ] I act silly and childish
    - [ ] I adopt a cool guarded manner
    - [ ] I dress with extreme modesty
    - [ ] I flaunt my wedding ring
    - [ ] I've never had to cope with it

16. What is your approximate annual salary?
    - [ ] Less than $5,000
    - [ ] $5,000 to $10,000
    - [ ] $10,001 to $15,000
    - [ ] $15,001 to $25,000
    - [ ] More than $25,000

17. What is your marital status?
    - [ ] Single
    - [ ] Living with a man
    - [ ] Married, first time
    - [ ] Remarried
    - [ ] Separated
    - [ ] Divorced
    - [ ] Widowed

18. What is the highest level of education you have completed?
- [ ] Primary school
- [ ] Secondary school
- [ ] Some university
- [ ] University graduate
- [ ] Some graduate work
- [ ] Advanced degree

19. Where do you live?
- [ ] Major NZ city (Name:)
- [ ] Town (Name:)
- [ ] Small country town (Name:)
- [ ] Rural district (Name:)

If you have also sent a response to the survey in the *Public Service Journal*, mark here [ ]

SEND REPLIES TO:
Committee on Women
The Treasury
Private Bag
WELLINGTON

Adapted from an article in the Public Service *Journal, March 1981, pp.12–13*

Leaflet (Ephemera B Women 1981, ATL)

8.4. Making the Connections
Feminists for the Environment (1981)

We believe that narrow definitions of feminist issues are no longer sufficient. The environment is a feminist issue because man's (sic) exploitation of the environment and man's oppression of women are closely interconnected. We cannot separate the violence done to nature from the violence done to ourselves. Men's conquering of nature, straightening of rivers, filling of estuaries, exploiting of resources, controlling, penetrating, drilling, reclaiming and subduing is part of a chain reaction that begins from their oppression of women: the burning of the witches, the takeover of childbirth, the binding of women's feet, the savage enfibulation practices, and rape.

Virginia Woolf made a connection between sexism (oppression at home) and war (oppression abroad); as she saw it, the two were inextricably linked. We extend her analysis to include man's exploitation of the environment; an act of the imposition of will rather than an act of understanding, respect, and working with.

We hesitate to say that women are innately more in touch with nature because of their biological makeup; this seems to us to stereotype women and deny men the possibility for growth. Rather we find a connection with nature for two reasons:

(1) Identification. We receive and have received the same treatment – abuse and exploitation.

(2) Because as bystanders, we perceive things more clearly.

Women have not been the destroyers, the warfarers, for century after century; instead we

have been involved in birth and nurturing. Hence we perceive the choices more clearly than men. Because we do not have a vested interest in preserving the status quo, we are more free to articulate new directions. If there is to be a hopeful future for the planet Earth, then those people who are in touch with growth, rebirth and nurturing must lead the way. At present those people are ourselves: women.

We cannot narrow down our definitions of what will make a better world. It is not just a world where we can control our fertility, get adequate child care and cease to be discriminated against for being lesbians. It is also a world where aggressive acts such as the aerial spraying of 2,4,5-T no longer take place, where the integrity of living ecosystems is respected, where co-operation rather than exploitation is emphasised, where we participate in decisions about our future, and where the power base is localised, not centralised.

The mind-set that results in the rape of the Clutha is the same that batters women and overrides their rights. The imposition of nuclear power stations and the denigrating of child care are connected.

The Issues

Power
New Zealand is at the cross-roads. The government is now making decisions which will drive us deeper into the HE (Hyper-expansionist) future. The National Development Act was passed to speed large scale industrial development without the 'interference' of grass-roots participation (grass-roots includes women!).

making the connections

We believe that narrow definitions of feminist issues are no longer sufficient. The environment is a feminist issue because man's (sic) exploitation of the environment and man's oppression of women are closely interconnected. We cannot separate the violence done to nature from the violence done to ourselves. Men's conquering of nature, straightening of rivers, filling of estuaries, exploiting of resources, controlling, penetrating, drilling, reclaiming and subduing is part of a chain reaction that begins from their oppression of women: the burning of the witches, the takeover of childbirth, the binding of women's feet, the savage entibulation practices, and rape.

Virginia Woolf made a connection between sexism (oppression at home) and war (oppression abroad); as she saw it, the two were inextricably linked. We extend her analysis to include man's exploitation of the environment; an act of the imposition of will rather than an act of understanding, respect, and working with.

We hesitate to say that women are innately more in touch with nature because of their biological makeup; this seems to us to stereotype women and deny men the possibility for growth. Rather we find a connection with nature for two reasons:

(1) Identification. We receive and have received the same treatment - abuse and exploitation.
(2) Because as bystanders, we perceive things more clearly.

Women have not been the destroyers, the warfarers, for century after century; instead we have been involved in birth and nurturing. Hence we perceive the choices more clearly than men. Because we do not have a vested interest in preserving the status quo, we are more free to articulate new directions. If there is to be a hopeful future for the planet Earth, then those people who are in touch with growth, rebirth and nurturing must lead the way. At present those people are ourselves: women.

We cannot narrow down our definitions of what will make a better world. It is not just a world where we can control our fertility, get adequate child care and cease to be discriminated against for being lesbians. It is also a world where aggressive acts such as the aerial spraying of 2,4,5-T no longer take place, where the integrity of living ecosystems is respected, where co-operation rather than exploitation is emphasised, where we participate in decisions about our future, and where the power base is localised, not centralised.

The mind-set that results in the rape of the Clutha is the same that batters women and overrides their rights. The imposition of nuclear power stations and the denigrating of child care are connected.

Broadsheet produced by Feminists for the Environment, an Auckland group, in 1981. *Ephemera Collection, Alexander Turnbull Library (Ephemera B Women 1981)*

This path means a second aluminium smelter, maybe a nickel smelter, an extended steel mill, more exploitation of native forests, exporting of our coal and Maui gas, and conversion of these resources into fuel for the private motor car instead of improving public transport systems. It means vast sums of money and greater multinational control. It means faster destruction of the environment. It means consolidation of centralised male power. It means women's voice will be even fainter than it is now.

The alternative SHE (Sane Humane Ecological) scenario favours both women and the environment. It is the path towards decentralisation, where small industries and self-sufficiency are encouraged. This 'small is beautiful' path tends to equalise power and encourage positive humanitarian values. Women must resist the HE scenario and insist upon the SHE.

War

$1,000,000 is spent every minute in the world on military activities; the stockpiles of weapons are large enough to kill every woman, child and man 20 times over.

It is the nature of the weapons developed and refined since World War II which endangers life on this planet as never before.

To prevent war by removing the instruments of war is not enough. Prevention of war demands a change in attitude towards people, resources and conflict. Women have a clearer view, a better chance at identifying new directions not only in the areas of personal and collective liberation, but also in the resolution of conflict and the care of the environment.

Town Planning

The structure of our cities reflects the split between home and (paid) work. Women are expected to put down roots and raise children in suburbs which lack transport systems, access to work and child care opportunities, and support facilities. Here, they are invisible to the decision-makers in the centres. Until there is integration of home, work and community life, women will remain victims of the planning process.

Pollution

Women and children are particularly susceptible to certain types of pollution, for example, nuclear pollution, agricultural chemicals such as 2,4,5-T and lead in petrol. Women must have

a strong voice on these issues. For too long we have been content to leave such questions largely in the hands of the scientists. It is now clear that the effect on human health of very low levels of physical insult cannot be ascertained by the scientific method. Lack of scientific evidence should not be taken as proof of safety.

Consumerism

Women have been turned into a captive consumer market through psychological oppression which gives us a view of ourselves as inferior.

Hence we have been easy victims for marketers who sell cosmetic goods to 'brighten up' the exteriors of ourselves and our homes. There is a connection between the consumerism that damages the environment and the consumerism that damages ourselves. We have enormous power to boycott environmentally and personally damaging products, to say *no* to needless consumption and to the manipulation of women.

Technology

Women must take their rightful place in the development and control of technology. We must ensure that the technologies chosen for society are on a human scale, protect our independence from centralised control, and encourage personal fulfilment.

Work

Women's traditional work is both unpaid and undervalued. In the paid work force the position of women is being threatened by economic restructuring and new developments in technology, such as the silicon chip.

The work ethic is not sustainable either from an environmental, social or economic perspective. We must reassess the relationship between work and income. We must share the work available, making sure it is socially just, ecologically sound, and fulfilling for women as well as for men.

Strategy and Tactics

We wish to work differently from other environmental organisations. Rather than duplicate their work we intend to:

– Highlight the feminist perspective on current issues;
– Mobilise grass-roots involvement of women on key issues, e.g. communicating to women that the second aluminium smelter proposal

concerns *them* directly; and
– Take up issues that have not been given priority by other groups.

This is the outcome of a year's reading, thinking

and discussion by a small group of women meeting in Auckland.

Leaflet, Auckland, 1981 (Ephemera B Women 1981, ATL)

8.5. Miss Wgtn Meat Market (1982)

On July 2 at Oliver's Cabaret the final of the Miss Wellington Beauty Contest will be held.

Meat markets of this kind, at which women's bodies are paraded and judged, are offensive to a great number of women. Beauty contests do not just degrade the individual women who enter them; they affect all women.

Our society puts tremendous pressure on women to measure up to commercially prescribed standards of cosmetic beauty. The majority of women do not have the time or money to mould themselves to fit the advertising world's image of an attractive woman, and are therefore made to feel inferior.

Beauty contests must be viewed in context of a society which conditions us from an early age to think that women are weak, passive, pretty ornaments who have no minds of their own. These attitudes are rammed down us every day in the form of advertisements, TV

programmes and in the media. Beauty contests are just one more mechanism which keep women in their place.

The attitude that women are just objects to be used at a male's will for sexual pleasure is so widespread that rape and physical abuse of women are excused in the courts and the woman is somehow blamed for exciting men's 'uncontrollable desires' or criticised for doing such provocative acts as walking home at night.

Women and men who oppose the exploitation of women should protest against the Miss Wellington Beauty Contest as a manifestation of the way commercial interests work to continue women's oppression as second class citizens.

PICKET: FRIDAY JULY 2, 7.30pm OLIVER'S CABARET, LLOYD ST, MOUNT VICTORIA.

Leaflet (Ephemera A Women 1982, ATL)

8.6. National New Zealand Women's Health Network Conference (1982)

Venues

Friday Sept 17: Professional Symposium Hotel Intercontinental (Ballroom)
Saturday and Sunday Sept 18/19:
North Shore Teachers' Training College (Women Only)

Overseas Speaker:
Two Women from the Boston Women's Health Collective

Statement of principles

Statement of Principles of New Zealand Women's Health Conference. Organised by New Zealand Women's Health Network.

'Knowledge is power. To get control of your own life and destiny is the first and most important task. But it begins with getting control of your body everywhere in your life.'

The Women's Health Movement aims to provide women with the means to control

and own their own bodies and thus to begin to be free to own and control their own lives. Through our long history of oppression, the patriarchy (the system of sexism, female oppression and male dominance), has used our bodies as a focus for control. Our bodies are our most basic and precious resource, yet women lack basic information about them. The special position of reproduction has been especially used as a tool of oppression.

The long term goals of the Women's Health Movement can be seen as:

1. Gaining control of our lives, our bodies and our reproductive processes.
2. Making the health system one which is fully representative and responsive to the needs of women (and of all people).
3. To make fundamental changes in the social system which creates inequality between people.

4. To educate all women so that they can demand their consumer rights in medicine.
5. To ensure that knowledge, experience and good health care are always available to women.

The Women's Health Movement has a definite ideology – that is a guiding set of principles that governs its everyday practice.

1. That women have the right to control their own bodies in every way. This means that each woman must be given all possible information and that all decisions must be made by that woman on the basis of informed consent.
2. That the conventional doctor patient relationship, existing as it does within a framework of professional male determined and technologically orientated health care, is exploitive and oppressive of women. Therefore, alternative structures must be developed which do not revolve around patriarchal structures.
3. That women themselves must develop and operate these alternative systems of health care in order to meet their own need.

Health is one issue which unites all women, cutting across ethnic, socio/economic and political boundaries. All women share a set of common experiences – menopause, menstruation, the need for and problems of fertility control, pregnancy and birth. Women must seek information and help for healthy functioning from the medical services attuned to a disease model – to illness. Additionally, the medical/health services are largely administered and controlled by men, whose socio-economic status as well as their gender, remove them from the experiences of the female population. The prevailing view of female behaviour and physiology is not complimentary to women, their behaviour and illnesses are judged psychosomatic, and professionals judge women to be less mentally healthy than men to begin with.

Programme

FRIDAY – PROFESSIONAL SYMPOSIUM
Topics of concern to women will be presented in a symposia format.
CHAIR: DIEDRE MILNE

8.30 a.m.: Registration (Ballroom)

9-10 a.m.: Women's involvement in Primary Health Care (presentation of research findings).
10 a.m.: Morning tea
10.30-11.30 a.m.: Mental Health
11.30-12.30 p.m.: Menopause and Menstruation

12.30-2 p.m.: Lunch

2-3 p.m.: Violence Against Women
3-4 p.m.: Research on Women
(meal cost extra)

FRIDAY EVENING – WINE AND CHEESE
7.30 p.m. at North Shore Teachers Training College (Akoranga Drive).

NATIONAL WOMEN'S HEALTH CONFERENCE
For a variety of reasons men will be totally excluded from the Friday evening, Sat/Sun sessions of this conference.

CONFERENCE CHAIRPERSON: SANDI HALL

SATURDAY
8.30-9.30 a.m.: Enrolments, tea and coffee
9.30-9.45 a.m.: Announcements and organisation
9.45-10.45 a.m.: Guest speakers
11-11.30 a.m.: Tea and coffee
11.30-1 p.m.: FIRST WORKSHOP SESSION
1-2.30 p.m.: Lunch and active displays
2.30-4.30 p.m.: SECOND WORKSHOP SESSION
4.30-7 p.m.: Tea break (tea not provided)
7.30 p.m.: PARTY – WOMEN'S MUSIC

SUNDAY (SUFFRAGETTE DAY)
9.30 a.m.: tea/coffee
10-11.30 a.m.: THIRD WORKSHOP SESSION
11.30-1 p.m.: Symposiums on creating change.
1-2 p.m.: Lunch
2-3 p.m.: Time for talking/consultations/future organising/geographic planning
3-4 p.m.: Final session
(meal costs extra)

WORKSHOPS – Validity of feminist therapy; staying healthy; lesbian health care; Maori women/third world women; assertiveness; adoption; abortion; violence against women; incest; coping with a handicapped child; disabilities; occupational health; sexuality/masturbation; vaginal infections; V.D.; rape; breasts; nutrition; menopause; menstruation/P.M.T.; childbirth; mental health; contraception; anger; guilt; patients' rights; fitness for health; alternative health such as homeopathy; iridology; bach flowers; herbs; spirituality; massage; acupuncture; reflexology; counselling; colour therapy; osteopathy; naturopathy, etc.

Registration form, National New Zealand Women's Health Network Conference, Auckland, 17–19 September 1982 (Ephemera A Women 1982, ATL)

8.7. First Yearly Meeting of the New Zealand Women's Political Party (1982)

Philosophy

The New Zealand Women's Political Party is committed to seeking successful answers to the common and individual concerns of women and of the community at large, putting aside with finality the possibility of war as a solution.

The Party affirms the rights of all women to choice and opportunity, including the right to control their own fertility.

The New Zealand Women's Political Party stands for the full representation of women by women in parliament, to speak freely and powerfully on the rights of all women.

Registration:
Friday 26/11/82
At: 'JUST DESSERTS'
  7 Airedale Street, City.
  Ph: 799 897
  From 3 p.m. onwards

Saturday and Sunday:
Venue: Auckland University
Fee $20.00 It includes morning tea, lunch and afternoon tea both Saturday and Sunday.

Covers the cost of the meeting, venue and creche facilities. Includes $1.00 interim membership fee, the actual membership fee to be determined at the meeting.

Saturday night: 8 p.m.
Revue by Renée Taylor. Followed by a women's concert. Venue to be advised and cost is extra to the registration fee. For members with membership cards available once membership fee determined the concert will cost $2.00

For others, price yet to be set and you will be advised at the meeting.
Open to Public.

First Yearly Meeting of the New Zealand Women's Political Party, Auckland, 26–28 November 1982 (Ephemera A Women 1982, ATL)

8.8. Nuclear Free and Independent Pacific Women for Peace (1984)

Nuclear Free and Independent Pacific

Te Reo Oranga O Te Moana Nui A Kiwi

Fakaata E Pasifika Ua Fakalavelave

Tu Galala E Na Pasifika

Pasifik bilong ol manmeri Pasifik tasol

Faaloto Pasefika

Hakologo Pahesika

'We fear for the life of this planet, our earth. We are young and old, we work at a variety of jobs – we are all daughters and sisters. We are in the hands of men whose power and wealth have separated them from the reality of daily life and from the imagination. "We will protect you . . ." they say. We have never been so endangered. We are right to be afraid.'
(extract from the Unity Statement by the Women's Pentagon Action Group)

As mothers, daughters and sisters, we do not believe that the deployment of nuclear weapons throughout the world can ever be a way of achieving peace. We reject the arguments put forward by our own and other governments, that nuclear weapons act as a 'deterrent' to war, and that the build-up of nuclear and other weapons is necessary for 'world peace'.

It is becoming increasingly clear that the superpowers are more interested in maintaining their own power bases than they are in maintaining the quality of life in the world.

We are finding that we cannot challenge the nuclear mentality without also challenging the mentality that counts things more than people, considers one culture superior to another, condones violence and rape against women.

It does not matter who presses the button first. We cannot afford to wait for some computer error to trigger a nuclear 'accident' to prove that this nuclear madness affects us all. For ourselves and for our children we say NO to the nuclear mentality.

We are part of the Pacific

There are now nine independent Pacific nations: Western Samoa, Nauru, Fiji, Tonga, Papua, the Solomon Islands, Tuvalu (formerly Ellice Islands), Kiribati (Gilbert Islands) and Vanuatu (New Hebrides).

The rest of the Pacific remains colonized to a greater or lesser degree by France, the UK, the USA, Indonesia, Chile, and Australia and New Zealand (themselves the result of colonial expansion).

Some like East Timor have no say in their future, so violently have they been suppressed. Others like the Kanak of New Caledonia, already a minority in their own country, are being systematically deprived of a voice.

Whether their colonial past stretches back 400 years, as does that of the Micronesian Islands, or is the result of annexation after the Second World War, like the Marshall Islands, all have suffered under colonial rule and continue to pay for the mentality of colonial expansion.

From the first use of the islands' natural resources to refit and supply trade ships, through to the development of those resources as trade goods: copra, bananas, cocoa and cheap labour; and the imposition of missionaries; from the exploitation of their mineral resources as in nickel rich New Caledonia, and the wealth of their seas, to the development of the area as a strategic military playground for testing nuclear weapons and dumping nuclear wastes; the Pacific still suffers.

The Pacific as a Military Playground

To imagine that the Pacific and Aotearoa/New Zealand can somehow remain above and beyond the power plays of the US and the USSR is naive. In May 1983 at the Williamsburg Summit, the US, Japan, France and other industrialised nations with interests in the Pacific, recognised that the Pacific is a potential proving ground for the forces of both superpowers, as currently both have access but neither has complete control.

Both superpowers are loud in their professed abhorrence of nuclear war, yet the prevalent US/NATO doctrine is one which predicts 'conventional' wars escalating into nuclear war deliberately or accidentally, on a limited scale. There is no reason to suppose that this view is not shared by Soviet military strategists.

France, also a nuclear presence in the Pacific and the principal colonial force in the region, maintains garrisons in both Tahiti and New Caledonia as well as at Mururoa. Their justifi-

cation for nuclear development and testing is that they are an independent force in the conflict between the superpowers, yet their operations to date have coincided with American interests with a complete disregard for the interests and well-being of the people of the Pacific.

New Zealand's existing role

New Zealand currently performs two roles for the US Government:

* providing small but vital spying and surveillance facilities such as:
  The UK/USA signals intelligence station near Waiouru; Tangimoana and the five RNZAF P3 Orions used to spot and target Soviet submarines.

* setting up a flexible 'Ready Reaction Force' which can be deployed quickly and sustained in the Pacific, South East Asia and the Southern Oceans to act independently or with New Zealand's allies to further New Zealand's 'wider interests and concerns'.

The justification for these operations and other bases is an unspecified Soviet threat in the Pacific and Asia. It is also the justification for joint operations such as: Cope Thunder – practising bombing runs into North Korea; Rimpac – a naval bombardment practice of the island Kaho'olawe in Hawaii; Operation Kangaroo – a counter insurgency exercise held in Australia, and Operation Northern Safari – a similar exercise recently conducted by New Zealand forces on Great Barrier Island.

Who and what is being threatened

The link between economic exploitation and military expansion is too well established to be disregarded. To preserve the existing order our government and others are prepared to suppress newly independent and emerging indigenous Pacific nations and to risk the future of all of us.

It is our lives and the future of our children that are being threatened in order to preserve the 'strategic balance' of the Pacific. It is the claim to self-determination by people in the Pacific that is being threatened in order to preserve a vast war machine that serves the interests of a very few.

Women for Peace

Women for Peace is a coalition of women from diverse life experiences who have been drawn together by a common concern about the arms race. We are a grass roots movement that encompasses the difference between women; of class, race, and sexuality.

Aims:

- to add our voices to the growing international women's peace movement;
- to be an action group – organise activities and provide information about the issue;
- to act as a support group for women acting for peace in other structures and organisations;
- to draw parallels between the nuclear threat/oppression and the poverty caused by the arms race.

We not only oppose nuclear stockpiling and the arms race but the intertwined injustices and

oppressions caused by this. In solidarity with indigenous people of the Pacific we wish to dismantle existing nuclear weapons systems which have disrupted and destroyed land and social conditions.

As women we do not see this as a single issue. If we turn our backs to the present nuclear madness we will also close our eyes to the systems that oppress – those systems that actually give rise to the nuclear threat.

We do not want any part of any nuclear system to be helped by us or our money or by any political system to which we belong.

Pamphlet, Wellington, 1984 (Ephemera A Women 1984, ATL)

8.9. Fight Violence Against Women
Women Against Pornography (1984)

Picket outside the 'Video Shack', Friday 27 July, 7 pm, Manners Street!

The contrast is at once established. The audience – made up almost entirely of men – line up in a formidable wall of shirts and ties, sweaters, beer mugs and dollar bills. The women cavort before them, one dressed as 'good girl' nurse, the other the 'bad girl' school teacher disciplinarian.

When they enter the kiddy pool – 6 inches full of red jelly – they become the same. Their clothes off, they represent Everywoman. Breasts, buttocks, vaginas and legs are their being. The women 'wrestle' with each other to the delight of the audience. Their bodies covered in red jelly could be covered in blood, so similar is its colour and consistency on the T.V. screen in front of us. At once, the combination of pornographic exposure and violence is established.

The above description is of a pornographic video which has NOT been seized by the police.

The Video Retailers Association is presently circulating a nation-wide petition calling for individuals to have the 'right' to watch what they choose in their homes. The petition was in response to the seizure by police of some 'Electric Blue' and 'Red Tape' video tapes.

Women Against Pornography challenges the 'right' of anyone to legally be able to view material which degrades, humiliates, and promotes violence against women and children.

Rape and murder of women isn't pornography?

(1) Denis Amiss, Secretary of the V.R.A. – 'The very worst material under question at the moment would not in most people's minds constitute pornography.'

- Much of the stock in video shops is pornographic. The word 'pornography', from the Greek, means literally the *depiction of prostitutes* or *female sexual slaves*. This is as opposed to the word 'erotica', from the Greek word 'eros' meaning *love* or *mutual passion*.

- The following are two examples of video tapes available in shops in N.Z. today. The first involves a gang of two men and a woman who kidnap a 'school girl' – a woman dressed in school uniform, buckled shoes, hair in pig-tails, and who speaks in a voice which tells the audience that she is meant to be around 9 years old. The entire film centres around this 'child' teaser, who is eventually raped, and who is portrayed as enjoying it.

The second video is of a woman who takes a job as a cab driver so she can indulge in as many sexual encounters as possible. It involves scene after scene of crass sex and pseudo lesbianism. With her as narrator, she recounts her first sexual experience – which can be construed as nothing less than rape – and of which she tells the viewers she enjoyed. The bad acting, the crassness, and the absurdity of the theme, cannot possibly prepare you for the final scene. She is

227

bashed semi-unconscious and then says 'I figured it would happen to a girl that lived the way I did.' After tying her up, she exclaims that she was 'brought to the depth of degradation, the bottom of the hole'. As she is raped she says she is 'beyond caring – I realised that only this man could give me what I wanted.' The scene moves on. 'I felt his hands around my neck – I was being strangled. I was being punished – if only I had chosen a different road.' The final camera shots are impossible to describe in words as they appeared on film. The camera moves to a picture of a naked woman on the wall, over to her face – mouth open, eyes glazed, then finally to her breasts, and crotch. There is total silence, and it is only in the final moments that the realisation sinks in – she is dead. Her final words relinquish her rapist and murderer from any responsibility – and relinquish too, any sense of shame and guilt that men who enjoy such brutality to women might just possibly feel.

Good 'entertainment'?

(2) Amiss – 'We don't want to be seen to be supporting pornography or excessively violent videos. Explicit horror or sex scenes might make videos off limits for some. Others might regard them as good entertainment.'

— Effects on children who watch video 'nasties' in Britain included nightmares, an increase in violent behaviour, physical illness, and even death in one case, literally of fright.

— Pornography has been shown to contribute to anti-women attitudes and behaviour in adult men, including rape and wife beating. Ex-Auckland Task Force chief Gideon Tait wrote in his book *Never Back Down*, 'It is a matter of police record rather than opinion that a great many offenders convicted of sex crimes possess libraries of pornographic books . . .'

'The responsibility lies with the head of the household'!

(3) Amiss on video audiences – 'The responsibility lies with the head of the household – normally if they are responsible citizens, which we've no reason to doubt, they would never allow others to watch them.' And, 'Retailers are very responsible.'

— W.A.P. have been told of two cases where

young children have arrived home from Video shops with 'Electric Blue' videos – to the horror of their parents.

— Recently a press report stated that a man was convicted for forcing girls of 12 and 13 to watch a pornographic video. We know of a case in Wellington where a young girl was forced to watch a 'Snuff' movie. (Where women are actually tortured and then killed.)

— In Britain 40% of children over 6 years have seen one or more video 'nasties'. 44% of parents couldn't guarantee their kids would not get access to them in other people's homes.

— Given the huge market for 'Snuff' movies in New Zealand, it is obvious to us that any talk of 'responsibility' is a smoke-screen. If men were 'responsible' then there would be no market for pornography.

Censorship? or demanding our right to dignity and safety?

(4) Amiss – 'It's their choice, not for us to dictate.'

— The censorship argument is a red herring. We speak of outlawing pornography in the same way that murder, assault, or *threats* of murder or assault, and defamation are outlawed. Pornography depicts and promotes all these things. There is also a law against inciting racial hatred – women must have that same legal protection.

Privacy in the home – freedom for whom?

(5) Amiss – 'This is clearly an area of in-home entertainment.'

— It makes no difference whether men watch pornography in a picture theatre or their own homes. The effects on women and children are the same. Rape, battering and child sexual abuse are all more likely to occur in the home than out of it, and are less likely to be reported to the police. Thousands of women and children do not have the right to safety and dignity in their homes, why is men's 'right' to pornography so fundamental?

— Individuals don't have the 'right' to take drugs in the privacy of their home, where is the cry of 'censorship' of individual right's in this area?

— The acceptance of men's right to watch pornography in the home has resulted in Hollywood producing pornography speci-

A Place to Stand

fically for Television. One can turn on T.V. at 8pm in the States and watch it. How will children be restricted from viewing it?

Profit before women's rights!

(6) The V.R.A. claim that they are not to blame for men's consumption of pornography. It is however, hardly in their interest to outlaw pornography or restrict it when they make so much money from it.

— Also, pornography is not only a mirror of many men's attitudes to women and children, but it also endorses and promotes those anti-women ideas. In Quebec, Canada, school nurses tell of young boys asking if it's true that for a woman to have an orgasm she has to be raped or beaten first.

Women Against Pornography is involved in a campaign to outlaw all pornography. This does not mean the banning of all remotely sexual material or nudity per se.

We support the depiction of the human body and human sexuality, however explicit, in a way which enhances the dignity of all human beings.

Pornography both promotes, and is itself, violence against women. It is plain that porno-graphic video tapes can hardly encourage positive sexuality, respect for women, or concern at the high incidence of violence against women by men.

What can you do?

• Support our picket. 7 pm outside the 'VIDEO SHACK', in Manners Street, on Friday, 27 July.

• Write to Members of Parliament, newspapers, Customs, Internal Affairs and the Police Department.

• Make your opposition to the Video Retailers' Association campaign and their present promotion and selling of pornography known to them.

• Tell your friends, etc. what we are doing, show them this leaflet.

• Donate money to Women Against Pornography – unlike the Video Association we do not have enormous resources, neither do we get equal access to the media.

To find out more about Women Against Pornography, please write to P.O. Box 475, Wellington.

Pamphlet, Wellington, 1984 (Ephemera B Women 1984, ATL)

8.10. We're Fighting for Our Lives – Against Pornography Women Against Pornography (1985)

MARCH – JUNE 7TH FROM THE LIBRARY TO PIGEON PARK (ASSEMBLE FOR 7PM START)

Why a march?

1. Women Against Pornography (WAP) had its beginning at a 'Reclaim the Night' march in January, 1983. It is appropriate that we launch this major campaign in a way which will publicly demonstrate the level of support its policies have gained since we began two and a half years ago.

2. The route of the march will take us from the Wellington Central Public Library; around the streets of central Wellington, to identify and reclaim places where women have been raped or subjected to the forms of sexual violence and exploitation (sex shops, strip clubs, video shops, areas like the Basin Reserve); and to Pigeon Park where we will celebrate our strength and confirm our level of commitment.

3. By marching together we can demonstrate and affirm our solidarity with each other

and with all women who are struggling against oppression.

Creche facilities will be available but the final details are yet to be arranged.

A pre-march film screening at 5.30pm is also being organised by WAP. This will take place in the Library Theatre, June 7.

Why are you invited?

1. All pornography, from sexist advertising to 'girlie' photographs to snuff movies, creates and endorses a climate of contempt towards women as individual people and as a class. The fact that men conceive it in vast quantities shows it has a ready audience and that it mirrors the attitudes that many men have about women. Those attitudes in turn allow all other forms of sexual exploitation and degradation of women and children to take place.

2. The fight against pornography, and against the attitudes it instils, should be part of the

229

agenda of all groups who are working for the liberation of women. In the same way, WAP is involved in assisting and supporting the causes of those other groups, and welcomes them to take part in the march and to use it as a focus for their own demands. We hope the march will include women from any group which acknowledges the connections that link pornography with anti-woman attitudes and with the injustices that are suffered as a result of those attitudes.

What are the issues?

For WAP, the fundamental issue is pornography, which we identify as woman-hating defamation and propaganda. Our commitment is to eradicate all forms of pornography and to work to change the social attitudes which provide a market for its lies. But that primary concern quickly spills over into other issues:

Currently we are demanding immediate action by Parliament:

1. To scrap Graeme Lee's Video Classification Bill – the bill would *force* video importers to label their videos accurately so that consumers of pornography could find exactly what they wanted as quickly as possible. There is no law stopping importers or distributors from doing that at present, and the bill does nothing to set standards which might help prevent pornography coming into the country.
2. To clarify the 'Freedom of Expression' provisions in the Draft Bill of Rights – It needs to be made clear that the balance between the pornographers' 'rights' to freedom of expression, and the rights of women to live freely and safely, protected from the dangers, lies and hatred created by pornography must be weighted in *favour of women*. The present wording of the Bill of Rights simply preserves the current imbalance in favour of the pornographers.
3. To legislate to give women effective redress against the distributors of pornographic material in a way which recognises pornography as a form of sexual harassment, sexual discrimination and class defamation. The Race Relations Act attempts to protect members of racial or ethnic groups from racial defamation. That Act has many shortcomings. We want it improved and extended to protect women from pornography.
4. To legislate to establish:
(a) a single tribunal structure to assess the material which currently comes within the jurisdiction of the Indecent Publications Tribunal, the Internal Affairs Department (film censorship), the Courts (material seized by the police), or Broadcasting House (radio and television programmes and advertisements);
(b) a uniform set of criteria for assessment of the material based on a recognition of the rights of *all* people to be considered and treated as full human beings;
(c) the principle that, where material under assessment contains any depictions of character(s) being subjected to violence, sexual attentions or denigration, the material will be assessed only by Tribunal members of the same gender, race and sexual orientation as the character(s) being depicted.
5. To extend the Sex Education Bill to provide for the introduction into all State and integrated schools, comprehensive education programmes on *all* aspects of human sexuality and relationships and also including assertiveness and physical self-defence training for girls.

A call to action:

If you support these demands, be sure you attend the March on June 7. (The march is for women only, but there may be a men's vigil or other action for mixed groups organised separately. Tel. Tim, – – if you are interested.) In the meantime, we are organising stalls, speak-outs, lobbying, publicity, liaison with other groups, telephone-trees, letter writing, music, street theatre, pickets, leaflets, posters, submissions, newsletters and a host of other activities.

If you can help, come to one of our next meetings:
Wed, April 24, 7.30pm – Newtown Community Health Centre
Wed, May 1, 7.30pm – tel. 893-038 for venue
Wed, May 8, 7.30pm – Newtown C.H.C.
Wed, May 15, 7.30pm – tel. 893-038
Wed, May 22, 7.30pm – Newtown C.H.C.
Wed, May 29, 7.30pm – tel. 893-038
Wed, June 5, 7.30pm – Newtown C.H.C.

OR: Let us know how we can contact your group. Tel. 893-038 (day)

AND: Don't forget DONATIONS to:
WAP, PO Box 475, Wellington

Leaflet, Wellington, 1985 (Ephemera A Women 1985, ATL)

8.11. Policing Pornography – A Repressive Strategy
by Allanah Ryan (1988)

Get your pens out women
It's time to write yet another
submission, this time to the
Committee of Inquiry into
Pornography

While the Inquiry gives a specific focus for the already considerable political activity around pornography, my fear is that it will do nothing more than provide space for a rehearsal of the now familiar call for stricter censorship of 'offensive' material.

What feminists need is an analysis and politics of pornography that is alive to both its oppressive features *and* the opportunities for pleasure that it offers. The dominant feminist approach to pornography, which sees it as a site of unmitigated male power and recommends censorship, is one which must be rejected. I believe there are three questions that must be addressed when examining the issue of pornography. Firstly, how should we define pornography? Secondly, what does pornography do? And finally, what should we do about pornography?

What is pornography?
Feminists are rather fond of distinguishing between pornography (which is bad) and erotica (which is good). However, as Paula Webster has suggested, 'There are no universal or unchanging criteria for drawing the line between acceptable and unacceptable sexual images'. Definitions of pornography and erotica depend more on 'personal taste, moral boundaries, sexual preference, cultural and class biases' than on an objective distinction between 'good' and 'bad' sexual images.

Part of the problem with trying to make hard and fast decisions about what is pornographic and what is erotic is that this approach neglects *how* images are used. We can take for example the hypothetical case in which a group of feminists agree that a particular image is erotic rather than pornographic, but a man on viewing it, jerks off and has negative feelings towards women. Does this mean the image is now pornographic?

The difficulty with trying to 'draw the line' conclusively between pornography and erotica is that it assumes the problem is in the content of the images rather than in their consumption

and the overall context in which they occur. For example, the sexual content of *Lesbian Nuns* is well integrated into the text and it has been well received by the feminist press. However, the same content changed its meaning when it was taken out of context printed in *Forum* as a titillating article. The problem was not with the sexual content per se, but the way that it was used.

In my view there is little point in trying to draw a line conclusively between pornography and erotica, because the line will shift with time and between different people (even different feminists). This is not to abdicate any of the analysis of what it is that pornography does. Rather, it is simply to recognise that there is no definitive distinction that can be held for every situation between a pornographic image and an 'erotic' one.

The most productive way to define pornography is to see it as a cultural product with specific social and historical conditions of existence. In our society pornography can best be understood as sexually explicit material which is designed to arouse its consumers. As Angela Carter so succinctly puts it, 'pornography is propaganda for fucking'.

Part of its appeal is that it is illicit, indeed it thrives on the fact that it is naughty. It is a multimillion dollar industry. It is frequently, although not always, sexist. It is often, but again not always, racist and violent.

As a cultural product it also reflects the other dominant ideological themes of our culture, e.g. fat women are ugly, old people are not sexual, and so on. It can also provide the space for an exploration of sexual identities, desires, practices and pleasures.

What does pornography do?
There are several different theories about what pornography 'does', i.e. what its effects and functions are. The main feminist argument against pornography is that it degrades women, is 'woman-hating' and that it causes violence against women. Much of the empirical evidence used to support these claims has been misinterpreted or exaggerated. Indeed much of what has come to be called the 'effects research' on pornography can be dismissed on methodological and theoretical grounds.

Psychological studies have been used to

231

show that viewing pornography arouses negative feelings in men towards women and that these are translated into aggression against women. Methodologically, many of these studies are weakened by using narrow samples (e.g. young male university students who were often paid for their participation in the research) or the instruments used to measure sexual arousal actually caused 'penile tumescence' (i.e. men 'got it up' without the help of the porn).

However, the most fundamental criticisms are those based on the theoretical inadequacy of the models used. Many of the studies use behaviourist assumptions. People are seen as being passive rather than active in their response to stimuli. In fact, they are thought to be automatons who respond almost mindlessly to any 'anti-social' stimulus.

As Thelma McCormack has argued, this ignores that we are 'continually surrounded by anti-social stimuli and opportunities to which we either do not respond, or if we do, it is in socially acceptable and responsible ways'. Men do not see pornography and simply take on board what is portrayed. Rather, there are many mediating factors that influence what use is made of pornography. There are vast differences between a rugby team watching a porn video to bolster their masculine identity and the same video watched in a family context where the images may be discussed and the messages rejected.

Rape scenes in porn may confirm the sexist views of some men, for others the same scenes may fill them with disgust and horror. Perhaps most importantly, pornography is only one site where sexual values, desires and behaviours are learnt, and it may conflict with ideas generated elsewhere.

It is naive to believe, as some feminists do, that male sexual arousal will be translated into aggression. Adrienne Rich has gone so far as to say that 'when the chord of sexuality is struck in the male psyche, the chord of violence vibrates in response'. Again, in this analysis, there is no account taken of mediating variables which influence behaviour. Content is divorced from context and the selective nature of human responses to images is ignored.

Anti-pornography feminists have not only relied on empirical studies but have advanced the theory that pornography is an important (and some say the most important) mechanism in maintaining male power. Lynne Segal has made a powerful critique of the idea that pornography reflects 'the imperial power of men' (an argument used by Andrea Dworkin, Susan Griffin and implicit in the work of WAP). On the contrary, Segal maintains that pornography has flourished at a time when women's economic independence has increased.

While it cannot be claimed that women have won all the battles, it is nonetheless true that there have been significant gains made by women. In this context pornography represents not so much male power as 'pathetic weakness – a gargantuan need for assurance that, at least in fantasy, women can remain eternally objects for men to use and abuse at will. It is the last bark of the stag at bay'.

Andy Moyle has reflected as a man on the function of pornography and he suggests that 'it works by denying the reality which men know and fear to be true. Sex (for men) is not unproblematic but is beset by complications and anxieties – those of sexual isolation, clumsiness, 'inadequacy', the tension attendant on 'doing it right', of not being or feeling sexually desirable. It is in the space between this anxiety and the fantasy realm of a perfect sexual world that pornography achieves its power'. If Segal and Moyle are correct, then, rather than being a manifestation of men's power, pornography is actually a reflection of sexual anxiety and paranoia.

In addition to claiming that pornography represents the apex of male power, some feminists have argued that pornography objectifies and fragments women's bodies and these processes help sustain female sexual subordination. This analysis, however, simplifies a more complex process.

Objectification is an unavoidable part of everyday life. We are constantly presenting ourselves as objects in the world when, for example, we decide what haircut we want and what clothes to wear. All images (even feminist ones) objectify what they portray. Images are obviously outside of us. In this way they are objects that are available for us to take what action we want with them. There is nothing inherently oppressive in this.

Some feminists have argued that porn, by reducing women to sexual objects, degrades women. And indeed, sexualised images of women's bodies are used everywhere from hard-core pornography to selling cars. This gratuitous use of women's bodies must be resisted.

However, surely women (and men) have a right (and many have a desire) to be sexual objects (i.e., the object of someone else's desire). This is in addition to the right to be sexual subjects where we can pursue our sexual desire for somebody else. In 'real life' it is of course often difficult to separate out when we act as sexual objects or subjects, and the task is to integrate both aspects in our lives.

Associated with the opposition to objectification is the claim that it is bad that pornography fragments women's bodies. The argument is that in the fragmentation of women's bodies, women's 'whole' personality and self is neglected or destroyed. This view maintains that we should desire the 'whole' person. However, I believe it is misguided and naive to claim we can ever know a 'whole' person (including ourselves). And I'm not sure there's anything wrong with fancying somebody on the basis of a fragmented image.

Mandy Merck questions 'Is the appropriate response to all this an insistence that sex can only be represented or conducted between old friends? And why do we often defend intellectual or social characteristics as less 'objectifying' than physical ones? Is it wrong to fancy someone because of the colour of their eyes – and right if they agree with you about this article?'

These critical comments about the effects of pornography should not imply that I believe pornography has no social impact or that it isn't frequently sexist. Clearly, pornography uses stereotyped images of men and women and it often endorses a view of sexuality which oppresses women. However, the process is a complex one that cannot be reduced to a notion that 'pornography is the theory, rape is the practice'.

What should be recognised is that pornography may use codes that endorse female sexual subordination. For example, the idea that women need men to feel complete, or that rape is a pleasurable experience for women. The point is that many of these codes are also found in non-pornographic material, and it is the codes we must reject.

There is a quote from Harlequin romance that I'm fond of using because it illustrates very clearly some of the same codes that are found in porn.

She had never felt so helpless or so completely at the mercy of another human being, a being who could snap the slender column of her body with one squeeze of a steel-clad arm. No taste of tenderness softened the harsh presence of his mouth on hers, there was only a savagely punishing intenseness of purpose that cut off her

breath until her senses reeled and her body sagged against the granite hardness of his. He released her wrists, seeming to know that they would hang helplessly at her sides and his hand moved to the small of her back to exert pressure that crushed her soft outlines to the unyielding dominance of his, and left her in no doubt as to the force of his masculinity.

This view of male and female sexuality is obviously sexist. It works on a narrow range of appropriate behaviours for men and women and it endorses the view that female sexuality is passive and opposed to aggressive male sexuality. What is more, women consume this kind of romantic fiction in huge quantities.

Some feminists have argued that romantic fiction is women's 'pornography' and that it needs to be addressed as strenuously as male porn. The eroticisation of domination in this kind of fiction may have as much, or even more, influence as pornography, on the form that oppressive sexual relations take.

However, while we might object to the messages that come through romantic fiction, we must be aware that women don't simply and uncritically absorb these messages. Many *feminists* enjoy this form of fiction because it offers a welcome escape from the hard slog of being 'strong' and 'in control'. In the fantasy of romance the reader can allow herself to be swept off her feet and have someone stronger 'make it better'.

Unfortunately, the role of fantasy in pornography has been largely ignored by feminists. Where it has been discussed, the tendency is to see a relatively uncomplicated connection between fantasy and reality. In fact the connections between images, fantasy, 'reality' and behaviour are extremely complex. If there was a direct connection between fantasy and reality then women who have rape fantasies would enjoy actual physical rape (which they clearly do not), and men who fantasize about being dominated by women would make themselves slaves for women (again a rare occurrence).

McCormack suggests that pornography can induce arousal and fantasies in both men and women. 'The fantasy may act as a substitute for an overt sexual act; it may act as an enhancement of sexual activity; it may lead to sexual activity . . . There is no systematic evidence that people copy what they see or read about in pornography. On the contrary, there is strong evidence that sex patterns, once established, are as difficult to change as any other social habits, and, in addition, there are strong inhibiting factors that intervene to keep our responses within the cultural norms.' Fantasy, therefore, cannot be taken as an indicator of actual behaviour. I am sure I'm not alone in fantasizing about acts and situations that in reality I would run a mile from. But as fantasies they serve as a means to explore themes of power and control, submission and domination, and autonomy and dependence in my sexual life.

Similarly, Segal comments that fantasies don't simply reflect reality, but rather, 'they draw upon all manner of infantile sexual wishes, active and passive, loving and hating, all the way back to our very earliest feelings of desire and pleasure in childhood'.

In summary, what pornography does is provide the space for a rehearsal of cultural attitudes about sexuality. In this respect it works using sexist (and other oppressive) codes. However, porn is only one place where we learn about sex. The sexual codes found in romantic fiction, advertising, TV drama etc, are also powerful influences on the cultural and individual forms of sexuality. What is important is to analyse and respond to the specific context and use of sexist sexual codes.

What is to be done about pornography?

If pornography is to be understood in the way that has been outlined here then the call for censorship is entirely inappropriate. Censorship will not deal with non-explicit sexual images and text that may be oppressive. As a process it closes off debate about sexuality rather than allowing space for its exploration. It ends up attacking sex rather than sexism. And censorship has not historically (and is not likely to in the immediate future), worked in favour of gay, lesbian or feminist sexual images.

A rejection of censorship does not mean that there is no work to be done on the issue. There are some general principles that should be applied to the question of a politics surrounding pornography. These are part of a project that has been called radical pluralist democracy. Briefly, this is a politics that accepts that there are many different forms of sexual expression. It maintains that this diversity is a good thing and that institutional arrangements should be made to safeguard differences.

What distinguishes this approach from a libertarian or liberal one is that it recognises the structural limits on individual and collective choices, and it works at loosening these. A radical pluralist position does not assume equality, but analyses the oppressive features of society and seeks a democratic approach to resolving conflicts. This should allow for community participation in decision-making.

So, decisions about what are 'good' or 'bad' sexual acts (or images) should be based on guide-lines that take into account context, consent and the quality of the relationship involved. This form of politics would not automatically assume that every depiction of female sexual availability was bad, but would work towards reducing the *over-abundance* of images that showed women being sexually available for men.

There are two strands to a strategy around pornography. Firstly, there *is* much that can and should be done to eliminate sexist porn and sexual codes found elsewhere. Secondly, the production of radical and exciting new sexual images must be fostered. In terms of getting rid of the 'bad' stuff, protest directed against particular manifestations of sexist material may be useful if it has an educational component.

Protest might seem like too little, too late, but it has the advantage over censorship of being democratic rather than authoritarian. It allows for a process whereby the community is involved in a public way with decisions about what is, and is not, acceptable.

On the legal front, stronger sexual harassment legislation is a good way to confront the gratuitous use of sexual images of women in workplaces. In this way, pornographic shots included in anatomy slides at med. schools, etc., can be challenged through a public process. This type of action is important because it encourages confrontation and negotiation about what is acceptable. It is also more likely to bring about broader cultural change than punitive and restrictive laws that seek to ban images at the outset.

Perhaps the most effective way to counter offensive sexual images is through creating alternatives. Many feminist, gay and lesbian cultural workers are producing new images. This is important work. However, it is constantly undermined by censorship, and is largely ineffective because of the monopoly that the porn empire, and other media, have on the market.

This implies that an important struggle should be around the democratisation of the cultural industry. In particular, it will be necessary to work towards a democratisation of arts funding. It is important that alternative and radical explorations of sexuality have the funds to be produced and widely distributed.

Sex education must also be widely available – but our current understandings of this have to be broadened. Schools may not be the best places for the subject and a broader community approach needs to be used.

The content of sex education should not only be about reproduction and relationships but should include a component that explores the more directly 'sexual' sphere and uses sexual images to explore identities and pleasures. The contradictions, ambiguities, pains and pleasures surrounding sex have to be addressed in a way that opens up possibilities.

To conclude, to eliminate sexual violence the proper target for protest and action must be found. Any submission to the Committee of Inquiry on Pornography must address the broader issues suggested here. Pornography is one place where sexual violence may be encouraged and learnt but it is not the most important site.

If space for an exploration and affirmation of diverse sexualities is to be created then censorship must be rejected. Sexual and reproductive rights for women and children need to be more firmly established, economic independence and security for women must be gained and the democratisation of culture and politics must be fought for. It is in these wider battles that sexual violence and oppression will be finally eliminated.

References

Mandy Merck. 'Pornography' in *Looking On: Images of femininity in the visual arts and media.*

Andy Moyle. 'Pornography' in *The Sexuality of Men.*

Thelma McCormack. 'Making Sense of Research on Pornography' in *Women Against Pornography.*

Lynne Segal. *Is the Future Female?*

Paula Webster. 'Pornography and Pleasure' in *Caught Looking: Feminism, pornography and censorship*

Broadsheet, *no. 158 (May 1988), pp.38–41*

8.12. Support the Homosexual Law Reform Bill
Lesbian Coalition (1985)

The Lesbian Coalition urges you to support the Homosexual Law Reform Bill
• Support age of consent of 16
• Support no discrimination on grounds of sexual orientation
• Support no criminalisation of lesbians

Why should I support the Bill?
If you support the Bill, you will be supporting the human rights of over 300,000 New Zealanders.

At the moment, lesbians and gay men are legally discriminated against in jobs, housing and access to services. Gay men can be imprisoned. This Bill affects our whole lives.

How can I support the Bill?
Write to your local MP asking her/him to support the Bill
Write letters to your local newspapers
Ring up talkback programmes
Come on the Lesbian and Gay Rights March Friday, May 24 7.00 pm, Bunny Street. Straight supporters urged to be there
Talk to your friends, relations, neighbours, work colleagues
Pass this pamphlet on to them
Come to public meetings and support us.

DON'T sign the Anti-Bill Petition
DON'T circulate the petition

Support Lesbian Rights
Who are lesbians and gay men?
Lesbians and gay men are people who relate emotionally, mentally, physically and sexually to other people of the same sex.

How many lesbians and gay men are there?
A conservative estimate based on research done by Kinsey puts the figure at 10% of our population. i.e. in excess of 300,000 people in New Zealand.

What sort of people are we?
We are women and men of all types, of all races, of all jobs, of all positions in the community, of all beliefs, of all religions, of all interests – daughters, sisters, brothers, parents, friends.

We are in all families, in all workplaces. In short, WE ARE EVERYWHERE!
LESBIAN AND GAY RIGHTS WEEK – 3rd week in May

Support Gay Rights
Is there any danger to children from lesbians and gay men?

Support Lesbian Rights

Who are lesbians and gay men?
Lesbians and gay men are people who relate emotionally, mentally, physically and sexually to other people of the same sex.

How many lesbians and gay men are there?
A conservative estimate based on research done by Kinsey puts the figure at 10% of our population. i.e. in excess of 300,000 people in New Zealand.

What sort of people are we?
We are women and men of all types, of all races, of all jobs, of all positions in the community, of all beliefs, of all religions, of all interests — daughters, sisters, brothers, parents, friends.

We are in all families, in all workplaces.

In short, **WE ARE EVERYWHERE!**

LESBIAN AND GAY RIGHTS WEEK — 3rd week in May

The Lesbian Coalition's pamphlet produced at the time of the campaign in support of the Homosexual Law Reform Bill, 1985. *Ephemera Collection, Alexander Turnbull Library (Ephemera A Lesbian 1985)*

Nearly all sexual assaults on children are perpetrated by *heterosexual men*. Over 90% of the victims are *GIRLS* If the Bill is adopted children will continue to be protected from sexual assaults by adults of either sex.

Why an age of consent of 16? Why not 18 or 20?
We are entitled to full equality with heterosexuals.

A higher age of consent promotes homophobia (fear of homosexuality) and increases the oppression of young gays.

Should heterosexuality be compulsory?
The freedom to express our sexual orientation is a *basic human right*.

To be able to do so in a way that is natural to us is a *basic human need*.

Enforced heterosexuality causes much pain.

What's happening now?
A petition against the Bill is being circulated and public meetings are being held around the country.

Extremists are stirring up hatred which inevitably leads to violence – and in fact, it already has.

This hatred and violence is based on ignorance, lies and fear.

Lesbians and gay men are living day-by-day and side-by-side with this hatred and violence.

IF YOU BELIEVE IN BASIC HUMAN RIGHTS FOR EVERYONE SUPPORT THIS BILL

LESBIAN AND GAY RIGHTS WEEK – 3rd week in May

Leaflet, Wellington, 1985 (Ephemera A Lesbian 1985, ATL)

8.13. Introducing the Ministry of Women's Affairs (1986)

WORKING FOR EQUALITY FOR WOMEN
• IN THE HOME   • IN THE COMMUNITY
• IN THE PAID WORKFORCE

What is the Ministry of Women's Affairs?
We are a small Government department, set up like any other department under the terms of the State Services Act. Like all other public servants, our staff are politically neutral. Our job is to implement the policies of the Government of the day.

The Labour Government has a policy of working towards equality of the sexes – and it is to that end that the Ministry of Women's Affairs was established on 28 March 1985.

What is our purpose?
The main functions of the Ministry are:
• to assess all Government policies in terms of their effects on women
• to monitor and initiate legislation and regulations to promote equality for women
• to advise the Minister of Women's Affairs on suitable women for nomination to various statutory bodies
• to advise the Minister on all Government matters relevant to women.

The Ministry's role is to ensure that the views of women are taken into account in the decision-making processes, to act as a resource centre for women, and to communicate and liaise with women throughout New Zealand.

Why do we need a Ministry of Women's Affairs?
We need it because women do not yet have equal rights with men in New Zealand society.

Although women are 51% of the community:
• They are only 13% of Members of Parliament.
• They are only 14% of local body members.
• They are only 9% of mayors.
• They are only 1% of the upper levels of the public service.
• There are only 3 women judges in New Zealand.
• There are no women as managing directors of major companies.
• Despite the Equal Pay Act, women earn on average only 75% of what men earn.
• The career system is still geared to the male life cycle – a 40-year, 40-hour week which takes no account of time spent in child rearing.

Men far outnumber women in all the decision-making bodies in New Zealand. Up till now, women have not had enough say in the decisions which affect them. That is why a special department is needed whose sole responsibility is the concerns of women.

237

How does the Ministry actually work?

Most of the Ministry's work involves monitoring policies and legislation and the work of all the other Government departments. That means being part of governmental working parties, official committees and review bodies; writing submissions and reports; and liaising with the other departments.

Ongoing liaison with women's organisations and individual women in the community ensures that information flows both ways – that women's views are conveyed to decision-making bodies and that women are kept informed of matters important to them. The Ministry is building on existing women's networks to put women's groups in touch with one another and to increase information exchange.

Written material from the Ministry gets information out into the community through a regular newsletter and through information sheets on special topics.

Funding for women's projects is administered through the Ministry's Project Fund. (A separate leaflet is available to explain the funding criteria.)

The Ministry also services the Women's Appointment File, a computerised file of curricula vitae of women who are willing to be nominated to statutory boards.

The Women in Agriculture network of 3,000 rural women is supported through the Ministry's funding of WagMag, the network newsletter.

Some of the working parties on which the Ministry has been represented have examined child care, domestic violence, tertiary assistance grants, parental leave, women's refuge and breast prosthesis benefits.

Written submissions from the Ministry have involved issues such as women's sport, the school curriculum, broadcasting, nursing planning, new birth technologies, cervical screening, video recordings, industrial relations, and advertising practice.

Does this mean that all women's issues will now be handled by the Ministry?

The Ministry believes that *all* issues are women's issues. Education matters still belong to the Department of Education, legal questions to the Department of Justice, and so on. The Ministry's job is to ensure that the other departments are giving the fair treatment to women which is their right. It also acts as a

clearing house, steering women through the bureaucratic red tape.

Of course there are certain issues which specially affect women: the value of unpaid work in the home and community, domestic violence, health care, childcare, women's portrayal in the media, equal pay and opportunity, parental leave from work, sexual harassment, and so on.

The Ministry will be looking at all these issues, but it will do so by working with other departments, not by trying to solve everything itself.

What sort of staff does the Ministry have?

The Ministry is starting off with a staff of 20, whose work is divided as follows:

The Policy and Programme Development Unit is responsible for planning and preparing Cabinet papers, policy reports, reviews of legislation, Ministerial correspondence and replies to Parliamentary Questions.

Te Ohu Whakatupu (The Maori Women's Secretariat) is responsible for seeing that the specific needs of Maori women are included in all areas of the Ministry's work.

The Information and Liaison Unit manages the information flow, publicity, and liaison with women's groups and other organisations. It includes the work of the library, Project Fund and Women's Appointment File.

These three units, together with the two heads of the department, the Secretary and Deputy Secretary, are serviced by an administration group.

The age range of the staff is from 18 to 57.

Is the Ministry only interested in women in the paid workforce?

Absolutely not. The Ministry entirely supports the choice of women to be full-time homemakers, and has as a priority the raising of the status of homemakers and those doing unpaid work in the community.

What does the Ministry hope to achieve?

It is hoped to raise the consciousness of those in decision-making positions so that they will in future take women into account in their planning, policies and decisions.

The Ministry hopes to give women themselves more power over their own lives, by giving them the kinds of information they need to be able to make decisions for themselves – and so that they will feel more confident about using 'the system'.

By acting as a watchdog to safeguard women's interests, and by giving a women's perspective on all issues, the Ministry hopes

to raise the status of women and eventually to achieve true equality for women in New Zealand.

Leaflet, Wellington, 1986 (Ephemera B Women, 1986, ATL)

8.14. Mate's Rates. Just what is a mother worth?
by Claire Parker (1987)

Mum's the word but the news is out – you're worth your weight in gold!

Chief cook, bottle washer and nappy changer be blowed. Today's mother is a home management executive with a job description and daily schedule as time consuming and demanding as any big-shot businessman.

On paper, according to our calculations, a mother and homemaker is worth around $80,000 a year. The fact is the country's hardest working, most loyal company executives who slog 15 hours a day plus, seven days a week, earn zilch.

They do it out of necessity and love.

But at the end of the day many people including home management executives themselves, wonder what on earth women at home do all day taking care of the family business.

'After all, Petal, you've got all the mod cons, from dishwasher to drier, from microwave to digital touchtronic gadgets galore. I mean, Petal, you don't have to stoke the copper any more, do you?'

'Well, love of my life, bright morning star, let's see how far Mr Businessman would get coping with this lot.'

For the average suburban mother – and if she's a cocky's wife you can throw in anything from milking the cows to sheep drenching and docking or driving the school bus – mother-hood, home-making, call it whatever you like . . . is a full-time job as prime care-giver, protector and mainstay of the family. If the woman of the house is an officially paid 'working woman' she's got two jobs – one paid, one unpaid. And few fellas would take that.

New Zealand Woman's Weekly was hoping for official recognition of our Supermum's executive status when we approached a top personnel company to help us with figures. But the response was: 'Oh no, we only deal with the upper range of executive jobs.' Sorry, Mum.

So the Labour Department and Drake Personnel in Auckland provided hourly and weekly rates for us to calculate in theory what

a mother could earn if she combined all her talents and usual activities, and then put a price tag on them. Our figures do not include special allowances, uniforms, meal allowances and travel. We've also underpaid rather than over-paid just to ease the shock, by generally using minimum rates.

A large part of a mother's life involves child care. We decided it was a 24-hour a day job spanning seven days a week. Therefore it forms the biggest chunk of our calculations. A person working in a licensed child care facility earns a minimum $5.15 an hour. However, people in-volved in temporary baby-sitting and nannying services can earn $6.50 an hour. We went for a median figure of $6 an hour which produces a flat rate of $1008 a week. There you are Mum, that's enough to make your eyes sparkle – $52,000 a year and we're not even off first base.

The hourly rate for rest home workers involved in budgeting, preparing and cooking food is $6.88. With three meals a day to plan and prepare seven days a week, together with all the home baking women do, we've allowed 25 hours a week so there's another $172 to add to Mum's pay cheque.

Domestic helps can earn about $8 an hour but an average rate is around $6.40 an hour. Add up all the washing, ironing, vacuuming, dust-ing, polishing, floor-mopping, toilet cleaning, bedmaking and general scrubbing and cleaning involved in keeping most homes ship-shape – three hours a day, maybe a little less at the weekends – and you get around $115 for 18 hours' work.

If mother is also organising payment of the family bills, doing the accounts, organising the maintenance of the home, including electrical appliances, she could collect between $10 and $15 an hour as an accounting assistant. We'll pay her $12 an hour – she's got heaps of experience and enthusiasm and a pleasant personality – for two hours' work. That's another $24 to the bill.

And who is it who plays nurse when the kids are sick? Mum, of course. We asked a nursing agency what an unqualified woman with lots of nursing experience could hope to earn. The answer was $8 an hour. Six hours of kissing better scraped knees and soothing measley, mumpy, grumpy little patients is a well-earned $48 a week.

A mother probably spends a lot of time on the road each week, doing anything from driving the kids to and from school – okay we know thousands walk and there are school buses – to taking care of business errands for her partner, driving to the supermarket and taking kids to extra curricular activities. The lowest hourly rate for driving a vehicle under 10 tonnes – we guessed that describes Mum's old bomb – is $6.29. We'll round several hours a week of that out to $20 on the bill.

And talking of supermarkets, we've decided to award mother $20 a week (not nearly enough) danger money for her grit, tenacity and general bravery in negotiating three kids and a trolley around the supermarket.

Some of mother's day will be taken up by duties which could be the function of a school care-taker. We're going to give her one hour a day at $7.57 which over seven days amounts to a total of $52.99. She is also going to do several hours gardening a week. That works out at $20.61 on an hourly rate of $6.87.

We've included in the never-ending list of manual chores an hour of painting and decorating – $7.79.

If she washes and valets her car or the family car once a fortnight that's half an hour a week on an hourly rate of $6.44 – please ring up $3.22.

She might spend four hours a week sewing and mending – we excluded knitting as many women look on this as a relaxation. A clothing machinist's minimum wage is $248.26 which gives her $24.80 for four hours.

She probably makes jam, bottles fruit and freezes vegetables, for an hour a week. Add another $5.90 for the minimum hourly rate in the canning and food-processing industry.

Auckland City Council swimming pool attendants earn a minimum of $248.28 a week giving an hourly rate of $7.10 if she's teaching the kids to swim.

The list could go on and on. Mum is also a psychologist, minder and walker of pets, story reader, party organiser, hostess and peace maker. But to save Finance Minister Roger Douglas a heart attack we stopped the clock at $79,529.32.

We thought about subtracting three weeks' wages for 'annual leave' but mothers know there's no such thing. And as our hypothetical mum had three kids – one is primary school age, one a pre-schooler and there's a baby – we reckoned she'd earned paid leave, rather than 'leave' without pay.

Mama mia, you're something else!

New Zealand Woman's Weekly, 11 May 1987, p.6

8.15. Abortion Decriminalisation: the arguments
Women's National Abortion Action Campaign (1988)

Decriminalisation of abortion, abolishing the Abortion Supervisory Committee, and removing the legal necessity for certifying consultants will enable women to get abortions without unnecessary delays.

Travel problems
A legal requirement on all Hospital Boards and Area Health Boards to provide abortion services will end the existing situation of many women having to travel out of their regions, sometimes more than once, to see certifying consultants and then to travel again to have their abortions. In some places there is regularly a delay of up to four weeks to get an abortion.

Some women find it hard to get referred to certifying consultants because their doctors do not consider that they have displayed sufficient distress.

If there were abortion clinics and professional non-directive counselling services available from all Area Health and Hospital Boards women would be more aware of the general availability of these services and would seek help as soon as they discovered they were pregnant.

The sanctity of life
Is a foetus a sacred life? The people who argue this are often not so respectful of human life in other circumstances. The same people who argue so vehemently against abortion are often those who make excuses for nuclear weaponry or the reintroduction of hanging. For them sanctity of life is limited to the foetus.

We are the people who stand for the sanctity of the real lives of human beings. A foetus is not an independent human being. It is clear that it is alive, as indeed is every sperm cell, but it cannot be claimed to be an independent *human* life. It is absurd to argue that a foetus should have more rights than the mother or any other dependents she may have.

Deformed foetuses

There are a variety of arguments about the necessity of abortion if there is evidence that the child will be deformed. The decision to have an abortion because of the foetus's abnormality must lie entirely with the woman. A woman has to consider her own capacity to provide the type of care the child will require, she must consider how she will maintain her own life and that of her other dependents and her partner. If a woman decides that she is incapable of providing the necessary care – physical, emotional and financial – for the child then she must have the right to an abortion. There is no logical conclusion to be drawn between a deformed foetus and abortion. Many women will not want an abortion on the grounds of deformity and their decision must be respected. Society and the state must provide the necessary supports to assist women who choose to continue their pregnancy and look after a disabled child.

Late abortions

The majority of abortions are performed in the first trimester, and this will continue to be the norm. However, we need to make it possible for women to have an abortion in the last trimester if that is necessary. Putting a time limit on legal abortions is arbitrary. With medical science continually making it possible to keep very young foetuses alive outside the womb at increasingly earlier stages this cannot be used as an argument to move continually backward the time at which abortion is legal.

Women seek abortions at this late stage for two reasons. (1) They have discovered only late in their pregnancy that the foetus is deformed. (2) The life of the woman is threatened and an abortion is the only option available.

Abortions over five months are very rare. Research has shown that the less restriction on access to abortion the earlier abortions are performed.

Fathers' rights

Does the father have no rights? No. If the father is not cohabitating with the mother-to-be then he has no rights whatever. If he is living with her, then his rights extend *only to the extent that he wins those rights from the woman* by assuring her of his economic, physical and emotional support. Unless he can provide the love and security which allow the woman to feel confident that conditions will be good for her and the child then he can have no claims. The law has no place here. The decision must be the woman's.

If men wish to insist on their right to have children, then they must begin to put their energy into enabling men to have babies. Let them produce their own progeny if they are so keen.

Killing Shakespeare

Is it not a crime to kill a foetus which might turn out to be a Shakespeare or an Einstein? To carry this argument to its logical conclusion it must be a crime to allow any ova or sperm to be wasted, any might just as easily become geniuses. If they are worried about destroying potential Einsteins the Moral Majority should be campaigning against chastity!

In fact this kind of genetic elitism has no basis in reality. Einsteins are made not born. Different circumstances, different family structures produce different people. We will produce the best people through building a society where children have the best circumstances and the best family structures, where parents have the emotional and material resources to look after their children well, and where the children are wanted.

Adoptee manufacture

Through abortion being too readily available, it is argued, there are too few babies available for adoption. The claim is that women, like cows and ewes in the farmyard, should be used for breeding machines. Women must not be denied fulfilment of their need for a truly human life. Nobody should be forced to go through nine months of discomfort and disruption of life (possibly losing her job and so on) in order to manufacture a baby for someone else. It is inhuman to force someone to develop a bond with the foetus she is carrying, only to have to give the baby away when it is born. The emotional ties between a woman and her baby are usually very strong and many women grieve for years for the child they gave up for adoption. We believe that women must have the CHOICE on the one hand of an abortion and on the other hand of taking the pregnancy to full term and either having the baby adopted or keeping it.

Backstreet abortionists

The decriminalisation of abortion, it is claimed, will open the doors to backstreet abortionists. This is nonsense.

Abortions have always been the last resort for women and have always been sought when contraceptive methods failed or were primitive or were not realistically accessible. In the days when almost all abortions were illegal women sought – and often found – abortions. Most women had to turn to backstreet abortionists but women of means were always able to get one under competent medical supervision. Safe abortions have for many years been the prerogative of wealthy women.

The current proposals are quite clear. Abortions are to be performed by medical practitioners in appropriate institutions under the control of Area Health Boards or Hospital Boards. It is not we who pave the way for backstreet abortionists but the people who oppose decriminalisation of abortion. It is when access to safe, legal, medically supervised abortions is limited that women are forced to seek backstreet abortionists. We have no wish to return to the days of poor women being the victims of punitive and unequally applied laws.

Safety of abortions

Does induced abortion lead to infertility? This is a theory that probably evolved from early abortion procedures in Japan and Europe. Also illegal abortion techniques may have been associated with sterility.

Recent studies, however, show no association between infertility and previous induced abortion. Major complications rarely occur (1 in 20,000 abortions in USA) that might require a hysterectomy, but this is a risk of childbirth as well.

One study found a subsequent lower pregnancy rate was in fact linked to the use of more effective contraceptives. This same study concluded that induced abortion status did not influence pregnancy rates except that women reporting three or more induced abortions had a *higher* subsequent pregnancy rate. (Obstet. Gyn. 63:186, 1984)

Barrier contraception plus back-up abortion is the safest method of birth control for women. The pill, IUD, Depo provera all have side effects and may not be appropriate for many women. Early abortions under local anaesthetic are much safer than child-birth or miscarriage.

Why rock the boat?

There is an argument that anyone who wants an abortion can get one today. However in fact many women who want an abortion find it very difficult to do so. If you live in any of the main metropolitan centres and know your way around the system then you can with relative ease find a doctor who is sympathetic to your situation and will refer you to a certifying consultant. If, on the other hand, you live in one of the main metropolitan centres and are not very confident about your rights and how to find a sympathetic doctor, getting an abortion is not easy. This situation is magnified many times for any woman who lives outside the main metropolitan centres. In some places you cannot get an abortion at all, and you must be able to travel away from home, falsify an address and find the certifying consultants. Many women find this difficult; others find it impossible.

People who wish to maintain the status quo are unable to appreciate what it is like to be faced with what seem to be the huge obstacles of the present non-system: obstacles involving lack of sympathy, obstacles of medical bureaucracy and a pose of professional infallibility, and obstacles of financial hardship. The status quo suits educated, financially better off and urban women.

The bill drafted by WONAAC/ALRANZ is for a change in the status quo of privilege and extends the same rights to all women regardless of economic, educational or residential status.

Abortion Decriminalisation: the arguments. A position paper from WONAAC, *Wellington, 1988 (Ephemera A Abortion 1988, ATL)*

8.16. State Sector Act (1988) (1988)

An Act –
(a) To ensure that employees in the State services are imbued with the spirit of service to the community; and

(b) To promote efficiency in the State services; and
(c) To ensure the responsible management of the State services; and

(d) To maintain appropriate standards of integrity and conduct among employees in the State services; and

(e) To ensure that every employer in the State services is a good employer; and

(f) To promote equal employment opportunities in the State services; and

(g) To provide for the negotiation of conditions of employment in the State services; and

(h) To repeal the State Services Act 1962, the State Services Conditions of Employment Act 1977, and the Health Service Personnel Act 1983 . . . .

PART V
PERSONNEL PROVISIONS

56. General principles – (1) The chief executive of a Department shall operate a personnel policy that complies with the principle of being a good employer.

(2) For the purposes of this section, a 'good employer' is an employer who operates a personnel policy containing provisions generally accepted as necessary for the fair and proper treatment of employees in all aspects of their employment, including provisions requiring –

(a) Good and safe working conditions; and

(b) An equal employment opportunities programme; and

(c) The impartial selection of suitably qualified persons for appointment; and

(d) Recognition of --

(i) The aims and aspirations of the Maori people; and

(ii) The employment requirements of the Maori people; and

(iii) The need for greater involvement of the Maori people in the Public Service; and

(e) Opportunities for the enhancement of the abilities of individual employees; and

(f) Recognition of the aims and aspirations, and the cultural differences, of ethnic or minority groups; and

(g) Recognition of the employment require-

ments of women; and

(h) Recognition of the employment requirements of persons with disabilities.

(3) In addition to the requirements, specified in subsections (1) and (2) of this section, each chief executive shall ensure that all employees maintain proper standards of integrity, conduct, and concern for the public interest.

(4) For the purposes of this section, 'employee' includes a member of the senior executive service.

57. Code of conduct – The Commission may from time to time issue a code of conduct covering the minimum standards of integrity and conduct that are to apply in the Public Service.

58. Equal employment opportunities – (1) The chief executive of a Department –

(a) Shall in each year develop and publish an equal employment opportunities programme for the Department:

(b) Shall ensure in each year that the equal opportunities programme for that year is complied with throughout the Department.

(2) The chief executive of a Department shall include in the annual report of the Department –

(a) A summary of the equal employment opportunities programme for the year to which the report relates; and

(b) An account of the extent to which the Department was able to meet, during the year to which the report relates, the equal employment opportunities programme for that year.

(3) For the purposes of this section and section 56 of this Act, an equal employment opportunities programme means a programme that is aimed at the identification and elimination of all aspects of policies, procedures, and other institutional barriers that cause or perpetuate, or tend to cause or perpetuate, inequality in respect to the employment of any persons or group of persons.

NZ Statutes, *1988, pp.225–226, 251–252*

8.17. So Chins Up, Girls: Things have never been better
by Alastair Morrison (1992, commentary on 8.16)

Good news for the majority. It's a great time to be a woman. Yes, indeed, things are buzzing ahead for the sisterhood.

Wherever she goes, Women's Affairs Minister Jenny Shipley says, women are telling her how pleased they are with the Employment

Contracts Act.

This positive breath of fresh air from Mrs Shipley was certainly needed to counter the spoil-sport State Services Commission's recent report on equal employment in the public service for the 1991-92 year.

There's Mrs Shipley with good stories to tell, and the commission has to remind us 76 per cent of women in the public service earn less than $30,000, men make up 90.7 per cent of management, disabled people are being turfed out of jobs at a greater rate than others . . .

Not one to be intimidated, Mrs Shipley counters by using Status of New Zealand Women 1992, the second government progress report to the United Nations Committee on the Elimination of Discrimination Against Women.

It shows great strides for the sisters. Two of the three reservations New Zealand expressed in its first progress report in 1986 have since been removed.

Back then, we opposed women working down the mines. Now they can pick away with the men. We didn't like them going into combat, either. Now they're allowed to jump in a Skyhawk, hop in a Scorpion or grab a Steyr and kill people.

The one remaining touchy issue is 'New Zealand's reservation concerning maternity leave with pay'. It's the 'with pay' bit we don't like.

The report skites about how government departments have to produce equal employment opportunity (EEO) plans, but it's a bit thin on the detail when it comes to how effective the plans are. The commission's report throws some light on that.

In 1991-92, 34 government departments were meant to send three reports to the commission; their EEO plans, progress made, and a statistical profile of staff.

The reports are required by law. Despite that, two departments didn't supply any of the three reports. How ironic that one of them should be that oracle of the law itself, the Crown Law Office! The other was the National Library.

Crown Law practice manager Alan Pollard doesn't know why the reports didn't go in last year because he has taken over only in the past year, but he says the office 'very much leads the industry in the promotion of women'. Five of its eight management team are women.

In the report area, the office is now 'very much up to speed'.

National Library human resources manager Kevin Jones says they were 'running late' but have since 'caught up'.

The excuses are pathetic. The departments had till March 1992 to report. Commissioner Don Hunn says there were 'several rounds' of written reminders for those who were late.

In addition to the two main offenders, five departments got only some of the three reports in: Housing Corporation, Audit Office, Ministry of External Relations and Trade, Justice and Parliamentary Service.

As for those that did report? Twenty-eight sent in EEO plans, and most were late, the commission says, which 'raises serious issues not only about departmental planning processes but also about whether plans were being implemented in the period they were designed for'.

Ten of the plans 'can be described as good, eight as adequate and ten as poor'.

Thirty departments sent in EEO progress reports. Two were so bad the commission couldn't work out what they had achieved. Eight 'achieved a substantial amount'. Four departments, among the largest in the public service, 'need to seriously reassess their approach to EEO'. Two showed 'a complete lack of understanding of the process of planning', and in at least three there was 'a lack of clear commitment to EEO from top management'.

Thirty-one departments sent in staff profiles. The data in one were 'too confused' to be of help. Twelve presented 'complete and well-analysed information', nine were 'adequate' and nine were 'incomplete or muddled'. Treasury, Labour and Education made 'spectacular improvement' in their data reporting.

It's not easy for the boys to give up their privileged position and switch to a system where merit is what counts, but the commission's report contains examples of good progress. For all that, it is littered with examples of non-compliance, incompetence in planning and reporting, and lack of commitment to EEO.

No government would tolerate such appalling management in 'important' areas, like budgeting. But Mr Hunn has a point when he argues EEO is a complex issue that involves changing behaviour, so long-term it's best to use the carrot rather than the stick.

Tolerance is wearing thin. This year offenders who did not report were named for the first time. It has worked. The reports for the 1992-93 year had to be in by October this year, five months earlier than last year. Assistant EEO director Margaret Hansen says the commission has '100 per cent of the documents' and at first glance there appear to be significant improvements.

Mr Hunn says this year the commission also intends naming departments whose reports show inadequacies.

The combination of EEO legislation and the commission's approach is proving effective, but is the Government backing that with good leadership?

In one section of her progress report to the UN committee, Mrs Shipley notes the participation of women in democratic organisations.

Many women have been attracted into public life through elected health boards. Researcher Jean Drage has shown women have increased their numbers, making up 53 per cent of representatives elected on to area health boards in 1989.

The report notes the boards are 'soon to be replaced by regional health authorities'. But it fails to add the members are appointed, not elected.

The Government has since made the appointments. Women make up only 25 per cent of both the authorities and the appointed Crown Health Enterprises that run hospitals, also once overseen by elected representatives. Apparently the Government has less faith in women than the public.

This is consistent with the Government's slashing of EEO provisions in legislation for the new health structure.

The four regional authorities and 23 crown enterprises must have EEO programmes and recognise 'the employment requirements of women'. In effect that amounts to little.

Unlike the old boards and hospitals, they won't have to develop and publish an annual EEO programme, ensure it is complied with, and report on progress.

This watering-down of employment equity was borrowed from Labour's legislation for the state-owned enterprises, where EEO is also regarded as less important. Governments, it seems, regard EEO as fine for social services but not commercial.

One of Labour Minister Bill Birch's first search-and-destroy missions was against the Employment Equity Act and the commission established to make it effective.

The commission had barely got off the ground when Mr Birch pronounced it ineffective. Of course he was anxious to see women get a fair deal, and promised 'a workable, lasting employment equity policy' instead.

Eventually a token $400,000 was budgeted for voluntary employment equity projects.

But the real linchpin in National's plan to liberate the sisters was the Employment Contracts Act. And it certainly seems to have captured their imagination. The stories Mrs Shipley hears everywhere she goes of how it has changed their lives for the better surely make Mr Birch a good friend of women.

So chins up, girls, things have never been better. Have they?

Dominion, 11 December 1992, p.11

8.18. Report of the Ministerial Committee of Inquiry into Pornography (1987–1988)

Terms of Reference

(a) Examine the relevant legislation (including the Indecent Publications Act 1963, the Films Act 1983 and the Video Recordings Act 1987), paying special regard to:
(i) the criteria for determining whether material should be prohibited or restricted;
(ii) the types of restrictions that should apply to different types of materials;
(iii) the nature of the body or bodies which should be responsible for determining whether material should be prohibited or restricted;
and recommend whether or not changes are desirable in the law;
(b) Consider what non-legislative measures should be adopted to counter the pro-

duction and distribution of prohibited or restricted material;
(c) Consider developments in communications technology and their implications for the transmission of such material across international boundaries;
(d) Consider whether the presentation of an indecent show or the exhibition of indecent material in a licensed liquor outlet should be a ground for suspending or revoking the operator's licence.

. . . .

Recommendations

1. That the Indecent Publications Act 1963, the Films Act 1983 and the Video Recordings Act 1987 be repealed and replaced by

one comprehensive statute dealing with the classification and rating of the works to which those Acts currently apply.

2. That the preamble to that comprehensive statute make plain the purpose and limitations of classification in a modern democratic society.

3. That the Justice Department administer the reformed classification system until such time as a department is created that is concerned, and identified, with matters of arts and culture and/or communications.

4. That the ultimate standard by which any printed, filmed or videotaped work should be assessed is that of the work's availability being likely to be injurious to the public good.

5. That material (i.e. a printed, filmed or videotaped work or part of such a work) likely to be injurious to the public good shall include material of the following kinds:

    (a) material that advocates or condones the sexual exploitation of children by adults;

    (b) material in the production of which children or young persons have been or seem to have been sexually exploited;

    (c) visual material that depicts detailed and/or relished acts of extreme violence or cruelty, whether or not in a sexual context, other than material that depicts such acts, in a non-sexual context, in order to report or condemn their occurrence; and

    (d) any material that advocates or condones acts of extreme violence or cruelty, whether or not in a sexual context.

6. That material of the following kinds be presumed to be likely to be injurious to the public good:

    (a) sexually violent material, which means visual material that depicts the use of violence or coercion in association with sexual behaviour, whether or not any person is depicted as suffering as a result of the violence or coercion, and any material that advocates or condones the use of violence or coercion in association with sexual behaviour;

    (b) visual material which depicts acts of bestiality, necrophilia, coprophilia or urolagnia and any material that advocates or condones any such acts.

7. That the above presumption be rebutted when those responsible for making classification decisions are satisfied, taking into account the seven factors set out below, that a work containing such material possesses such overriding merit (i.e. value or importance in relation to social, cultural, scientific, educational, artistic or literary matters) that its availability would not be likely to be injurious to the public good.

8. That the factors to be considered in classification decisions be as follows:

    (a) the dominant effect of the work as a whole;

    (b) the extent and degree to which and the manner in which the work depicts, includes, or treats anti-social behaviour, cruelty, violence, crime, horror, sex or offensive language or behaviour;

    (c) the extent and degree to which and the manner in which the work demeans any particular class of the public by reference to the colour, race, ethnic or national origins, sex, sexual orientation, disability or religious beliefs of the members of that class;

    (d) the extent and degree to which and the manner in which the work depends upon the demeaning portrayal of any person;

    (e) the extent to which the work has merit, i.e. value or importance in relation to social, cultural, scientific, educational, artistic or literary matters;

    (f) the persons, classes of persons, or the age groups of the persons to whom, and the circumstances under which, the work is most likely to be made available;

    (g) the impact of the medium in which the work is presented.

'Terms of Reference', and 'Recommendations' from the Report of the Ministerial Committee of Inquiry into Pornography, *Wellington, 1988, pp.11 & 165*

8.19. Employment Equity Bill: Introduction by Helen Clark (1989)

Hon. HELEN CLARK (Minister of Labour): I move, *That the Employment Equity Bill be introduced.* The Bill establishes procedures to bring about equality of opportunity for groups disadvantaged in the work-force, and to bring about fair pay for women. In recent decades Parliament has passed many measures that were aimed at bringing greater equality for women to the work-force. Prior to 1960, awards and agreements generally stipulated different rates of pay for men and women who undertook the same or similar work. In those days it was argued that men required sufficient income to maintain a family, while women did not. By 1960 the Labour Government of the time accepted that such differences in pay were discriminatory. Parliament passed into law the Government Service Equal Pay Act 1960. That Act provided for the elimination of differences based on sex in pay rates for Government employees as soon as practicable after 1 April 1963.

It was expected – perhaps naively – that women's pay in the private sector would follow the 1960 Act. Unfortunately, it did not. Legislation was required to bring equal pay to the private sector. That ensured that women in that sector, as in the State sector, were paid the same as men when undertaking the same or similar work. While the Equal Pay Act 1972 certainly succeeded in narrowing the pay gap between men and women in New Zealand, it could not eliminate it. Even now, in 1989, women still earn a little under 81 percent of average male hourly earnings. In 1986 the Labour Government commissioned an equal pay study to identify why the pay gap persisted. The study showed that the pay gap was related to the narrow distribution of women across occupations, the low levels of seniority reached by women in the work-force, and the historical undervaluation of work traditionally undertaken by women.

The study recognised that women were not the only group disadvantaged in the labour market. Maori people, Pacific Island people, other ethnic minorities, and people with disabilities were also identified as being disadvantaged. In 1987 the Government set up a working-group to bring down recommendations on equal employment opportunities and equal pay. The report of the working-group was published in May last year. Submissions were called for and a final report was presented to the Government in November 1988. Thereafter the Government agreed in principle to introduce legislation incorporating both the concepts of equal employment opportunities and pay equity.

This Bill is the outcome of a long and very thorough period of deliberation on how to implement those concepts practically. I think that the Bill is practical and workable. The pattern of history in some ways repeats itself in the Bill. Equal pay provisions were first developed in the State sector, and later expanded into the private sector. This Bill also takes some provisions that were introduced, first, to the State sector – as in the State Sector Act, which required State agencies to promote equal employment opportunities – and applies similar provisions beyond the public sector into the private sector. The Bill also provides a mechanism for eliminating gender bias in pay rates.

I think the processes that the Bill puts in place will lead to more equal opportunities for women and other groups that are disadvantaged in the work-force, and to a more equitable pay structure for women in those occupations that have been female-dominated. Further, the Bill recognises economic realities by ensuring that both the equal employment opportunities provisions and the pay equity provisions are phased in so that they are affordable. It is important to remember that the Equal Pay Act 1972 was similarly phased-in, in that case over a period of 5 years.

The pay equity provisions of the Bill take into account many market factors, such as recruitment and retention, and differences in pay by region. By allowing pay equity payments to be phased in over time the parties can be assured that costs will not be unmanageable. The pay equity provisions have also been designed to fit in with the current labour relations framework. Unions and employers will be able to bargain collectively on pay equity, while established labour market institutions – the Arbitration Commission and the Labour Court – will oversee progress.

I come now to the detailed provisions of the Bill. Part I provides for the appointment of an Employment Equity Commissioner. The commissioner will be accountable to the Minister of Labour, with the Department of Labour providing managerial, advisory, administrative, and other services, as necessary. The objectives of Part II are to promote equal opportunities for women, Maori people, Pacific Island people, groups of workers with the same ethnic or national origin, people with disabilities, and individual groups that the Employment Equity Commissioner determines should be a designated group.

Equal employment opportunities programmes will be designed to eliminate inequality in recruitment, promotion, and other employment practices or policies from all forms of paid employment in the public and private sectors. In the first year of operation this part of the Bill will apply only to those employers who employ 500 workers or more. In the second year the provisions of the Bill will apply to those who employ 100 workers or more. Thereafter they will apply to those who employ 50 workers or more. At the end of the 2-year interval from the beginning of implementation, and each year thereafter, employers should review the implementation of the equal employment opportunities programme and determine whether changes are necessary.

The Employment Equity Commissioner may, at any time, review the programme and its rate of implementation. After 2 years the commissioner may decide whether the programme needs to be replaced, or managed to achieve its objectives. The first equal employment opportunities programme that the employer lodges needs to meet the requirements set out in the schedule to the Act, and any further minimum requirements that the commissioner might determine in that case. The employer's programme will name the person responsible in the firm for overseeing the development and implementation of the programme. The programme will outline the form of consultation to be undertaken with unions and workers about the programme.

The second programme – year 2 – to be lodged by the employer will review the extent to which the first is being implemented, and establish whether it needs changes at that stage. It will establish a timetable for implementation and set realistic targets. The commissioner is responsible for establishing minimum requirements for the equal employment opportunities programmes, and for designating the particular groups they should aim to assist in that firm. The commissioner can advise and assist employers to monitor the lodging of programmes, scrutinise the programmes, undertake research and education programmes on equal employment opportunities, and initiate proceedings, when necessary, for compliance with the Bill. Compliance can be secured by taking a compliance order in the Labour Court, along the same lines as the procedures set out in the Labour Relations Act.

Part III deals with pay equity. A union with coverage of, or an employer's organisation that employs workers in, a female occupation can request that the Employment Equity Commissioner undertake a pay equity assessment. The Bill defines a female occupation as one in which 60 percent or more of the workers employed are female. A group of 20 or more female workers may also request an assessment if there is no union, or if the union fails to act or to act promptly in requesting a pay equity assessment.

The Employment Equity Commissioner is charged with consulting interested parties to determine the boundaries of the pay equity assessment. The parameters should include the definition of the female occupations to be assessed, and the selection of two or more male occupations to be used as comparators. A male occupation is similarly defined as one in which 60 percent or more of the workers are male. In the first instance at least one of the male comparator occupations should be employed in the same work-place, or same kind of work-place, as those in which a significant number of the workers in the female occupation are employed. In addition, the first male comparator occupation should also require broadly similar levels of physical, mental, and interpersonal skills, and of knowledge and experience, as the female occupation requires of its members. The second male comparator would also be one that requires, in an overall sense, broadly similar levels of skill, knowledge, and experience, but need not be from the same work-place or same kind of work-place.

If there is no suitable male comparator in the same work-place or same kind of work-place, both comparators would still be required to meet the test of requiring broadly similar levels of skill and experience. The purpose of the assessment is to assess the extent of gender bias, if any, in remuneration. The assessment will consider the difference between actual remuneration for the female occupation, and the remuneration that would be paid within a male occupation in which members work in similar conditions and have broadly the same skills, knowledge, and experience. In the assessment, the commissioner may consider any extraordinary working conditions. That consideration allows recognition of dangerous, hazardous, or stressful working conditions that might affect pay.

The commissioner shall take note of differences in remuneration between each of the main metropolitan areas, and the rest of the country. That allows recognition of different market pay rates in different regions. The commissioner shall also recognise differences in pay that can be attributed to recruitment and retention factors. That allows for recognition of supply and demand. When an assessment is completed and a report produced, unions or employers can lodge a pay equity claim as part of negotiations for an award or agreement. The claim would take the form of a schedule of pay equity payments supplementary to the award or agreement. Therefore unions and employers are provided with the opportunity to bargain on pay equity, along with bargaining on all other wages and conditions affecting the workplaces concerned.

However, if the pay equity claim is not settled within 60 days, either party can refer the claim to the Arbitration Commission for final-offer arbitration. The commission will determine the claims separately for each relevant work description or position designation, and, where applicable, for each region. The Arbitration Commission will also determine the relationship between the provisions of the award or agreement and the schedule of pay equity payments. It will determine, at the same time or subsequently, the time within which the pay equity determination, if any, is to be implemented. The time-frame for that implementation shall be 3 years, unless the commission determines that a longer or shorter period is warranted.

In deciding that, the Arbitration Commission would consider the need to achieve fair pay for women, and the need to minimise the impact of the cost to employers, the Government, and the economy. The Government would have the opportunity to present submissions to the commission on the overall economic and fiscal impact of any determination. No further pay equity claim may be brought within 5 years of the date of determination, or the date of final implementation, whichever is the latter. Part IV has miscellaneous provisions, the most important of which is that the decisions of the Employment Equity Commissioner are subject to judicial review in the Labour Court, and that strikes by female occupations in relation to any part of an award or agreement while a pay equity claim is before the commission are unlawful.

In conclusion, the Bill provides processes that increase opportunities for those women disadvantaged in the labour market, and ensures them fair remuneration. It does so in a way that is carefully moderated, and is affordable to the economy, as, indeed, the Equal Pay Act was when introduced. I commend the Bill to the House.

New Zealand Parliamentary Debates, vol. 503 (1989), pp.14333–14336

8.20. Films, Videos and Publications Classification Bill: Introduction
by Jenny Shipley (1992)

Hon. JENNY SHIPLEY (Minister of Social Welfare), on behalf of Minister of Justice: I have the honour to move, *That the Films, Videos, and Publications Classification Bill be introduced.* The Bill represents the culmination of a number of years' work to bring consistency to, and to strengthen, our classification legislation. This work includes input from the ministerial committee of inquiry into pornography, the previous Government, and effort and commitment by the current Government, its women's caucus, and my colleagues the Minister of Justice and the Minister of Internal Affairs.

The Bill proposes a comprehensive revision of New Zealand's censorship laws. The new statute is to be enacted to replace the Indecent Publications Act 1963, the Films Act 1983, and the Video Recordings Act 1987. The Bill will send some very clear messages about the society we want to live in and the types of behaviour that we believe are totally unacceptable.

In 1988 the committee of inquiry into pornography reported that clear, coherent, and purposeful legislation was required to rationalise the approach to classification of visual and printed matter, to revise and reform the criteria of classification, and to facilitate public access to the classification system. In 1991, I and other Ministers called for further submissions from the public. This Bill is the result of both extensive consultation and careful deliberation.

The main features of the Bill include the establishment of a new Office of Film and Literature Classification. The classification office will be responsible for the legal classification of all material covered in the Bill. A uniform set of revised classification criteria is to be introduced. An enhanced access by members of the public to the classification system will be facilitated. Controls on the display of restricted material in public places will be delivered. There will be rationalisation of offences and a substantially increased penalty for those offences. There will also be the introduction of an offence for possession of prohibited material.

Legislation to consolidate and amend existing law is long overdue. The present system is complex, and difficult to access readily. Currently, books, magazines, sound recordings, and other publications are dealt with under the Indecent Publications Act 1963. Films intended for exhibition to the public must be approved by the chief censor, pursuant to the Films Act 1983, and video recordings intended for sale or hire to the public must be labelled and classified pursuant to the Video Recordings Act 1987. The courts, too, have a residual jurisdiction of rule to the status of other publications that are not dealt with by any of those three bodies. The material itself is classified according to criteria that vary across each of those three enactments. This has led to an untidy situation, which has been able to be manipulated. It has allowed some pornographic material to escape classification, and is not a satisfactory situation.

The classification system will be as follows. Existing bodies are to be replaced by a unified system for the classification of publications. The Bill applies to all printed and visual matter covered by the three existing statutes. However, the definition of 'publication' in the Bill also covers some material not caught by the current law, including, for example, computer discs and other electronic or computer-generated articles by which material representations can be produced. The new legislation will also cover video-parlour games.

The system will be more straightforward and accessible to the public. The classification office will consist of a chief censor, a deputy chief censor, and a pool of classification officers. The classification office will have the sole jurisdiction to determine the legal status of all publications. When material is the subject of court proceedings, any question about the classification of the material must be referred to the classification office. The responsibility for the exercise of the functions of the office and its powers rests squarely with the chief censor and the deputy chief censor. The general rule is that classification decisions cannot be issued without the authority of both the chief censor and the deputy chief censor.

The system will be much more straight-

forward and accessible to the public. The role of the information unit will be to publicise the work of the classification office, provide a forum for complaints, and examine applications from the public for a publication to be received for classification. The classification office and the chief censor will be more accessible to the public under this new legislation.

Clause 15 specifically addresses the process by which a member of the public may make a complaint. An information unit is to be established within the classification office. One or more of the staff of that unit will be appointed as complaints officers. The task of the complaints officer is to receive complaints and submissions of material from members of the public and to forward recommendations on those complaints and submissions to the chief censor. This will ensure that the chief censor is not directly inundated with public queries, while he or she will retain the final say on whether a complaint merits action. All complaints and submissions are thus considered by the chief censor and cannot be dismissed by any other persons. This is vital for the public perception of the accessibility of the classification system.

The bill is structured in such a way as to allow lay people to follow easily how the various bodies are established, and how functions performed under the legislation fit together. The information unit will also have a research function. Members of the public will be able to submit a publication to the classification office through the new information unit, and will also have the right to seek a review, by leave, of decisions made by the classification office. Persons who can show an interest in proceedings before the classification office will be able to make written submissions. The power of the censors to consult is retained. In addition, the classification office will have the power to classify material on its own instigation. When warranted, this will enable the office to act promptly without the need for an official or a member of the public to take the initiative on any matter of concern.

The Film and Literature Board of Review will be established to hear applications for a review of decisions made by the classification office. An appeal from the board of review on a point of law will be available to the High Court, and from there to the Court of Appeal.

There will be a combined labelling regime for films and videos. All films and videos intended for supply or exhibition to the public are required to be rated or classified before they are made available to the public. An expanded industry-labelling body will perform that function in exactly the same way as the current video-labelling body works. The Bill cures the deficiency in the current system by establishing a single, coherent classification structure.

In relation to the new classification criteria, one of the most important features of the Bill is clause 3, which explicitly outlines the type of material that will be prohibited or restricted. This clause defines the standard for prohibition and describes the criteria to be employed in the classification process.

The provisions of that clause have two main objectives. First, it is necessary to update the law so that it deals in a satisfactory way with the kind of material available in New Zealand and about which the public has expressed significant concern. Second, as far as possible the censors and their assistants should be given clear statutory guide-lines so that they can be applied sensibly to the material that comes before them.

The decision to prohibit or restrict the availability of any publication is a serious matter. The Bill proposes that a decision be made according to a uniform set of statutory criteria. The decision to prohibit a publication turns on whether that publication is objectionable. The term 'objectionable' replaces the term 'indecent', which is used currently in both the Indecent Publications Act and the Video Recordings Act. For the purposes of the Bill, clause 3(1) provides that 'a publication is objectionable if it describes, depicts, expresses, or otherwise deals with matters of sex, horror, crime, cruelty, or violence in such a manner that the availability of the publication is likely to be injurious to the public good'.

However, one category of material is marked for prohibition on its own terms. The Government has decided that all forms of child pornography will be banned outright. Banned material does not apply only to sexual violence but also to extreme violence and cruelty, which comes in for special attention in this new legislation. Clause 3(2) provides that 'A publication shall be deemed to be objectionable' if it 'promotes or supports, or tends to promote or support,' any of the following: '(a) The exploitation of children, or young persons, or both, for sexual purposes; or (b) The use of violence or coercion to compel any person to participate in, or submit to, sexual conduct; or

(c) Sexual conduct with or upon the body of a dead person; or (d) The use of urine or excrement in association with degrading or dehumanising conduct or sexual conduct; or (e) Bestiality; or (f) Acts of torture or the infliction of extreme violence or extreme cruelty.'

The Government believes that it is not acceptable for this type of material to be available, so the opportunity for abusers of any type to have the use of this pornography to excite themselves, or to condition their victims, will no longer be available.

For publications not caught in clause 3(2) and banned outright, there is a second important stage of inquiry. These publications may also be prohibited and given another classification.

The test for prohibition is the standard of injury to the public good with regard to the list of statutory criteria detailed in subclauses (3) and (4). Therefore the Bill continues to employ the contextual approach to censorship matters, which has long been a feature of New Zealand censorship law. The essence of that approach is that censors must have regard to the context in which a publication deals with particular subject-matter.

While that approach is a necessary and appropriate feature of good classification law, the Government now considers that it is desirable for particular factors to be given special weight in the classification process. Pursuant to subclause (3), censors will be directed to give particular weight to the extent to which, and the manner in which, publications describe, depict, or otherwise deal with certain subject matter. The important point here is that censors are being directed to scrutinise very closely the way in which those matters are described or portrayed. The provision provides a much sharper focus than the factors described in current law which, on their own, seem rather bland and ineffectual.

I will mention briefly some factors that now must be given special weight or attention in subclause (3). For example, subclause (3)(a) deals with material that describes or depicts a range of extreme violent behaviours. Subclause (3)(b) deals with exploitation of nudity of children or young people. Subclause (3)(e) relates to material that represents, either directly or by implication, members of any particular class of the public to be inherently inferior to other members of the public by reason of their colour, race – ethnic or national origin – sex, physical or intellectual capacity, or religious beliefs of members of those classes.

In summary, the Bill retains the useful features of existing law but builds upon them to provide classification authorities with much clearer, firmer, and more workable guide-lines.

Some brief comments need to be made about clause 4, which deals with the evidence of injury to the public good. In 1987 a question arose in the context of the Indecent Publications Act about whether it was necessary to establish by means of direct evidence that material was injurious to the public good. The question was decided by a full bench of the High Court in the case of *Comptroller of Customs* v *Gordon and Gotch*. In that case, the High Court held that the Indecent Publications Act did not require there to be evidence of witnesses, or other concrete evidence of injury to the public good, before a publication could be classified as indecent within the meaning of the Act.

The court said that an expert body such as the Indecent Publications Tribunal was entitled to reach its decision on that question on the basis of the publication before it, any evidence before it, and, in particular, on the expert knowledge and the experience of the members of the tribunal. However, 'injury to the public good' was not a matter that had to be proved in the ordinary way. It is an inherent feature of the censorship process that the censor must, in the end, exercise judgment about the likelihood of injury to the public good. The purpose of clause 4 is to codify, for the purposes of the new classification procedures contained in the Bill, that decision of the High Court.

I want to talk about restrictions on public display. It is essential in any classification system that publications classified as restricted, such as R16 and R18 material, are available only to those restricted classes. The ministerial committee of inquiry heard evidence that restricted material is often displayed in dairies, in service stations, and in other places in a manner that allows children access to it. Furthermore, many people, especially women, are offended by the way in which some publications are openly displayed.

It is a legitimate object of the Bill to minimise the scope for such material to cause offence to people who are simply going about their business. Accordingly, the Bill will empower the classification office to impose conditions on the public display of publications that have been classified as restricted.

The classification office will be able to require that the public display of a book be subject to any one or more of the following conditions: the clear display on its cover, or any package in which the book is kept, of the classification assigned to it; display only in a sealed package; where the book is displayed in a package, that the package be of opaque material; display only in premises or in a part of premises set aside for the display of restricted publications; or that the book not be openly displayed at all but made available only to persons who specifically ask for it. Similar conditions will be available in relation to films and to video recordings.

I want to talk about penalties and enforcement. The Bill introduces new offence provisions. The offences have been rationalised and separated out. The current level of penalties under existing law are well out of date. The monetary penalties are, therefore, substantially increased, particularly in respect of the production of objectionable material and commercial dealing. Furthermore, any equipment used in the production of objectionable material will be liable to confiscation upon conviction. One of the most effective ways of targeting people who produce that kind of material, in addition to confiscating the product, is to take away their tools of trade.

In addition, the Bill proposes a new offence of simple possession of objectionable material. Possession of prohibited material in itself is not an offence under current law. However, the Government considers that to be a serious gap in the law. There is little point in classifying material as objectionable on the basis that it should not be available, if there are no mechanisms for dealing with material that has found its way into circulation. As the law stands, publications that contain child pornography and the like can be lawfully kept, provided that they are not circulated to others. The Government believes that that is totally unacceptable. Possession of objectionable material should be prohibited. Moreover, there should be power to seize the material and to remove it from circulation. Such a power is contained in clause 98 of the Bill.

Clause 121 creates a corresponding offence of possession of objectionable material. The clause applies to possession of both classified and unclassified material. The first category is material that is found in a person's possession that has already been classified as objectionable under this enactment; or, that has been classified as indecent under existing law. It will also be an offence to have possession of material that is not classified at the time of possession but is subsequently ruled to be objectionable. That approach is necessary because most hard-core pornography never enters the classification system when it first becomes available to those who want to possess it. The Government has decided that there should be no general defence available to a person charged with possession. Clause 121, therefore, is a strict liability offence.

Some will argue that that is a matter of personal rights or freedom. That is not my view, nor is it the view of many thinking New Zealanders, for it is women and children who are almost always the victims of such indulgence. The Government has decided to introduce the Bill taking that firm stand, and it looks forward to hearing evidence put to the select committee on whether it is reasonable to say that there is no defence for having objectionable material in one's possession.

I point out that we should be mindful that we are not speaking about erotic behaviour between consenting adults when we talk about objectionable material. We are speaking about degrading, dehumanising, and extremely violent behaviour that promotes and condones all manner of excesses. The Government believes that the public wants to see a stop put to that kind of behaviour.

The important message today to those who have material in their possession is that if people are in any doubt they must take action between now and when the Bill is due to be passed. One

can, of course, either destroy the material or seek advice from Department of Internal Affairs link centres about the possibility of having that material classified. Clause 121 has implications for the New Zealand Bill of Rights Act 1990 about which the Attorney-General will speak in this debate.

In future the imposition of strict liability will require consumers to think very carefully about the material that they are purchasing or that they may have in their possession. It is my view that that is a good thing. In future it will be the responsibility of individuals to face up to this issue, rather than the wider society always being left to prove damage as has been the case in the past.

In conclusion, I believe that this is a very important Bill that we are introducing this afternoon. I have had time to summarise only some of its major features. I believe that it is likely to attract very wide public interest, and, as with all social policy matters, it is likely to lead to strong public debate. The Government welcomes that; it is determined to bring into force a censorship regime that can take New Zealand forward. This Bill will be sent to the Internal Affairs and Local Government Committee. The membership of the committee on the Bill will be the member for Bay of Islands in the chair, the member for West Coast, the member for Western Hutt, and one other. The Opposition will be free to put whoever it wants on the committee. I hope that all members in the House today will support the Bill.

New Zealand Parliamentary Debates, *vol. 532, (1992), pp.12757–12762*

Index